The Definitive BARRACUDA & CHALLENGER GUIDE 1970–1974

Scott E. Ross

CarTech®

CarTech®, Inc.
838 Lake Street South
Forest Lake, MN 55025
Phone: 651-277-1200 or 800-551-4754
Fax: 651-277-1203
www.cartechbooks.com

Edit by Paul Johnson
Layout by Monica Seiberlich

ISBN 978-1-61325-236-9
Item No. CT558

Library of Congress Cataloging-in-Publication Data Available

Written, edited, and designed in the U.S.A.
Printed in China
10 9 8 7 6 5 4 3 2 1

Front Cover:
Although Chrysler was a late entry to the pony car wars, the Dodge Challenger and Plymouth Barracuda became stand-out muscle cars of the era because they carried the full range of high-performance engines. The Challenger T/A and AAR 'Cuda were two fine-handling and powerful Trans-Am race cars and the Hemi 'Cuda and Challenger RT 426 Hemi ruled the quarter-mile. (Photo Courtesy Jerry Heasley)

End Papers:
Highly optioned Challengers like this 1971 R/T bring big money at auction. This one is equipped with the 426 Hemi, factory-installed sunroof, front and rear spoilers, as well as 60-series raised-white-letter tires on 15-inch Rallye road wheels. (Photo Courtesy David Newhardt)

Frontispiece:
Seen here is the standard Challenger interior, with the non-tachometer-equipped instrument panel, plus optional center console, Music Master AM radio, and 4-speed manual transmission. (Photo by David Newhardt, Courtesy Mecum Auction Company)

Title Page:
Dodge's first foray into the "pony car" market segment was the 1970 Dodge Challenger. Thanks to its larger-than-Mustang size, engine choices ranging up to the 426 Hemi (which this car has), and chassis hardware borrowed from the midsize B-Body platform, the Challenger was more of a muscle car than a pony car. (Photo Courtesy Mecum Auction Company)

Contents Page:
One of Bob Ackerman's renderings prepared while the 1972 styling update for the Dodge Challenger was underway. It shows a grille that more closely resembles the black-painted grille that went into production as the standard Challenger Rallye grille. Also note the Shaker hood scoop above the grille. (Photo Courtesy Bob Ackerman)

Back Cover Photos
Top:
For 1971, few visible changes were made to the Dodge Challenger. This 1971 Challenger R/T shows off its new grille, the R/T's simulated scoops just forward of the rear wheels, and the painted-steel-wheel-with-hub-cap wheel treatment, which was the only wheel choice with the 426 Hemi in 1971. (Photo Courtesy Mecum Auctions)

Bottom:
Standard graphics were vivid, even if the spelling of "Six Pack" didn't match that on the air cleaner.

Author note: Some of the vintage photos in this book are of lower quality. They have been included because of their importance to telling the story.

OVERSEAS DISTRIBUTION BY:

PGUK
63 Hatton Garden
London EC1N 8LE, England
Phone: 020 7061 1980 • Fax: 020 7242 3725
www.pguk.co.uk

Renniks Publications Ltd.
3/37-39 Green Street
Banksmeadow, NSW 2109, Australia
Phone: 2 9695 7055 • Fax: 2 9695 7355
www.renniks.com

CONTENTS

ACKNOWLEDGMENTS

In preparing this book, help came from many sources, which are gratefully acknowledged here.

Thanks for granting kind permission for me to photograph their E-Body Mopars are due to Larry Gibb (owner of the Panther Pink 1970 Dodge Challenger T/A), Grant Brundage (original owner of the 440 Magnum green 1970 Plymouth 'Cuda, and Mike Lundein (blue 1972 Plymouth Barracuda). Dana and J. Barrie Breska and Michael Thomas (1973 Barracuda); Street Side Classics (1974 Challenger). Special thanks also to Eldon Meyers, owner of the *Olsonite Eagle* 1970 Plymouth 'Cuda AAR, as well as Richard Goldsmith, owner of the #77 Autodynamics 1970 Dodge Challenger T/A race car, and Bill Ockerland, owner of the #42 1970 Plymouth AAR 'Cuda race car, for supplying insights to those cars' histories and current conditions. Also, thanks to Chris Brown and Howard Cohen for their photos of the 1974 Dodge Challenger "Chrysler Kit Car" prototype.

Overall and detail shots of many 1970–1974 Challengers and Barracudas seen in this book are courtesy of the Barrett-Jackson Auction Company. Special thanks to Craig Jackson and Rodney Scearce for their assistance in bringing those E-Body images to you.

Grateful acknowledgment is also due to Mecum Auctions, and to Dana Mecum and Christine Giovingo, for supplying images of spectacular 1970–1974 Challengers and Barracudas for this book that crossed their auction block, as well as images of "competitive" Fords, Mercurys, Chevrolets, and Pontiacs.

Additionally, Russo & Steele provided images of E-Body Challengers and Barracudas that crossed their auction block, and many thinks are due to them. Special thanks are due to Russo & Steele's Drew Alcazar and Darin Roberge.

The insights of those who were involved with the E-Body Challengers and Barracudas, from initial concept through styling, engineering, production, sales, marketing, and service were also extremely valuable in the writing of this book, and I will always be grateful for the opportunity to chat (in person or online) with many of these people. They include Burton Bouwkamp, who headed up Chrysler's product-planning team during the E-Body's creation; Plymouth Exterior Styling Studio head Gerry Thorley; stylists Ben Delphia, John Dickerson, Tom Gale, Max Kenney, Chester Limbaugh, John Samsen, and Diran Yasajian; engineers Bob Cox, Bob Davis, and Paul Gritt; plus former Chrysler Chelsea Proving Ground technician Dave Langstone and John Parsons, who was in assembly operations at Chrysler's Hamtramck, Michigan, Assembly Plant.

In researching this book, the collection of original 1970–1974 dealer literature, salesman's pocket guides, technical service bulletins, and other information in the online library of the Hamtramck-Historical.com website was most valuable, and that site is a must-read for not only restorers, owners, and lovers of the E-Body Mopars, but those who are interested in all other 1955–1979 Chrysler-produced vehicles. Kudos to Barry Washington for assembling and sharing such an impressive collection!

Thanks also to other online sites consulted: NHRA.com (for information about the Pro Stock Challengers and Barracudas of the early 1970s), MyMopar.com (for 440 Six Pack/440 6-barrel production information), ClassicPonycars.com, ClassicAMX.com, 'Cuda Corner, TheCamaro.com, MustangRegistry.com (for help regarding the E-body's competitors), and TheIndyChannel.com (for information about the 1971 Challenger Indy Pace Car).

My thanks to fellow authors for their insights, which were quoted in this book from their previously published works. That includes the late Paul Zazarine, Robert Genat, Peter Grist, Jeffrey Godshall, John Gunnell, Steve Magnate, Mike Mueller, Joe Oldham, James Schild, Roger Struck, Eugene Piurkowski, and Bill Wetherholt at allpar.com.

Thanks also to R. M. Clarke for compiling the original magazine road tests of the E-Body cars into the *Dodge Muscle Portfolio 1964–1971*, *Plymouth Muscle Portfolio 1964–1971*, and *Original Barracuda and Challenger 1970–1974*. (And thanks to amazon.com, where you can find those books, as well as those by the authors listed above, to add to your Mopar reference library.)

My special thanks go to David Tom for his excellent history of the glory years of the SCCA Trans-Am Series, *The Cars of Trans-Am Racing 1966–1972: Road Racing Muscle from GM, Ford, Chrysler and AMC,* which is also a CarTech publication.

A number of former colleagues from my magazine days also contributed to this book, including Butch Noble and Randy Bolig. Butch provided spectacular trackside photography from Laguna Seca and Infineon Raceways while I was *DRIVE!* magazine's first full-time editor; and Randy was my editor and supervisor during the years that I wrote for *Mopar Muscle* magazine. I'd also like to thank former colleagues Alan Colvin, Kevin Di Ossi, and Bill Moore for their support.

As this is my first work to be published in book form, I will always be grateful for the kind assistance and support given by my editor at CarTech Books, Paul Johnson.

My most grateful thanks go to my family for their encouragement and support during this project, including Pat Ross (my mom and longtime editor), Stuart T. Ross (my dad, who was a PhD metallurgist in Chrysler's materials lab in Highland Park when I was born), along with Douglas T. Ross and Doreen Ross (my brother and sister-in-law). Special thanks are also due to Mom and Dad for allowing me to compile my automotive reference archive over the years, information and images from which are also included in this book, along with bits and pieces here and there that I've remembered.

Finally, my deepest thanks are due to you, the Mopar enthusiast, whose passion for products that wear the car and truck brands of Chrysler Corporation and its successors made the writing of this book a joy to perform!

INTRODUCTION

Are the 1970–1974 Dodge Challenger and Plymouth Barracuda "pony cars" . . . or muscle cars?

That's a question based on the heritage, and mechanical layout, of Chrysler's E-Body cars, whose lifetime spanned the late 1960s when they were styled, engineered, and entered into production; and the first five years of the 1970s, a time when changes (not all of them good) confronted the U.S. automakers on an almost-daily basis.

Until the fall of 1969, my family lived outside Detroit, in Bloomfield Township, near where more than a few car-company stylists and styling executives lived. Gerry Thorley, head of Plymouth's exterior styling studio, lived a short distance away, and his sons were grade-school classmates of my brother and me.

Also living nearby were Richard Baird, who'd been De Soto's last exterior styling studio head before De Soto's operations were merged into those of the Chrysler brand in 1959, and Dave Holls, whose career at General Motors included stints in Cadillac, Buick, and Opel's exterior styling salons before a move to Chevrolet's advanced styling studios around the time that the second-generation F-Body Camaro and Firebird were in the works.

The northern end of Woodward Avenue's legendary "cruise strip" was within earshot on warm summer nights, when the high V-8s of those looking to race heads-up north of 16 Mile Road could be heard from my bedroom window.

Into all of this, for the 1970 model year, was coming an all-new Dodge Challenger and Plymouth Barracuda. If you were "plugged in" to the goings-on in the car business back then, as a large number of people (of all ages) in greater Detroit were at that time, you knew that this could be huge for both Dodge and Plymouth.

Unfortunately, factors not considered back in 1967 such as high insurance rates and surcharges, as well as limited supplies at the nation's gas stations, negatively impacted the E-Body Mopars' success. That, along with plenty of competition from General Motors, Ford, and AMC (and even within Chrysler itself) was also a factor.

But can you say that the E-Body Challenger and Barracuda, both of which had only a five-year production run, were total failures? You can't say that as long as there's a demand for reproduction parts to restore them to factory-original condition (and a demand for those parts that have yet to be reproduced), up to and including reproduction 1970 Challenger hardtop bodies, which are available from Dynacorn.

And you can't say that about a car that's been revived in the 21st Century, a derivative of Chrysler's LX rear-drive platform, styled to look like the 1970 Challenger yet includes modern-tech powertrain and chassis hardware and electronics, and boasts a standard Hemi V-8 whose output rivals many 1960s muscle car engines, and includes a 707-hp Hellcat version.

In this book you'll find out why Chrysler went with the E-Body to compete against the Mustang, Camaro, and related pony cars, what it went through to get them into production, what was available on those cars, and why after 1971, it appeared that Chrysler was putting as little as it could into the Challenger and Barracuda, offering them as long as Ford and General Motors built price-class competitors.

You'll also find many "I didn't know that!" items in the text, images, and related information.

Many of the books produced previously about the E-Body Challenger and Barracuda have been heavy on photos of them: trackside, in the show field, on the street, wherever they can be found. This book does not replace them; in fact, it's a volume that can be enjoyed alongside them, with the information here, especially those items that have never before been published, adding to the body of knowledge about these cars.

I hope that this adds to your body of Mopar knowledge and is as fun for you to read as it was to compile.

CHAPTER 1

BIRTH OF THE E-BODY

Development of the Barracuda and Challenger

On April 17, 1964, Ford introduced its Mustang, a "sporty compact" that shared the Falcon and Comet's powertrain, chassis, and mechanical features, as well as the small Fords' cowl, firewall, floorpan, and other sub-structural members, underneath a sharply styled two-door body, available at first as a convertible or coupe.

Reaction to the Mustang was sensational, to say the least. Ford, which had figured it would sell approximately 70,000 to 80,000 Mustangs in the first year, sold 22,000 Mustangs on that first day, and its first-year production and sales totals exceeded the 417,000 that Falcon had recorded for 1960.

At Chevrolet, thoughts of the revised-for-1965 Corvair competing against the Mustang were soon lost in a cloud of figurative sales dust, as more and more Mustangs were seen on the American road as the spring of 1964 rolled into the summer. By the time the 1965-model cars went on sale in September, Chevrolet had stopped all development work on the Corvair and its rear-engined platform (despite a massive reworking for 1965) and had begun a crash program to get a front-engined "Mustang fighter" into production as soon as it could. Target date: the start of model year 1967 production.

At that time, though, Chrysler did introduce the sporty compact Valiant Barracuda on April 1, 1964. It was not regarded as a direct competitor to the Ford Mustang, as it was based on the A-Body Valiant Signet. (Many observers described Barracuda as a "Valiant Signet wearing a fishbowl" due to the small Plymouth's large, compound-curve glass fastback rear window.)

Chrysler sold 23,443 Barracudas over its shortened 1964 model run. Compare than with Mustang's sales success, especially on Mustang's first day. As for Dodge, it had its top-of-the-line Dart GT hardtop and convertible, but (as with Barracuda) these were not considered "true" Mustang competitors because they were a version of Chrysler's A-Body compact platform. Although the Mustang was based on the same Ford platform as its compact Falcon and Mercury Comet, it did not share any body panels or interior trim items, unlike the top-line Chrysler compacts, which were clearly extensions of its two compact-car lines.

The next two model years, 1965 and 1966, brought minor visual changes to the small Plymouths and Dodges, along with mechanical upgrades, including a high-performance version of the 273-ci LA engine, which arrived for 1965. Equipped with a solid-lifter camshaft, 4-barrel carburetor, 10.75:1 compression, and low-restriction exhaust system with a single rear resonator and tailpipe, the 273 Hi-Po was rated at 235 hp, a figure that many who drove it say was low by a good 10 to 25 hp, if not more. The A-833's standard shift linkage was sourced from Hurst, the leading name in aftermarket manual-transmission shifters, which was expanding its OEM offerings.

In 1966, Dodge offered the 273 Hi-Po in a special run of Dart GT hardtops that were known as the D-Darts, because their factory equipment was intended to make the car legal to race in NHRA's D/Stock class for production-based cars. (Chrysler had already established mastery in the Stock and Super Stock classes with the

In 1970, the Barracuda was offered with a variety of powertrain packages and trim levels, and that included the AAR 'Cuda. Designed to race head to head with the Camaro and Mustang in the Trans Am Series, Chrysler had to sell a requisite number of street cars in order to the meet racing rules. (Photo by David Newhardt/Mecum Auction Company)

Max Wedge and 426 Hemi B-Body Plymouths and Dodges that had ruled the "doorslammer" classes on the strip from mid-1962 onward.)

For 1967, Chrysler had plenty of ideas in mind for its A-Body small-car platform. It received fresh slab-sided styling, but the Barracuda (even though it gained Valiant's former hardtop and convertible body styles) still had to use an exterior shell that looked a lot like its plain-Jane Valiant counterparts. The same was true for the Dodge Dart hardtop and convertible models.

At the start of 1967 production, and for much of that model year, the LA-series V-8 was the largest engine available from the factory in the A-Body cars, despite the competition having big-block engines available as options (Ford, Mercury, and Chevrolet) or standard (Pontiac).

In the spring of 1967, a big-block V-8 joined the Barracuda and Dart option lists, thanks to Chicago Dodge dealer "Mr. Norm" Kraus. At his Grand Spaulding Dodge dealership, a 383-ci "B" engine was stuffed into a Dodge Dart GT hardtop, which Kraus then drove to Chrysler's engineering shops in Highland Park, Michigan. Once the engineers took a good look at it and figured out what was needed to install a big-block "B" engine on the assembly line, the 383 became a factory option for the

Chrysler's "sporty compact" of the mid-1960s, the Plymouth Valiant Barracuda. It was essentially a Valiant Signet with a different roof and trunk; it also had a large, compound-curved window between them and a fold-down rear seat under the glass. Power came from a standard 225-ci Slant Six, or an optional 273-ci V-8. From this rear-corner view, the first-generation Barracuda's A-Body compact car roots are apparent. Some called it "a Valiant Signet with a fishbowl." (Photo Courtesy Mecum Auctions)

Available as an option in the first- and second-generation Barracudas was Chrysler's LA small-block V-8, which entered production (and joined the Valiant and Dart option lists) midway through the 1964 model year, and was a Barracuda option from the beginning. This particular Barracuda is equipped with air conditioning. Note that the engine bay does not have much room around it to permit factory installation of a B/RB-series big-block V-8, let alone a 426 Hemi. (Photo Courtesy Mecum Auctions)

The second-generation Barracuda gained convertible and hardtop body styles starting in 1967, but was still built on the same A-Body platform as the Plymouth Valiant. Those cars' scarcity today is not only explained by the passage of time, but also by the fact that Chrysler sold far fewer A-Body Barracudas than Ford did Mustangs, especially convertibles, including this 1968 Barracuda Formula S. (Photo Courtesy Mecum Auctions)

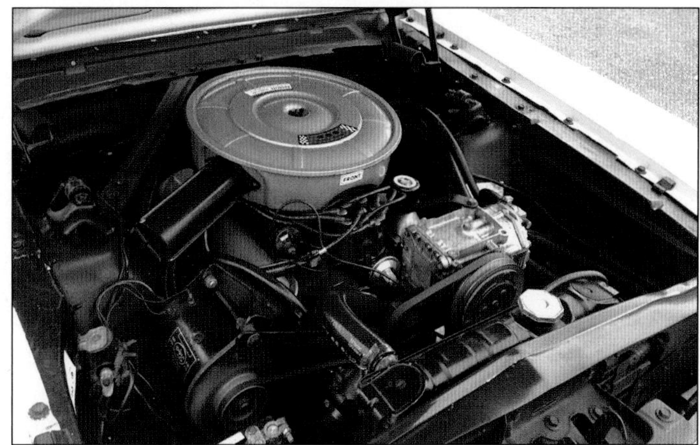

Ford's Windsor series of V-8s was a Mustang mainstay from the first day of production through the Windsor's discontinuation as a passenger-car engine after the 1995 model year. Note how this 289-ci V-8 fills the engine bay that was derived from the Falcon. A widening was needed for optional FE-series big-blocks, which became available for 1967. (Photo Courtesy Mecum Auctions)

sporty A-Bodies. However, power brakes, power steering, and air conditioning were not available, because the 383's width and length left no room in the A-Body engine bay for a factory-installed power brake booster, power steering pump, or air conditioning compressor. Also, a special "up and over" exhaust manifold for the left side was needed for the 383 Barracudas and Darts, to clear the steering shaft.

Another "Valiant" Effort?

As the 1967 model year progressed and the sales reports came in to Chrysler's top brass in Highland Park showing just how far behind the Mustang and Camaro the Barracuda and Dart were, they saw that they had to do something more than just run a re-skinned Valiant to compete with Mustang and its pony car competitors Chevrolet, Mercury, and Pontiac.

The Mercury Cougar was the upscale Ford Mustang, and Dodge Challenger competed directly against this Cougar during its four-year model run.

The first step was to ditch the A-Body platform, which Plymouth stylist Jeffrey Godshall says was all wrong. "What the Barracuda really needed was to be its own car with its own platform, one that would allow more adventurous styling, not to mention the use of Chrysler's really big engines, to do battle with 400-ci Firebirds, 396 Camaros, and 428 and 429 Mustangs. For 1970, things were different.

"The Barracuda would get a brand-new body, its own, code named E-Body, shared with only its new companion, the Dodge Challenger. Chrysler's midsize B-Body cars were donating their underpinnings, and that meant that those big engines could be stuffed underhood. The disadvantage, of course, was that the Barracuda would now cost more to produce. (By the way, the Barracuda and Challenger shared no common sheet metal. The Challenger even rode on a wheelbase that was longer by 2 inches. Externally, the two cars shared only their windshields.)

"Dimensions were juggled so that Barracudas got wider, shorter, and squatter. Although the wheelbase remained at 108 inches, overall length was reduced 2 inches to 50.9, and overall width was stretched a whopping 5 inches to 74.9. The tread was also increased, to 57.5 inches up front [up 2.2 inches] and 61.3 inches in the rear [up 5.7 inches].

"The new styling, however, made the most of the new measurements. Hoods and decks were flat, with single headlights and slotted taillights firmly planted at each of the car's four corners."

Starting in 1967, the pony car segment of the U.S. new-car market grew to include competition from General Motors, namely the Chevrolet Camaro. This is a 1970½ Camaro Z-28. This year's Camaro featured the LT-1 350 engine with solid lifter cam that pumped out 360 hp.

The "Mustang Fighter" Proposal

To receive Chrysler's upper management approval for the new car concept, Burton Bouwkamp, who was then Chrysler's director of product planning, made his pitch to the corporation. "At the Corporate Product Planning Committee meeting, I promised management that we would sell 200,000 cars a year. Manufacturing loved the plan because 200,000 cars a year was perfect: two eight-hour shifts at 60 cars per hour. Finance calculated that we would make money at 200,000 per year, and consequently the program was approved."

At that time, Chrysler's product planners estimated that the pony car segment of the U.S. new-car market would reach 1.5 million cars a year by 1970. "We told management that we should be in it with fully competitive products," said Bouwkamp. "We projected a Chrysler market penetration of 15 percent of this 1.5 million [vehicle] segment, which would be 225,000 cars a year."

But, at that same time, Chrysler's product planners also saw how big-block V-8s were changing the sporty compact market. They were not just factory options like Mercury's and Ford's 390-ci FE-series V-8, Chevrolet's 396-ci Mark IV V-8, or any of Pontiac's big-block V-8s from 326 to 400 ci, but special cars that had larger-displacement engines swapped into them by performance-minded dealers, in the case of 427 Camaros, or by outside companies that a manufacturer contracted with for that work, in the case of Ford and Shelby Automotive's collaboration beginning in 1965.

Chrysler already had two platforms in production that could handle its existing B/RB line of big-block V-8s. The full-size C-Body and the midsize B-Body could be fitted with the big-blocks, and both had been extensively restyled for 1965 and 1966, respectively. The latter was also the platform into which the 426 Hemi was installed starting in 1964 and developed for racing. It became a regular-production option for 1966 in slightly detuned Street Hemi form. Chrysler's engineers let it be known that any new vehicle intended to compete in the same size and price class as the Mustang would also have to have the same factory big-block capability as Mustang and its competitors had. Bouwkamp adds, "We knew that we could not get a competitive sporty proportion and B/RB engine options with an A-Body platform."

Thus, it was decided that the new "Mustang fighter" would be wider and heavier than its predecessor A-Body Barracuda, which had been designed and engineered around the Slant Six and, to a lesser extent, the LA-series V-8. Bouwkamp also noted that the proposed Mustang-fighter would have to be wider than the A-Body, to fit larger (up to 15-inch diameter) wheels, as well as the new "low profile" tires that the tire makers were developing for 1967 model-year introduction. With that added width, Bouwkamp pointed out, came an improved appearance, at the cost of adding extra weight to what was supposed to be a relatively small car, one shorter in length than the midsize B-Body Dodges and Plymouths.

It was also decided that the underpinnings of this new car would be shared with those of another new-car program that was in the works. According to Diran Yasajian, who worked in the Dodge Exterior Styling studio at that time, "The windshield, cowl, and firewall . . . was designed for the 1971 B-Bodies, and they actually pulled all that stuff ahead for the E-Bodies."

With styling and engineering lead times what they were, that meant the soonest that the E-Body would reach Dodge and Plymouth dealers would be at the start of the 1970 model year.

Styling the New E-Body

There was a lot of work to be done, and a stampede of competitors that Chrysler hoped to catch and pass with the E-Body cars, and not much time to get it all done. It was already February 1967 when Chrysler's Advanced Styling studio, under the

Early styling concepts for Chrysler's next-generation "Mustang fighter" (which succeeded the A-Body–based Barracuda) began appearing in the fall of 1964. This sketch by John Samsen shows a car with a long hood and short deck; what the Ford Mustang had by then, and what the E-Body eventually had. (Photo Courtesy Brett Snyder)

direction of Cliff Voss, set the dimensions including overall length and wheelbase (the "hard points") plus details such as the size of the glass area and the size and rake of the windshield. Chet Limbaugh, who worked in the Chrysler Advanced Styling studio then, explains what would go into a new vehicle's package: "We'd start with a bunch of dimensions and concepts. Then, we'd go through a phase where we'd do a car concept of some sort, then have a presentation. Then, at that point, they [Chrysler management] would decide whether they would continue with that program."

Once the package of dimensions (overall length, width, height, wheelbase, front and rear tread, etc.) was finalized, initial styling work on the E-Body was done by the Plymouth Exterior and Interior Styling studios. (At the time, each Chrysler brand had its own exterior and interior styling studios, along with an advanced styling studio. The concept of "platform teams" that covered all aspects of new-vehicle design and engineering was not introduced at Chrysler for many years.)

Limbaugh added, "Chrysler bosses wanted something contemporary, so under the guidance of Plymouth studio manager Gerry Thorley and assistant Irv Ritchie, a team that included Milt Antonick, Dave Cummins, John Herlitz, and John Samsen pooled their ideas to come up with the new 1970 pony car. [Chrysler Styling boss Elwood] Engle told the stylists that the sales division wanted a car with long hood/short deck proportions like the Mustang, but with a unique look. The Plymouth designers were very pleased to be able to move away from the slab-sided, Ford-looking designs being offered on the larger corporation cars."

Both the Dodge and Plymouth Exterior Styling studios developed styling concepts based on Advanced Styling's package, but Chrysler's top brass picked one that would be the basis for the E-Body, with the "losing" studio then tasked to give that winning design the character of its brand. "We would all

About five months after the Ford Mustang went on sale, this rendering by John Samsen from the fall of 1964 shows a long hood/short deck fastback coupe with side-mounted exhausts. Note the sharp lines of the front of the car, which suggest an engine mounted close to, or under, the firewall and windshield. The "blue streak" tires were likely suggested by Goodyear's Blue Streak sports car tires of the era. (Photo Courtesy Brett Snyder)

Front view of the long hood/short deck fastback coupe by John Samsen, again from the fall of 1964. Note the Barracuda "fish" logo next to the left headlight. Also note the rectangular headlights, which were not legal for U.S. production vehicles at that time (they did not appear on Chrysler products until 1977), and the "ironing board" on the hood, which appears to add clearance for the proposed car's engine. (Photo Courtesy Brett Snyder)

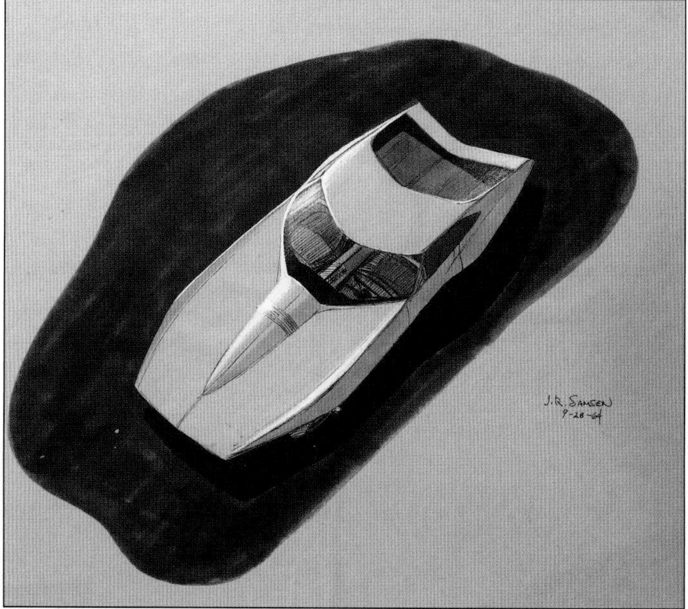

Overhead view of the long hood/short deck sport coupe styled by John Samsen in the fall of 1964. The length of the hood is much longer than any production Chrysler product of the era, as is as the cabin, which features bucket seats similar to those in the production Barracuda, along with a long center console (similar to the Barracuda's optional console), an extremely swept-back windshield and large rear window, and what appears to be a two-seat cabin between those large expanses of glass. (Photo Courtesy Brett Snyder)

do designs to get the program going, then the best designs were picked to go into clay models," recalled Plymouth stylist John Samsen. "Then, our body would compete with the Dodge [body], and [as in the case of the E-Body] the Plymouth Body won out over the Dodge proposal. So, then the Challenger had to be made out of the Plymouth basic design."

Diran Yasajian recalls that despite the intra-brand competition between the two styling studios, the proposed new car's styling program was not one that was out of the ordinary, nor a "crash" program like the sudden redesign and downsizing of the 1962 full-sized Plymouths and Dodges was. "The process was just a normal design program," he recalled. "The designers made sketches and put them on the wall, the big bosses came in and picked them [those they approved of], and they clayed them up. That was the process that we used for all cars."

The process came with the executive decision to accommodate the B/RB and Hemi engines in the new car, which would provide big savings for Chrysler.

That "borrowing" of the upcoming 1971 B-Body's cowl and firewall, as well as its front floorpan and substructure forward of the cowl, likely appealed to Chrysler's management on the basis of cost and time. Using the B-Body structural members (and the powertrain and chassis parts that bolted to them) saved untold millions of dollars in design, engineering, and tooling costs. This also led to further cost savings, from the engineering and development time that was saved in the process. If this sounds familiar, it's exactly what Ford's upper management did in 1962, when it chose to base its first-generation Mustang on the existing Falcon/Comet platform.

Yasajian adds that early sketches that "borrowed" some styling themes for a then-in-progress (and now legendary) vehicle design for the B-Body turned out to be wrong for the E-Body. "We tried putting the 1968 Charger theme on that car. It didn't really work that well; it just wasn't suited for that size car." He adds that John Herlitz is credited by many for the E-Body's basic silhouette. "In an interview many years ago with *Musclecar Review*, he recalled, 'I wanted to put the rear quarters as high as possible and spank the roof down as low as possible and just get the very high hunched look in the rear quarters, allowing the front fenders to become the long, leading design element that ran out past the powerplant to give a very dynamic thrust.'"

Samsen adds that a number of elements from his work made it onto the production E-Body cars, which he says was a team effort. "I had a design that I still have images of, which the lower part of the body is a lot like what I had. But the roof, cab, and so on were different."

Although Herlitz and the Plymouth Exterior Styling studio team (managed by Gerry Thorley and included Herlitz, Samsen, Milt Antonick, Shinski "Matty" Matsura, Dave Cummins, Pete

This styling sketch by Chester Limbaugh, dated November 15, 1966, incorporates the long hood/short deck theme seen in the John Samsen sketches, along with a windshield and A-pillar that look like the ones that made it into production on the E-Body cars for 1970 and on the Plymouth and Dodge B-Body cars for 1971. The distance between the windshield and rear window suggest a four-seat configuration inside. Note also the "skirted" rear wheels, a feature seen only on production C-Body Chryslers and Y-Body Imperials at the time. (Photo Courtesy Tom Limbaugh)

Dated February 1967, this sketch by Chester Limbaugh shows his concept of what a long hood/short deck sports coupe would look like. Note the flat hood, which suggests an engine location similar to that of production 1967 Chrysler Corporation vehicles, instead of the location in the 1964 John Samsen sketches, which suggested the engine would be mounted rearward of the front wheels. Also note the covered headlamps, which look similar to the ones that Oldsmobile used on its production 1966–1967 Toronados. (Photo Courtesy Tom Limbaugh)

In this Chester Limbaugh sketch from July 1967, the windshield and A-pillar look similar to the ones that made it onto the production E-Body (and 1971-later B-Body) cars, though more steeply raked than what made it into production. Note also the flat hood, similar to the hood in the Chester Limbaugh sketch of February 1967. (Photo Courtesy Tom Limbaugh)

Loda, Don Hood, John Herlitz, Bill Shannon, Fred Schimmel, and Neil Walling) did the E-Body's advance work; they were not just working on one for Plymouth alone.

Dodge also received its version of the new car, but with different door outer skins, which (per Bouwkamp) gave it a different appearance. It also received a 3-inch-longer wheelbase and was projected to have a $100 higher market price than the Plymouth.

The E-Body's larger, B-Body-derived size presented problems that Gerry Thorley pointed out. "The car was too big [and] too wide," he remembers. "The seating was no longer intimate."

While the new car (code-named E-Body) was in the clay-model stage, other changes were made, including moving the main character line ("B" line, in styling slang) on each body side higher, at the suggestion of Chrysler chairman

This sketch by Bob Hubbach shows a four-headlight front-end treatment for the Dodge Challenger. Note that the shape of the grille above the bumper appears similar to the production 1970 Challenger grille, while the below-the-bumper grille foreshadows the 1972–1974 production Challenger grille. Also note that a variation of this headlight/grille theme later appeared on the production C-Body 1973 Plymouth Fury. (Photo Courtesy Brett Snyder)

This front-end concept sketch by Bob Hubbach shows an "egg-crate" grille entirely below the front bumper. Had this design made it onto a production vehicle, it likely would have been severely altered by the Federal Motor Vehicle Safety Standards (FMVSS), which required 5-mph front-impact protection beginning with 1973 model-year vehicles. (Photo Courtesy Brett Snyder).

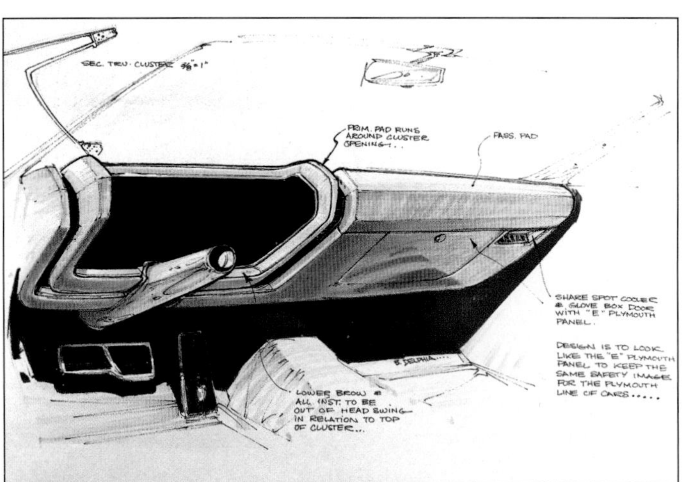

The proposed E-Body Challenger and Barracuda was the first new-vehicle program where Chrysler stylists had to consider upcoming Federal Motor Vehicle Safety Standards, inside and out. This instrument panel concept sketch by Ben Delphia for the 1971 B-Body cars notes the safety concerns, as well as using the already-approved Plymouth E-Body glove box door panel and spot cooler designs. (Photo Courtesy Brett Snyder)

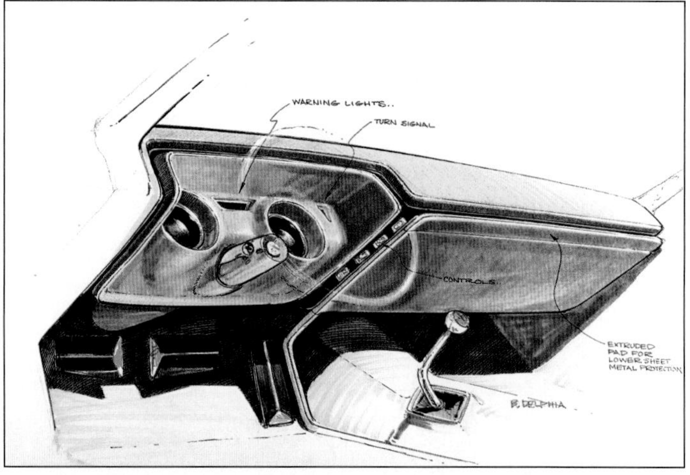

In this undated Ben Delphia instrument panel sketch, the pad on the top of the panel appears identical to the one that made it into production for the 1970 Challenger and Barracuda. The large round gauges of this particular concept did not make production. The large gauge on the left is similar to the speedometer on the standard-model, non-"Rallye"-instrument-cluster-equipped 1970-later Barracudas and Challengers. Note also the gear shift lever location, angled to the left side of the transmission. This location did not make it into production. (Photo Courtesy Brett Snyder)

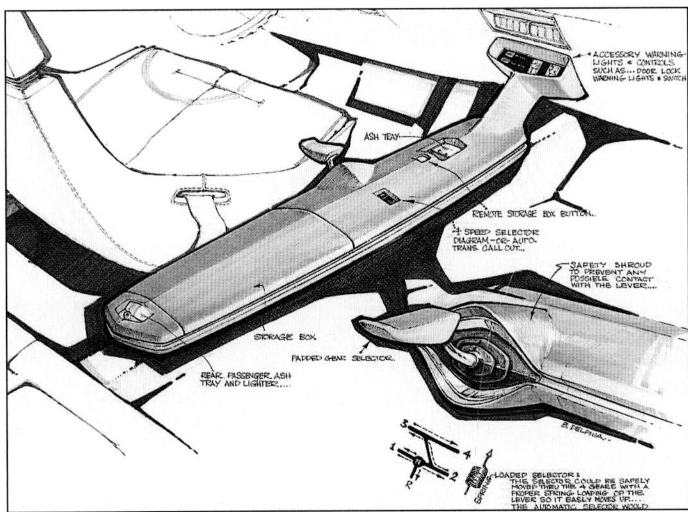

This is an undated concept sketch by Ben Delphia for a center console with floor-mounted gear shift lever. The overall shape of the console's top appears similar to the production 1970 E-Body console, minus the crease on top. Note the novel spring-loaded manual transmission gear shift lever, located on the left of the transmission similar to the shift lever in another Ben Delphia sketch. Note also the accessory warning lights and controls pod at the front of the console. For the production 1970 Barracuda Gran Coupe and Challenger SE, that pod was located above the console on the inside of the roof, just aft of the windshield header. (Photo Courtesy Brett Snyder)

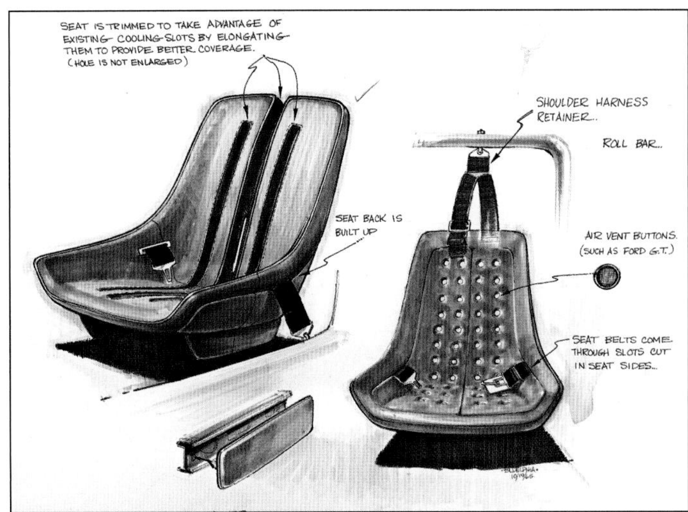

Two front bucket-seat concepts by Ben Delphia from October 19, 1965, incorporated cooling slots (such as on the seat at the left), or cooling holes similar to what Ford's race-only GT-40 used. Note also the "racing-style" seat belts and shoulder harnesses, and roll bar (to which the shoulder harness retainer is mounted). It would have been interesting to see designs like these on the production 1970 Plymouth 'Cuda AAR and Dodge Challenger T/A, along with those cars' other unique parts that were included to make them legal in SCCA's Trans-Am racing series or any other production-based racing series such as those run by NASCAR and NHRA. (Photo Courtesy Brett Snyder)

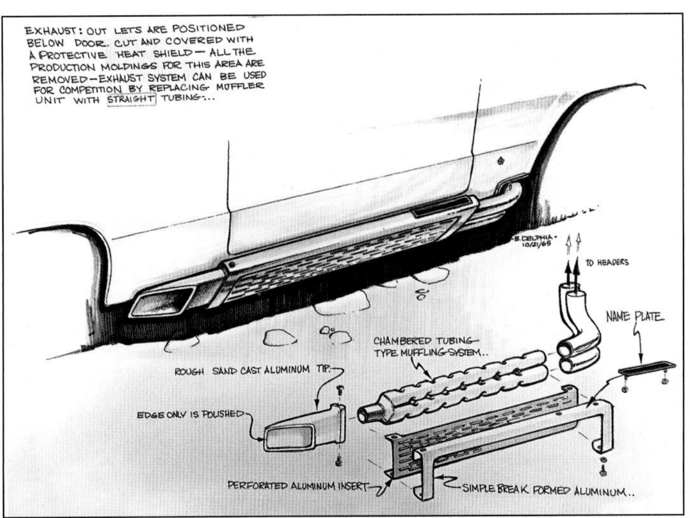

Along with interior design concepts, Ben Delphia also worked on designs for exterior components. In this sketch dated November 21, 1965, he devised this side-mounted chambered exhaust system. Note that these exhausts are for use with tubular exhaust headers, not cast-iron production exhaust manifolds. Had these made it into production, either by Chrysler or an aftermarket company, imagine the sound that a 426 Hemi would make through them, even with the chambered "mufflers" installed. (They would probably have made a Slant Six sound like a P-51 fighter plane!) (Photo Courtesy Brett Snyder)

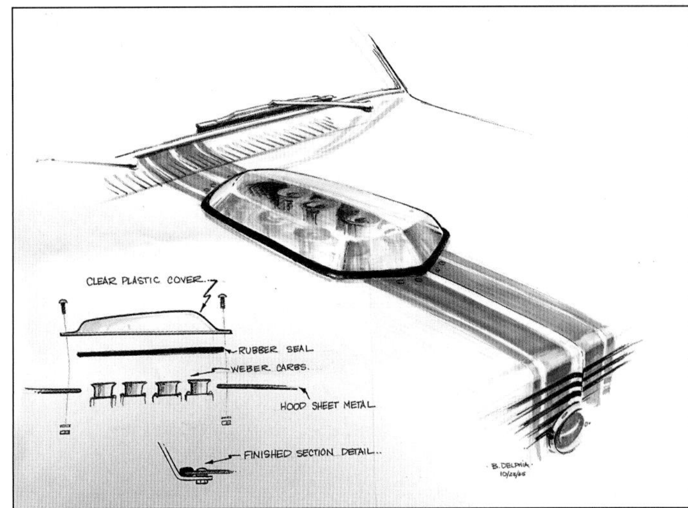

Dated October 22, 1965, this Ben Delphia sketch foreshadows the hole-though-the-hood look that the "Shaker" hood scoop gave the production 1970–1971 'Cuda and Challenger R/T models. Seen here on a possible modified production 1966 Barracuda, it features a clear plastic cover over a set of eight Weber carburetors. The mechanically fastened cover looks as if it could have been easily removed for competition purposes, where engine heat combined with air flowing through those Webers may have led to massive deformation of that cover! (Photo Courtesy Brett Snyder)

Lynn Townsend to Dodge exterior-styling head Bill Brownlie. Townsend thought the change would give that line less of a "dragging" appearance.

Also while the E-Body was still in the clay-model stage, the exterior styling received further refinements. As Plymouth stylist Milt Antonick explains, "We utilized two clay models, which allowed for four variations. At that point, the centerline profile was set, and small bodyside variations were being evaluated. Remember, we received the package from the [Cliff] Voss [Advanced Styling] studio. This included a 58-degree windshield. We later managed to develop a 60-degree windshield for the B-Body;the argument was night vision refraction of headlamps as a double image.

"The Voss package also defined the curvature and tumblehome of the side glass and the sill or rocker position, which is a structural member shared with the B-Body. The rear glass was not defined, but we were told not to do a fastback. They wanted to tie the structure together in the C-pillar area. We added some front overhang and reduced the rear overhang as much as possible while still clearing the spring hangers, similar to the [Studebaker] Avanti approach.

"I think we spent about eight weeks developing the clay. I wanted to provide a gill or engine vent on the A-Body Barracuda as a visual update, but could not because it would require re-tooling the fender from scratch. The stamping people said we could define an area for a fender update in the original fender design, and that is how we managed to add the fender vents [nonfunctional] on the 1971 models. They were designed by Don Hood."

Regarding the grille, taillights, and other styling details, Antonick explains how the Plymouth Exterior used techniques from their counterparts in Dodge Exterior Styling to add those details to their E-Body, with similar details going on the Dodge. Quoted by author Peter Grist in his book *Dodge Challenger, Plymouth Barracuda: Chrysler's Potent Pony Cars*, Antonick says, "We utilized paper overlays for grille, tail lamps, and other details before committing the time and effort to clay modeling. At the time Chrysler was utilizing leaf spring rear suspensions, which prohibited the E-Jag[uar] or 'duck butt' undercut form below the rear bumper.

"We borrowed the Avanti approach of covering the rear spring shackle with a vertical nerf-bar form, which allowed the surface to be modeled forward of the springs. Had we modeled the shape to the springs, the result would have been a 'baggy pants' look, instead of the cool undercut look. Since the sheet metal was a separate piece, we managed to get the exhaust to run through the part. This did not come easily, as the Manufacturing department was concerned about maintaining enough clearance to the rectangular pipe extensions. They preferred a simple notch at the bottom of the panel, [and] they also preferred a simple hole."

Design and Development

As with any new-vehicle program, challenges arose during the time between final approval of the body designs and the start of production. Once Chrysler's top management approved what Styling had created for the E-Body project, it was time to turn those ideas and concepts into production automobiles, fast.

Conventional auto-industry wisdom determined the time needed for a new-car program to be at least 24 months from the date that management approved a new car's styling to the date that the new car would start rolling off the assembly lines. Chrysler was mindful of what a "rushed" styling job could do in terms of build-quality glitches leading to a drop in sales. Its high-finned line of 1957 "Forward Look" cars leaked water into the cabin whenever it rained, and they began showing visible rust within a year of their assembly. Chrysler body engineers later said that they needed at least another six months to fix those "bugs," time Chrysler management didn't give them.

The E-Body cars would benefit from post-1957 engineering advances, as well as from the corporate strategy of pulling the upcoming 1971 B-Body's underpinnings (cowl, firewall, A-pillars), front floorpan, front frame rails, and K-member crossmember forward a year for use with the E-Body, so engines bigger than the LA small-blocks would fit.

By definition, a pony car of the 1960s was derived from an existing small-car platform that was designed for a 6-cylinder engine, with no thought toward the factory installation of a large V-8 engine. This underhood view of a 426 Hemi 1970 Dodge Challenger R/T coupe shows the benefit of pulling forward the 1971 B-Body engine bay, so that Chrysler's largest (and most powerful) engine could easily be installed at the factory with options such as power steering and power brakes. (Photo Courtesy Mecum Auctions)

"We were planning a new B-Body type of car for about 1971, and we were trying to get something out there as soon as we could," said Bob Davis, who worked in Chrysler's Advanced Chassis Engineering section. "About the only way that [E-Body] car was going to get sold [to upper management] was if we could use a lot of the same parts that you didn't see underneath the car, between the E-Body and the B-Body." Davis added that the "commonization" of parts between E-Body and B-Body platforms brought the costs for both projects down to where Chrysler could afford two distinctive-looking E-Body cars.

While the approved design concepts were translated from two-dimension sketches and renderings and three-dimension clay models, Chrysler's engineers developed "mule" test cars that had the same dimensions as the approved E-Body cars. Bob Davis said that was done by taking existing B-Body cars and resizing them by removing sections from their centers, making them longer forward of the windshield and shorter from the rear window on back, not just for engineering them for street duty, but also for road racing such as in SCCA's Trans-Am series.

As Davis explains, "We had cobbled up some cars, and we took a 340 engine and knocked it down to 305 ci, which was required. The race guys put all the equipment on that they thought they needed, and then we took those out [to track-test them]. The Trans-Am races would be on one week, and we'd have the track rented for the second week, and the racers would take them out and try to fine-tune them, and see how they compared with the lap times of guys such as Parnelli Jones, Mark Donohue, and other greats. These early mule cars served that purpose.

"So that gave us a head start on at least trying to get into the Trans-Am [series]. You probably know that Chrysler signed up Dan Gurney [and his All-American Racing team, to field the Plymouth 'Cuda AAR].

Author note: Dodge signed Autodynamics to field the Challenger T/A in SCCA Trans-Am racing, driven by Sam Posey and others.

"The other thing that we found with these cars was that if you ran the rough roads on the Proving Grounds with those modified cars, the rear axle went into a condition called 'tramp,'" said Davis. "If you could picture looking at the back of the car where the axle assembly is, and then when driving on those rough roads the wheels would alternately jump up and down and have a sort of dance, and start pulling the rear end off the side of the road. That, if you ever look in the trunk area, is why you see the shock-absorber mounts looking like afterthoughts, and they were. That's because we had to straighten up the shock-absorber mounts to make them more vertical to control that condition. Once we had that worked out, then we had a pretty stable car."

And not just a car that was stable on the racetrack. As Davis recalls, their work on the E-Body project also found its way into the coming-for-1971 B-Body Dodges and Plymouths. "We kept the torsion bar length the same, but there were a lot of changes in torsion bar sizes for not only the stiffer suspensions, but also because the B-Body was eventually going to have heavier station wagon versions of them as well. The B-Body was going to be built with a short wheelbase for the two-doors and the pillared hardtops [which did not make it into production], and the station wagons and four-door sedans were going to have a longer wheelbase."

Located just inboard of the rear wheelwells of this production 1970 Dodge Challenger R/T hardtop are the shock-absorber mounts that Bob Davis mentioned, which were located in this position to eliminate the rear axle "tramp" that was discovered in track and proving grounds testing of "mule" prototypes cut and sized to the E-Body's dimensions. (Photo Courtesy Mecum Auctions)

When the E-Body Dodge Challenger and Plymouth Barracuda went into production in August 1969, they did so with the longest doors ever used on a production Chrysler Corporation passenger car to that time, and the heaviest ones, too. Note the size of this 1970 Dodge Challenger SE R/T's door in proportion to its front fender and rear quarter panel. (Photo Courtesy Mecum Auctions)

E-Body Doors: Identical Functions, Different Looks

One area of the E-Body that Chrysler's engineers devoted a lot of time to was its doors. The final styling concepts called for a pair of long doors, with frameless window glass and no vent windows. That resulted in doors that were among the longest ever made by Chrysler (much longer than the ones used in the 1964–1969 Plymouth Barracuda and same-years Dodge Dart) and among the longest in the industry.

Bill Wetherholt, a longtime employee of Chrysler's Twinsburg, Ohio, stamping plant, says they were among the heaviest, too. "These doors weighed 87 pounds, and they didn't have any hardware on them, they didn't have any glass, they were just an inner and an outer door, with an impact bar for safety, for side impact." He adds that the size and weight was a problem for the Twinsburg plant. "They had little cranes overhead that had hooks, where you could pick up the door and maneuver it into the rack. Well, they didn't work at the time, so when you got to work, you had to pick them up by hand, and I mean these things were *heavy*, and you didn't get any breaks, other than your normal scheduled breaks for lunch, or every two hours."

One solution proposed to keep the finished doors' weight down was a one-piece inner panel to be made from polypropylene. Less weight and lower cost were its strong points, compared to other materials, so it was chosen for production.

Unfortunately, producing door inner panels with that material led to unforeseen problems. As Roger Struck recalled, "Colin Neale [chief of interior design] loved the sculptured look of the plastic molded door trim panels. He said he would 'soften' the hard touch of the molded panel with a textured surface. Well, it was still hard, texture or no. The good characteristics were that it had a cost advantage, as well as the 3-D freedom of a molded part, but it was unfriendly to the touch and had no sound-dampening quality and, therefore, exaggerated any rattles in the door."

Polypropylene door inner panels were not only hard to the touch, but that material was unstable, leading to every door panel being a little different dimensionally. That made it a problem for line workers installing them, one they solved thanks to that material's flexibility.

Tom Gale, who later became Chrysler's design chief, agrees that those door panels (and the rear-quarter trim panels located just aft of the doors) were the biggest challenges that he and his Advanced Engineering colleagues faced. "At that time, those were the biggest injection-molded parts that had ever been done in the industry. They required platen sizes and presses to be larger, and they required engineering for thermal coefficients of expansion to take care of the stretching, warm temperatures versus cold. Also, the fact that they were polypropylene meant at that time they couldn't be painted. So, you had [issues such as] injection-molded color, color-match, and graining."

Gale adds that despite those problems, Chrysler learned a lot about injection-molded door and interior panels, information it used in future years' passenger cars.

There was another problem that cropped up that involved the doors, and the tendency for their frameless window glass to rattle. Dave Langstone, who worked for Chrysler Engineering at the company's Proving Grounds at Chelsea, Michigan, describes how that problem was solved and the "colorful" name a line worker at Hamtramck Assembly's came up with for the curative part. "As originally designed, and unfortunately produced, the car's door glass got side-to-side support only on

An inside view of a production E-Body door, in this case a 1971 Dodge Challenger R/T. Note the size of the door, as well as its one-piece molded polypropylene inner panel. Soon after production began in 1969, a "fuzz"-coated steel bracket was designed to keep the large door window from shaking while lowered, and that bracket was installed on the assembly line before the inner panel went on. (Photo by Teddy Pieper/Courtesy Mecum Auctions)

Another view of a production E-Body door inner panel on a 1970 Dodge Challenger SE R/T hardtop. Note the size of the door hinges (right), which were subject to fatigue loading from the heavy door, especially when open. This, in turn, tended to make the door sag (and more difficult to close and latch) over time. Also note the optional remote-control mirror, "Special Edition" nameplate, and wood-grain trim. (Photo Courtesy Mecum Auctions)

Visible in this view of a 1974 Plymouth 'Cuda door opening are the door hinges previously mentioned, along with the large one-piece rubber weather strip that ran from the bottom to the top of the A-pillar, then along the roof header to the B-pillar. The 1970–1971 convertible models utilized a multiple-piece weather strip in that location. Also note the two-spoke "Tuff" steering wheel, which entered production in 1972. (Photo Courtesy Mecum Auctions)

the outside surface. You probably understand that the glass had no frame around it. Thus, when you shut the door with the glass up, there was no problem; it seated against the door seals. However, when the glass was lowered partway or all the way, it would travel inward when the door shut and then rattle back and forth several times.

"The impression was really bad, but somehow the problem didn't get corrected until after production started. I remember someone making a cartoon of the E-Body with the door glass rattling and the caption 'The Window Rattler.'

"Soon after production started, a part got released that corrected the problem. It was a U-shaped stamping, with a fuzzy surface on one side, which bore against the glass. The other side of the U bolted to the door structure. In any case, one day a group of engineers made a trip to the Hamtramck [Assembly] plant to see how the installation was going. While they were there, the installer, an older woman I was told, provided some entertainment. She ran low on parts and then yelled out, 'Send down another load o' them fuzzyfuckers, will ya?' This event resulted in the parts having a new name among those close to them."

Author note: There is no proof that Chrysler ever changed the name of that part on its parts drawings/blueprints to "Fuzzyfucker," and no reproduction parts have ever, to my knowledge, been produced with that name.

The E-Body cars were the first Chrysler products without front vent windows in decades. Those were "shaved off" the full-size C-Body cars and the Y-Body Imperials starting in 1969, and left off of the 1971 B-Body cars altogether.

Under the new sheet metal and ventless door glass, the E-Body cars would be like the 1960 Valiant in one regard: They would be the Chrysler products to adopt advanced-engineering ideas and practices. But, unlike Valiant, those advances in engineering were needed to comply with Federal Motor Vehicle Safety Standards (FMVSS) from the start of the new-car-development process, as opposed to modifying existing production cars to comply, as Chrysler (and all other automobile manufacturers who sold cars in the United States) had to do when those standards took effect on January 1, 1968.

Safety with Style

Inside, those new federal safety standards represented another challenge. Max Kenney, who worked in the interior-lighting lab in Chrysler Engineering's Highland Park, Michigan, facility, explains. "The only thing that we really had [that had to comply with the new standards] was the collapsible steering column, for 1970. Eventually, we had to mock up the column, and they wanted an actual column, which we didn't get [from Styling] until early 1969."

Kenney adds that the two-piece, lap-and-shoulder belts that the E-Body hardtops would have to meet the federal safety standards for front-occupant restraint (convertibles were exempt from that requirement, at that time) were something they already had experience with. "In 1968, they had already

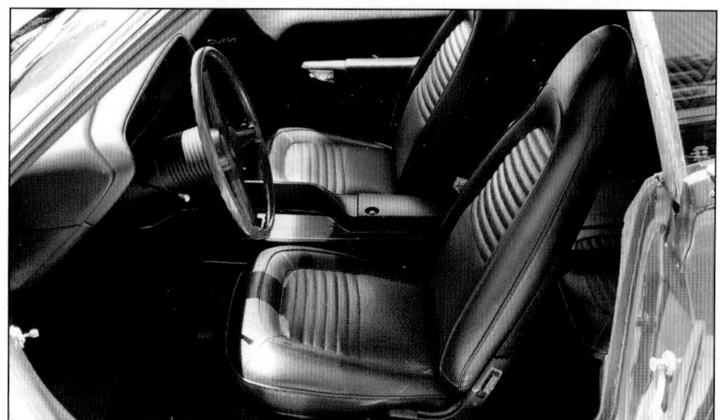

Federal Motor Vehicle Safety Standard (FMVSS) compliant features are visible in this 1970 Plymouth 'Cuda hardtop's cabin, including the accordion-shaped collapsible steering column and the production front bucket seats that incorporated an integral head restraint in the seat back, instead of the separate, adjustable headrest that Chrysler Corporation used on its 1969 models. (Photo Courtesy Mecum Auctions)

added the shoulder belt, which was located up above the front door windows. It was optional to use. We knew that we were [eventually] going to go to three-point belts, but nobody really knew what the finalization was going to be, and we were trying to beat it with that third belt clipped up above the window."

Another area now needing attention to comply with the new federal safety standards was the dash and instrument panel. Safety-standard compliance wasn't the only area where Chrysler's engineers needed to shine the light of progress. They also needed to shine it on the E-Body cars' dash lighting itself. Afterall, Illuminating Research = Better Lighting.

Max Kenney says that lighting up the new cars' recessed instrument clusters was their biggest challenge. "There were two versions that were proposed. One was backlighting, where you put the light bulbs in back of the gauges. The other one was floodlighting. This was something new. Nobody had done floodlighting of an instrument panel before. They did end up going with floodlighting [on the E-Body; it was later used on the C-Body Chryslers and Y-Body Imperials]." Kenney adds that floodlighting the instrument cluster would also cut costs over lighting up each gauge individually.

Once how to light the instrument panel was chosen, it was time to solve problems that cropped up with it, as Kenney explains. "There were problems with the plastic lenses; they had to have the right opaqueness to pass the light rays, the dials had to be at certain indices. That's when we started learning about day-glow reds on the pointers, to bring out the pointer at night. Here again, you get into that possible problem with low voltage when people turn their [instrument panel lights'] intensity down at night, if they live in the country. They'd lose some of the smaller dials. And, of course, you can't lose the speedometer; that was mandated by law.

"So, that went on. Floodlighting is what won the day."

Interior Style: A High-Performance Look

Some aspects of the E-Body cars' interior designs weren't received by Engineering to develop into production items until they were less than a year away from the start of production. Kenney says that included the steering wheels. "We didn't get [it] until early 1969, and in mid-1969, they didn't know if they were going to use the 'Tuff' in the E-Body, or use it in the A-Body. They ended up going with the 'Tuff' wheel in the Plymouth [Duster]."

Author note: The Tuff steering wheel was used in the E-Body cars starting in 1972 and in the B-Body Charger/Satellite in 1971.

The Pistol Grip Shifter

One interior item that debuted with the E-Body cars for 1970 was the Pistol Grip shifter handle for the optional 4-speed manual transmission. Bob Cox, who was a transmission and powertrain engineer with Chrysler in the late 1960s, relates how that now-iconic shifter handle came to be. "[Fellow engineer] Bruce Raymond and I had this old Dodge Coronet around that we'd cut up, and put different shifters in, trying different locations and beefing up the shift rods. Part of the thing was, you wanted something kind of long that gave a good

Visible in this through-the-door-opening view of a 1970 Dodge Challenger R/T hardtop's cabin are the three-spoke "flat" steering wheel (whose design wasn't finalized until just months before the start of production), as well as the four-pod "Rallye" instrument cluster (inside an instrument panel that closely resembles Ben Delphia's concept sketches), and the console-mounted Slap Stik shifter for the optional TorqueFlite automatic transmission. (Photo Courtesy Mecum Auctions)

Here's the Pistol Grip shifter, as installed in a 1970 Dodge Challenger R/T convertible. Note the "Hurst" lettering stamped on the shifter handle and the rubber boot at the shifter's base. The new shifter design, and the Hurst brand name, caught the eye of performance-minded new-car buyers back in 1970, those who hadn't been scared off by high insurance premiums and surcharges for 4-speed cars. (Photo Courtesy Mecum Auctions)

Close-up of a Pistol Grip shifter handle inside a 1970 Dodge Challenger R/T convertible. Although Chrysler Corporation's 1970 new-vehicle warranty didn't specifically say it, you were guaranteed not to get any wood splinters in your hand from prolonged shifting of one of these 4-speeds, despite the realistic appearance of the shifter handle. (Photo Courtesy Mecum Auctions)

A close-up of the top of a Pistol Grip 4-speed shift lever shows the transmission's shift pattern. Reverse was engaged by moving the shifter to the left, then up, which also lit up an amber indicator light on the instrument panel. Note the short throw from third gear to fourth gear. (Photo by Teddy Pieper/Courtesy Mecum Auctions)

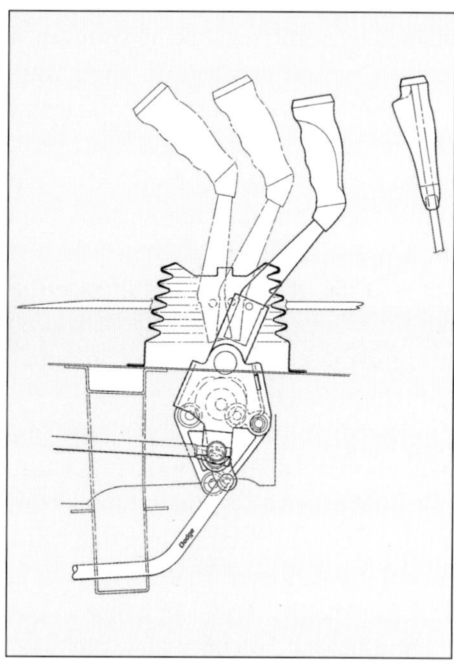

In this schematic diagram, supplied by former Mopar Muscle *editor Randy Bolig, the Pistol Grip 4-speed manual transmission gear lever and shifter assembly are seen in a left-side view, and the Pistol Grip handle is also seen in a front-view detail (right). The shifter seen here is for all E-Body cars, and was also used on B-Body 1971–74 Plymouth GTX/Road Runners/Dodge Chargers that were equipped with bucket seats and a center console. Bench-seat B-Body Pistol Grip shifters utilized a longer handle, shaped to clear the seat's bottom cushion. (Photo Courtesy Randy Bolig and Chrysler Historical Services)*

This non-console-equipped 1970 Plymouth 'Cuda hardtop's Pistol Grip 4-speed shifter is identical to the shifter seen above. Also visible are the buckle ends of the 'Cuda's separate lap and shoulder belts, as well as the "Engine Starting" instruction card on the turn-signal stalk that was included with every new Chrysler Corporation vehicle back then. (Photo Courtesy Mecum Auctions)

mechanical advantage, but looked short. For a while, we had a Hurst shifter in there that had a round ball on it. We looked at that and said, 'How about doing one that looks like a hockey stick?'" Soon after, Raymond carved a pistol-grip-shaped shifter out of walnut, camped it on the existing shifter stick, and what became another iconic Chrysler design was born.

Cox adds that when Styling and Product Planning each received a look at that carved-walnut handle, they liked what they saw. "Their eyes lit up a little bit, and they said, 'Oh yeah; we can do something like that.'"

When the Pistol Grip shifter eventually made it into a prototype E-Body car that would see testing duty, one problem cropped up. Dave Langstone recalls an incident involving a 440 Magnum/4-speed test car at the Chelsea Proving Grounds, which had its roots in the earlier version of the Chrysler A-833 gearbox, one day when a test car was being driven hard to evaluate shift quality. "This was a red 440 4-barrel convertible that was pretty beaten up at this point. My boss was driving and power-shifting through the gears. These transmissions took a lot of effort to shift, so naturally he was applying all his strength to that shift lever. The session culminated with him making a really hard 1-2 shift and having the lever uproot from the isolator, fly close to my ear (I remember the *ZZZZ*) and land in the backseat. The memory of almost getting brained by a shift lever being swung as hard as my boss could swing it has stuck with me through the years."

Langstone explains that problem (determined to be a tang in a stamped rectangular sleeve in the middle of a rubber isolator at the base of the shift lever, which held in place the shifter's attachment to the isolator) had its roots in the earlier versions of Chrysler's A-833 gearbox. "When the 4-speed came out in 1964, it had a Hurst linkage that shifted pretty well, but since there was no rubber isolation between the transmission and the shift lever, a lot of powertrain noise and vibration got transmitted to the car.

"From 1966 until mid-1968, an Inland linkage was used that had rubber isolation, but was a functional disaster. [Auto writers of the day called it the "Inland Steel Toilet Flusher," or worse!] It got replaced by a Hurst linkage that had a rubber isolator at the base of the shift lever. That isolator was junk. It allowed a lot of shift lever motion even when new and would crush and let the lever wobble all over after a few thousand miles.

"The isolators went away sometime around 1971. There was a bit of noise created, but people didn't seem to complain."

But that wasn't the only manual-gearbox-related problem that needed solving.

New Platform, New Clutch

A much bigger challenge involved the clutch to be used with the A-833 manual transmission behind the 440 and 426 Hemi engines. In the larger, B-Body cars, Chrysler used an 11-inch-diameter clutch. However, in the E-Body cars, there was a big problem, as Bob Cox explains. "There wasn't enough ground clearance when we used the 11-inch clutch; we missed it by about a 1/2 inch."

At the time, Cox and his colleagues were experimenting with a two-disc clutch, a concept that did not make it to production in a Chrysler product, but did appear in just 102 Chevrolet Corvette Stingrays as an option in 1969. "We were going to go with a 9½-inch, two-plate clutch that had two discs in it. The design of the clutch also affects how hard the shift efforts are; the bigger the clutch, the harder it will be to shift it.

"We worked for a year, year-and-a-half with that, and the two-plate clutch worked fine. It lasted well, but the problem was that you couldn't power-shift it. It wouldn't release properly; it was like the clutch was hanging up all the time. We really worked with Borg & Beck [Chrysler's clutch supplier] on that; they were certainly committed to the two-plate clutch. But we finally got to the point where we said, 'No, we've got to do something else.'"

That "something else" involved a feature that was already in production. "The 10½-inch Police and Taxi clutch had holes scalloped out in its cover that would clear the heads of the bolts [that hold it to the flywheel]. We looked at that and said, 'We can do that. We can put an 11-inch clutch where a 10½-inch bolt circle clutch would fit, if we did the scallops.'

"The real concern with the scallops was that we'd be using them on clutches in performance vehicles with Hemis that had a redline of 6,200 rpm or so. We needed to make sure that the clutches would not explode at high RPM. Borg & Beck didn't think they could do it, from their experience. For a sufficient safety factor, we had to double the engine speed, up to 13,500 rpm.

"We had burst chambers in the Mechanical Lab that we'd use, and we'd run the clutches up to where they'd explode."

But the "scalloped" clutches proved themselves in the research lab and went into production for the E-Body cars,

Close-up view of a production clutch disc and pressure plate, as used with the 440 and 426 Hemi engines in 4-speed-manual-transmission 1970 and 1971 Dodge Challengers and Plymouth Barracudas. Note the "scalloping" between the bolt holes; this was done to permit use of the heavy-duty clutch while not adversely affecting the E-Body cars' already-low ground clearance any further. (Photo Courtesy Brewer's Performance)

Full view of a "scalloped" clutch assembly for a 440/426 Hemi 1970–1971 Dodge Challenger or Plymouth Barracuda. This is an aftermarket unit, manufactured by McLeod, which can also be used on any other Dodge or Plymouth 4-speed application such as A-Body Dusters, Barracudas, and Darts, as well as on all 4-speed B-Body cars. Note the "scalloping" around the outside of the pressure plate. (Photo Courtesy Brewer's Performance)

Formerly known as "Dodge Main" (the complex where all of the Dodge Brothers Motor Company's operations were concentrated when it opened in 1914), Chrysler's Hamtramck Assembly Plant was a massive facility located in Hamtramck, Michigan, a city located entirely within the city limits of Detroit. It became a Chrysler plant when Chrysler bought Dodge Brothers in 1928 and was in operation until January 1980, when it closed for good. (Photo Courtesy Chrysler Historic Services)

as well as any 1970-later B-Body car factory equipped with a 440 or Hemi.

Hardware that helped the E-Body Dodge and Plymouth go fast was one thing. They also needed braking power that was up to their engines' power, given the state of the art in the late 1960s.

Braking System Development

Another crucial area of the E-Body was its braking system. Fortunately, they and their related parts were already in production, and readily available. Paul Gritt, a brake engineer for Chrysler when the E-Body cars were being developed, says that most of the system shared parts with the B-Body's brakes. "The front disc brakes had a 2.75-inch, pin slider caliper from Kelsey Hayes with vented rotors. The rears were 10 x 2½–inch drums, dual servo. The booster was, I believe, a 10½-inch single from Bendix or from Midland-Ross. The Bendixes were black, and the Midland-Rosses were gold.

"At that time, we were starting to make our own calipers (a 2.6-inch one and a 3.1-inch one at Toledo), and the 'Cuda had 2.75 [inch] calipers that was a pin-slider [design] instead of a rail-slider from Kelsey-Hayes, which was a little better brake, actually, a little more efficient. Because it was Kelsey-Hayes, it still had the chrome-plated steel piston."

But not all E-Body Barracudas and Challengers would be factory-equipped with front disc brakes. Manually assisted four-wheel drum brakes would be standard on the Slant Six and 318 V-8 Challengers and Barracudas, with front disc brakes available as an option, or included with the larger and high-performance engines.

One other question remained during E-Body development: Where would it be built?

E-Body Production Begins

Production for the E-Body Dodge Challenger and Plymouth Barracuda was assigned to Hamtramck Assembly in Hamtramck, Michigan. The former "Dodge Main" plant, which had been assembling automobiles since 1914, had the capacity needed to build the new Barracuda and Challenger, alongside the A-Body compacts Dodge Dart and Plymouth Valiant.

But it was far from state-of-the-art, or at least as modern as Chrysler's newest assembly plant at the time, Belvedere (Illinois) Assembly, a single-level plant that opened in 1965.

Hamtramck Assembly, by comparison, was made up of the original 1914 building, plus others added over the years, with the portion of it devoted to final assembly stretching some eight stories tall. The task of turning out 60 cars per hour, between two assembly lines (one E-Body and one A-Body) would lead to the in-process bodies making multiple up-and-down trips between floors, depending on assembly operation, instead of it staying on one level such as at Belvidere, and at the nearby Lynch Road Assembly Plant, which was built in 1928 as the primary Plymouth plant.

John Parsons, who worked at Hamtramck's Production Department, describes the process involved in building Chrysler's newest car line in its oldest plant, starting on its sixth floor. "Major body framing for each body was done in two vertical

Chrysler's Hamtramck Assembly Plant, in its heyday. This aerial view shows the front of the complex, with Joseph Campau Boulevard running diagonally from left center to lower right. Assembly operations were contained in the long six-story section of the building at right center. The lot at the right of the photo is where new cars were driven after final assembly to await shipment to dealers. (Photo Courtesy Chrysler Historic Services)

fixtures, called 'gates,' into which the workers clamped the A-pillar, the inner front fender, the quarter panel, the rocker panel, and the roof rail, along with smaller parts. These gates traveled on rails until they were completed, at which point the pairs would be lowered to the fifth floor, where they would be clamped to the appropriate floorpan; then an inner and outer roof would be added and that would complete the uni-body. Occasionally, the gate fixtures would get out of sync and a 'Challacuda' would be constructed, comprised of a Challenger on one side and a Barracuda on the other. Although the two cars had wheelbases that were 3 inches different, workers usually didn't notice the problem until they tried to weld on the outer roof."

After that, and after lead-solder filling of the roof/C-pillar joint for non-vinyl-roof cars, the "bodies in white" (industry slang for unpainted body assemblies) would return to the sixth floor for the start of the primer-and-paint process. Vinyl-top cars would get a Plastisol filler in that joint before they entered the paint shop.

As the production body advanced from Paint to Body Trim to Chassis and Final Assembly, it traveled from Hamtramck Assembly's sixth floor to the fifth, then from the fifth to the fourth floor, then down to the third floor. This vertical journey may have been state-of-the-art when John and Horace Dodge planned the complex to build the cars that bore their name, but by 1969 it was obsolete. John Parsons, who worked in Hamtramck Assembly's Production Department, says that plant's build quality was far from the best in the industry at that time. "Assembly quality was not Chrysler's forte, and a huge number of cars were towed, or driven, to a repair stall or to a vast outdoor repair yard."

Body quality was a weak point, according to Parsons, who blamed it on what he called "very crude" body engineering and tooling (compared with competitors such as General Motors and its Fisher Body Division), and body stampings produced from a separate division of Chrysler, which had its own cost priorities. "Another problem was that, due to the general atmosphere (general odors, flying sparks from the spot-weld guns, an undercurrent of concern about the lead-solder dust and its distance from the exits), the Body Shop was the least desirable work assignment. As a result, it drew the newest employees who, having the least investment in their 'career,' were most apt to, let's say, behave irresponsibly."

Parsons also says that chassis and engine engineering, and their production, were right in Chrysler's "wheelhouse." "I remember visiting a supplier who did engine prep on Chrysler and Ford NASCAR engines. Appropriately, he wouldn't take me through every operation he performed on the Ford engines, but he did say that it was vastly more than he had to do to make the Hemis live for 500 miles."

After all of the work that Product Planning, Styling, Engineering, and Production put into the new "Mustang fighters" going back to 1967, the 1970 Dodge Challenger and Plymouth Barracuda were ready for production to begin at Hamtramck Assembly on August 1, 1969.

Other than the streetcar line along Joseph Campau Boulevard (which was replaced by buses in 1956), and the absence of the pedestrian overpass over Joseph Campau, there's little visible difference between the "Dodge Main" shown here and the Chrysler Hamtramck Assembly Plant where the bulk of E-Body production took place from 1969–1974. (Photo Courtesy Chrysler Historic Services)

This overpass allowed Hamtramck Assembly Plant workers to cross Joseph Campau Boulevard at shift-change time, as well as at lunchtime. (Note the bars along Joseph Campau.) Also note the new 1963 Dodges atop the overpass: the mid-size B-Body Dodge 440 and compact A-Body Dodge Dart were assembled at Hamtramck, while the full-size C-Body Dodge 880 (right) was assembled at Chrysler's Jefferson Assembly Plant a short distance away. Like the Hamtramck Assembly Plant itself, this overpass was demolished following the plant's closing in 1980. The site is now occupied by General Motors' Detroit/Hamtramck Assembly Plant. (Photo Courtesy Chrysler Historic Services)

CHAPTER 2

1970 DODGE CHALLENGER
The Long-Awaited Pony Car Arrives

Anticipation had been building for months for the new 1970 Dodge Challenger by the time it went on sale on September 23, 1969 (along with the rest of the 1970 Dodge lineup). That was thanks to advanced information released from Highland Park through the Dodge Division to all its dealers, while at the same time the motoring press presented the last of its preview articles and "spy" photos.

That's how Dodge described its new E-Body car in its early-1970 promotional pieces and advertising copy. That difference was the extra room inside its cabin, thanks to a 3-inch-longer wheelbase than its E-Body Barracuda sibling. As experience had taught the American motoring public, any extra room inside a car that was competing with Mustang was welcome, especially in the backseat.

Dodge even went as far as calling the Challenger Special Edition (SE) coupe their "little limousine," thanks to that additional interior room, and the "formal" (smaller) rear window that was included with that option group.

But the big difference, compared to the A-Body Dart GT and Dart GTS that had been the "hot" small Dodges through 1969, was under the hood. There was finally room in the engine bay to not only house the B and RB big-block V-8s, the 426 Hemi also fit and could be installed on the Hamtramck assembly line, instead of at an offsite plant that Hurst used in 1968 to convert a fleet of Dart hardtops and Barracuda fastbacks into 426 Race Hemi Super Stock drag racers. Furthermore, Challengers equipped with those optional engines could be fitted with power steering and power brakes at the factory, something that the B/RB-engines' width and the A-Body's designed-around-the-Slant Six confines prevented.

Also, if a customer wanted a Challenger factory-equipped with air conditioning and a big-block V-8, he could get one, as

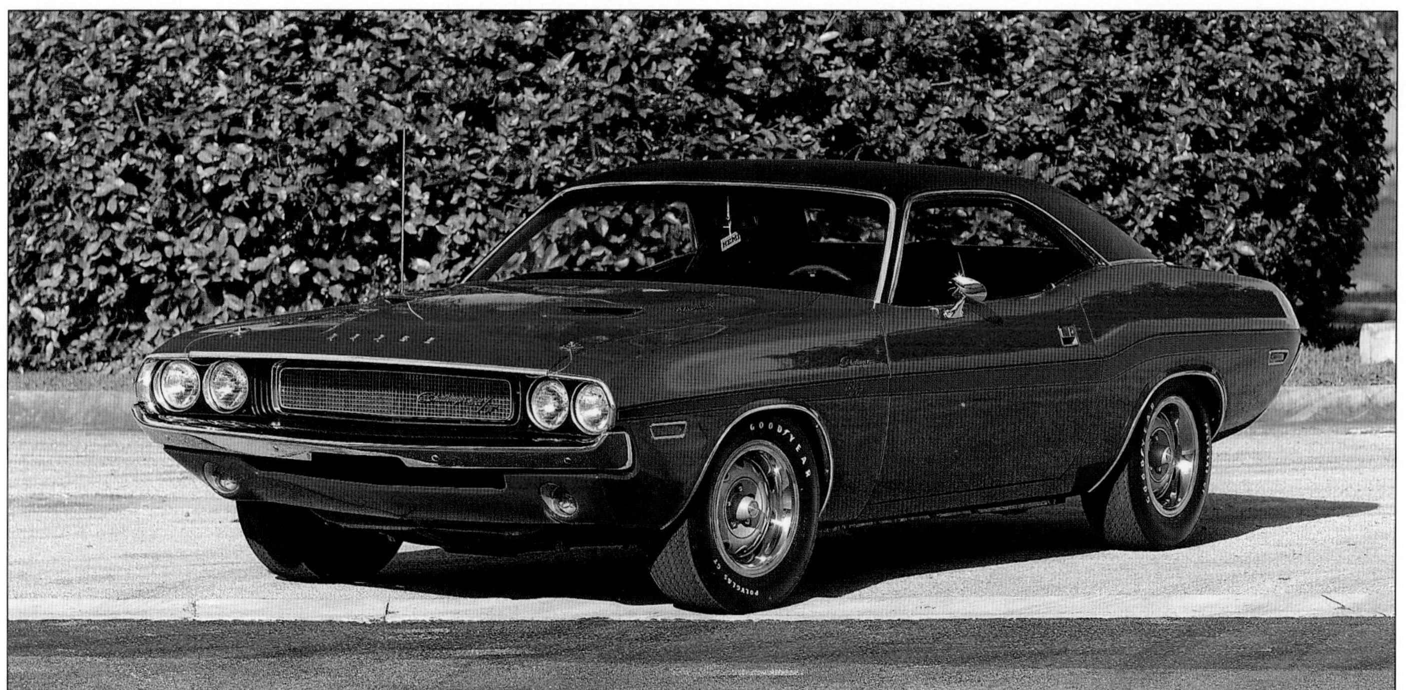

Dodge's first foray into the pony car market segment was the 1970 Dodge Challenger. Thanks to its larger-than-Mustang size, engine choices ranging up to the 426 Hemi (which this car has), and chassis hardware borrowed from the midsize B-Body platform, the Challenger was more of a muscle car than a pony car. (Photo Courtesy Mecum Auction Company)

The Challenger was available as a hardtop or convertible (seen here), in your choice of base series, R/T, or Special Edition trim. (Photo Courtesy Mecum Auction Company)

long as he wasn't ordering it with the available Shaker hood scoop, which took up room at the front of the engine where the Airtemp air conditioning system's compressor would go.

As Dodge had delivered on the promise of performance in the styling of its Charger starting in 1966, so it delivered performance with its new Cougar-and-Firebird-fighter. Firebird, GM's upscale entry in the pony car field, featured an all-big-block line of V-8s, and the Mercury counterpart didn't offer any engine smaller than 351 ci, so Dodge had to be ready with a performance version that rivaled anything Pontiac or Mercury could offer.

The Challenger R/T was all that, and then some. Offered in two body styles, hardtop and convertible, the Challenger R/T had plenty of high-performance hardware underneath its all-new styling. For openers, the same high-performance 383 that was standard in the Coronet Super Bee, and optional in Coronet and Polara police cars, was standard. Underneath was a chassis featuring heavy-duty front torsion bars and front sway bar, heavy-duty rear leaf springs plus heavy-duty shocks all around.

A heavy-duty 3-speed manual transmission was standard on the R/T, but many buyers who wanted to grab the gears opted for the Chrysler-built A-833 4-speed manual gearbox, which featured the Hurst-built Pistol Grip shifter that was new for 1970.

The big reason why the Dodge Challenger and its Plymouth sibling, Barracuda, were so big: the 426 Hemi, a regular-production, factory-installed option. Note that the engine bay has plenty of room for a power brake booster and the battery. (Photo Courtesy Mecum Auction Company)

If a high-performance buyer wanted an automatic transmission, the proven TorqueFlite was an option, with center-console Challengers receiving a Slap Stik gear selector that made high-speed power shifting easier (and is detailed below).

In back, the reliable 8¾-inch rear axle assembly (named for the diameter of its ring gear) was standard on the R/T, with the ultra-heavy-duty Dana 60 rear end available with the highest-performance engine options.

That included the 426 Hemi, which was now available in a Dodge line smaller than the B-Body Coronets and Chargers, with room under the hood for a factory-installed power brake booster and power steering gear.

It was one of nine engines available in Challenger for 1970, more than in any other Dodge line that year.

The Special Edition trim and features option was available on base-series and R/T Challengers (seen here), adding leather-and-vinyl seats, a roof-mounted consolette, and a smaller "formal" rear window to the Challenger hardtop. (Photo Courtesy Mecum Auction Company)

Central to Dodge's introductory publicity for its new Challenger was a cutaway illustration of a Challenger hardtop, with bullet-point captions detailing features that Dodge's new E-Body car had as standard or as options. These included a range of exciting new features, such as the ventless door glass (Challenger's standard "flow-through" interior ventilation system eliminated the need for door-mounted vent windows), and a clean, uncluttered look with concealed windshield wipers.

The Challenger R/T was fitted with a twin snorkel performance hood that had aggressive lines, and it was also included with the 340 V-8. Other exterior treatments included new-for-1970 steel "Rallye" wheels, available in 14- and 15-inch sizes and aerodynamic outside mirrors (painted to match body color). Included inside the car were head restraints built into front seatbacks, an energy-absorbing steering column and steering wheel, and steel side-impact protection, built into both doors, which enhanced occupant protection.

Functional features included a dual exhaust system, standard on all engines except the 225 Slant Six, 318, and 383 2-barrel. V-8s. Heavy-duty torsion bars were standard on R/T models and with 340 V-8. The tires were E60x15 fiberglass-belted, black sidewalls with raised white letters. Front power disc brakes were installed. A heavy-duty sway bar was standard on R/T models and with 340 V-8.

The full-line Dodge sales brochure for 1970 and the specific, large-page-size Challenger sales brochure weren't the only Dodge factory publications that showed off the new Challenger. There was also the Dodge Scat Pack brochure. The Scat Pack had been a Dodge marketing mainstay since 1968, when Dodge began calling its high-performance cars the Scat Pack and whose available rear bumblebee stripes were a striking visual cue.

In that Scat Pack brochure, which was loaded with testimonials about the 1970 high-performance Dodges by some of the leading race drivers who competed with them, was "Big Daddy" Don Garlits's assessment of the new Challenger R/T.

Garlits, who had used Dodge power for many of his *Swamp Rat* dragsters over the previous decade, and who would go on to win 17 Top Fuel Dragster season-championship titles during his career, had plenty to say about the new Dodge.

"Now Dodge has gone and done the real thing. Built the pony car of all pony cars," the brochure quoted Big Daddy. "They watched the whole pony car thing develop, then built their own super-tough version, the Challenger R/T. Compact like a Dart. Wide like a Charger. Just the right size for anyone who likes his own personalized backyard bomb. Dodge should sell a million of 'em. The Challenger, and especially The Challenger R/T, are young peoples' cars with young persons' price tags. The standard R/T engine is the 383-ci Magnum V-8, and you can go from there to [the] 440 Magnum and 426 Hemi if you want more zap.

"What turned me on was the turning radius. It's really tight, which means you get a taut handling package in the stock Challenger.

"Another thing I like is the return to gauges, you know, gas, oil pressure, amps. No warning lights, but true calibrated gauges on the Challenger R/T.

"Dodge told me that Challenger R/T comes in three body styles. Two-door hardtop, SE hardtop, and convertible. There's loads of options including a 4-speed full-synchro transmission and 3-speed TorqueFlite automatic with stick shift [Slap Stik]. And the new colors are something else, really wild. The one I drove is Go Mango.

Although Challenger and Barracuda shared the same E-Body platform, the Challenger was nearly 5 inches longer overall, with a 2-inch-longer wheelbase. Other than the roof stampings, very little of the exterior sheet metal was interchangeable between the two lines. (Photo Courtesy Mecum Auction Company)

The Challenger's cockpit featured standard all-vinyl front bucket seats and a three-spoke steering wheel, along with an available Rallye Instrument Cluster, which included a tachometer, clock, and fuel/oil pressure/temperature/electrical gauges, plus the new Pistol Grip shifter for 4-speed manual transmissions. (Photo Courtesy Mecum Auction Company)

"Fantastic Performance! If I ever leave dragsters, you can be sure I'll run a super stock Challenger R/T.

"If you want to see what Dodge did to pony cars, stop by your Dodge Dealer's, and give the Scat Pack Challenger a test drive. You can challenge the world with Challenger R/T."

Author note: "Big Daddy" eventually drove a Challenger in NHRA Competition, but not an E-Body one. Instead, his *Swamp Rat 37* was an LC-Body Challenger Drag Pak car built in 2009.

The new Challenger was available as either a two-door hardtop or convertible, both with a 110-inch wheelbase, 191.3-inch overall length, 76.1-inch width, 50.9-inch height, with a front track of 59.7 inches and rear track of 60.7 inches. Headroom was 38.2 inches front and 36.4 inches rear, more in the convertible with the top down.

Two Series and More

The 1970 Dodge *Dealership Data Book* noted that the Challenger was available in two series (standard and R/T) with a "Special Edition" option for both series. "The Special Edition model of the two-door hardtops creates the totally different look of still a third series: vinyl roof, formal roof line with small rear window, leather and vinyl bucket seats, and many distinctive exterior and interior trim choices." This was an answer to Chevrolet's strategy with the Camaro: Offer the high-level trim (in Chevy's case, the Rally Sport package) as a regular-production option available on all Camaros.

On the outside, the Challenger looked like no other Dodge before it. Its low, wide stance was accented by a large, rectangular grille opening with four headlights in front and two wide taillights flanking a single rear backup light. A character line on each side of the body "kicked up" as it went over the rear wheelwells, and a snap-open, "racing-type" fuel filler was located on the right rear quarter panel.

Doors were long, stretching from the A-pillar to just in front of the rear wheel openings, featuring curved, ventless windows that took up almost all the room between the front and rear roof pillars and pull-open door handles. Unlike the similar-functioning door handles that Dodge had used over a decade earlier, these

Unlike the pull-to-open door handles that Dodge used in the late 1950s and early 1960s, Challenger door handles fit flush with the door's outer skin, with the lock cylinder integrated in the handle assembly.

Long taillights accentuate Challenger's width. The Challenger SE's "formal" rear window is evident here, as are the special exhaust tips and under-bumper rear valance panel unique to the Challenger R/T. (Photo Courtesy Mecum Auction Company)

From the front, the look is wide, shared by all 1970 Challengers. This R/T wears the scooped hood that was standard on R/T models, as well as the wide, low-profile wheels and tires that came with Challenger's performance version. Hood-retaining pins were a factory option, and insurance against a hood latch failure at high speeds causing hood or windshield damage. (Photo Courtesy Mecum Auction Company)

The Challenger R/T's rear "bumblebee" stripe was painted on, instead of a vinyl stick-on. (Photo Courtesy Mecum Auction Company)

The standard Challenger interior, with the non-tachometer instrument panel, plus optional center console, "Music Master" AM radio and 4-speed manual transmission. (Photo by David Newhardt, Courtesy Mecum Auction Company)

The all-new Challenger's interior included one-piece molded door panels, with the door lock located in the armrest just below the triangular Dodge logo. Remote-control body-color outside mirror was optional or included in certain option packages.

were mounted flush with the body, adding to the door's long and smooth look.

Standard Challenger models had a flat hood with two front-to-rear character lines in it, while the R/T's received a standard "sport-type" hood, with two nonfunctional scoops that could be opened up by removing the trim/block-off plates from the openings, and a "bumblebee" stripe around the car's rear end. Under the stripe and below the rear bumper, the R/Ts were equipped with a pair of chrome-plated exhaust tips, with two rectangular openings on each side, nestled into an opening that was stamped in the R/T's unique rear valance panel.

Dodge's Pony Car Cabin

The Challenger's front bucket seats featured high-rise seatbacks that integrated federally required head restraints into the seat backs, instead of separate pieces added on as the 1968 and 1969 Dodges used. The dashboard held a standard array of gauges (speedometer/odometer, gas gauge, coolant temperature, and ammeter) in a panel covered by the dashboard's padded top, with controls for the standard heater and defroster (and available Airtemp air conditioning) below the gauges on the left side of the steering column, and the available sound systems were located to the right of the steering column, below the gauges.

Manual-transmission Challengers received a chrome-bezeled reverse-indicator light that was located in the middle of the dash, above the standard ashtray, and all Challengers had the "Challenger" script on the dash's padded top (which overlapped downward to the glove box door). Unlike the A-Body Darts, whose ventilation/air conditioner outlets were located under the dash (and would stay there until the end of A-Body production in 1976), the Challenger featured ventilation and air conditioning outlets built into the dashboard.

In back, a single bench seat, trimmed like the front buckets, made use of the Challenger's rear cabin. Rear headroom was given as 35.6 inches and rear legroom as 30.9 inches, which resulted in a rear seat that was somewhat larger than its General Motors and Ford competition but was less than ideal for accommodating adult-size passengers on anything but short trips. Convertible models made use of a different rear seat assembly and rear interior side panels to make room for the folding top and its workings.

The Challenger's door inner panels were the one-piece molded design that Styling had envisioned, and combined with Engineering to bring into production reality. They featured a long, molded-in armrest along with "Challenger" nameplates, a recessed door handle that fit flush with the front of the armrest, and either a crank to roll up the door window or a switch to operate the power window's lift, if that car was equipped with the power windows option.

Standard steering wheel for the Challenger was an all-new, non-convex three-spoke design, which was combined with an all-new steering column. That column incorporated a crash-energy-absorption system in its "bellows"-style construction, as well as an integrated steering wheel lock and ignition switch. Its design and construction satisfied federal motor-vehicle standards for driver protection and theft prevention that had been phased in for the 1970 model year.

Only one transmission control was available mounted on the steering column, the one for the available TorqueFlite automatics. No column-shifted three-on-the-tree manual gearbox was ever developed or offered on the 1970 Challenger.

Pistol Grip or Slap Stik

The 4-speed equipped Challengers received the Hurst-sourced Pistol Grip shifter, with its curved handle and wood-grained, hand-friendly knob. Non-console 4-speeds received a Pistol Grip shifter with a longer handle, shared with the B-Body Dodge Charger, Charger R/T, Coronet Super Bee, and Coronet R/T.

Unique to the E-Body cars was their console-mounted automatic transmission selector. Called the Slap Stik Shift, its construction enabled drivers to either shift into Drive and leave it there for fully automatic shifting, or they could shift to Low and shift manually to Second and Drive without worrying about missing Drive and going instead (through Neutral) into Reverse, causing the transmission's instant, shrieking death if done at speed. Unlike Plymouth, which used a black T-shaped handle on its Slap Stik shifter, Challengers so equipped had a chrome lever with a large wood-grained knob with a spring-loaded pushbutton that allowed the driver to select any gated PRND21 position.

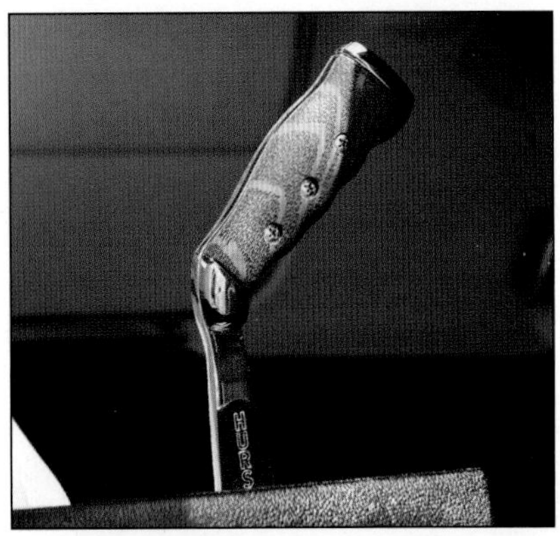

Hurst was the original-equipment vendor for the 4-speed manual transmission shifters, which featured the new "Pistol-grip" handle for 1970.

A look inside a Challenger Special Edition's cabin shows the optional console-mounted Slap Stik TorqueFlite automatic transmission shifter, as well as the E-Body's energy-absorbing steering column. (Photo Courtesy Mecum Auction Company)

A Full Selection of Mopar Power

For its inaugural year, there were two standard engines. The 6-cylinder Challengers received Chrysler's venerable 225-ci Slant Six, the "Leaning Tower of Power," which had been a mainstay of the Dodge engine lineup for the previous decade. Designed and engineered with a 30-degree slant to the passenger side to fit under the original Valiant's low hood line, it featured a cast-iron block and cylinder head, a 3.40-inch bore and 4.125-inch stroke, 8.4:1 compression, and single-barrel carburetor that made it regular-gas-friendly, rated by Chrysler at 145 hp at 4,000 rpm and 215 ft-lbs of torque at a low, get-moving-from-a-stop 2,400 rpm. For 1970, this was the only 6-cylinder engine offered in the Challenger, as the smaller-displacement Slant Six standard in the Dart (which received a displacement bump from 170 ci to 198 for 1970) was only available in the A-Body compacts for 1970.

V-8 buyers had another venerable Chrysler powerplant as standard equipment: the 318-ci version of the LA (Light A) engine series that debuted as a midyear option in 273-ci form in 1964 and was based on Plymouth's polyspherical V-8 that first appeared in 1955. The 1970 318 shared very little with the early "poly" engines other than the cubic inch displacement, courtesy of a 3.91-inch bore and a 3.31-inch stroke. Features included hydraulic valve lifters (which reduced valvetrain noise and did away with periodic lifter adjustment needed with mechanical/solid lifters) as well as a single-plane intake manifold with a 2-barrel carburetor, new-for-1970 pistons that reduced compression to 8.8:1 (to reduce hydrocarbon emissions, per Chrysler) and was factory-rated at 230 hp at 4,400 rpm and 320 ft-lbs of torque at 2,000 rpm.

Non-R/T engine options progressed to a pair of 383-ci "B" engine series big-block V-8s, versions of the powerplant that had been a Dodge mainstay because it replaced Dodge's Red Ram hemispherical-head V-8s in 1959. Both 383s utilized the "low deck" Chrysler big-block architecture with a 4.25-inch bore and 3.38-inch stroke; cast-iron block, cylinder heads, intake and exhaust manifolds, and a solenoid-operated mechanism that retarded ignition timing when the throttle was closed, part of Chrysler's Cleaner Air Package, along with lower-than-1969 compression to meet 1970 federal and California emission standards.

The differences in the standard Challenger's 383s came in compression (8.7:1 or 9.5:1) and carburetion (2- or 4-barrel). The 4-barrel 383 also included dual exhausts and a double-snorkel air cleaner, plus a different grind of camshaft, which helped it develop 330 hp at 5,000-rpm and 425 ft-lbs of torque, compared to the single-exhaust, 2-barrel version's 290 hp at 4,400 rpm and 390 ft-lbs of torque at 2,800 rpm.

Standard Challengers also had an available high-performance engine not available in the Challenger R/T: the 340-ci LA V-8. Introduced in 1968, it was a high-revving, high-output engine that was more than a match for competitive-sized powerplants. There was a forged-steel crankshaft inside its cast-iron block; high-flowing cast-iron cylinder heads with 2.02-inch intake ports; a double-roller timing chain and a special-grind camshaft that enabled high-RPM operation by keeping the valves open longer at high engine RPM; 4.04-inch-bore pistons with 10.5:1 compression requiring premium fuel; an unsilenced air cleaner; and dual exhausts. The factory horsepower rating was 275 at 5,000 rpm with a factory torque figure of 340 ft-lbs at 3,200 rpm, which many who drove cars so equipped said may have been lower than the engine's peak output.

For the performance-oriented Challenger R/T, the standard engine was the 383 Magnum shared with the B-Body Dodge Super Bee, as well as Dodge's Coronet and Polara police vehicles. Variations from the standard Challenger's 383s included cylinder heads shared with the 440 Magnum engine; an unsilenced air cleaner; special high-lift performance camshaft (again, for high-RPM operation) and a windage tray atop the oil pan that cut down on power-robbing drag caused by oil splashing on the crankshaft. For 1970, it saw its compression drop to 9.5:1 for emissions reasons, but its output was still where the previous 383 Magnum's was: 335 hp at 5,200 rpm and 425 ft-lbs of torque at 3,400 rpm. Needless to say, premium fuel was required.

Not only was the Challenger's engine bay large enough to fit the 426 Hemi without special modifications like Ford needed to fit their Boss 429 into the Mustang, the big-block B and RB engines easily fit, even with power steering and power brakes, like this 440 Six Pack Challenger has. Note the "up-and-over" exhaust manifold on the engine's left side (screen right) that clears the steering gear. (Photo Courtesy Mecum Auction Company)

Thanks to the E-Body's wider and longer engine bay than the A-Body Dart's, power steering, power brakes, and Airtemp air conditioning were available as factory options with the big-block V-8s.

Next up on the Challenger R/T's option list was a pair of RB ("raised B") big-block V-8s. Also a mainstay of the Chrysler Corporation engine lineup since 1959, the RB engines' cast-iron blocks were about an inch taller, to make room for longer-stroke connecting rods and crankshafts that gave them added displacement. For 1970, the 440 Magnum also featured, along with its 4.32-inch bore and 3.75-inch stroke and high-performance cylinder heads, a special 4-barrel carburetor; a special, longer-duration camshaft and low-restriction exhaust manifolds. It had also seen a compression ratio drop for emission-control purposes, down to 9.7:1, but it still required premium-grade fuel. Horsepower was 375 at 4,600 rpm per Chrysler, with 480 ft-lbs of torque at 3,200 rpm.

The other available 440 in the Challenger R/T was the 440 Six Pack, which added a trio of Holley 2-barrel carburetors with their own unique linkage, intake manifold, and air cleaner to the 440 Magnum. When this engine was first offered as an option by Dodge in the B-Body Coronet Super Bee in the spring of 1969, its intake manifold was an aluminum casting made by Edelbrock; however, Chrysler took production of that part in-house for 1970, and changed its material from aluminum to iron. Unlike the 4-barrel 440 Magnum, the 440 Six Pack had a compression ratio of 10.5:1 and was rated at 390 hp at 4,700

The 426 Hemi speaks for itself. Note factory-style marking on the left-side valve cover and the factory emissions-certification sticker near the brake master cylinder at screen right. (Photo Courtesy Mecum Auction Company)

rpm and 490 ft-lbs of torque at 3,200 rpm. It also came with a different limited powertrain warranty than the other Challenger engines (only for 12 months/12,000 miles) instead of Chrysler's five-year/50,000-mile powertrain warranty, which had been a selling point for all Chrysler Corporation passenger cars since its inception in 1963.

One engine option remained: It had been derived from an all-out racing engine developed by Chrysler to win the Daytona 500 back in 1964, the 426 Street Hemi. On its unique cast-iron block sat a pair of cylinder heads with huge, hemispherical-shaped combustion chambers and double-rocker valvetrain that was covered by an enormous pair of black valve covers. Inside, the solid-lifter camshaft that had been part of the Street Hemi (with slightly less lift and duration than the Race Hemi's camshaft) was replaced starting with the 1970 model year by one with hydraulic lifters, with no sacrifice in power; factory ratings were still 425 hp at 5,000 rpm and 490 ft-lbs of torque at 4,000 rpm.

Additional features of the 426 Hemi included two huge 4-barrel carburetors atop a cast-iron, inline intake manifold; a maximum-performance fuel pump and special 3/8-inch-diameter fuel line to keep the mighty Hemi fed at high RPM; dual-breaker distributor; and a look (and sound through its unsilenced air cleaner and dual exhausts) like no other engine.

Like the 440 Six Pack, it was also offered with a 12-month/12,000-mile limited powertrain warranty instead of the five-year/50,000-mile one, owing to the Hemi's likely use in competition, sanctioned or otherwise. After the start of the 1970 model year, the 426 Hemi's warranty was cut back to just six months and only available to the original owner.

One item that all Challenger engines, from the Slant Six to the 426 Hemi, shared at the start of the 1970 model year was a drop-forged-steel crankshaft. A Chrysler hallmark for many years prior to 1970, it was fabricated with large overlaps between connecting rod bearing and main bearing journals for strength, and each one was also statically and dynamically balanced at the Chrysler engine plant that assembled it (the Mound Road Engine Plant in Detroit for all but the 426 Hemi, which was built at Chrysler's Marine and Industrial Engine Plant in Marysville, Michigan) before installation in a production engine. Although more costly to manufacture, forged crankshafts were stronger than comparable cast-iron crankshafts, and better able to survive the stresses put upon them by high-RPM engine operation, even if the Challenger that engine was installed in would never see action on a racetrack, let alone an unsanctioned street race or a "stoplight grand prix."

Transmissions

Backing the Challenger's engines was a selection of manual and automatic transmissions. The standard heavy-duty 3-speed manual gearbox with its shifter located on the floor (mentioned above) was the same fully synchronized unit shared with A-Body and B-Body Dodges. At the start of the 1970 model year, it was the standard gearbox for all Slant Six, 318 and 340 Challengers, as well as both 4-barrel equipped 383s, but was not available with the 2-barrel 383, the 440s, or the 426 Hemi.

The optional manual gearbox was Chrysler's A-833 4-speed, which came in two versions from Chrysler's New Process Gear Division plant in DeWitt, New York. One version, which had a 23-spline input shaft and a 2.47:1 first-gear ratio, was available with the 318, 340, and 383 engines. For the 440s and the 426 Hemi, Dodge used what enthusiasts call the "Hemi 4-speed," a heavy-duty version with much stouter internal components, including an 18-spline input shaft and a 2.44:1 low gear. Both versions were built with aluminum cases and the Hurst-built Pistol Grip shifter.

Axle Options

The Challengers were equipped with different rear-axle assemblies, depending on the engine selected. Slant Six and 318 V-8 Challengers received a light-duty axle assembly with a 7½-inch-diameter ring gear and gear ratios ranging from a standard 3.23:1 to a 2.76:1 rear gear for TorqueFlite 318s and Slant Six (standard with the 6, optional with V-8).

The Challengers with higher-output engines other than the 426 Hemi and 440 Six Pack received heavier-duty rear axle assemblies based on the one with an 8¾-inch-diameter ring gear shared with the B-Body Chargers and Coronets. Available gear ratios ranged from a standard 3.23:1 to an available-with-an-automatic 2.76:1 rear gear to 3.55:1 and 3.91:1 gears that

Restored 8¾-inch rear end wears factory-style marking on its center cover. Also note the special rear leaf springs, shock absorbers, rear sway bar, and forward-exiting mufflers under this Challenger T/A.

were available with the optional rear-axle option packages described below.

For the 426 Hemi, a special heavy-duty rear axle assembly sourced from the Dana Corporation, known as the Dana 60, was standard. It had proven itself behind Hemi since that engine's debut in 1964 (and as a production "street" engine for 1966) and was now sized to fit under the Challenger. Originally designed and engineered for 3/4-ton and 1-ton trucks, and equipped with a 9¼-inch-diameter ring gear, the Dana 60's available gearing ranged from a standard 3.23:1 to available 3.54:1, 3.91:1, and 4.10:1 rear gears.

All Challenger rear axle assemblies were available with Chrysler's limited-slip Sure-Grip differential, which, in circumstances where one wheel lost traction, directed power from the engine to the other wheel, enabling both wheels to keep rolling under power, instead of one wheel losing traction completely.

Proven Unibody Construction

Regardless of powertrain selected, all Challengers were built with Chrysler's "Unibody" unit-body construction, which had been used on every U.S.-made Dodge passenger car since 1960. Per the *Dealership Data Book*, "all of the sheet metal is reinforced with a web of rigid, box-section steel girders. The entire structure is welded into a single, rigid unit. Body shake and vibration, major sources of noise in other cars, cannot happen in Unibody. Tests have proven that Unibody is better able to resist twisting and bending forces than the separate body and frame construction. [None of Challenger's sporty-compact class competitors used body-on-frame construction in 1970.] Less shaking and less twisting mean a more comfortable ride, and a ride that makes for better handling and control."

The Challengers had additional structural features over and above those used by Chrysler since 1960. To meet federal side-impact standards, a two-piece beam of high-yield-strength steel was welded to the inside of every Challenger door. Plus, a box-section, sheet-metal roll-over structure was welded into Challenger hardtop bodies under the roof panel near the rear window, for what Dodge called "greater roof strength." For obvious reasons, Challenger convertibles did not get this structure.

Once Challenger unit-body assemblies were constructed, they were subjected to Chrysler's multi-step, dip-and-spray corrosion prevention treatments. As the *Dealership Data Book* described it, "Each Dodge Unibody (was) thoroughly cleaned, bonderized [coated with a phosphate solution], and coated inside and out with corrosion-resistant primer by being passed through seven large tanks, plus being sprayed. Special solvents (were) used to remove dirt and drawing compounds [which may have been transferred from the inside of the dies used to stamp the steel body components]."

Corrosion prevention was something that Chrysler had learned about the hard way. When Chrysler totally restyled its five passenger-car lines (Plymouth, Dodge, De Soto, Chrysler, and Imperial) for 1957 with long, low lines and sweeping fins at the rear, many areas inside each passenger-car body were not coated at all. That led to premature rusting in the first year those cars were on the road, one factor behind a drastic drop in all Chrysler Corporation car sales in 1958. That also factored in the demise of the De Soto brand early in the 1961 model year, despite the anti-corrosion processes and procedures mentioned above, which Chrysler adopted for 1960, when all of their passenger car lines except Imperial switched from body-on-frame to Unibody construction. (Imperial didn't receive Unibody until 1967.)

Once the body-fabrication-and-rust-protection processes were complete, Challenger bodies went into the paint shop, where they received two coats of acrylic enamel paint over two coats of epoxy primer (which was sprayed over the primer applied during the dip-and-spray process).

The Challenger's Chassis

Underneath each Challenger was the latest version of Chrysler's "Torsion Aire" suspension system, first seen on Dodges in 1957. In front, tempered-steel torsion bars (.86-inch diameter on Slant Six models and .088-inch diameter for all non-R/T V-8s) served as the front springs, twisting and untwisting as they absorbed bumps from the road, while 1-inch-diameter shock absorbers helped level the car after each bump. They were connected to angled upper control arms, which exerted a lifting force on the front end and kept the front end level during braking.

In back, asymmetrical leaf spring bundles were combined with 1-inch-diameter shock absorbers. Those rear leaf springs also received thick rubber isolators, intended to keep road-induced vibrations out of the passenger compartment.

The Challenger R/T models received a heavy-duty version of this system, with torsion bars up-sized to .90-inch-diameter heavy-duty rear leaf springs with 4¼ leaves on each side, plus a front sway bar and 1-inch-diameter heavy-duty shock absorbers. The 340 Challengers also received a rear sway bar, which was not factory-installed on any other Challenger. The 440 and 426 Hemi Challengers received their own suspension upgrade: larger, extra-heavy-duty rear leaf spring bundles containing six leaves on the left side and 5½ leaves on the right.

The Challenger's brakes, while state-of-the-art for the time in the late 1960s when the E-Body platform was designed and engineered, may seem primitive by today's standards. The standard brake system used on Slant Six and 318 Challengers used hydraulic drum-and-shoe brakes at each corner, with 10 x 2½-inch drums with an effective lining area of 195.2 square feet, and no power assist. (That was a factory option.) All other drum-brake Challengers received 11 x 2½-inch drums (the same ones that had been used on Dodge police cars since the late 1950s) with an effective lining area of 234.1 square feet.

Disc brakes had only been available on Chrysler Corporation passenger cars since 1966 and available on Dodges starting with the full-sized C-Body Polara/Monaco models, starting in 1967. They were optional on all Challengers and included with several of the available performance-axle packages, and power brakes were a required option with factory discs.

All Challenger brake systems were equipped with dual master cylinders, ensuring braking if one brake line leaked. This was adopted by Chrysler in 1967, the same year that Ford and General Motors also adopted dual-circuit brakes, which American Motors pioneered in the U.S. market in 1963.

Colors Inside and Out

Dodge offered 22 exterior colors on the 1970 Challenger, including 10 new "High Impact" colors, intended to increase "curb appeal" over the standard Chrysler Corporation color selection.

Those High Impact colors were SubLime (Code J5), Go Mango (Code K2), Hemi Orange (Code V2), Plum Crazy (Code C7), Top Banana (Code Y1), Bright Green (Code F6), and Citron Yella (Code Y3) at the start of the 1970 model year, for $14.05 extra. Two additional High Impact colors, Green Go (Code J6) and Panther Pink (Code M3), joined the Challenger color selection at midyear.

If Challenger buyers wanted one of the standard Dodge colors, they had these choices for 1970: Silver (Code A1), Light Blue (Code B3), Bright Blue (Code B5), Dark Blue (Code B7), Bright Red (Code E5), Light Green (Code F3), Dark Green (Code F8), Dark Burnt Orange (Code K5), Beige (Code L1), Dark Tan (Code T6), Light Gold (Code Y4), White (Code W1), and Black (Code X9).

Inside, the Challenger's cabin featured standard all-vinyl bucket seats in front and a matching all-vinyl bench in back for base and R/T hardtops and convertibles, available in blue, red, burnt orange, black, green, tan, and white (the latter with a black dash and carpets). Optional on the base Challenger hardtop was an all-vinyl split-bench front seat in blue or black only, which required the column-shift TorqueFlite automatic transmission.

The Challenger SE's interior was spiffed up with standard wood-grain trim and "Special Edition" script nameplates on the door inner panels, while the seats were covered in either a leather-and-vinyl combo (leather seating surfaces with vinyl

Although white was specified as this Challenger T/A's interior color, the dash, carpets, console, steering column, and steering wheel center are black. Stereo equalizer under dash is an aftermarket item.

Choosing the cloth-and-vinyl upholstery option on the Challenger SE, as seen here, instead of the standard leather-and-vinyl seat trim, took $48.25 off the car's sticker price. (Photo Courtesy Mecum Auction Company)

SE door trim included the "Special Edition" script nameplate and wood-grain insert. (Photo Courtesy Mecum Auction Company)

bolsters and backs) available in black, tan, or burnt orange. But, if you preferred cloth instead of leather, you could credit-option a cloth-and-vinyl combination that was available in burnt orange, green, black, or blue. That same cloth-and-vinyl trim option was also available on base Challenger and R/T hardtops.

Factory Model and Option Pricing

The following pricing and availability information is from the *1970 Dodge Salesman's Pocket Guide.*

Base pricing for 6-cylinder and V-8 powered base Challengers and Challenger SEs differed by about $100. The Challenger hardtop Manufacturer's Suggested Retail Price (less taxes and delivery charges) started at $2,851 for a Slant Six one, or $2,953 for one with a 318-inch V-8, while the convertible started at $3,120 (Slant Six) or $3,222 (318) and the SE hardtop's base sticker price started at $3,083/$3,185.

R/T models with their standard 383 Magnum and heavy-duty chassis hardware were priced slightly higher. R/T hardtops started at $3,266 (SE R/T hardtops sticker prices started at $3,498), and prices for R/T convertibles started at $3,535.

Then came the options, which allowed dealers to offer a variety of Challenger models to customers who bought from a dealer's stock, and to buyers who wanted a factory-customized one and didn't mind waiting approximately six weeks for Chrysler to build one and ship it to their Dodge dealer.

Dodge offered several option groups on Challengers and Challenger R/Ts, combining a number of options in one group at a price less than they were if ordered separately. That included the Light Group (Code A01), which added glove box, trunk lights, map light, ashtray light, ignition-switch light with time delay, headlights-on reminder buzzer, fender-mounted turn signal indicators, and a time delay for the instrument panel flood lighting. Not available on R/T models, it added $41.15 to the sticker price ($30.45 if ordered with a 340 engine).

The Challenger's Radio Group (Code A04) combined the available pushbutton Music Master AM radio with power steering, variable-speed windshield wipers and electric windshield washers, deluxe wheel covers, and a left-side remote-control mirror. On base Challengers with 14-inch wheels, it was priced at $198.95, but $177.65 if the car was ordered with 15-inch Rallye road wheels. On R/Ts, which had the variable-speed wipers and electric washers standard, this option group was priced at $188.35 with 14-inch wheels, or $167.05 with the 15-inch Rallyes.

The additional chrome accent moldings and Astrotone-painted taillight panel that were standard on SE were available in Molding Group A (Code A63), which was $37.23 extra. For $57.90 extra ($43.25 on 340 Challengers), the Challenger Protection Group (Code A05) included vinyl-insert body-side moldings, door-edge protectors, and front and rear bumper guards with rubber inserts. Upgrading from the standard black front and rear seat belts was the Code C15 Seat Belt Group, which added $13.75 for color-keyed buckles, loop guides on buckle ends and buckle stowage brackets, and a "Fasten Seat Belts" light on the dash with time delay.

The Challenger for 1970 was also offered with an optional trailer towing package (Code A35), which enabled towing a trailer whose maximum loaded weight was 4,000 pounds, or anything with a gross weight between 2,000 and 4,000 pounds. If a customer wanted to tow something heavier, Dodge's bigger cars, and especially their D-Series pickup trucks, were more than up to the job.

The A35 package included a maximum-capacity cooling system with a high-capacity radiator, a larger transmission fluid cooler, seven-blade cooling fan with shroud and hood seal, a heavy-duty performance axle with a 3.23 rear gear set, heavy-duty suspension front and rear with a front sway bar, heavy-duty brakes, trailer-towing wheels, a variable-load turn-signal flasher, and a heavy-duty stop-lamp switch. Recommended options were either of the 383s, Sure-Grip differential, high-output 50-amp alternator (which was standard with AC), heavy-duty 70-amp battery, power brakes and front disc brakes, power steering, Airtemp air conditioning, and automatic speed control. The A35 required the optional TorqueFlite automatic transmission and was not available with the Slant Six, 440 Six Pack, or 426 Hemi engines. With a 318 or 2-barrel 383, it was $48.70 extra; $34.80 with the 4-barrel 383 or 340; or $14.05 with the 440 Magnum.

Performance Option Packages

From there, the available option groups focused on performance. The Code A66 Challenger 340 4-Barrel Engine Package, for base-model Challengers only, combined the 275-hp 340-ci V-8, with a sport-handling suspension system that included front and rear sway bars. Priced at $258.90, it required 15-inch Rallye wheels (Code W21) and a collapsible spare tire (Code W34) as must-also-order options.

Then came high-performance rear-axle packages for the R/T models, based around Chrysler's 8¾-inch rear end or the ultra-heavy-duty Dana 60 9¾-inch rear end. The Code A31 High Performance Axle Package for 383 R/Ts included a 3.91:1-ratio rear gear set and a Sure-Grip limited-slip differential, a seven-blade torque-drive fan, the "Hemi Suspension Handling Package," and a 26-inch high-performance radiator with fan shroud. Not available with air conditioning, A31 added $102.15 for R/Ts equipped with it.

Next up was the Code A32 Super Performance Axle Package. Only available with 440 Magnum, 440 Six Pack, and 426

Hemi engines equipped with the TorqueFlite automatic transmission, it featured a 4.10:1-geared and Sure-Grip Dana 60, power disc brakes, and the 7-blade fan and 26-inch high-performance radiator and was not available with AC or heavy-duty (drum) brakes. It added $250.65 to the 440 cars' sticker prices, and $221.40 to the Hemis'.

If you wanted those rear-end options on a 4-speed 426 Hemi or 440 Magnum/Six Pack, you ordered the Super Track Pack (Code A34), whose $235.65 tariff included the heavy-duty 4.10-geared and Sure-Grip Dana 60, along with power disc brakes and the 26-inch radiator/seven-blade fan combo, and was not available with air conditioning.

The Code A33 Track Pack left off the A32's power disc brakes and substituted a 3.54 rear gear set, but included a Sure-Grip Dana 60 and 26-inch radiator and seven-blade fan for $142.85 extra on 4-speed 440 and 426 Hemi R/Ts without air conditioning.

Finally, the Code A36 Performance Axle Package, available only on TorqueFlite 383s, 440 Magnums and Six Packs, and 426 Hemis, utilized the 8¾-inch rear axle assembly with a 3.55 gear set and Sure-Grip differential, the Hemi suspension handling package, and the 26-inch radiator with fan shroud. With a 383, it was $102.15 extra, $92.25 with either of the 440s, or $64.40 with the 426 Hemi.

Limited availability of air conditioning with the high-performance engines and axle packages was for several reasons: The power draw that the system's compressor had on the engine, which cut down on engine output; the possibility that the belt from the engine that drove the compressor could fly off at sustained high speeds or under hard acceleration; the system's additional weight; and the compressor's location at the front of the engine, which interfered with the 426 Hemi's and 440 Six Pack's air cleaners and the "Shaker" hood scoop.

Speaking of the optional Code H51 manual-temperature-control air conditioner with heater, which was made by Chrysler's Airtemp division, it was one of Challenger's most pricey options at $357.65 extra. Tinted glass was recommended (Code G11, $32.75 extra), and all AC-equipped Challengers, like all other AC Chrysler Corporation passenger cars, received an "Airtemp Air Conditioning By Chrysler Corporation" decal on the inside lower-rear-corner of the right rear window. That made it easier for new-car shoppers searching a dealer's lot for an AC car to find one and gave owners of cars so equipped a "brag factor" on hot and humid days.

The 440- and 383-ci Challenger engine options fit easily in the E-Body engine bay. Note the power steering pump and power brake booster, items that didn't fit under the hood of 383 A-Body 1967–1969 Dodge Darts. (Photo Courtesy Mecum Auction Company)

Powertrain Options

As mentioned above, base-series V-8 Challengers were available with a choice of 383s: the 2-barrel equipped, regular-fuel version was $69.75 extra and only available with a TorqueFlite automatic, while the non-Magnum 4-barrel version was $137.55 extra and was available with TorqueFlite, or the 3- or 4-speed manual gearboxes.

Optional engines for the R/Ts were the 440 Magnum (Code E86, $130.55 extra and not available with air conditioning and a 4-speed); the 440 Six Pack (Code E87, which required the Code A33 or Code A34 axle packages with a 4-speed and added $249.55 to the sticker price); and the Code E74 426 Hemi, which also required the A33 or A34 axle packages with a 4-speed, and which cost a mere $778.75 extra.

To back those standard and optional engines, Challenger buyers could choose either the Code D34 TorqueFlite automatic or Code D21 4-speed manual gearbox. The 4-speed, with its Hurst Pistol Grip shifter, not available with the Slant Six or 2-barrel 383 engines, required either the Code A33 Track Pack or Code A34 Super Track Pack option groups with the Hemi or the 440s, and was priced at $194.85. As for the TorqueFlite automatic, it added $190.25 to the sticker of a Slant Six Challenger and $202.05 to a 318 car; it was $216.20 extra with the 340 or 2-barrel 383 and $227.05 extra with the 4-barrel 383, both 440s, or the 426 Hemi.

To help keep all that power from those nine engine choices propelling a customer's Challenger forward was the Code D91 Sure-Grip limited-slip differential, priced at $42.35 extra but standard with all the optional axle packages.

Mechanical Options

Mechanical options included a 50-amp alternator (Code F11, $11.00 extra, but standard with AC on V-8 Challengers); optional axle ratios, your choice (2.76:1 or 3.23:1) only $10.35

extra, or no charge with the D91 Sure-Grip Differential or the A35 trailer-towing package; Code F25 70-amp battery ($12.95 extra, standard with the 440s and Hemi); heavy-duty drum brakes (Code B11 standard on R/Ts but $22.65 extra on base Challengers, not available with disc brakes or on Slant Six cars); Code B41 front disc brakes ($27.90, which also required the Code B51 power brake option, which was $42.95 extra); and Code S77 power steering ($90.35).

Code S13 Rallye front and rear suspension with sway bar was a $14.75 option that was standard on R/Ts, with the A35 trailer-towing package and with the 340 and 4-barrel 383; Code S15 extra-heavy-duty front and rear suspension (standard with 440 and Hemi engines) was an option on 340 and 383 Challengers for $18.25 extra, and Code S25 firm-ride shock absorbers, which were standard on 440 and Hemi-equipped cars and with extra-heavy-duty suspension, were $3.55 extra on all other Challengers. The Code N88 automatic speed control was $57.95 extra, but not available with the Slant Six, 340, Hemi, or 440 Six Pack, and required B51 power brakes on 383 and 440 Magnum cars. All Challengers could also be ordered with the optional Code J55 undercoating and hood silencer pad, for $16.60 extra.

California-bound Challengers were equipped with two required options: the Code N95 evaporative control system ($37.85) and Code N97 noise-reduction package for Hemi and 440 Six Pack cars (no charge).

Interior Features and Options

Interior options included cloth and vinyl bucket seats on hardtop Challengers ($16.25 extra on base and R/T models, but Dodge knocked $48.25 off the sticker price if they were ordered on an SE hardtop), and leather-faced seats that were standard on SE but $64.75 extra otherwise. A vinyl bench seat with a center armrest was available on TorqueFlite base Challengers for $16.07 extra, while Code C62 was a six-way manual adjuster for the driver's side bucket seat ($33.90); Code C13 front shoulder belts for convertibles or Code C14 rear shoulder belts for hardtops (your choice $26.45 extra); the Code A62 Rallye gauge cluster with tachometer (standard on R/Ts, $90.30 extra on V-8 Challengers only); Code J21 electric clock (standard with the A62 Rallye gauge cluster and on R/T models, but $16.50 extra otherwise); Code J25 variable-speed windshield wipers, which were standard with the A62 Rallye gauge cluster and on R/Ts, but were $10.60 extra on all other Challengers; Code C16 center console ($53.35 extra, only available with bucket seats); Code H31 rear window defogger ($26.25 extra, not available on convertibles); Code C92 rubber floor mats ($10.90); Code L42 headlamp time delay with lights-on reminder ($13.00 extra with the A01light package, or $18.20 without A01); Code J41 pedal dress-up ($5.45); and a choice of steering wheels: Code S83 with a "rim-blow" horn switch in the wheel's rim ($24.60) or a partial horn ring on the standard steering wheel (Code S83, $5.45 extra).

For factory-installed sound systems, choices without the A04 Radio Group were the solid-state Music Master AM radio with push-button tuning (Code R11, $61.55 extra), an AM radio with stereo 8-track tape player (Code R22, $196.25 extra), or the Code R25 multiplex AM/FM stereo radio with pushbutton tuning, priced at $213.60. Choose the A04 Radio group, and the AM/8-track combo only cost $134.75 extra, while the extra charge for the multiplex AM/FM stereo radio with A04 was $152.20. If you wanted a rear speaker in your Challenger hardtop, Code R31 either got you a single rear speaker for your Music Master AM radio for an extra $14.05, or dual rear speakers with your stereo radio for $25.90 more (rear speakers were not available on convertibles). If you wanted to hear just the sounds of the engine and road and wind noise (or if you wanted to keep weight off your race-intended Challenger), a plastic block-off plate covered the factory radio opening in the dash, for no charge.

Exterior Appointments

Outside, Challenger buyers had a big choice of available appearance and trim items, headed up by the High Impact paint colors ($14.05 extra); two-tone paint on base and R/T hardtops ($31.70), longitudinal thin-dual paint stripes ($15.15, not available on R/T or with the 340); and Code V21 Hood Performance Paint Treatment ($24.30 for all 340 Challengers and R/Ts). R/T buyers could choose between the no-cost optional longitudinal tape stripe or rear bumblebee paint stripe, and they (and 340 Challengers) had Code J45 hood tie-down pins available for $15.40 extra.

For body-side dress-up and protection, chrome door-edge guards were Code M05 and $4.05 extra, while Code M25 sill moldings cost $21.75 and body-side vinyl-on-chrome rub rails were available on base Challengers that weren't equipped with

Snap-open "racing-type" fuel filler on the right rear quarter panel. A locking cap underneath was a factory-installed or dealer-installed option.

optional tape stripes for an extra $29.45 ($14.80 with the A66 340 package).

The standard manually adjustable chrome rearview mirror on the driver's door could be upgraded to a remote-control one (Code G33, for $15.15 extra) and paired with a matching, manually adjustable one on the right side door (Code G31, for another $10.95). Body-color-painted racing-style mirrors, with a sleeker shape than the chrome mirrors, were new to Dodge for 1970 and available on Challengers as Code G34 left-side remote control ($15.15 extra) and Code G33 manual-control for the right side (for $10.95 more).

For added style in back, and a bit more luggage space, all Challenger buyers could get a chrome luggage rack on the trunk lid (Code M91, $32.35 extra), plus front and rear bumper guards with rubber inserts (Code M85) were $23.80 extra, and a locking gas cap under the standard snap-open filler in the right rear quarter panel (Code J46) was priced at just $4.40 extra as a factory option.

Wheels and Tires

Inside the wheelwells, choices abounded. Base-level Slant Six and 318 Challengers wore E78-14 bias-ply blackwall tires on body-colored 14 x 5–inch steel wheels with Dodge's "dog dish" chrome hub cap, while 383 base Challengers were equipped with slightly larger F78-14 bias-ply blackwalls and the standard tires on 383 R/Ts were F70-14 raised-white-letter bias-plies, which debuted on Dodge factory equipment lists for 1970.

Slant-6 and 318 Challengers could have their factory tire selection upgraded to E78-14 whitewalls for $26.45 extra (Code T26); F78-14 bias-plies, either blackwall (Code T35, $15.40) or whitewall (Code T34, -$44.55). Or, they could choose from F70-14 tires on 318 base Challengers that required the S13 heavy-duty suspension option and either heavy-duty drum or front disc brakes, Code T86 whitewalls or Code T87 raised-white-letter tires, both priced at $65.35 extra.

The 383 base Challengers' tire upgrades used the same option codes as on the Slant Six and 318 cars, but were priced differently. The F78-14 whitewalls were $29.25 extra, while the choice of F70-14 tires cost $50.10 extra.

The Challenger R/Ts could be upgraded from their standard tires with Code T86 F70-14 whitewalls for no extra charge, or Code U82 E60-15 low-profile raised-white-letter tires ("Racin' tars," as commercial pitchman/"Dodge Safety Sheriff" Joe Higgins called them in 1970 Challenger TV ads) were $47.95 extra, but not available on 440 convertibles or with the A35 trailer towing package.

Those big, 60-series tires (the widest ever offered by Dodge to that point) made the optional W34 collapsible spare tire a necessity, thanks to their size and the Challenger's trunk opening and (lack of) room under the lid.

A temporary-use tire that was no larger than the 15-inch rim it was mounted on, it inflated with an attached aerosol bottle, was priced at $12.95 extra on Challenger hardtops (it was standard on convertibles), and was a required option on all 340 and Hemi Challengers. Convertibles could get the Code W08 conventional spare tire for no extra charge, as long as they didn't have a 340 under the hood or 15-inch tires all around.

Those tires either rode on the stock steel wheels, which were body-colored with the standard chrome "dog dish" hub cap, or painted "chassis black" when covered by one of the optional wheel covers: the same 14-inch deluxe wheel covers shared with Dart, Coronet, and Charger (and which flew off the black 1968 Dodge Charger R/T the bad guys drove in the movie *Bullitt*), deep-dish, cone style covers that were also shared with Dart, Coronet, and Charger, and dented easily when "shared"

"Space-saver" spare tire was required on all Challengers equipped with 60-series wide-tread tires. Aerosol bottle was used to inflate the spare to a size suitable for getting the car to a tire-repair shop.

The Challenger's limited trunk room (8.0 cubic feet) shows why the "space saver spare" was a good idea for any Challenger, not just the wide-tire ones. (Photo Courtesy Mecum Auction Company)

Call them "dog dishes," or "poverty caps," but this chrome-plated hub cap was the standard wheel trim on base-level Challengers and Challenger R/Ts. The Challenger T/A added the chrome trim ring and E60-14 wide-tread tires. Although the stamping is similar to Plymouth's standard hubcap, this version was unique to Dodge in the early 1970s.

A popular option in 1970 on all series of Challengers was the all-new steel Rallye road wheel, which came with the chrome trim ring seen here. (Photo Courtesy Mecum Auction Company)

The "fender tag" attached to the left front inner fender under the hood was where the codes for engine, transmission, interior and exterior trim, optional equipment, and the car's build date were denoted. This 440 Six Pack/ TorqueFlite Challenger R/T SE was built at Hamtramck Assembly on November 12, 1969. (Photo Courtesy Mecum Auction Company)

with curbs while parking; and 14-inch wire covers that gave the look of wire wheels for much less cost than real wire wheels, an item that was a long time off of any Dodge option list.

Pricing for those covers depended if the A04 Radio Group was chosen, which included the deluxe covers (Code W11 and $21.30 if ordered without A04). Code W13 deep-dish covers were $44.90 extra without A04 or $23.75 with it; and the Code W15 wire covers were priced at $64.10 without the Radio Group, or $42.85 with it.

If Challenger buyers wanted an optional road wheel instead of wheel covers, they had two choices for 1970, one of them the all-new Rallye Road Wheel (Code W21). It was a replacement for the cast aluminum road wheel option the year before that was recalled before the 1969 Dodges went on sale, because of bolt tightening and related cracking issues that Chrysler and supplier Kelsey-Hayes could not solve. The new wheel was made of steel and featured a chrome trim ring and center cap. The W21 with the A04 Radio Group on base-model Challengers was a $21.95 option ($43.25 without A04). The five-spoke Code W23 road wheel with a chrome trim ring, carried over from the 1969 Chargers and Coronets, was priced at $64.95 with the A04 package, or $86.15 without it.

Options

Does that sound like a lot of confusing choices for prospective Challenger buyers? It may today, but back then long option lists were a way to satisfy customers while maximizing profits per car. Drawbacks included additional costs involved with the production, delivery, and stocking at the plant of all those items of optional equipment, which likely drove the bean counters in Highland Park crazy. That long option list also added complexity on the assembly line, where line workers had about a minute to read the "broadcast sheet" that specified what alpha-numeric-coded item was to be installed on the car on the line that was moving past their work station, select the item called for, and install it before the next car came down the line.

The Challenger in Print

Probably no Chrysler product (and no Dodge) had been so eagerly anticipated by the monthly motoring press. Finally, there would be a pony car–class competitor that wasn't based on the lowly A-Body platform, and finally, Dodge would have one of their own to compete against the Pontiac Firebird and Mercury Cougar.

Car and Driver was more critical of the Challenger, writing in the November 1969 issue: "In the flesh, it's a highly stylized Camaro with strongly sculptured lines, more tumble-home,

MAGAZINE TEST PERFORMANCE FIGURES

Sports Car Graphic tested a 440-Magnum Challenger SE R/T hardtop, while *Car and Driver* and *Road Test* each had 426 Hemi R/T hardtops. Here's a sample of their test data:

Acceleration

0–30 mph

Road Test: Not given
Sports Car Graphic: 2.7 seconds
Car and Driver: 2.3 seconds

0–60 mph

Road Test: Not given
Sports Car Graphic: 6.4 seconds
Car and Driver: 5.8 seconds

0–100 mph

Road Test: Not given
Sports Car Graphic: 16.9 seconds
Car and Driver: 13.4 seconds

Standing 1/4-mile

Road Test: 14.00 seconds/no speed given
Sports Car Graphic: 14.80 seconds at 95 mph
Car and Driver: 14.10 seconds at 103.2 mph

Skid Pad (maximum lateral g, left/right)

Road Test: Not given
Sports Car Graphic: .69/.67
Car and Driver: Not given

Braking 60–0 mph

Road Test: 190 feet
Sports Car Graphic: 148 feet
Car and Driver (80–0): 294 feet
Author note: All three recounted rear-wheel lockup during high-speed braking tests.

Observed Fuel Consumption

Road Test: Not given
Sports Car Graphic: 13 mpg (average)
Car and Driver: 7 to 12 mpg

and a grille vaguely in the Charger tradition. There's no doubt it is a handsome car, but it also has a massive feel that is totally unwelcome in a sporty car, a massive feeling that results from a full 5 inches more width than a Mustang, and a need to sign up with Weight Watchers."

Road Test magazine, in the June 1970 issue, took note not just of the new E-Body Dodge's styling, but also its effect on B-Body Charger sales. "Challenger styling must be rated as pleasing though surprisingly, sales are disappointing. Combined Challenger and Charger sales are less, so far this year, than were the Chargers alone for the equivalent period in 1969, indicating that the newcomer is "feeding" off the latter. When compared to competitive General Motors and Ford products, the Challenger shows a refreshing absence of unnecessary chrome, particularly in the grille area. Some might say it's excessively wide for a true pony car configuration, measuring 76.1 inches compared to the Mustang's 71.7, but this is noticeable mostly when you are seated behind the wheel."

What about acceleration? That was the E-Body Dodge's strong suit. "The '440's' kick-in-the-back in normal street operation predicted glorious things," reported *Sports Car Graphic* in their November 1969 issue. "Their auto-box was a joy in town, but don't expect it to think for you on the strip, as it insists on shifting at around 4,000 rpm. We don't ordinarily hold automatics in lower ranges, but to be fair, we experimented and found that the acceleration *g* curves crossed at about 5,000 rpm, which is the scientific way of determining shift points for any kind of transmission. The result: a quarter mile of 14.8 seconds and 95.0 mph. Not the fastest we've tested, but certainly the quickest automatic sedan we've had the pleasure to instrument."

Handling? That's where things got a bit dicey. "Normal street driving is typically Detroit," reported *Sports Car Graphic*. "Ride, good. Brake and throttle response, good. Maneuverability, good, if you can remember where the fenders are because you sure can't see them."

But when they took their test car to the skid pad, *Sports Car Graphic* called it "a waste of time." "We expected new lateral acceleration records, judging by the fat F70 x 14 Goodyears and the wide track; however, they alone do not a handler make. The first runs in a counterclockwise direction were uneventful in that the engine kept discontinuing from a lack of fuel in the carb: Either the pump won't pump left or the floats won't float right.

"More exciting were the right turns, which were interrupted by the photographer running onto the track, yelling, 'You're on fire! You've blown! Bail out!' But since the oil pressure gauge was still sane, all the blue smoke from the left two tailpipes must have been that oil which wouldn't drain out of the left cylinders and valve covers under the combination of roll and lateral forces, and thereby worked past the rings and valvestems.

"However, by pitting on each lap to allow the fluids to flow properly, we finished the test, and .67 g right and .69 g left are just average. Understeer was just average also, but with the power available, throttle oversteer lurks for the unwary. Checking the tires for adequate 'scuff-in,' we noticed that the rubber compound was super soft, somewhere between eraser-tip and bubble gum, and we suspect that if you use the traction, you'll lose the tread."

Car and Driver was equally as tough describing its 426 Hemi Challenger R/T's handling. "Before we go any further, we should make it clear that the test car is perfectly satisfactory for normal maneuvers like going to church and fetching grandma, but you don't buy Hemis for that kind of duty. Strong understeer is apparent in places where you might try to hurry, like expressway entrances and really flogging on a twisting road or a tight road course is a waste of time. The car just won't cooperate.

"The Hemi's road course performance was hamstrung by two distinct difficulties. First, the carburetors cut out so badly in turns that the whole operation is deprived of the power necessary to negate the understeer, and you end up moving very slowly on a very erratic line.

"The idea of a 'sporty' car weighing within 100 pounds of a comparably equipped Road Runner or Super Bee is ridiculous. Along with all of the weight comes a weight distribution problem: 58.9 percent on the front wheels of the Hemi test car. What has happened is Chrysler has built itself a 'performance' car that is 300 pounds heavier than a Cobra Jet Mustang, and almost as nose-heavy. Nice going, you guys."

Interior comfort, roominess, and general utility? *Car and Driver* put it this way, in their road test's sub-headline: "Lavish execution with little or no thought toward practical application."

Road Test noted the pluses, and minuses, of their test car's cabin. "As long as 'comfort' is not used in the strictest sense of the term and applied to the ungiving relationship of the suspension to city pavements, the Hemi Challenger is a pleasing car and indeed, quite plush in the R/ T form tested. It was nice in particular to sit on cloth-covered seat cushions for a change (this is but one of the many options) and not be subjected to the extremes in temperatures served up by vinyl and leather on the first contact of the day.

"A purist could quarrel with the molded plastic material used to cover in one piece the entire inside area of each door as well as each side of the rear compartment. It is difficult to impart a look of richness to this material, or at least Dodge stylists haven't succeeded, and the armrest molded into it is somewhat less comfortable than the padded types on other cars.

"Headroom, legroom, except in the rear, driving position, and control accessibility must all be rated as good for normal-sized people. The instrumentation pictured is part of the R/T package and complete, including coverage of all engine functions, a tach and a rally clock with a large, detailed second hand. Tach and speedometer, though, are obscured by the wheel rim, necessitating adjusting the seat to a position that may not be the most comfortable for the individual.

"The normal glove bin is too small to hold much in the way of items that you might wish to conceal under lock, but console-equipped cars offer an additional covered storage area, plus an odd indentation at the end that serves no known purpose. At first we thought that the rear ashtray had been stolen and rear seat passengers used it as such, causing smells like plastic makes when it's too hot. No one in the Dodge organization has yet been able to explain this feature to us.

"The heating and ventilating system worked well although on this test, its hardest task being to dissipate windshield fog from parking out overnight. There are no vent windows but the forced-air system will handle at least one cigar smoker. Cracking a front window will serve only to blow ashes all over."

However, *Sports Car Graphic* was kinder than *Car and Driver,* though not with the front bucket seats. "The front buckets aren't, really, and are more like individual bench seats because of a lack of lateral support, but otherwise comfortable with practical and unobtrusive headrests."

They added, "Driver comfort and convenience are the best features of the car, though it takes a lot of comparison-driving to be aware of all the mistakes they didn't make. Everything you need is right there when and where you need it, everything works like it ought to and is understandably labeled, and everything is right in sight, except the wipers now. Along with hidden wipers, they have also arranged and finished the dash and cowl so that you get no sun reflections no matter how hard you try. And at night, the panel illumination is literally 'out of sight,' a green-tinted beam shining out of nowhere over the entire cluster, but again, not reflecting on the windshield."

All of them took note of the roominess of the trunk, or lack of it, with *Sports Car Graphic* stating that, "You'll have to hold any luggage on your lap, because the trunk is the smallest in the United States, and worse, not even a small suitcase will fit because the spare is square in the center of it."

But, did they like it? Said *Road Test,* "Just driving a Hemi is an experience. Owning one is almost a full-time project. If brute power over all other considerations is your forte, the Hemi is still boss on the street and if you'll note what most people put under a supercharger in Top Fuel Eliminator, it's boss on the strip as well. Don't, though, expect sophisticated handling, or much in the way of ride.

Sports Car Graphic put it this way. "We loved the car, as long as it went in a straight line."

Car and Driver concluded its road test article with, "If Dodge's sporty car is like everyone else's, success will depend entirely upon public acceptance of its looks. We've never accused the Mustang of being a wizard car, but it sells like one and we think the Challenger has got it covered in the looks category. Still, we are disappointed that looks are awarded such a high priority over function, and we think Dodge has had enough time to build a more purposeful car. It's our humble suggestion that, to avoid similar ineptitude in the future, all of the Challenger product planners fall on their swords immediately."

Sales by the Numbers

Just how good (or bad) were Challenger's sales in 1970? Instead of totaling half of the 200,000 to 225,000 number that chief product planner Burton Bouwkamp projected back in 1967 to get the E-Body program approved, the Challenger's numbers were close but not close enough. They totaled 83,032 for the 1970 model year, per Ward's Automotive Yearbook (1971).

Although the 1970 sales figures did not reach expectations, there was still reason at Dodge to be optimistic for the future. The Challenger was now in production, and Dodge finally had a car that could take on Pontiac and Mercury in the pony car class. Unfortunately, the cost of insuring one of these cars (even if it had a standard, regular-gas engine) was beginning to climb into the unaffordable range, and surcharges for items like a floor-mounted shifter or a tachometer didn't help, either.

Also, what sales success that Challenger may have had quite probably cut into Charger's sales for 1970. Dodge sold 89,200 1969 Chargers and Charger R/Ts, per *The Standard Catalogue,* but that number dropped to 49,768 for the three-model (base, R/T, and new midlevel Charger 500) 1970 Charger lineup, which was also hit with the same high insurance rates and surcharges that the Challenger was.

Coming out of the 1970 model year, Dodge was positioned to compete in 1971 with a lineup ranging from economical compact Darts, newly styled midsize Chargers and Coronets, a roomy full-size line of Polaras and Monacos, the sporty Challengers, and light trucks that were becoming more and more

1970 DODGE CHALLENGER SALES (FULL 1970 MODEL YEAR)

- Challenger hardtop: 53,337
- Challenger convertible: 3,173
- Challenger SE hardtop: 6,564
- Challenger R/T hardtop: 14,889
- Challenger R/T convertible: 1,070
- Challenger SE R/T hardtop: 3,979
- Challenger T/A hardtop: 2,400

Here is the breakdown of that 83,032 total:

- Challenger R/T hardtop with 426 Hemi: 287 (150 TorqueFlite, 137 4-speed)
- Challenger SE R/T hardtop with 426 Hemi 58 (37 TorqueFlite, 22 4-speed)
- Challenger R/T convertible with 426 Hemi: 9 (4 TorqueFlite, 5 4-speed)
- Challenger R/T hardtop with 440 Six Pack: 1,640 (793 TorqueFlite, 847 4-speed)
- Challenger SE R/T hardtop with 440 Six Pack: 296 (161 TorqueFlite, 135 4-speed)
- Challenger R/T convertible with 440 Six Pack: 99 (38 TorqueFlite, 61 4-speed)
- Challenger R/T hardtop with 440 Magnum: 2,802 (1,906 TorqueFlite, 916 4-speed)
- Challenger SE R/T hardtop with 440 Magnum: 875 (733 TorqueFlite, 142 4-speed)
- Challenger R/T convertible with 440 Magnum: 163 (129 TorqueFlite, 34 4-speed)
- Challenger R/T hardtop with 383 Magnum: 8,939 (6,014 TorqueFlite, 2,570 4-speed, 335 3-speed)
- Challenger SE R/T hardtop with 383 Magnum: 2.476 (2,076 TorqueFlite, 400 4-speed)
- Challenger R/T convertible with 383 Magnum: 684 (516 TorqueFlite, 149 4-speed, 19 3-speed)
- Challenger hardtop with 340: 8,837 (6,933 TorqueFlite, 1,830 4-speed, 343 3-speed)
- Challenger convertible with 340: 264 (178 TorqueFlite, 66 4-speed, 20 3-speed)
- Challenger T/A: 2,400 (1,411 TorqueFlite, 989 4-speed)

car-like in styling and features. Add in a line of "subcompact" cars built by Mitsubishi for Dodge that were set to enter the market during the year on the West Coast, and there was plenty of reason to be optimistic at Dodge for 1971. For 1970, 83,032 Challengers were sold, and the model and option breakdown goes as follows.

The Challenger T/A: Race-Inspired Performance

There was one more member of Dodge's "Scat Pack" come midyear 1970; one whose production run was short (fewer than 3,000 cars total) but whose impact was felt beyond the sales floor: the Dodge Challenger T/A. "T/A" stood for "Trans Am," short for the Sports Car Club of America's Trans-American Sedan Championship, or "Trans-Am" series, which Dodge had competed in with limited-factory support in 1966, with an extremely limited-production car, the so-called D-Dart, which was also raced in NHRA's D/Stock class back then.

The Trans-Am series was production-based, which meant that the cars that raced in it had to use production-based bodies, engines, suspension, and chassis hardware, and the manufacturers that made the cars that raced in that series had to build a minimum number of so-equipped cars to qualify it as a "production car."

Tom Gale, Chrysler's former design vice president, says that it was that SCCA rule alone that led to the Challenger T/A's development, along with its Plymouth sibling, the AAR 'Cuda (which will be covered in Chapter 3). Chrysler released the road-going Challengers to meet the SCCA homologation requirements, but the corporation had to do a lot of work to make that happen. And many were not happy about it.

For 1970, SCCA's Trans-Am rules increased the number of specially equipped cars that had to be built to qualify as "production" cars. For Dodge, that number would be 2,500, and not just the first 2,500 Challengers off the assembly line with any engine, transmission, or suspension options, but 2,500 equipped with powertrain and chassis hardware that would also go on the race versions. Fortunately, SCCA's 1970 rules also permitted "destroking" of existing production engines, which meant that Chrysler's potent 340-ci small-block V-8 could qualify without the corporation going to the expense of making a run of 2,500 engines that conformed to the SCCA's 5-liter (305.5 ci) rule with expensive, low-volume parts like smaller-bore cylinder blocks or smaller-stroke crankshafts and connecting rods.

But a special "TA" engine block (a stouter casting with provisions for four-bolt main-bearing cap) was OK'd for production in the Challenger T/A and its Plymouth counterpart, as well as special "TA" cylinder heads with offset valves and more material cast in to allow for porting, and an induction system using three Holley 2-barrel carburetors, an aluminum intake manifold, plus carburetor linkage and air cleaner similar to those used on the 440 Six Pack.

The process to bring the Challenger T/A into production reality was helped along by an Action Letter from J. T. Brown at Chrysler's Engineering Planning Section dated October 2, 1969. In it, these callouts for chassis components were made. For the steering system, a 24:1 manual steering was to be standard, quick ratio power steering optional, about 14:1, quick-ratio manual gear 16:1 to be dealer-installed option. For wheel and tires, the following upgrades were to be made: 15x7 wheels, Rallye type standard, tires to be G60, the Challenger front rework to be determined, and collapsible spare tire. The rear axle was to be equipped with a Sure-Grip 3.55 standard.

For the street-going versions of the road-racing E-Body, these body callouts were also included in that action letter

Built to homologate the stouter engine block, special cylinder heads, and fiberglass hood for SCCA Trans-Am competition (as well as for any other production-based race series), the Challenger T/A joined the Dodge lineup in the spring of 1970. This Panther Pink with a white interior example is one of only two surviving T/As with this color combination.

The 340-ci "LA" engine was a stout performer in base 4-barrel form, but the 3x2-barrel Holley carburetor induction system (atop a cast-aluminum intake manifold sourced from Edelbrock) took the 340's performance to another level.

of October 2, 1969: a new fiberglass hood with forward facing fresh air hood scoop to be designed at Creative Industries (which had performed the post-assembly conversion work on the 1969 Charger Daytona), development to be coordinated with Product Planning Special Performance Events Department; a flush-mounted grille to be styled and engineered at an outside source; deck-lid stabilizer to be an advanced "G" series universal stabilizer with an outside source to do styling and engineering; front spoiler under nose; fenders reworked to provide tire clearance; and dual body-colored outside mirrors.

Finally, that letter of October 2, 1969, concluded with these items, including a 14½-inch soft steering wheel, Rallye instrument cluster, competition seat to be an option for driver's side only, and unique paint striping and distinctive trim to be developed.

The projected number of units to be produced was 2,500 for Challenger, and 2,800 for Barracuda, the minimum requirements for Trans-Am racing per SCCA's rules for 1970. The deadline to finalize the package for submission to ACCUS-FIA for their approval was January 15, 1970, and the projected life expectancy for this program was put at "the 'F' Series and beyond." Detailed Product Planning letters were to be issued at a later date to cover available colors and trim.

Author note: The lettered series designation for A-Body cars was first used in 1965, with those Barracudas denoted as the A Series. Following in that sequence, the F Series denoted the 1970 models, G Series the 1971s, and H Series the 1972s. That designation was discontinued in 1972, and all E-Body cars from then on were identified by model year.

Also worth noting is the "ACCUS-FIA" callout and deadline. ACCUS was the Automotive Competition Committee of the United States, the American arm of the Federation Internationale de l'Automobile, the international motorsports rule-making body under whose rules the SCCA operated. The deadline to submit their homologation paperwork that showed what special parts were going on the batch of street T/As and AAR 'Cudas, as well as the production plans and scheduling information for cars not yet built, was January 15, 1970.

On October 15, 1969, an Engineering Action Letter went out for the F Series E-Body Trans-Am 340 over J. T. Brown's signature. At the top of this one, the box, "This item has been approved subject to the availability of Engineering manpower resources," appeared, requesting man-hour and material estimates from body, chassis, vehicle engineering, and materials operations groups within Chrysler Engineering.

That action letter went on to describe some of the features of the street version of the road-race cars: "Engine: Exhaust system and engine sounds, a Z-28 noise level. Pending a successful design and development program, dual-pass mufflers are to be considered in conjunction with NASCAR type side exit exhausts. Brakes: Four-wheel discs will be sold only as a special order for racing purposes. Transmission: The close-ratio 4-speed is a 2.47 ratio with fine pitch gears. Steering: The conventional 15.7 ratio power steering gear is also to be made available as an option. The quick-ratio power steering option is dependent upon successful design and development activity. Wheels and tires: G60x15 tires are to be used on rear wheels, and E60x15 tires on the front wheels. Challenger rework will not be required. Rear Axle: All axles must accommodate a 60.7-inch rear track. Body: No fender rework is required. Miscellaneous: The 14½-inch steering wheel is not to be made available for these cars. Usage of existing wheels will be defined by a supplemental letter."

Note the change in tire sizes: the original plan, per the October 2 Action Letter, was to use the G60x14 tire. It was the

The decision to put E60-14 tires on the Challenger T/A front wheels instead of G60-14s meant that stock front fenders, and not the special "rolled" ones used on 426 Hemi Challengers, could be used on the T/A.

The G60-14 tire's width isn't evident here, but it fills the fenderwells. It was the widest tire ever factory-installed on a Dodge car up to that point in time.

A stock grille, instead of the flush-mounted one similar to the 1969 Dodge Charger 500s, resides between the stock front bumper and the T/A's fiberglass hood.

This Challenger T/A shows how the fiberglass hood tended to "bow." (Photo by David Newhardt, Courtesy Mecum Auction Company)

widest ever used on a Chrysler Corporation passenger car to that point, all around. Unfortunately, when fitted to a prototype Challenger, it rubbed against the top inside of the wheel opening on the regular-production Challenger's front fender. Front fenders for 426 Hemi Challengers, which would use the huge 60-series rubber all around, had their inner lips rolled to provide clearance. However, those fenders would not be produced in quantity for use with what became the Challenger T/A. The change in front tire size to E60x14 permitted the use of the regular-production Challenger front fender, thereby solving the clearance problem while keeping costs down.

On October 31, 1969, yet another Action Letter went out regarding the Trans-Am Street Package program. On its front page was mention of the F Series and G Series E-Body cars. As that intra-company correspondence and the one of October 2 suggested, Chrysler's plan for what turned into the Challenger T/A and AAR 'Cuda was for them to remain in the E-Body production lineup beyond 1970.

Some items mentioned in those Engineering Action Letters never made it onto the production Challenger T/A. The flush-mounted grille, similar to the one fitted to the limited-edition Dodge Charger 500 in the spring of 1969, was left off, in favor of the production Challenger grille. The four-wheel-disc brake and driver's-side competition seat options for dealer installation were also dropped before the T/As began rolling off the line at Hamtramck Assembly. Also, while the Plymouth version would use the Rallye wheels as mentioned above, stock-type steel wheels, painted black and adorned with a chrome trim ring and the standard Dodge "dog dish" hub cap, was the standard wheel treatment for the Challenger T/A.

But the fiberglass hood did make it into production, with steel hood pins holding the front of the hood down (the stock hood latch was not used on the Challenger T/A), with stock hood springs at the rear. Unfortunately, that led to the hoods not fitting flush with the fender line, "bowing" upward in the middle. Tom Gale, who worked in Advanced Engineering then, and later became Chrysler's design head, told me in a January 2015 interview, "The problem was the fiberglass hoods were made off-site, and the hood springs and hinges were working against the hood pins, which would cause them to bow."

One solution to the problem of fiberglass hood bowing (and subsequent cracking from normal opening and closing) was what Challenger T/A owner Larry Gibb used when he restored his Panther Pink T/A, which included repairing that cracked stock hood. "I went ahead and put metal bars inside [along the sides of the hood] to get it flattened out," he told me during the May 10, 2015, photo shoot of his Panther Pink T/A.

Thanks to a little remedial work, the hood on Larry Gibb's Challenger T/A fits flat and flush with the fenders.

Side-exit exhausts with chrome "megaphone" tips were unique to the T/A and not available from the factory on any other Challenger. The tips and curved tailpipe that connected them to the mufflers were shipped in the trunk for dealer installation.

Decklid-mounted fiberglass spoiler was an integral part of the Challenger T/A's standard equipment.

Under the triple Holleys and Edelbrock intake manifold is the special "TA" block and cylinder heads, the reason why Dodge had to build so many production Challenger T/As if they wanted to use them in SCCA's Trans-Am series.

"The stock hood hinges bolted right through to those, and I epoxied them in." As the photos of his T/A show, the hood lies flat, as the Styling and Engineering teams at Dodge envisioned it would way back in 1969.

Once all the preproduction problems were solved, the Challenger T/A went into production, at Hamtramck Assembly. Production began on March 10, 1970, and ended two months later, on May 10.

Standard equipment on the Challenger T/A included (along with the special engine block and cylinder heads, and the 60-series wheels and tires) Chrysler's A-833 4-speed manual transmission, with a heavy-duty Torquefite automatic optional; either the 3.55 or 3.91 rear axle ratios, inside a Sure-Grip differential; heavy-duty suspension with front and rear sway bars and shocks; special side-exit exhausts; and power front disc brakes. Not available was air conditioning, drum brakes, the G81 "wing" rear spoiler that joined the option list during the 1970

The exhaust outlets' front-exit mufflers, unique to the Challenger T/A, are seen here, along with its standard special chassis hardware.

model year or the chrome luggage rack, automatic speed control, five-spoke road wheels, the A04 Basic Group and the S15 extra-heavy-duty suspension option, and the A35 trailer-towing package.

Another Challenger T/A distinction: The antenna on factory radio-equipped T/As was located on the right rear quarter panel.

Standard graphics were vivid, even the spelling of "Six Pack" didn't match that on the air cleaner.

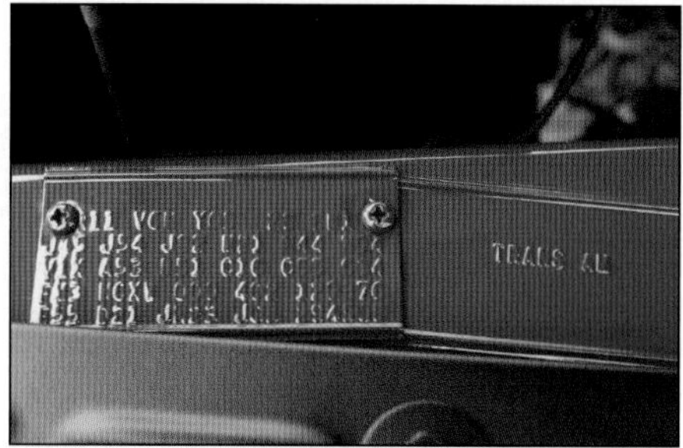

Special equipment on the Challenger T/A made it a "two-tag" car, with the special indication "Trans Am" on the second fender tag (right).

AUTODYNAMICS' CHALLENGER T/A

At the same time that the production Challenger T/A was taking shape in Highland Park, the race versions began their transformation from an idea, bodies-in-white and a stock of parts, into two cars ready to race in the SCCA's Trans-Am Series. Time was of the essence. The first race, at Laguna Seca on California's Monterey Peninsula, was scheduled for April 19–21, 1970. About a month before then, the first on-track test session for the racing Challengers and their Plymouth AAR 'Cuda siblings was scheduled for Riverside Raceway in Southern California. And the shop where the Challenger T/As would be constructed, and call home that season, hadn't even been set up as of the day that the production Challengers went on sale in September 1969.

Chrysler chose one shop to convert production E-Body hardtop bodies-in-white into ones that race cars could be built from, with those bodies chemically milled ("acid dipped") to reduce their weight, with steel tube roll cages then welded in. From there,

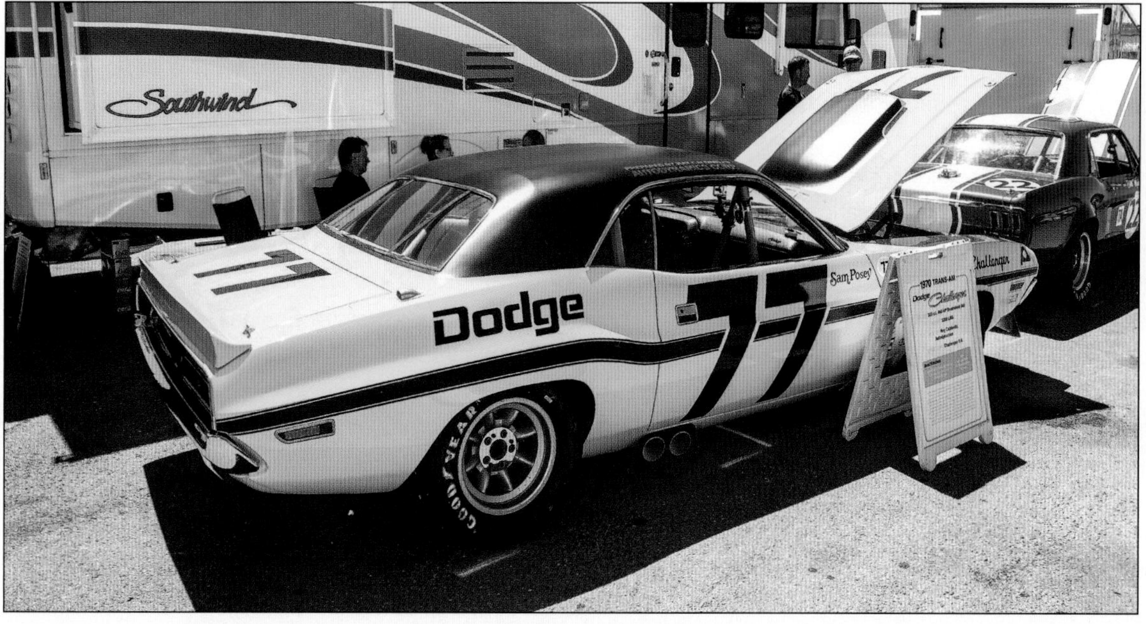

Only raced one year, and now restored and running in Historic Trans Am races, is the #77 Autodynamics Challenger T/A. Once raced by Sam Posey, it's now owned by Richard Goldsmith. (Photo Courtesy Michael Campos)

AUTODYNAMICS' CHALLENGER T/A CONTINUED

separate shops for the Dodge and Plymouth teams would turn those partial vehicles into race cars.

When Chrysler made the public announcement of its 1970 Trans-Am program on October 16, 1969, Dan Gurney's All-American Racers shop had been picked not only to build and race the Plymouth AAR 'Cudas, but also to perform the preliminary body preparation. Dodge chose another race shop, Autodynamics, to build and race the Challenger T/A.

"A small New England company with formula and sports racer background was chosen to develop the Challengers," said David Tom in *The Cars of Trans-Am Racing 1966–1972: Road Racing Muscle from GM, Ford, Chrysler and AMC*, adding, "Pete Hutchinson, Chrysler's head of racing, perhaps influenced by top line driver Sam Posey, chose to separate the two brands by more than 3,000 miles."

Autodynamics, which was based in Connecticut, had constructed sports-racing and Formula Vee cars, which SCCA racers competed with from coast to coast, but this was their first venture into professional racing with production-based cars and factory support.

But Dodge wasn't the first automaker that Autodynamics had been in touch with regarding a factory-supported Trans-Am team. In the late summer/early fall of 1969, they had been in touch with American Motors about racing a factory-sponsored Javelin for 1970. When Dodge first contacted them about building and racing the new Challenger in Trans-Am, Autodynamics turned them down. But when it came time to sign the deal with AMC, Ray Caldwell found that Roger Penske had, instead, been given the AMC factory deal to race Javelins with Mark Donohue as their lead driver.

Autodynamics then turned to Dodge, and Dodge finally had a team they could provide factory backing to. Once the deal with Dodge was done, Caldwell set up a West Coast shop. He picked Reith Automotive in Long Beach as the location for Autodynamics West, as that location was not only close to the All-American Racers shop in Santa Ana where the Challenger bodies would be prepared, but it was also close to the Riverside and Willow Springs racetracks where they would test. Keith Black Racing Engines, chosen to build the "destroked" 340 race engines, was not far away, either.

Bob Tarozzi, chosen by Chrysler racing boss Pete Hutchinson to oversee the engineering development of the factory E-Body race cars, details his and All-American Racers' involvement with the Dodges before Autodynamics got them. As Tarozzi told David Tom, "We were also doing the basic builds on the Dodge Challengers for the [Autodynamics] team. This made our tasks harder or at least more time-consuming, but overall cut the Chrysler team's development time. When we had the basic Dodge chassis done, we sent them to Ray Caldwell's boys to finish as they wanted."

Under the hood sits the restored Keith Black–built racing engine, destroked to meet SCCA's 305.5-ci (5 liters) limit. (Photo Courtesy Chad Raynal)

Unfortunately, there was a problem with one of the Challenger bodies when it went though the acid-dipping process. "When a car body or any metal is acid dipped, the acid etches, or eats away at the metal until it is neutralized," Tarozzi told Tom. "All of our bodies were dipped, but the Dodge bodies did not get the proper neutralization, so they continued to etch. The Dodge team had continuing problems, especially in the floor of the car where the crossmembers of the unit body were weak and getting weaker. Even before the season started, we knew that there was a problem and we applied some additional bars to strengthen the floor."

Once the acid-dipped bodies were put on the Phil Remington–built chassis fixture, Autodynamics West turned them into race cars.

For power, Keith Black Racing Engines, who had done the preliminary development work on the 1970 Trans-Am engine program for Chrysler, supplied the destroked 340s for the Dodges, which now displaced just under 304 ci, that were built using the production "TA" engine block and cylinder heads. (All-American Racers, after the development work that Keith Black's did for them, built their AAR 'Cuda race engines in-house.)

"We both had good engine programs," recalls Sam Posey. "But in the end, ours was better, because the Keith Black engines

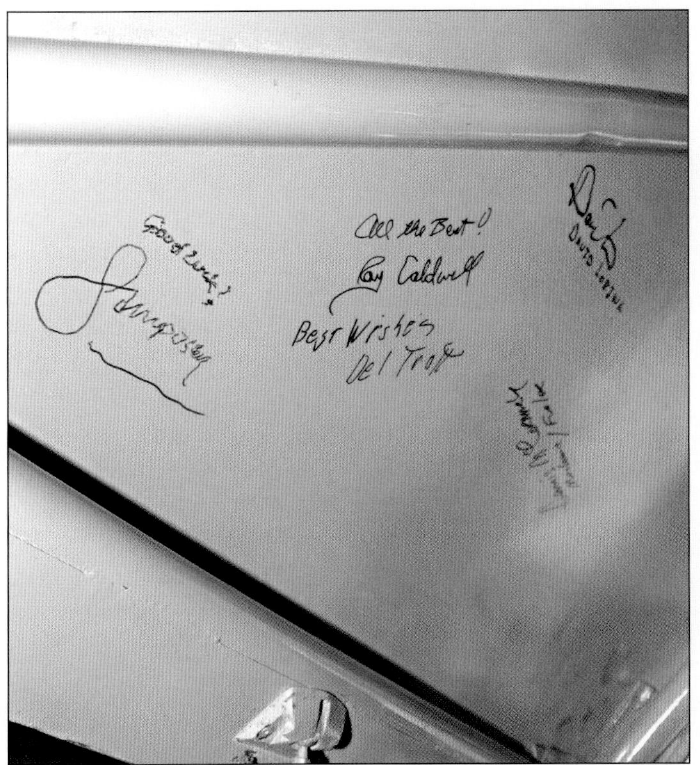

On the underside of the roof, autographs include Sam Posey's, as well as Autodynamics chief Ray Caldwell. Also visible, parallel to the roll bar tubing, is the weld used to graft a new roof on to the acid-dipped Challenger body before it could run in its first race. (Photo Courtesy Chad Raynal)

were just that one hair more reliable, and I think we had every bit the horsepower they did." Posey added, "The inherent features of the Chrysler engine were first class, and I think what Keith Black did with them made them first class *plus*."

For the chassis, Ray Caldwell chose to use the same "full-floating" rear axle design that he'd used with their Can-Am road race cars with the E-Body leaf-spring rear suspension system, while the front suspension was based on the production (torsion bar) design.

As for what color the Challenger T/As would wear on the track, instead of the bright red that Dodge used as its corporate-identity color, they specified the High Impact color SubLime. Sam Posey suggested that the green be toned down somewhat by painting the roof and car numbers black, while adding a black front-to-rear stripe along each side, similar to what the production Challenger R/Ts used.

Once the cars were completed and tested in March at Riverside, it was time for their first race at Laguna Seca. And that's

A view of the #77's dash and gauges, removable steering wheel, and Hurst competition shifter. Note repair welds on floorpan, necessitated by the car's acid-dipped body. (Photo Courtesy Chad Raynal)

Where Sam Posey operated the #77 Challenger T/A from during the 1970 season, and where his son John drove it at Lime Rock Park many years later. Roll cage tubing was designed and installed by Dan Gurney's All-American Racers shop before the body was delivered to Autodynamics to build into the race car seen here. (Photo Courtesy Chad Raynal)

AUTODYNAMICS' CHALLENGER T/A CONTINUED

where the problems with the acid-dipped body started showing up, starting with its first race there. Pre-race technical inspection resulted in an inspector putting his thumb through the car's chemically milled roof panel.

Richard Goldsmith, the current owner of the #77 Challenger, confirms the errant-tech-inspector and roof-replacement story. "It's the real deal," he told me in an interview in April 2015. "It's still got Sam Posey's signature on the inside, where they replaced it in 1970, after they failed tech inspection. And then, they went down to a [Dodge] dealer in Monterey, cut the roof off another car, and put it on. You can still see the very rough welds on the inside where they did that job, when they cut that old [roof] off and put the new one on."

Once the new roof was welded on and painted, the car was reinspected, and passed. But when Sam Posey took it to the track, the acid-dipped Unibody's strength (or lack of it) became apparent. As Bob Tarozzi explained to David Tom, "Basically, the car (any race car) needs a rigid platform, or you cannot make lasting setup changes. Every time we took the car on the track, it came back sagging a little. When I say 'a little,' I mean too much to get whatever baseline or constant setup we applied. It was a continuing problem for the Autodynamics team."

Tarozzi also told David Tom that Sam Posey said that after every race that season, they needed to weld up cracks that appeared in the #77's floorpan. "We fixed our problem with torsion-bar sag right away," says Tarozzi. "I think the Challengers suffered throughout the season from that critical problem."

Keith Black Engines was tapped to build the destroked 340s for Autodynamics, and this one's been restored to race-ready condition. (Photo Courtesy Chad Raynal)

The result was a fast car that did not handle well, one which Tarozzi added his own, "See, I told you so."

"The Caldwell guys spent too much time and effort trying to get their Can-Am-style suspension to work on a leaf-spring rear. It just wasn't going to work." One of its problems was lots of rear wheel-hop under hard braking, which resulted in hard vibrations transmitted to the transmission, many times shortening its race-day life.

While the #77 Autodynamics Challenger with Sam Posey at the helm may have qualified well, and may have run strong in each 1970 race's early going, too many times it wasn't around at the finish. Posey finished in sixth place in the season-opener at Laguna Seca (which Parnelli Jones won in a Bud Moore–built Mustang Boss 302), then third at the next race at Lime Rock Park in Connecticut three weeks later. Unfortunately, the #77 Challenger T/A was again three laps behind Parnelli's winning #15 Mustang. Then, at Bryar Motorsport Park at Loudon, New Hampshire, three weeks later, the #77 car only lasted four laps before a clutch failure put it behind the wall.

Also unfortunate for the Autodynamics team was the reduction in factory support from Dodge. They had actually entered two cars at Bryar, the #77 for Sam Posey and the #76 Challenger (painted the same as Posey's car) for Skip Barber. Unfortunately, the #76 car was a no-show for the race. The #76 car was also entered for the Trans-Am race at Bridgehampton, New York, on June 21, but it spent the race on the trailer as a back-up car instead. Only at the season's last two races (at Seattle International Raceway in Kent, Washington, and at Riverside) did both Challenger T/As race.

Before then, the frustrations grew race by race. To be honest, the frustrations grew for every other Trans-Am team except the Fords, that (in the hands of Parnelli Jones and George Follmer) ran away from the field, winning seven of the 1970 season's ten races.

Mid-Ohio in early June brought another third-place finish for Sam Posey in the #77 Challenger, but once more he was three laps behind the race winner, Parnelli Jones. At Bridgehampton, a throttle failure led to Posey's dropping out of the race after 54 laps, a race won by Mark Donohue in the Penske Javelin. On July 5, at what was then called Donnybrooke Raceway in Minnesota (now called Brainerd International Raceway), Posey (driving the #76 Challenger) only lasted 13 laps before retiring.

But two weeks later, at Road America at Elkhart Lake, Wisconsin, Posey drove the #77 car to another third-place finish. This one was much closer, with Posey, Swede Savage, and Donohue battling for the lead in the late laps, and Donohue taking the checker .90 second ahead of Posey and just .58 second ahead of

Savage in the #42 AAR 'Cuda. At the Trans-Am's next stop at Circuit Mont-Tremblant in St. Jovite, Quebec, Posey again brought the #77 Dodge home in the top five, this time a fourth-place finish, one lap behind winner Mark Donohue.

But a DNF after just 24 laps at Watkins Glen in mid-August was a harbinger of bad luck yet to come for the #77 car. At the next to last race at Seattle International Raceway, that car (with Ronnie Bucknum driving) dropped out with transmission trouble after 29 laps. Sam Posey drove the #76 car in that race, and racked up his third 3rd-place finish of the year, again finishing one lap behind the winning Mustang of Parnelli Jones.

Then, at the 1970 season finale at Riverside, both Autodynamics Challengers failed to finish, due to engine problems. Sam Posey's #77 lasted just 20 laps, while Tony Adamowicz and the #76 Challenger T/A ran 64 laps before the engine packed it in.

In the final 1970 manufacturers' points standings, the Dodge team finished fourth, with 18 points, well behind the 40 points that Chevrolet scored that year, AMC's 59, and the championship-winning Fords' 72 points. No driver's points championship was awarded in Trans-Am for 1970, but Parnelli Jones, who won five times, likely would have run away with it.

Following the season, one would think that the teams that took part in the 1970 Trans-Am season would look forward to an off-season of further refinement and development, and a return to action for 1971. Sadly, that was not the case. As mentioned above, word came out of Highland Park that Chrysler wasn't going to fund its race teams as it had for 1970, in NASCAR and USAC stock-car racing, as well as in SCCA's Trans-Am.

Before the Seattle race, Chrysler told both of its Trans-Am teams that only one of them received factory support for 1971, the team that finished the highest in the manufacturer's points standings. But, by the time the series reached Riverside for the 1970 season finale, all Chrysler support for Trans-Am racing was gone.

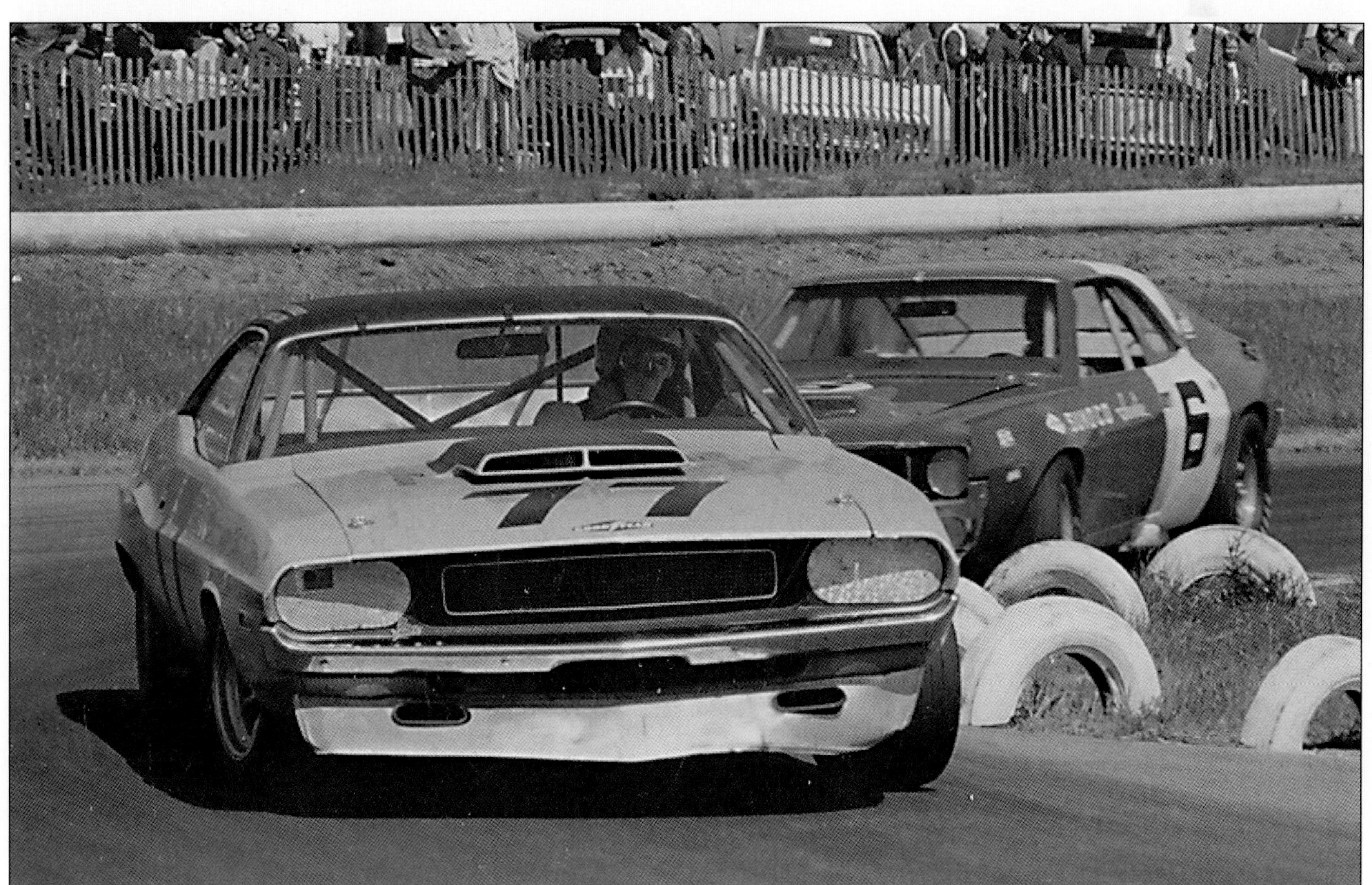

Sam Posey battles Mark Donohue's Penske-prepared AMC Javelin during the first 1970 SCCA Trans-Am race at Laguna Seca. (Photo Courtesy Butch Noble/Mazda Raceway at Laguna Seca)

It's very likely that Chrysler used the practice of "batch building" when it scheduled the Challenger T/A for production, owing to the lead time needed for the special components like the fiberglass hood, front "chin whiskers" spoiler and rear-decklid spoiler, mufflers and side-exit tailpipes, and the special TA engine block and cylinder heads, to be produced and then incorporated into the E-Body production process.

Dodge's experience in "batch building" high-performance cars dated back to the mid-1950s, when it began installing more than just higher-output engines in its lightweight Coronet sedans for police duty. Those cars also received a number of upgraded steering, chassis, suspension, and body/frame reinforcement pieces, which led Dodge's production-scheduling office to schedule them to be built in batches, when the police-specific parts would be available for factory installation.

Chrysler's Departure from Trans-Am

Without additional factory support from Chrysler, or a well-heeled commercial sponsor willing to put its logo and colors on the Autodynamics Challengers, competing in the Trans-Am series for 1971 was out of the question. If that financial support had been forthcoming, it's very likely that some of the problems that tended to plague a new race car in its first season of competition would have been cured. One was the wheel hop that the #76 and #77 Challengers experienced, due to the construction of the cars' rear suspension systems. "Ray Caldwell insisted that the Challenger would handle better with a rear suspension derived from his earlier Can-Am and open-wheel chassis development," says David Tom. "Bob Tarozzi felt it would not work, but was coerced to engineer it anyway. It turned out to be a handful, and not as good as expected."

On that point, Richard Goldsmith agrees. "One of the biggest problems that Sam had was the wheel hop he had going into the corners, and it would tear things up [in the transmission]," notes the #77 Challenger's current owner. "Those guys drove 'em awful hard, so I don't think there's a piece on the car they didn't have trouble with."

Without sponsorship for the two Challengers, Autodynamics closed their West Coast shop in California after the 1970 racing season and shut down altogether before the end of 1972.

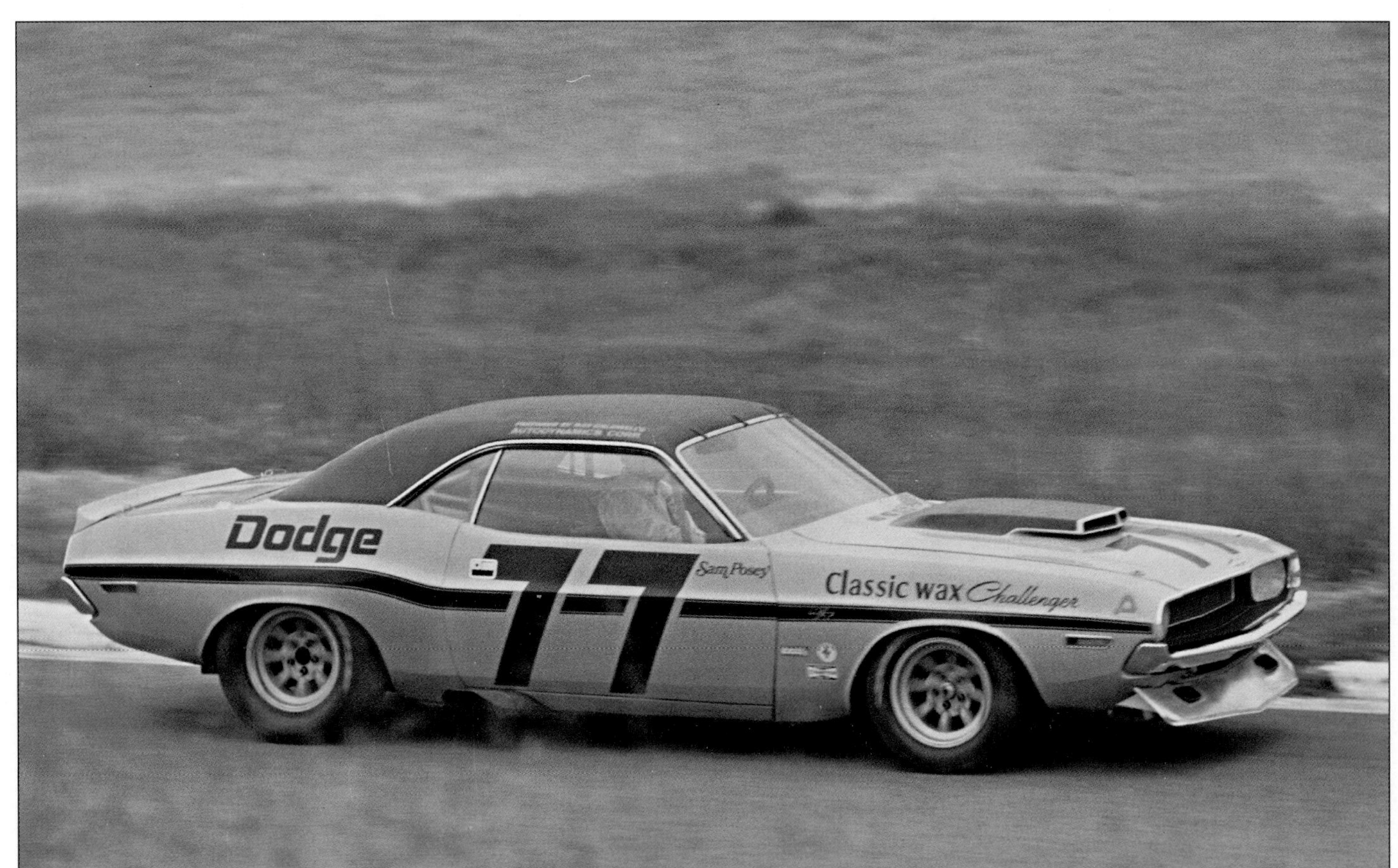

Sam Posey and the #77 Autodynamics Challenger T/A had their share of problems during the 1970 SCCA Trans-Am season. The disappearance of factory support from Chrysler meant that the #77, and Autodynamics' #76 Challenger T/A, would not race in Trans-Am the following year, or take to the track until many years after their restorations. (Photo Courtesy Butch Noble/Mazda Raceway at Laguna Seca)

There were a number of dark clouds looming over factory-supported motorsports operations as 1970 rolled on. Not just over Chrysler's, but those of the entire domestic auto industry as the 1971 model year approached. The Big Three, AMC, and the United Auto Workers were about to sit down at the bargaining table to work out new contracts. The UAW picked General Motors as the "strike target" as a part of their "pattern bargaining" process, where once the strike target and the union agreed on a new deal, similar ones would then be negotiated with the other automakers. The resulting new contract would not come cheap, and Chrysler had to look for spending they could cut to afford the new labor deal.

Add to that the recession of 1970 that hurt all car sales, plus the softness of the sporty-compact market (as mentioned below), and there was no corporate money for Trans-Am for Dodge for 1971.

Unfortunately, racing-sponsorships like the big-money consumer-product sponsor deals of recent years had yet to materialize. In fact, the off-season of 1970–71 is when the ball began rolling in that direction, with NASCAR team owner/legend Junior Johnson contacting the R.J. Reynolds Tobacco Company about sponsoring his race team for 1971. RJR, with the coming demise of broadcast advertising of its cigarettes, was looking to sponsor more than just one race team, and they ended up putting their Winston brand and millions of dollars into NASCAR's top stock car division beginning in 1972. Before then, Junior Johnson solved his sponsorship problem by hiring driver Bobby Allison, who had his own sponsor deal with Coca-Cola, which he brought with him to Johnson's team.

Also, television coverage of motorsports had yet to grow beyond the edited-film coverage that *ABC's Wide World of Sports* provided, interspersed with events such as figure skating and wrist-wrestling championships.

Still, if there had been a deal to show the Trans-Am races, and if non-manufacturer sponsor money began to show up like it did later in NASCAR, it's possible that the Autodynamics Challengers would have raced in 1971, albeit with 1971 grilles and taillights, and possibly a new, sponsor-driven color scheme.

What became of the two Challengers they built? They both survive (as mentioned above); the #77 is owned by Richard Goldsmith. "I've had it for only 2½ years, and it was in pretty good shape when I got it," he said in April 2015. "The car that's been competing in the Vintage Trans Am Series since about 1998. Ken Epsman had the car before I did."

As for who did the restoration work, Goldsmith says, "The restoration work was done by the Skanes family. This car is still very, very original: original-style transmission, and it still has the 303.8-ci destroked 340 [with the original 'T/A' block and cylinder heads]."

Bryan Skanes told David Tom he discovered that car for sale via the Special Interest Auto Club (SIAC). "It was made up of a group of avid owners/fans who were keeping the E-Body Mopars alive and well, but especially the Plymouth AAR 'Cuda and the Dodge Challenger T/A."

As luck would have it, his father, Ed Skanes, was headed to Houston on business and would see the advertised Challenger while there. "When he got home, we reviewed the pictures [he'd taken of the Challenger T/A], and the condition of the race car," he says. "Several people [had previously] owned it, and each one had made modifications to the car, but it came with a lot of parts. It was a very interesting restoration to consider."

Soon after, the Skanes (who had been restoring rare Dodge and Plymouth muscle cars in the late 1970s) bought that Challenger, along with the AAR 'Cuda they'd seen in the SIAC's publication. (See Chapter 3.)

How does that restored #77 Challenger T/A perform on the track? According to current owner Richard Goldsmith, "The car works very well. Not with me driving, but with Kenny [Epsman] driving, it's always at the front of the pack." Also, the problems with the acid-dipped body have been addressed. "The lower tub has been modified, and I would assume replaced at one point," he says. "It's still got a lot of cracks in it, that get welded all the time. It may be the same bottom on it, too."

Goldsmith says that the #77 Challenger has been reunited with Sam Posey, and driven once by his son. "I saw Sam when we were at Lime Rock in 2013. I had met Sam when I took the car to the Amelia Island Concours, in early 2013. It was a phenomenal thing, sitting there with Sam Posey and Dan Gurney, both of them sitting on the fender of the car swapping stories about the old days. That was an amazing adventure for me.

"Then, when we went to Lime Rock, Sam was just 10 minutes away. He actually stopped by, and I had my wife with me, and we met with his wife and Sam, and we talked about everything, about life, my son, who's an artist, just opened up an art gallery in San Francisco, so we had a lot to talk about. His wife is also an artist.

"He mentioned that his son John had started getting involved in car racing over the last couple of years. He was doing SCCA Mazda Miatas and stuff. I offered, and was gladly accepted, to let John take the Challenger out at Lime Rock for one of the practice sessions. He did great. He did real well in it.

"I'm sitting in Turn One with Sam (being in ill health, he was in a golf cart). I think it was as emotional for him as anything; he was tearing up watching John go around the track. To hear John and Sam talk about how much they bonded over that whole thing, because it's a big part of Sam's life that John wasn't a part of, because he was younger than that. Now, they can swap stories about the Challenger, John has a different perspective over what that was like. It was a great thing to be a part of."

CHAPTER 3

1970 PLYMOUTH BARRACUDA

An All-New Flyin' Fish

The E-Body Barracuda was an entirely different Fish, one with bigger teeth in the form of its engine choices, with a "school" full of standard features and options different from the A-Body Barracudas. Essentially the E-Body utilized the Chrysler B-Body, but it was wider and shorter. Best of all with the new platform change, the Barracuda shed its image as an economy car and established a reputation as a genuine pony car. While the Barracuda and Challenger shared the E-Body platform, these were distinctly different cars. The Barracuda rode on a wheelbase of 108 inches, which was 2 inches shorter than the Challenger. And as a result, no body parts interchanged between the two models. As far as options go, for 1970, all that remained the same about the Plymouth Barracuda from 1969 was the name, the convertible and hardtop body styles, some of the powertrain choices, and very little else.

In the spring of 1969, Chrysler-Plymouth Dealers across North America began receiving advance information about the new products on the way for 1970. Along with photographs of prototype models, the advance-information kit included information about the changes coming to the returning Fury, Belvedere/Satellite/Road Runner/GTX and Valiant line (including the new two-door Valiant Duster). The kit let Chrysler-Plymouth dealers know what was new for their sporty compact.

Under the heading "What's New About Barracuda For 1970?" it spelled it out: "Barracuda for 1970 is an all-new specialty sports car, available only in hardtop and convertible models. Bodies are completely new. The line-up includes basic Barracuda, the 'Cuda performance series, and a new luxury model: Gran Coupe. The Gran Coupe provided a luxury option package that was comparable to the competition, such as the Ford Mustang Grande and Mercury Cougar XR-7.

The Gran Coupe option certainly added some amenities, style, and appointments that were definitely higher scale. In particular, the stitched leather bucket seats delivered more comfort and style. The overhead console was an important feature

This InViolet 1970 Hemi 'Cuda convertible is owned by Craig Jackson. It is one of only 14 drop-top 1970 Hemi 'Cudas ever made, the only one wearing this color combination, and the only one exported. (Photo Courtesy Barrett-Jackson Auction Company)

All new for 1970, Plymouth's Barracuda was a whole different kind of fish, especially in 'Cuda hardtop form, as seen here. More engine options were available for 1970, thanks to the longer and wider engine bay under the Barracuda's new, longer hood. The 'Cuda was now a separate series, as was the all-new-for-1970 Barracuda Gran Coupe.

Head-on angle shows the standard 1970 Barracuda grille and hood. All non-'Cuda Barracudas received this grille; 'Cuda models had theirs blacked out. This car was likely built with either of Barracuda's standard engines (the 225 Slant Six or 318 V-8), as it wore no badges with the engine displacement on them.

Even in base convertible form, the 1970 Plymouth Barracuda showed a clean design devoid of any styling tack-ons. This convertible is one of the rare ones that hasn't been converted into a "tribute" Hemi 'Cuda yet.

of the package that included indicator lights for low fuel and door ajar. Other key upscale features included wood-grain dash and styled door panels. (See Appendix C for the complete feature and option list for the Gran Coupe.)

New Series and New Engine Availability

Instead of a single series with an optional 'Cuda package, the E-Body Barracuda now had three distinct series: the standard Barracuda, the plush-for-its-price Gran Coupe, and the performance-oriented 'Cuda. All were available as either a two-door hardtop or a convertible.

Like the Dodge Challenger, Barracuda offered nine available engine choices. Base-level and Gran Coupe cars had either the 225 Slant Six or 318 V-8 standard, with the regular-gas 383s available as options. The 'Cuda's engine selection started with the 383 Magnum that was also Road Runner's standard powerplant (and optional in the Belvedere and Fury police cars), with the high-winding 340 as an extra cost option, along with the 440 Magnum and 440 6-barrel (Plymouth's name for what many Mopar lovers call the 440 Six Pack, regardless of it being in a Dodge or Plymouth). Plus, the 426 Hemi was finally available as a regular-production option.

Unlike powerplants of the past, these engines were shared by Plymouth and Dodge instead of being unique to each division, as had been the case within Chrysler up to 1959, and were built at the same engine plants, "M&I" for the Hemi and Mound Road Engine for the others. (The engine specifications in the preceding chapter apply to the 1970 Barracuda engines.)

1970 BARRACUDA ENGINES

Engines	Barracuda	Gran Coupe	'Cuda
225 Six	Standard †	Standard †	N/A
318 V-8	Standard †	Standard †	N/A
340 V-8	N/A	N/A	Optional
383 2-barrel*	Optional	Optional	N/A
383 4-barrel	Optional	Optional	N/A
383 4-barrel	N/A	N/A	Standard
440 4-barrel **	N/A	N/A	Optional
440 6-barrel	N/A	N/A	Optional
426 Hemi***	N/A	N/A	Optional

† Original factory literature lists both engines as "standard"
** Available with TorqueFlite automatic only*
*** N/A with 3-speed manual*
*** N/A with 3-speed manual or with air conditioning*
Author note: The second 383 4-barrel engine is the 383 Magnum shared with the Road Runner.

Under the Hood: Power and Economy

When Chrysler released the new E-Body in 1970, it marked the first time that you could get any of their production engines in the Barracuda. When introduced in 1964, the choices were the Slant Six and the new-that-year LA small-block V-8, which were also the only factory-installed engines available when the second-generation Barracuda appeared for 1967.

But now, all four Chrysler engine "families" were available on Barracuda, in an engine bay that had plenty of room for them, as well as factory-installed items like power brake boosters and power steering pumps, as well as Airtemp air conditioning compressors on the optional single-4-barrel big-blocks.

The Slant Six was an engine that Chrysler-Plymouth dealers had grown to love since its 1960 introduction. Low operating cost and spirited performance (compared with other car makers' sixes back then) made the Slant Six an easy sell, and dealers had little trouble selling them in either compact, mid-size, or full-size Plymouths.

Likewise the 318, which was a larger-displacement version of the LA small-block that, by 1970, had replaced the 273-ci version in the Plymouth engine lineup. Easy on fuel, yet powerful enough to serve as the standard engine in the Belvedere and Fury lineups, the 318 would prove to be an easy choice for someone who wanted more power without the cost of premium gasoline.

If a buyer wanted a little more (again, without paying a lot more) then the 2-barrel 383 was a good choice. That was especially true if that buyer considered towing a small trailer with their Barracuda, or wanted an engine they knew wouldn't bog down with the optional air conditioning on, as some competitive engines back then tended to do.

When it came to the "Magnum" 383, it was a known quantity, but not just because it was the standard Road Runner Engine. Optional in Plymouth police cars since 1963, more than a few would-be speeders changed their minds once a patrol car known to have this engine in it appeared in their rearview mirror.

The performance reputation of the other high-performance 'Cuda engines was well-known by 1970. The 340, because of its high-revving nature and enough power to make one think the

Add a black vinyl top, "hockey stick" stripes along each flank, and a big green paisley tie, and this 1970 Hemi 'Cuda would look like the one on the Barracuda sales brochure cover. Without them, it's still very well dressed! (Photo Courtesy Mecum Auction Company)

This 1970 Barracuda wears Gran Coupe badging and 'Cuda's scooped hood and "hockey stick" stripes on the show field inside the Daytona International Speedway's infield.

factory 275 hp was more than a little low; the 440 Magnum because of its success in turning the squared-off 1967 Belvedere GTX into a real screamer; the 440 6-barrel because it was an ultra-high-performance engine ready for the street or drag strip; and the 426 Hemi . . . because it was the Hemi, the same engine that led a 1-2-3 finish at Daytona in 1964 and was now available in a smaller Plymouth than the B-Body Belvedere series.

What was the Hemi's secret? Deep-breathing, per the *1970 Plymouth Dealer Data Book* that showroom shoppers could peruse. "The Hemi-engine design offers the ultimate in power breathing. Combustion chambers are dome-shaped with big intake and exhaust valve ports located directly across from one another. This permits large-volume fuel-air charges to enter from the intake port, deliver tremendous power to the piston, and exhaust directly across the chamber with minimum loss of flowing momentum. At high speeds, the Hemi breathes with ease, where ordinary engines have their power choked off."

As the specifications for the high-performance engines have previously appeared in this chapter, the specifications below are for the standard-performance engines: the 225 Slant Six, 318, and the 383s that were available in the base Barracuda and Gran Coupe series. (See Appendix D for Mopar engine specs.)

Transmissions

Backing Barracuda's nine engines was a choice of 3-speed manual, 4-speed manual, and TorqueFlite automatic transmissions, which were also used in the Dodge Challenger. The 3-speed manual gearbox was fully synchronized in all forward gears, preventing the gear clashing/grinding common with "crash-boxes" (non-synchronized manual gearboxes) when shifting into lower gears while moving. A floor-mounted straight stick with a round knob embossed with the shift pattern was the only shifter available with the 3-speed, as Chrysler did not tool up a "three-on-the-tree" steering column–mounted shifter for it.

Just as with the Challenger, two versions of the A-833 4-speed manual transmission were available: the Hemi heavy-duty 18-spline version used behind the 420 Hemi, 440 6-barrel, and 440 Magnum; and the 23-spline version used behind the 383 and 340 V-8s. And, just like Challenger, the Hurst Pistol Grip shifter was how you stirred the gears.

For automatic transmissions, Barracuda buyers had the proven TorqueFlite automatic as their choice, with a choice of a console-mounted Slap Stik shifter, which used a unique-to-Barracuda T-Handle selector handle, or a column-mounted gear selector. And, as with the New Process Gear-built A-833 4-speed, there were different versions of Chrysler's tried-and-true 3-speed automatic: a light-duty A-904 version for the Slant Six and 318, and the A-727 version for the 340, 383s, 440s, and 426 Hemi.

A photo of the available center console detailed the new-for-1970 Slap Stik shifter for TorqueFlites, of which the *Dealer Data Book* said, "'Slap-Stik' . . . enables the driver to shove the lever quickly and positively into the next range without visually checking his shifts, or to place the Torqueflite in Drive and let it shift automatically if he chooses. It offers all the fun and sportiness of a quick-shifting manual without losing the advantages of an automatic. Perfect for 'his' and 'hers.' The shift pattern is illuminated in color for night driving. The shift handle is T-shaped for added convenience and control." (See Appendix E For a complete list of available transmissions for 1970 Barracudas.)

1970 'Cuda

Before 1970, Plymouth didn't market its high-performance cars as a group, the way Dodge did with its Scat Pack starting in 1968 and Chevrolet did with its Super Sport models starting in 1961 (and the Chevrolet Sports Department, which began appearing in Chevy ads in 1968).

For 1970, Plymouth changed that with its Rapid Transit System, the grouping of all their high-performance cars under one label. Unlike the rapid-transit mass transit trains that were in various stages of proposal, design, and construction back then, this was a grouping of Plymouths that were indeed rapid methods of transportation (weather, road, and traffic conditions, and law enforcement permitting).

And, like the Dodge Scat Pack, the Rapid Transit System also had its own factory publications, including a sales brochure and other showroom materials. Like the Scat Pack, it highlighted those who raced Plymouths, including Pro Stock drag racers Ronnie Sox and Buddy Martin, as well as Don "The Snake" Prudhomme and Tom "Mongoose" McEwen.

The System also included special high-performance parts that could be ordered through the Chrysler-Plymouth dealers' parts departments like high lift/long duration camshafts, aluminum intake manifolds, high-compression pistons, and steel-tube exhaust headers. It was also the way that "performance clinics" were presented by Sox & Martin and Don Grotheer at Chrysler-Plymouth dealers around the country in conjunction with those racers' appearances at local drag strips for NHRA/AHRA competition or match races with other Pro Stock/Super Stock teams.

Plymouth showed that it had something for everyone interested in high-performance, be it for the track, the street, or for a young lad not of legal driving age who could send away for a Plymouth racing-team jacket and wear it to his hometown Ford, Chevrolet, AMC, or Volkswagen dealers, who would then chase him away, while the young lad made "Beep-Beep!" sounds like the cartoon Road Runner as he made tracks off the lot.

When it came to the road-going Rapid Transit System Barracuda, the 'Cuda was featured prominently. The Rapid Transit

'Cuda from the front for 1970. Fog lamps and scooped hood were standard equipment for the first time in 1970. In later years, the hood would be available as a separate option, and the fog lights could be installed by a dealer as accessories.

'Cuda's engine size was proclaimed by optional "hockey stick" stripes on the rear quarters that flanked its short rear deck.

New for 1970 was an all-new steering column with integral ignition switch. It's seen here with the optional column-mounted TorqueFlite automatic transmission lever.

There are hockey sticks, and then there are hockey sticks that make a big visual impact. (Photo Courtesy Mecum Auction Company)

The 0–150 mph speedometer, tachometer, oil pressure gauge, and clock; the Rallye Gauge Cluster kept 'Cuda drivers well informed. (Photo Courtesy Mecum Auction Company)

New-for-1970 high-back front bucket seats did away with separate head restraints that were required by federal safety standards since 1968. Seen here is the all-vinyl interior trim, which was standard in base-series and 'Cuda hardtops and convertibles.

Your everyday, standard-trim 1970 'Cuda hardtop, with optional Rallye road wheels and a 426 Hemi under the hood. (Photo Courtesy Mecum Auction Company)

System's brochure showed a 'Cuda at speed on what appeared to be the high-speed oval at Chrysler's Chelsea, Michigan, Proving Grounds, with text like this accompanying it. "Sooner or later, we knew our guys would have to step in and show the rest of the pony car builders what pony car biz' is all about.

"Not that there's anything wrong with other people's pony cars, *per se*. Indeed, the average specimen *looks* the part: the long hood, the short trunk, the plethora of spoilers, airfoils, racing stripes and fake scoops.

"But in the beginning, most pony cars were designed to be little more than personalized compacts. And despite the demands of car enthusiasts for something gutsier, many pony cars still cling to their spindly legged ancestry.

"We figured it was time someone gave equal time to the pony car's dark side: its chassis, the suspension, brakes, driveline, and so on. We figured our pony car ought to begin life as nothing less than a bona fide Sports/GT car.

"The result of our efforts is called, simply, 'Cuda.

"You can obtain 'Cuda in any of five high-potency formulae: 340, 383, 440, 440 6-barrel, or 426 Hemi. We'd suggest that if you're a Gran Turismo bug, order the 340 because of its excellent weight distribution, rear anti-sway bar and resultant great handling. If you're a straight-liner, dial a bigger number, like maybe our new triple-carbureted 440. In between, there's our 383, which is standard. If all else fails, order the Hemi; by George, that oughta do it.

"Whatever its propellant, though, every 'Cuda carries the most over-engineered underside in the industry. In fact, the entire chassis setup is virtually the same used on our intermediate-size Supercars: torsion bars, shock absorbers, rear springs, spindles, wheel bearings, axle shafts, driveshafts, bolt circles, control arms, front and rear track, U-joints, anti-sway bars, even the brakes, which are big 11-inch units. All this, to underpin a body configuration that's as lithe as they come."

High-performance devotees tended to skip the factory patter and turn directly to the specifications table, which detailed each available 'Cuda engine, transmission, and rear-gear ratio, plus specs for chassis features like brakes and front/rear suspension. (See Appendix D for a complete listing of engine specifications. Also, see Appendix X for all available rear axle ratios.)

New Features and Options

The Pistol Grip and Slap Stik shifters, and the big-block and Hemi engines, weren't the only new features for 1970. While other manufacturers offered interesting options, the Barracuda options for 1970 were well integrated, bold, and attention getting. Chrysler had done its homework and the myriad of options offered suited the car well. The Rallye wheels were a popular stamped-steel wheel that were common on many Barracudas. A Shaker hood designated that it was a big-block car, either 440 6-barrel or 426 Hemi. Plymouth also offered "A" and "B" appearance packages.

Package A featured a front bumper in nine body colors, bright belt molding, and racing mirrors while Package B featured front and rear bumpers in red only, racing mirrors in red only, bright belt molding, and rear deck surround molding with black paint treatment. (See Appendices A–I for a complete features and options list.)

More Options and Option Packages

Once prospective Barracuda customers had been drawn to their local Chrysler-Plymouth dealers by the all-new E-Body Fish, and once they'd read the sales brochures and seen the new cars on the dealers' showroom floors, there was a source of information which told them of all the new-for-1970 Barracuda features, as well as its standard and optional equipment: the *Dealer Data Book*.

After a multi-page table that denoted whether the features shown on it were standard, extra-cost options, or not available on the three Barracuda series, it went into detail about those features and options, starting with the available accessory groups and options packages. By checking one item on the order form, a dealer (ordering for inventory or for a customer) could have a car equipped with a number of options, priced lower than if those options had been ordered separately. It also simplified the assembly process.

Performance Axle Packages

Chrysler offered a full lineup of axle packages to handle the torque and stresses from the variety of Mopar powerplants. What good is the power of an engine like the 426 Hemi if the rear-axle assembly downstream of it cannot handle all that power without breaking? Or what good are rear gears that don't make the most of that engine's power? Chrysler's engineers labored long to come up with their 8¾-inch rear-axle assembly, as well as the 9¾-inch unit built for them by Dana Corporation (the legendary Dana 60).

For 1970, as with the Challenger, a choice of performance-option packages centered around those two heavy-duty rear-axle assemblies were offered as factory-installed options, saving customers the trouble of chasing down aftermarket "low" (high numerical) rear gears to use on the drag strip, much less a rear-axle assembly that could handle their car's power.

Chrysler offered five heavy-duty axle packages that were suitable for high-performance street, trailer towing, and racing. Each one of these axle packages contained premium components, limited slip differentials, and was offered in 8¾- or 9¾-inch Dana axle setup. Those option packages were Performance Axle Package (Code A31), High-Performance Axle Package (Code A36), Super-Performance Axle Package (Code A32), Track Pak (Code A33), and Super Track Pak (Code A34). Of course these axle packages included more than just axle components.

The first two axle packages were designed for high-performance and severe duty street use. The Performance Axle package was available for certain 340-, 383-, and 440-equipped Barracudas while the Super Performance Axle Package offered an upgraded drivetrain and suspension for street-going 340- and 383-powered Barracudas. The Super Performance Axle Package (A32) was designed for the 440 Barracudas for street and strip service. The Track Pak (Code A33) and Super Track Pak (Code A34) were expressly offered for racing use only. Both offered for the 4-speed A833 transmission, included the super heavy-duty Hemi suspension and high-performance radiator.

The Track Pack included a 3.54 gear ration while the Super Track Pack had the 4.10 gear ratio. (See Appendix H for a complete list of features in each package.)

Unibody in a Mod Suit

Although the Barracuda was slightly shorter than the Challenger (with a 3-inch-shorter wheelbase), it was built with Chrysler's "Unibody" unit-body construction, just as the Challenger was, and all Barracudas since 1964 had been built with.

That meant that structural members like front and rear frame rails were welded to the car's floorpan, eliminating a separate frame and its extra weight. For 1970, Unibody added the same "roll bar" box-section steel beam to Barracuda Hardtops as was used on the Challenger, located just ahead of the rear window. (Thinking back to the "fishbowl" 1964–1966 Barracudas and their roof forward of their massive rear window, such a "roll bar" would have added weight above the car's center-of-gravity that would have negatively affected the car's handling without major suspension reworking.)

And, like the Challenger, all 1970 Barracuda doors would be constructed with steel beams inside them, to prevent incursion in the event of a side impact crash, complying with Federal Motor Vehicle Safety Standard 214. (The E-Body cars would be the first Chrysler products to include these "214 beams" from the time of the car's creation, instead of retrofitted to an existing model.)

Once the Barracuda's Unibody was welded together, it received the same seven-step dip-and-spray, corrosion-protection process that Challenger bodies received, before their trip to the paint shop.

There, they would be treated to two coats of acrylic enamel paint, whose color selection included extra-cost High Impact colors like Challenger, with different names for each color as was common Chrysler practice then to give different names to each color for use with Plymouth, Dodge, Chrysler, or Imperial.

Color Codes

At the start of the 1970 model run, Barracuda's color selection numbered 13 standard, solid, and metallic colors: Blue Fire Metallic (Code B5), Lime Green Metallic (Code J5), Deep Burnt Orange Metallic (Code K5), Sandpebble Beige (Code L1), Rallye Red (Code E5), Burnt Tan Metallic (Code T6), Black Velvet (Code X9), Citron Mist Metallic (Code Y4), Ice Blue Metallic (Code B3), Jubilee Blue Metallic (Code B7), Ivy Green Metallic (Code F8), Yellow Gold (Code Y3), and Alpine White (Code W1).

For an extra charge, five vivid High Impact colors were available: TorRed (Code V2), In Violet Metallic (Code C7), Lemon Twist (Code Y1), Lime Light (Code J5), and Vitamin C [Orange] (Code K2).

At midyear, two more hues joined the extra-cost High Impact colors: Moulin Rouge (Code M3) and Sassy-Grass Green (Code J6).

Dressing Up the Fish

For 'Cuda models, an available "hockey stick" sport tape stripe on the rear quarter panels announced the car's engine (340, 383, 440, or Hemi) and was available in white or black. Adding an accent color along the sides of base Barracudas and Gran Coupes was an optional protective vinyl bodyside molding ("rub rail," as they were commonly called), which were

Newly available outside "racing" mirrors were either chrome-plated, as seen here, or body-colored.

These manual driver's seat adjusters were also new for 1970: Lever at left controls fore-and-aft adjustment; other lever controls up-or-down settings.

available in green, blue, red, black, or white, with the color selection color-keyed to the car's main body color.

Two convertible top colors were available (white or black), and they were available with any of the above-listed Barracuda colors, without restriction. The same was true for standard-grain vinyl tops for hardtop models: your choice of either black or white.

Newly available for 1970 was a "Gator Grain" vinyl top, available only in black. Per the *1970 Plymouth Color and Trim Selector,* it was only available with certain exterior and interior color combinations: Order it with Ivy Green Metallic, Lime Green Metallic, Yellow Gold, Citron Mist, or Burnt Tan Metallic exterior colors, and any interior color was available.

With a Sandpebble Beige, Alpine White, or Black Velvet Barracuda, 'Cuda, or Gran Coupe, you could only get a green, tan, white-and-black, or green-and-white interior with it.

If a customer chose Deep Burnt Orange Metallic on the outside with a Gator Grain roof, the only interior color choices were black, white-and-black, or burnt orange-and-white. With TorRed, Gator Grain could only be combined with black or white-and-black interiors. And if you wanted a Gator Grain vinyl top with an Ice Blue Metallic or Blue Fire Metallic–painted lower body? Your only interior color choices were blue, black, white-and-black, or white-and-blue.

Two "Mod Top" floral-pattern vinyl top choices (one blue, one yellow) were also available, which had been on the Barracuda's exterior trim selector since 1968. However, they were only available with certain paint colors: the yellow Mod Top with Citron Mist, Yellow Gold, Alpine White, and Black Velvet exterior colors and black, white-and-black, or gold-and-black interior colors. Exterior colors Lime Green Metallic and Ivy Green Metallic were dropped from the yellow Mod Top exterior-color choices after the start of production. The blue Mod Top was only available with Ice Blue Metallic, Blue Fire Metallic, Alpine White, and Black Velvet exterior colors, and black, white-and-blue, black, or white-and-black interiors.

New Seats, New Colors

Speaking of interior color and trim choices, they started with new-for-1970 and exclusive to the E-Body all-vinyl front buckets and rear bench seat in the Base Barracuda and 'Cuda, and progressed to your choice of a deluxe vinyl "houndstooth" cloth and vinyl, or leather-and-vinyl, depending on the series chosen. Those standard vinyl seats came in black, blue, tan, dark green, red, and white (the latter with white seats, door, and side panels with black carpets, dash, roof headliner, and steering wheel).

The white-and-black all-vinyl buckets were available with any exterior color, but the other all-vinyl color choices were only available color-keyed to certain exterior colors: Red with Bright Red, Sandpebble Beige, Alpine White, and Black Velvet; Blue with Ice Blue Metallic, Blue Fire Metallic, Alpine White, and Black Velvet; Green with Lime Green Metallic, Ivy Green Metallic, Sandpebble Beige, Alpine White, and Black Velvet; and Tan with Sandpebble Beige, Burnt Tan Metallic, Alpine White, and Black Velvet.

During the 1970 model year, white buckets also became available with red, blue, or green interiors, with the same exterior-color restrictions as the blue and green buckets had, respectively.

Next up was the split-front bench/rear bench seat option, which combined the same seat backs as the standard buckets with a folding center armrest and a bench-seat bottom. Available for base-level Barracudas and 'Cudas, it was available in green, blue, black, and white, with the same exterior-color availabilities that their corresponding all-vinyl buckets offered. (During the year, the white seats also became available with either blue or green dash/carpet/steering wheel and hardtop headliner.)

Leather was the next interior choice for all Barracudas and 'Cudas, while being standard on Gran Coupes. Seating surfaces were leather, but the seats' bolsters and front seat backs were a matching color vinyl. Three color choices were available: Black (available with all exterior colors), Tan (available with BL1, FT6, Alpine White, and Black Velvet on the outside), and White (with black carpets, roof headliner, dash, and steering wheel) was available with any 1970 Barracuda exterior color.

Gran Coupe had two more interior-trim choices, one an all-vinyl interior that had a richer look than the base all-vinyl Barracuda and 'Cuda interior did, was available in Black Frost, Red, Tan, Blue, Green, White, Gold, and Burnt Orange, with the same exterior color-keying as the vinyl and leather interior choices, and was a credit option that knocked $48.25 off the sticker price.

Gold was only available with Alpine White, Black Velvet, Citron Mist, and Yellow Gold, while Burnt Orange was only available with Black Velvet, Alpine White, Deep Burnt Orange Metallic, and Sandpebble Beige. Also, white seats in this style were available in Gran Coupes with blue, green, or red interiors, again with the same exterior color-keying as the other interior trims.

The other Gran Coupe interior choice consisted of houndstooth-pattern cloth and vinyl seats, with cloth seating surfaces on vinyl seats, available either in black-and-white (available with any Barracuda exterior color), or Burnt Orange (available only with Alpine White, Black Velvet, Deep Burnt Orange Metallic, or Sandpebble Beige exterior colors). And, like the all-vinyl option, it also knocked $48.25 off the sticker price for choosing this over the standard leather/vinyl trim.

The round item is the servo for the optional cruise control, another new-for-1970 Barracuda option.

1970 Barracuda Pricing

Since its introduction in 1928, Plymouth had always been Chrysler Corporation's high-volume/low-price brand, aimed squarely at those American car lines that were priced the lowest, especially Ford and Chevrolet. Each Plymouth model was targeted at comparable Blue Oval and Bowtie models, with features engineered in by Chrysler to advance them ahead of their low-price competition, and keep them on the road longer. Since its introduction in 1964, Barracuda had been priced just above the Valiant sedans but well within the price range for comparable U.S.–built compact cars and their sporty-compact offshoots.

When Chrysler released the E-Body Barracuda for 1970, the option list was new as well. Its Manufacturer's Suggested Retail (sticker) Prices for the standard-equipped cars, and for factory-installed options, were comparable to what its 1970-model competition offered.

For example, base Barracuda hardtop sticker prices started at $2,764 for the 225 Slant Six version, and $2,865 for the 318 base hardtop, while Barracuda convertible prices started at $3,034 (Slant Six) and $3,135 (318). Gran Coupe prices started at $2,934 for the 6-cylinder hardtop and $3,160 for the Slant Six convertible, while the V-8 Gran Coupes started at $3,035 and $3,260, respectively.

For the base level 383 'Cuda, sticker prices began at $3,164 for the hardtop and $3,433 for the convertible. Those prices also included federal excise tax, plus "handling and other charges, and factory retail provision for dealer new-car preparation of $20.00."

By contrast, sticker prices (per Ford's *1970 Armchair Estimator* price sheet) for Ford's mildly restyled 1970 Mustang, started at $2,721 for the coupe, $3,025 for the convertible, $2,771 for the SportsRoof (fastback), $2,965 for the "upscale" Grande coupe, $3,021 for the base Mach I (which sported a 2-barrel 351-ci engine), and $3,720 for the Boss 302. Prices for the base-level coupe, convertible, Grande, and SportsRoof were with the standard 200-ci inline six, add $101 for the base 302-ci V-8.

If the base prices for Mustang were lower, they were for an older car, one that had seen its last major restyling in 1967 (which made room for optional Ford FE-series big-block V-8s) and its last "sheet metal update" for 1969. Also note that Barracuda's standard engines had larger displacements, and in the case of 'Cuda, was a 4-barrel big-block instead of the Mustang Mach I's 2-barrel small-block.

Option Package Pricing

Barracuda buyers were also keenly interested in the prices of optional equipment. Although Chrysler printed retail-price sheets for customers to pick up along with sales brochures and paint-chip/interior-color guides, Barracuda retail prices were available in the *Plymouth Salesman's Pocket Guide*.

For Barracuda's optional equipment groups, it was $36.00 for the code A01 Light Package and $182.55 for the Code A04 Basic Group (or $171.55 if ordered with the A62 Rallye Instrument Cluster, or with 440 6-barrel or Hemi engines). If you wanted the Code A21 Elastomeric Front Bumper group, that added $81.50 to the base Barracuda, $68.00 to 'Cudas and Gran Coupes without the A04 package, and $66.50/53.00 if ordered with A04.

For the Code A22 Elastomeric Front and Rear Bumper Group (only available with Rallye Red exterior paint), the extra charge was $94.90 on A04-equipped 'Cudas, $107.75 for Gran

Coupes, and $121.30 for base-series Barracudas with the A04 package, or $110.00/$122.85/$136.40 without A04.

If you wanted to dress up a base-series Barracuda with the Code A46 Exterior Trim Group, that added $51.30 to the sticker price. And, if you wanted to dress up the dash with the Code A62 Rallye Instrument Cluster, that added $79.75 to the sticker of Hemi and 440 6-barrel 'Cudas, and $90.30 to the retail price of all other Cudas, Gran Coupes, and Barracudas.

"Package-deal" pricing for the Code A35 Trailer-Towing Package was $48.70 for Barracudas and Gran Coupes powered by a 318 or 383 2-barrel, $34.80 with the 340 or 4-barrel 383s, or $14.05 with the 4-barrel 440. "Tow a trailer with a Hemi or a 440 6-barrel? Are you *nuts?*" is what you may have heard from your Chrysler-Plymouth dealer if you asked about adding the A35 package to an E-Body with either of the two most powerful engines in the lineup, along with his finger pointing at the "N/A 225 6-cyl., 426 Hemi, or 440 6-barrel. Engines" callout in the *Pocket Salesman's Guide* for the trailer-towing options group. Besides, those two mega Mopar V-8s were best at putting their on-track competition "on the trailer," rather than towing one.

Speaking of option packages intended for on-track or "Stoplight Grand Prix" competition, the selection of performance rear-axle packages combined the features listed for each group (from Performance Axle Package to Super Track Pak) and added just one options-group price to the sticker, instead of a likely higher price if those options were ordered separately.

The Code A36 Performance Axle Package added $102.15 when combined with a 340 or 383 and either a 4-speed or Torqueflite transmission, $142.85 with a 440 6-barrel/ Torqueflite 'Cuda, or $64.40 with a 426 Hemi/Torqueflite powertrain combo.

For the Code A31 High Performance Axle package for 340 and 383 'Cudas, Gran Coupes, and Barracudas, an extra $102.15 went on the sticker. The Super Performance Axle Package (Code A32) for Hemi and 440 'Cudas equipped with the heavy-duty A727 version of the Torqueflite automatic transmission added $250.65 with the 440s or $221.40 with the Hemi.

The two rear-axle packages that boasted the ultra-heavy-duty Dana 60 rear end also boasted premium prices in 1970 that seem like a bargain in 2015. The 3.54-geared Code A33 Track Pak added $142.95 to the retail prices of 440 and Hemi 4-speed 'Cudas so equipped, while the Code A34 Super Track Pak (and its factory-installed 4.10 rear gear) retailed at $235.65. Just try to find a complete original E-Body Dana 60 rear end at a swap meet at anything near those 1970 prices.

Optional Engines and Transmissions

Optional engine prices also look like a bargain when viewed through the prism of 2015. For Gran Coupes and base-series Barracudas, the Code E61 383 2-barrel was an extra $69.75 over the base 318. Moving up to the 383 4-barrel, that was $137.55 extra for the "non-performance" version for the base Barracudas and Gran Coupes, while the "Magnum" version (with cylinder heads shared with the 440s) was standard in the 'Cuda series and not available on base/Gran Coupe models. The E55 340 was a no-charge option on 'Cudas, and like the 383 Magnum, not available anywhere else in the Plymouth E-Body lineup. Then came the 440s: the E74 4-barrel added $130.55 to the 'Cuda's sticker price, and the 440 6-barrel went for an extra $249.55.

And, if you wanted a 426 Hemi, if you *really* wanted one, then its $871.45 extra charge over the 'Cuda's 383 Magnum wasn't enough to scare you. Neither the 426 Hemi nor the 440 6-barrel engines were available with Chrysler Corporation's five-year/50,000-mile powertrain warranty, only a 12-month/12,000-mile warranty that was limited to the original purchaser only.

For the optional transmissions, the A-833 4-speed manual was Code D21, and $194.85 was the extra charge over the standard 3-speed gearbox.

As for those who wanted a Torqueflite in their new E-Body Plymouth, the option was Code D34, but its price varied depending on the engine it was installed behind. With the 225 Slant Six, it was $190.25 extra. Choose it with a 318, and the extra charge was $202.05. Add it to a 340 'Cuda, 383 2-barrel Barracuda, or Gran Coupe and the price was $216.20. And, if you wanted a Torqueflite behind the 4-barrel 383, either of the 440s or the Hemi, D34 added $227.05 to those cars' sticker prices.

Other Mechanical Options

Additional mechanical options on the 1970 Barracudas included a choice of optional rear-gear ratios (2.76 or 3.23, Codes D51 and D53, respectively) for Slant Six, 318, and 383 cars that were $10.35 extra, or no charge with the Code D91 Sure-Grip differential (which was $42.35 extra if ordered without any of the performance-axle packages). Heavy-duty suspension (Code S13) was $14.75 extra on base Barracudas and Gran Coupes, while the Code S15 Extra-Heavy-Duty Handling Package was $18.25 extra with a 340 or 383, and standard with the 440s and the Hemi. S15 also included firm-ride shock absorbers, which were just $3.55 extra by themselves (Code S25). And, if you wanted to add a Shaker hood to a 440 4-barrel 'Cuda, that was Code N96, $97.30 extra.

Power assists included Code B11 heavy-duty power drum brakes that were included in the A35 trailer-towing package (Code B11, $22.65 extra, on Gran Coupes and base Barracudas, standard on 'Cuda). Front disc/rear drum brakes (Code B41)

The Shaker Hood emblem designates that the wedge 440 lies underneath the hood, and it's good for at least 375 hp.

RB-series 440 Magnum big-block V-8 fits comfortably in the 1970 'Cuda's engine bay, along with the optional AC compressor, power steering pump, and power brake booster, which didn't fit under a big-block A-Body 'Cuda's hood.

were $27.90 extra, and they also required the Power Brakes (Code B51) option, which was an additional $42.95. Power steering (Code S7) was priced at $90.35 extra if not ordered in any of the option packages that included it. Power windows were available when you checked Code P31 and added $105 to the sticker, and a power convertible stop (Code P37) was $52.85 extra; a price many convertible owners were more than willing to pay for easy-up, easy-down convenience.

Fender-mounted turn signals were included in Barracuda's most illuminating option package: the A04 Light Group.

Comfort and Convenience Options

In 1970, Barracuda buyers had a big choice of other comfort and convenience options. They included the Code C62 manual six-way adjuster for the driver's seat ($33.30 extra); Deluxe seat belts (Code C15, $13.75); front shoulder belts for convertibles (Code C13) or rear shoulder belts for hardtops (Code C14), both priced at $26.45 extra; three-spoke "rim blow" steering wheel (Code S83, $24.60 extra); center console (Code C16, $53.35); color-keyed floor mats (Code C92, $10.90); outside rearview mirror choices ranging from a single chrome remote-control one on the driver's side (Code G33, $15.15, or add another $10.95 for the Code G31 "racing style" remote left-side mirror) to the Code G36 color-keyed dual racing mirrors, left side remote ($10.95 with the A04 Basic group, $10.95 with A04 or no charge with the A21 Elastomeric front bumper package); glove box lock (Code J11, $41.0 extra, but standard on convertibles); and an electric clock without the A62 Rallye Gauge Cluster (Code J21, $16.50).

If those weren't enough convenience and comfort features, then buyers could also choose from variable-speed windshield wipers (Code J25, $10.60 extra but standard with the Shaker

Alongside the 440 Magnum in a 'Cuda's engine bay. Note the room between the left exhaust manifold and the brake master cylinder, which was a tighter fit (with no room for a power brake booster) on RB-engined 1967–1969 'Cudas. (Photo Courtesy Mecum Auction Company)

Hood Rallye Instrument Cluster, 426 Hemi or 440 6-barrel engines); headlight time-delay and warning signal (Code L42, $18.20); automatic speed control (Code N88, $57.95 extra and only available on Torqueflite/318, 383, or 440 4-barrel cars); tinted glass (Code G11, $32.75 extra, for all glass except the convertible rear window, or $20.40 for the G15 tinted windshield only); or a rear window defogger for hardtop models only (Code H31, $26.25 extra).

Airtemp Factory Air

But the most prominent comfort-and-convenience option had to be air conditioning (Code H51), made by Chrysler's Airtemp subsidiary. For 1970, the AC outlets were now built into the Barracudas' instrument panels, instead of "hung on" the bottom of the dash, as had been done with the 1969 and earlier A-Body Barracudas (and on all A-Body Plymouths until the end of their production run in 1976). The factory air conditioning option was not available with the 426 Hemi, 440 6-barrel engines, or with the 4-barrel 440 and a manual gearbox, and it added $357.65 to a new Barracuda's sticker price.

Dress-Up Options

When it came to dress-up items, the Barracuda's option list was a long one in that regard; and the prices tended to vary, depending on whether or not option packages like the A46 Exterior Trim Group or the A01 Basic Group were chosen. Without them, the Code W11 deluxe wheel covers were $21.30 extra, Code W15 wire-spoke wheel covers were $64.10 more, while the Code W21 Rallye Road Wheels were an additional $43.10 and the Code W23 five-spoke Chrome-Style Road Wheels were $86.15 extra. With the A46 package, those wheel-treatment prices came down to no charge for W11, which was included with A46, while the W15 wire covers were $42.85, the W21 Rallye road wheels were $21.95 extra, and the five-spoke W23s were $64.95 additional.

A Slap Stik shifter in the console, and an Airtemp AC control panel and Rallye gauge cluster in the dash. This 'Cuda was (and still is) well-equipped.

Optional Tires

Optional tires were also priced according to engine size or option-package choice. Standard on the Barracuda and Gran Coupe's Slant Six and 318 hardtops and convertibles were E78-14 blackwall bias-ply tires. Same-size whitewalls (Code T26) were $26.45 extra, while upsizing to F78-14s cost $15.50 for the Code T35 blackwalls, or $44.55 for the Code T34 whitewalls. Choosing the wide-tread F70-14 tires on base Barracudas and

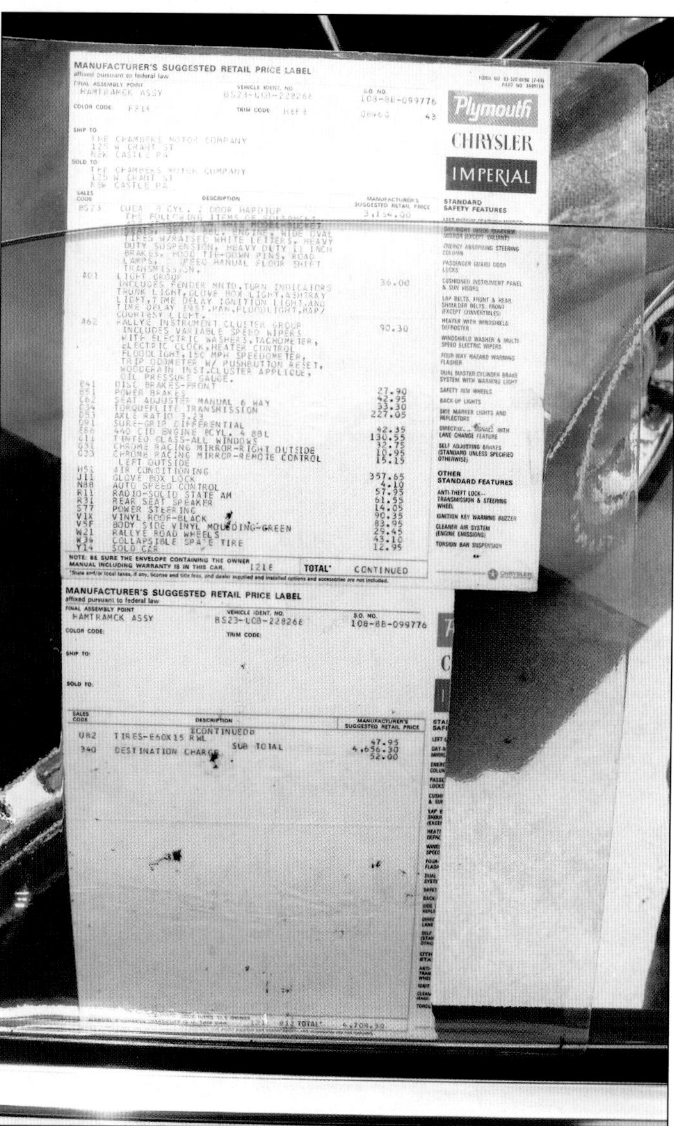

Options, options, options! Fully loaded 1970 Barracudas often needed two window stickers to show all the extras that were ordered with it.

Gran Coupes added an extra $65.35 for either the whitewall (Code T86) or raised-white-letter (Code T87) version.

F78-14 blackwalls were standard on non-'Cudas with the 383, and the Code T34 whitewalls in that size were $29.25 extra, while F70-14s added $50.10 for your choice of the Code T86 whitewalls or the Code T87 raised-white-letter ones. If you ordered the 2-barrel 383 with these tires, then you had to order the B11 or B41 brake options with the whitewalls, or B11/B41 and S13 heavy-duty suspension with the raised-white-letter E70-14s.

'Cudas tire selection started with the standard F70-14 raised white letter bias-plies, and had but two other choices: Whitewall F70-14s (Code T86-no charge) or Code U82 E60-15 blackwalls, which were $47.95 extra on all but the Hemi 'Cuda, whose E60-15 RWLs were standard.

Plus, the collapsible spare tire that was standard on convertibles was a $12.95 option (Code W34) on all hardtops (required with the E60-15 tires) and a regular spare tire was a no-charge option on convertibles (Code W08) with 70- or 78-series tires.

Interior Options

Inside, you could choose from the bucket or split-bench seats described above, with cloth-and-vinyl front buckets, or split-bench front seat, knocking $48.25 off the Gran Coupe's sticker if you chose them over the standard leather seats, which were $118.90 extra on all other hardtops, and $64.75 extra on 'Cuda and Barracuda convertibles.

As for your choice of factory sound systems, there was the Code R11 solid-state pushbutton AM, Code R22 AM/8-track tape player combo, or the Code R35 AM/FM Multiplex radio. Pricing was with or without the A04 Basic group; without it, the AM radio was $61.55 extra, the AM/8-track was an additional $196.25, and the AM/FM radio option cost $213.60 extra. Combined with the A04 option package, which included the AM radio, the AM/8-track was $134.75 more, while $152.20 more got you the AM/FM radio.

If you wanted front-and-rear speakers in your hardtop, a single one (Code R31) was $14.05 extra and required the R11 AM radio. Dual rear speakers required your choice of the R22 AM/8-track or R35 AM/FM sound systems and $25.90 extra.

What's another way to tell what a 1970 Barracuda was built with? Check the "fender tag" under the hood. It tells you what engine (440 Magnum in this one), transmission (TorqueFlite), colors (green with black vinyl top, stripes, and seats), and the build date (January 8, 1970).

Do all those option codes, and option prices, sound confusing? If they do now, they were even more confusing to buyers back in 1970, to the point that Chrysler began adding more option packages to all of its passenger-car lines starting in 1971. Those made it easy for buyers to order the car they wanted equipped the way they wanted it, and it made the bean counters in Highland Park happy by cutting down on the number of possible building versions of each car, thus cutting costs. Especially the Easy Order Package, which took the items in the A04 basic group and added a Torqueflite automatic transmission at no extra charge. A Luxury Equipment Package went further, adding Airtemp air conditioning, plus high-level trim inside and out, at a package price that was significantly lower than those options' separate cost.

However, those were still in the future in 1970. Barracuda buyers chose the features and colors they wanted from the factory selection and then waited six to eight weeks for their specially ordered car to arrive at their dealer, or they took their pick of what their dealers had in their inventories, sometimes shopping at multiple dealers to get a car with the features they were looking for.

The Production AAR 'Cuda

The Sports Car Club of America (SCCA) set rules for production-based road racing cars. If a manufacturer wanted a particular vehicle with a specific powertrain and chassis to be eligible, it had to build a specified number of them for retail sale. If you wanted to race one of the all-new E-Body Barracudas with an LA series small-block V-8 whose cylinder block was strengthened for possible race use (and whose cylinder heads made better power under race conditions than the regular-production heads) then a production vehicle so equipped with them was needed.

As a result, the AAR 'Cuda joined the Barracuda lineup in the spring of 1970. The goal was to beat Ford and Chevrolet at their own game when it came to ultra-high-performance-small-block pony cars. Ford had led the way with the first "High Performance" version of their 289-ci Windsor V-8, adding a four-bolt-main-bearing block, special cylinder heads, a solid-lifter camshaft, high-compression pistons, and a large, 4-barrel carburetor that combined to produce 271 hp, compared to the hydraulic-lifter 4-barrel 289's 225 hp. Carroll Shelby then added his touches to Ford's 289 HiPo, resulting in a 306-hp version that the Shelby GT350 Mustangs were powered by, starting in 1965.

Chevrolet upped the ante for 1967, using a combination of readily available high-performance parts for their 283- and 327-ci small-block V-8s to create a 290-hp, 302-ci special-performance small-block V-8 that would be legal, as part of the Regular Production Option Z28 Camaro Special Performance

Mid-year entry into Plymouth's Rapid Transit System: the AAR 'Cuda. The Rapid Transit System was Plymouth's group name for its 1970 muscle cars, of which the AAR 'Cuda was a mid-year entry. Its special engine block, cylinder heads, side-exit exhaust system, and fiberglass hood were among the parts made legal for production-based racing by inclusion on the street-going version. (Photo by David Newhardt, Courtesy Mecum Auction Company)

Package, for SCCA's A/Sedan and Trans-Am classes. Thanks to its use of off-the-shelf parts, this 302 Chevy engine pleased Chevrolet's and General Motors' bean counters, who had done away with direct factory support of race programs in 1963, and kept a sharp eye on any costs relating to developing high-performance engines and powertrains ever since.

Ford upgraded its Windsor V-8 with new "tunnel-port" cylinder heads for its now-up-to-302-ci Windsor V-8. Unfortunately for Ford and the teams that raced that engine, they proved troublesome and weren't used after that season. However, help arrived for 1969 in the form of the Mustang Boss 302, which featured a Windsor V-8 with heads based on those used in the new-in-1969 Ford "Cleveland" engine platform, as well as other heavy-duty internal hardware, that resulted in a factory horsepower rating of 290.

With Ford's Mustang Boss 302 and Chevy's Camaro Z28 showing the colors on the track, as well as on the street, one had to wonder if and when Plymouth would get involved with this segment of the pony car market, which was created to make thousand-car runs of specially equipped cars SCCA-legal.

Under the SCCA's 1970 rules, Plymouth would have to prove the AAR 'Cuda, and its special components, were indeed regular-production items by building 2,800 production AAR 'Cudas to make the race version legal for the production-based Trans-Am class. (That number had been increased from 1,000 cars, which had been the SCCA's homologation total in 1969.)

Also in the 1970 SCCA rules package, "destroking" of production engines was now allowed, which allowed engine builders to swap in a shorter-stroke crankshaft and connecting rods to get the engine's displacement within the SCCA's 305.5-ci (5-liter) engine-displacement rule.

Fortunately for Plymouth, they didn't have to use an engine different from the one used in the Challenger T/A. Credit for that can be given to Chrysler's engine-standardization program from over a decade earlier, when the unique lineup of engines produced by and for each division (namely the Plymouth "Polyspherical," Dodge "Red Ram," De Soto "Firedome," and Chrysler "Firepower" V-8s) were replaced by one small V-8 based on the Plymouth engine, and a new

"340 6-barrel" was Plymouth's name for the AAR 'Cuda's special 340, which boasted a beefed-up cylinder block casting and high-flow cylinder heads, an Edelbrock aluminum intake under three Holley 2-barrel carburetors, and more than the standard 340's 275 hp! (Photo by David Newhardt, Courtesy Mecum Auction Company)

This AAR 'Cuda was given in 1970 to "Ozzie" Olson, head of the Olsonite company, one of the sponsors of Dan Gurney's All-American Racing. It's now been fully restored. Eldon Meyer's "Olsonite Eagle" 70 'Cuda AAR. (Photo Courtesy Eldon Meyer)

big-block with wedge-shaped combustion chambers that replaced the Dodge, De Soto, and Chrysler hemispherical-head engines. Simplifying the engine lineup (and using a new engine plant on Mound Road in Detroit constructed for that purpose during the late 1950s), Chrysler saved millions in what it viewed as redundant costs. Unfortunately for drag racers and other high-performance enthusiasts, it led to the demise of the first-generation Hemi engines.

As with the Dodge Challenger T/A, making the 340 TA cylinder block and head (along with the 3x2-barrel carburetor induction system) production items on the AAR 'Cuda also made them legal for use in other production-based racing series, especially drag racing, where their production status made them eligible for Stock classes in NHRA and AHRA racing.

To go along with the special 340, a number of special chassis parts (same as used on the Challenger T/A, and detailed by Chrysler-Plymouth communications below) also went on the AAR 'Cuda.

The AAR 'Cudas would also receive a unique strobe stripe treatment along each side, forward of the "AAR 'Cuda" lettering at the top-rear of each rear quarter panel. Starting at the rear and moving to the front, the strobe panels would increase in size by 4 percent.

The newest Barracuda was introduced to Chrysler-Plymouth dealers in an intra-company memo from F. G. Hazelroth, Chrysler-Plymouth Division's General Sales Manager, dated March 4, 1970. "Plymouth is proud to announce the newest entry into the sport compact market, the AAR 'Cuda. Featuring optimum handling and braking packages with 340 6-barrel performance, the AAR 'Cuda earns its affiliation with America's best known road racer, Dan Gurney. Named after Dan Gurney's All-American Racers, the AAR 'Cuda represents the cars he will campaign in 1970 Trans-Am competition.

"Distinctive in appearance, the AAR 'Cuda features a new hinged fiberglass hood with functional hood scoop, ducktail type rear spoiler, side outlet exhausts, biased tire sizes (G60x15 rear and E60x15 front) and the new AAR 'Cuda body-side strobe tape stripe. AAR 'Cuda identity is strengthened by the flat black grille, hood and fender top paint treatment and the deleted wheel lip, sill and belt moldings.

"Mechanically, the AAR 'Cuda further displays its Trans-Am affiliation. Powered by a new 340 6-barrel. engine with special head and block castings and equipped with special rear springs and shocks and new front and rear sway bars, the AAR 'Cuda provides performance unmatched in the pony car market. Coupled with its superior handling characteristics, the AAR 'Cuda features disc front brakes and new 11-inch rear drum brakes to provide the ultimate in stopping ability."

Similar to the Boss 302 and Camaro Z28, the AAR 'Cuda production car that was the basis for a road racer, and therefore it was equipped with a 340 6-barrel V-8 rated at 290 hp. A 4-speed manual transmission was standard, or a 3-speed TorqueFlite automatic transmission was available at extra cost. A 3.55 axle ratio or 3.91 axle ratio in limited-slip or Sure-Grip differential was offered. The handling package featured heavy-duty suspension with front and rear sway bars, heavy-duty shocks, and stopping duties were aided by power front disc brakes, G60x15 rear and E60x15 front white raised letter tires. (See Appendix L for the complete list of standard and optional equipment on the AAR 'Cuda.)

The AAR 'Cuda had the same warranty as offered on other 1970 'Cuda 340 models, with a manufacturer's suggested retail price of $3,966.

Hazelroth's memo to the Chrysler-Plymouth dealer body concluded, "Demand for this type of special quality pony car has been strong. The exclusive three 2-barrel version of a special performance 340 CID engine and strong exterior identity will attract many appreciative buyers to Barracuda. Place your order now for this limited-production AAR 'Cuda so that you can take full advantage of this unique sales and profit opportunity."

Plymouth's advertising crew wasted little time putting the word out to the public about the new AAR 'Cuda via a two-page magazine ad:

Production of the AAR 'Cuda, at Chrysler's Hamtramck Assembly Plant, began on March 11, 1970, and was completed 40 days later, on April 20. Like the Challenger T/As, it's likely they were "batch-built," a common Chrysler practice at the time where special runs of cars with identical equipment were built at the same time, instead of scheduled on the assembly line in between other production E-Body cars. Plymouth police and taxi vehicles had been "batch built" by Chrysler for years, and they had also used the process to construct the 440 6-barrel Plymouth Road Runners that hit the dealers (and the nation's drag strips) in the spring of 1969.

As was implied in the magazine ad and the letter to Chrysler-Plymouth dealers, the AAR 'Cuda was indeed a limited-production car. Just 2,724 were built during its production run in early 1970, and an AAR 'Cuda for 1971, which had been planned, per Chrysler intra-company correspondence cited above, was canceled.

How did this midyear Mopar go over with the motoring press of the day? When the AAR 'Cuda entered production in the spring of 1970, *Sports Car Graphic* got one to test, and not just "any" production AAR 'Cuda. "We got the No. 1 AAR 'Cuda off the assembly line," said author Don Mathews.

The 340 6-barrel's performance was, in a word, impressive. "About that 290 advertised hp. We don't believe it . . . there's got to be more," wrote Mathews. "If that engine don't put out about 325 hp at the clutch plate when properly tuned, sucking clean air and on a test stand, then my name ain't . . . "

As for its handling, and the 340 6-barrel's performance at speed, Mathews said, "The AAR 'Cuda is one of the best-handling special-edition cars that we've driven. It has to be *driven,* because that's what it was designed for. At low speed the ride is *very* firm; below 3,300 rpm the engine snaps, crackles and pings on the best of fuels. But drop down a cog, stomp your foot on a straightaway and get it up in the hills and you'll find little dip, sway or roll, strong, predictable cornering power and, for its size, near-great engine response as those other two Holleys open up for the pull. The Pistol Grip Hurst shifter takes a bit of practice, but after a while there's never a doubt either upshift or down."

However, there were some flaws, some of which Mathews ascribed to the car's first-one-off-the-line status. "[It] had trouble living down the poor, warped fit of the fiberglass hood. And the flat-black paint looks like it was applied with a brush. The auxiliary driving-light switch is poorly located under the dash near the parking brake pedal where you can accidentally knock it on and not know it. The bottom seat belt is OK, but the diagonal shoulder strap turns into a throat strap. The heating system works fair, but that insidious draft of cold air seeping in from the base of the steering column has got to go. The starter motor sounded like it was moonlighting as a metal-masher. The bucket seats aren't bad, but I prefer more lateral support in a performance vehicle."

Beyond those flaws, Mathews saw plenty of good in the AAR 'Cuda. "The big scene is what counts, and the All-American Racers 'Cuda makes it. You can't call it a muscle car because it doesn't have a big, monster engine. But it goes too strong to call it a mere pony car; it's more than that. So, let's call it an Impulse Car, because from little impulses giant muscles grow."

The Press and the 1970 'Cuda

Just as the motoring press was anxious to get their hands on the E-Body Dodges (as was detailed in the 1970 Challenger chapter), so were they looking forward to trying out the new-for-1970 E-Body Barracuda, as soon as they could get their hands on one from the Chrysler press fleet.

As with the Challengers in the press fleet, there were 426 Hemi ones, as well as ones with the other high-performance engine options. But, unlike *Car and Driver's* E-Body Hemi test, which was mostly negative, a Hemi 'Cuda convertible got plenty of praise from the staff of *CARS* magazine when they tested an early-production Tor-Red Hemi/4-speed convertible in November 1969, for publication in their May 1970 issue. "Love That Hemi-Cuda!" the feature's headline proclaimed, with a subheading, "It was love at first blast when our ex-funny car digger turned up the stereo, buried his size 12 in the water pump, and blew the 440 Six Pack's doors back to Hamtramck!"

CARS had bad experiences with 426 Street Hemi-equipped Plymouths in the past, so their expectations were low when they got their hands on this one. "Not only did the test car look good, but it wailed. In fact, it even made our CHT (Chief Hemi Tester) Joel Kim rap for hours on the merits of the Mopar Mauler." Kim, per the story, had driven a fuel-injected Hemi Funny Car in competition and was (to say the least) very enthusiastic about

From the side, you see the "Olsonite Eagle" markings and the distinctive AAR 'Cuda strobe striping and a 1970 Michigan license plate. (Photo Courtesy Eldon Meyer)

Chrysler's strongest production engine. "All it took was a couple of runs as a passenger next to Kim and then at the helm myself, to realize that this year's Street Hemi works out," said the unnamed *CARS* staffer who wrote the feature. (Joe Oldham said many years later that he wrote the story, which *CARS* didn't give him byline credit for.)

"The main reason is that the 1970 Street Hemi runs a hydraulic cam rated at 292/292 degrees with 68 degrees overlap, and seems to work out better at the bottom end. It still has plenty of punch at the top end as well. And, the engine is relatively quiet. And, as an added bonus, [Joe] Oldham had the distributor and timing taken care of." (Author note: See below about Joe Oldham's experiences with this car in 1969 and many years later.)

Three trips down the strip at New York International Raceway resulted in time slips that read 13.40 seconds at 105.10 mph, 13.45 at 105.00, and 13.50 at 103.70. "All runs were made with traffic-scarred plugs, closed pipes, and the [E60-14 Goodyear] Polyglas GT tires pumped up to 45 psi."

When it came to the Hemi 'Cuda convertible's handling, the *CARS* crew was impressed again, contrary to what the *Car and Driver* testers experienced with their Challenger R/T hardtop. "The 'Cuda oversteered, as would be expected, but Kim managed to stay out of serious trouble by carefully steering by throttle and wheel at the same time. Cornering was even flatter than expected, thanks to the wide total-contact Polyglas GT tires, stiff suspension and big torsion bars. We couldn't make the wheels hop regardless of how hard we came out of the corners."

They also couldn't make the power front disc/rear brakes lock up and fade under high-speed stop conditions. "For three passes in a row, we tried to lock up all four wheels at 103 to 105 mph and induce brake fade. Impossible. Each time, the car came to a safe, sane stop with hardly any trace of swerving or lockup."

To cap off the article, *CARS* ran the Hemi 'Cuda test car against a 440/4-speed Challenger that had been dyno-tuned for optimum on-track performance. "After the smoke had cleared, it was Kim by quite a few car [lengths], and he managed to blow the Challenger's doors right back to Hamtramck." They closed the story by saying, "It's the Shotgun Express of the Rapid Transit System."

Road Test also got their hands on a 1970 'Cuda to test, this one a 383 hardtop that impressed them, despite its "small" engine (compared to the 440s and the Hemi). "True High Performance at a Reasonable Cost," headlined the March 1970 story, which opened, "Take away the spoiler, racing stripes and 5-inch-high '383' signs on the rear fenders, all of which are delete options, and you'd have a spirited, reasonably comfortable car not inappropriate for general family use as well as fun. It's also a safer car than the Hemi version because it's a better balanced package."

Specifically, they liked the 383's output. "The nicest thing about the 383 was its agility in the passing range. Throttle downshifting at 40 brought us to 60 mph in 3.37 seconds and 50 to 70 mph was almost as fast in 4.20 seconds. No matter what our Secretary of Transportation has to say about the horsepower race, passing acceleration like this spells safety. It's particularly safe when the power doesn't burst forth like the blast from a shotgun. We wouldn't recommend full throttle passing on a wet pavement, but there are no control problems at all when the surface is dry."

When they took it to the track, the 3.91:1-geared, Sure-Grip 'Cuda shone. "Unlike the Hemi tested in this issue, the tires were able to handle the power and the quarter-mile was achieved in 14.40 seconds with a terminal speed of 98.97 mph. This is very close to our Hemi figures, but it must be remembered that the Challenger is slightly heavier and more importantly, we were unable to get decent traction from the Hemi with street tires. Obviously, the 383 is not a competitor in that league when both cars are properly prepared."

As for handling, that was another strong point of this 'Cuda 383, in *Road Test's* view. "Aside from its inordinately stiff low speed ride, the [383] 'Cuda had better balance and feel than the Hemi. Driving it felt a little less like hanging on to the end of a slingshot. It oversteered, of course. But the 383 is at least 150 lbs. lighter than a Hemi, and every pound of this saving contributed to better handling."

Their test car's brakes had been mashed on repeatedly by a television production crew, who filmed a commercial with it before *Road Test* tested it, but *Road Test* said (in normal use) the brakes would not be a problem. "A 'Cuda equipped as was our test car will stop [from 60 mph without locking the wheels] in 190 feet."

When it came to comfort and convenience, *Road Test* had good things to say about the 383 'Cuda. "Cuda upholstery styling is different from the Challenger, but the bucket seats are just as well contoured and provide good lumbar support. The range of adjustment is adequate for most any size person. If you're an average 5 feet 11 inches [tall], the far rear position will prevent you from even reaching the pedals, and it will also prevent anyone from sitting in the rear seat. Headroom in front is a bit marginal for those who wear hats, and hats must be taken off in the rear."

The B-engined E-Body also drew praise from *Road Test* for its fuel economy. "The 4V 383 is a surprisingly economical engine when driven easily, although, of course, it requires premium fuel. On one uninterrupted stretch of Interstate, cruising at the legal maximums of 65-70 [mph], we registered 16.2 mpg. Another tankful checked while driving around town showed a consumption of only 14.4 mpg. There was never a trace of overrun when switching off, and oil consumption was negligible.

"Another 383 economy is widespread familiarity with the design on the part of mechanics. As it has been around for 12 years. Also, parts are readily available in any dealership, whereas only a minority stock parts for the Hemi.

"Perhaps the biggest economy of all, though, is the fact that a 383 doesn't tend to scare insurance companies. They're familiar with it and don't associate it particularly with high performance, whereas mention of the 426 Hemi, or the 440, on an application is like wearing red long johns in a barnyard."

Britain's *Motorcade* magazine got their hands on a 1970 Hemi 'Cuda, and they found much to like about it for their July 1970 feature story. "The Hemi 'Cuda seems an ultimate factory extension of what just a few years ago was a racy little fastback compact whose claim to fame was a rear seat back that folded flat for a variety of purposes. The ultimate extension comprises an engine tried, tested and virtually unbeatable over a span of years, plus a re-engineered, re-styled body as long and sleek as the killer fish whose name it bears. It used to be that Hemi 'Cuda meant the ultimate extension in drag racing. Hemi 'Cuda now means the ultimate extension in Plymouth street-and-strip sports machinery. The car carries the name well."

Foremost among *Motorcade*'s likes was the 426 Hemi's performance. "Even though the car tested by *Motorcade* was quickly off absolutely perfect tune, the TorqueFlite automatic Hemi 'Cuda turned quarter-mile ETs in the mid-14s at trap speeds in the range from 105 to 110 mph. With gross weight of car and driver at more than 4,000 pounds, that's the best that can be expected of a slightly ailing engine. In proper tune, the Hemi 'Cuda should operate in the mid-13s and approach 112 to 115 mph at the end of the quarter."

Unlike *Car and Driver*'s experience with a Hemi E-Body, *Motorcade* found their test Hemi 'Cuda to be a capable-handling car, too. "The car is powerful, quick and fast, but that isn't all the pick of Plymouth's performance line does well. With so-called rally suspension installed, the Hemi 'Cuda is a true handler on strip, turnpike and/or those crooked secondary roads where steering, suspension, tires and brakes are put together in a test of any street machine's true mettle. The 1970 'Cuda's power steering is quick, positive and precise, with no unnerving free play, no unnecessary number of wheel turns for rapid response.

"The hydraulic steering system turn, however, lacks 'feel,' that transmission of road shocks, tire scrub vibration and the forces of changing loadings under cornering stresses. Steering should telegraph the car's intentions to the sensitive driver to enable him to approach more closely the limits of performance.

"Suspension on the Hemi 'Cuda is specially designed for acceleration. Rear springs of two different rates, plus control arms, locate the 'Cuda's live axle firmly and prevent the slewin loss of directional control on full blastoff that is common among more softly spring, less thoroughly engineered Supercars. Torsion bar independent front suspension is augmented with a stiff anti-roll bar, almost one inch in diameter. Firm shock damping all around with the competition style springing delivers a distinctly stiff, sled-like ride that is somewhat harsh, yet not unpleasant.

"Solidity of this sort means the driver knows where the Hemi 'Cuda is, to where it is pointed. In cornering, the Hemi 'Cuda feels like a Group 7 racing car looks: flat, tight in the bend, tracking securely. The Goodyear Polyglas GT F60-15s fitted to the test car provided sufficient bite for anything but the most violent stomps on the throttle. Deliberate feeding in of power as the car moved off the line minimized wheelspin and, as best run times proved, eliminated slippage entirely in some cases. The wide, adhesive contact pad of these tires also contributes to the previously discussed exceptional cornering capability of the 'Cuda."

When it came to braking, the Hemi 'Cuda that *Motorcade* tested performed well, despite its nose-heavy weight bias. "The wide tires also are of major assistance with braking chores. However, the Hemi 'Cuda carries almost 60 per cent of its weight on its front wheels. Under hard braking, the apparent forward weight transfer takes effective poundage away from an already light rear end. When the rear end becomes overly light the tires lose their effective bite, a wheel locks up and directional control departs. Because of this imbalance between front disc and rear drum brakes, the driver is unable to use those discs to their fullest; he must ease up on the brakes to regain control, then try again to brake hard without breaking tire adhesion at the rear end. It's a contest of human skill against the automobile's inertial forces.

"Under sustained hard usage (numerous all-on panic type stops) those vented discs showed not a trace of fade or gave any other indication they would fail. The Plymouth people would do well to give their Hemi 'Cuda better front/rear weight distribution, or at least provide forces to squelch that sudden rear wheel lockup. Either way, those great front discs should be given a better opportunity to achieve their full potential."

As for the TorRed Hemi 'Cuda convertible that *Cars* tested back in late 1969, Joe Oldham had the rare opportunity to see it again many years later. "In 1989, 19 years after my article was published, I was walking through a car show in New Jersey with Cliff Gromer. We saw a red Barracuda convertible down the row of cars. I thought it looked familiar. As we got closer, I said to Gromer that it looked like the car I had tested back in November 1969." A look underneath to see if a telltale transmission-fluid leak that was present in 1969 was still there (it was) confirmed the car's history to Oldham.

Nearly two decades later, in 2006, Oldham saw that Hemi 'Cuda again. "When I opened the driver's door and looked in at that red, redder, reddest interior, I could almost feel a shiver go through my body. The interior was still all original. So when I sat down in that seat, my butt would be in exactly the same place it was 35 years before. It was weird. I felt very much in touch with the past, as if I was about to go back in time, to relive a past experience that I thought had been gone forever, a mere memory in the passage of time."

This time, he drove it. "I climbed into the driver's seat and settled in. The seating position was better than I remembered, but the steering column still felt too long and too close. All that was forgotten as I twisted the key and the big 426 Street Hemi bellowed to life.

"Man, what a sound. Blip the throttle. *Brraap, brraap, brraap!* I'll tell you something. I've driven every car made in the last 40 years. And I would be the first to admit that the lowliest Dodge Neon can run rings around any Mopar muscle car of the sixties in terms of ride and handling and driving comfort. But as far as ambience from the driver's seat, no amount of modern technology can match the sheer thrill of being the master of 426 ci of leashed fury. I just sat there as the twin exhaust pipes gurgled."

1970 'CUDA PRODUCTION NUMBERS

A further breakdown of production totals reveals just how few of the ultra-high-performance 'Cudas were built and sold. The following data is from 1970 'Cuda production numbers online at 'Cuda Corner (angelfire.com/md3/cuda_corner/prod.html).

- 14 Hemi 'Cuda convertibles (9 built with TorqueFlite automatics, and 5 with 4-speeds)
- 652 Hemi 'Cuda hardtops (368 TorqueFlites, 284 4-speeds);
- 1,755 440 6-barrel 'Cuda hardtops (852 TorqueFlites, 902 4-speeds)
- 29 440 6-barrel 'Cuda convertibles (12 TorqueFlites, 17 4-speeds)
- 952 440 Magnum 'Cuda hardtops (618 TorqueFlites, 334 4-speeds)
- 34 440 Magnum 'Cuda convertibles (28 TorqueFlites, 6 4-speeds)
- 4,445 383 Magnum 'Cuda hardtops (2,540 TorqueFlites, 1.905 4-speeds
- 200 383 Magnum 'Cuda convertibles (137 TorqueFlites, 63 4-speeds)
- 2,724 AAR 'Cudas with the 340 6-barrel (1,604 TorqueFlites, 1,120 4-speeds)
- 6,884 340 'Cuda hardtops (3,392 TorqueFlites, 3,492 4-speeds)
- 243 340 'Cuda convertibles (155 TorqueFlites, 88 4-speeds)

What came next was no mere around-the-block spin, not when the *CARS* road-tester in 1969 had the opportunity to drive it again the same way. "I mashed my foot down through the linkage detents, and all eight barrels opened up. There's no real way to describe in words the sound of eight Carter AFB barrels opening up on top of a 426-ci Hemispherical Combustion Chamber engine. But I'll try. It starts as a low moan, slowly rising into a wail that eventually turns into a shriek, a shriek that threatens to suck not only the surrounding air but also the hood itself and the closest two fenders directly into the shaker hood scoop."

How did the three-decades-plus-old car perform on the drag strip? "On the clocks, the car ran a couple of mid-14-second passes at just less than 100 mph, eventually recording a best of 14.32 seconds at 99 mph, almost identical to the box stock times of 35 years ago. And guess what? The [TorqueFlite] transmission was doing it to us again, not quite shifting properly on the 2-3 shift, even hanging up on one run. Some things never change."

1970 Barracuda Sales

When Burton Bouwkamp proposed what became the 1970 E-Body cars, he projected that they would take 15 percent of the sporty-compact market, or about 225,000 cars out of a 1.5-million-car new-vehicle market segment.

Unfortunately, just like Challenger, Barracuda missed its sales target for 1970, totaling just 55.499 Barracudas in all, per the *Standard Catalog of American Cars 1946–1975* and *allpar.com*. (Author note: Some online sources put 1970 Barracuda production at 48,887; this is likely the calendar-year 1970 total, not including those cars built between the start of E-Body production in August 1969 and year's end.)

That 55,499 total included 25,651 base Barracuda hardtops and 1,554 base Barracuda convertibles; 8,183 Gran Coupe hardtops and 596 Gran Coupe convertibles; 18,880 'Cuda hardtops and 635 'Cuda convertibles; and 2,724 AAR 'Cudas.

THE ROAD-RACING AAR 'CUDAS

How serious was Plymouth at competing on the nation's racetracks in 1970? Richard Petty was lured back to Plymouth, after switching to Ford for 1969, with the wind-tunnel-engineered Road Runner Superbird that was intended to put the Bird, and Plymouth, back out in front on the high-speed ovals in NASCAR's Grand National Series.

So, how serious would Plymouth's SCCA Trans-Am Series race program be? How about serious enough to lure racer and constructor Dan Gurney away from Ford?

However, there was a big difficulty that Gurney didn't mention in that article: the difficulty of starting a race team from scratch, when competitors like Roger Penske and Bud Moore had been racing (and winning) in that series for years.

The #48 AAR 'Cuda that Dan Gurney drove in his last-ever race at Riverside in 1970 is now in Craig Jackson's collection, ready to run in Historic Trans-Am races. That's Craig on the right, next to Dan Gurney. (Photo Courtesy Barrett-Jackson Auction Company)

THE ROAD-RACING AAR 'CUDAS CONTINUED

The big announcement was made on October 16, 1969. "Dodge and Plymouth chose Dan Gurney's All-American Racers to build all the chassis for Chrysler's programs. The teams, however, operated separately. Ray Caldwell's Autodynamics team prepared the Challengers and Gurney prepared the Barracudas. Gurney's AAR shops completed both makes' basic chassis/unit-body construction."

Dan Gurney added, in a story published in 1970 by *Popular Mechanics Monthly*, "When our relationship was announced, Glen E. White, vice-president of Chrysler Corporation and general manager of the Plymouth Division, said, 'We know what we are up against in the Trans-Am series, and we know that we are getting a relatively late start. There is a tremendous amount of work required to make the Barracuda competitive this year after a three-year absence from the racing scene.'"

Key to both teams that would race the E-Body in the Trans-Am series was a young engineer that Chrysler racing chief Pete Hutchinson picked to head up their engineering development, Bob Tarozzi. As he related to David Tom, "Hutchinson's job was to supervise the teams, administer the budget of this huge undertaking, and oversee the development of the 305-ci engine programs for Chrysler." Tarozzi recalled later, "One was an Indy Car [engine], and one was for the SCCA Trans-Am. It was casually mentioned that my name had come up as a possible chassis guy for Dan Gurney's new Trans-Am team. I didn't even know about that deal."

Before Tarozzi relocated from Michigan to California, he stopped by his old office at Chrysler Engineering in Highland Park. "Gurney asked me to go over to Chrysler and get all the drawings that I had worked on previously for the earlier Chrysler racing programs," he recalled. "I used my expired badge, and walked right in. They were more than happy to give me the drawings. I even got some old computer data that we had done in 1967. Try that today!"

That information was just about all that All-American Racers had to build its race cars when Tarozzi arrived at their Santa Ana, California, shop. "When I got to California, they had no car, no parts, and no drawings, but they had an engine," he explained to David Tom. "Now I know why they had me get the old drawings. The engine was about all there was there, except for a bunch of promises."

Tarozzi's first task was to put together a chassis fixture, upon which the modified bodies-in-white could be mounted for their assembly into race cars. Fortunately, Tarozzi had help in building that fixture, the best kind of help there was. "The Gurney operation had already been using Phil Remington as part of its design team, and he was assigned to me. Imagine being the boss of a guy who had been instrumental in most every successful racing operation in Southern California.

"We finally got the chassis fixture made, because Phil had experience in that area, and insisted that we do it exactly the way he wanted. I was the boss, so I said okay."

The first step in the race cars' preparation, after the bodies-in-white had been welded together at Chrysler's Los Angeles Assembly Plant (the only other Chrysler plant that would build E-Body cars other than Hamtramck) was their chemical milling, or "acid dipping," to remove weight from them. "The target weight of our Trans-Am Barracuda is 3,200 pounds with 22 gallons of fuel on board: minimum weight under the rules," Gurney told *Popular Mechanics.* So, every pound saved by use of lightweight materials such as aluminum (and reducing the weight of the all-steel body) was crucial to getting the race 'Cuda down to the SCCA's minimum weight.

Cutting weight from the as-welded but unpainted production steel body was accomplished by dipping it in an acid bath, then removing it and subsequently immersing it in a neutralizing solution to stop the acid from eating away at the body any further.

According to Bob Tarozzi, the same facility that dipped the Mopar bodies also acid-dipped production bodies for other factory Trans-Am teams. "The plant that did the acid bath was booked solid with Camaros, Mustangs, Firebirds and Javelins getting the treatment," he recalled. First in of the E-Bodies, per Tarozzi, was a Barracuda, which he said would be their test car. "Then, we did a Dodge, a Plymouth, the other Dodge, and finally the third Barracuda. As soon as the Plymouth was back from dipping, we mounted it on the fixture, and the fun began for me."

Although the other All-American Racers' employees may have frowned on the newcomers who worked on "taxicabs" instead of "real" race cars such as the Eagles they built for the USAC Indy Car series, Tarozzi said they all knew and respected Phil Remington, from his prior race car work at shops across Southern California. "I designed the stuff, and Phil fabricated it, or showed others how to do it," he said. "Whatever he wanted done was done, and done quickly. It was a good thing, because we got the cars right after Christmas, maybe even in January, [while] the first test was slated for March, and the first race for mid-April. That is not much time to build a go-kart, let alone a brand-new Trans-Am car. We hired several guys who had been with Shelby, since his Trans-Am program was shut down [by Ford, following the 1969 Trans-Am season], and those guys helped out a lot."

With the E-Body being a new car for 1970, and the AAR shop never before having built a steel-bodied, production-based race car (Dan Gurney's NASCAR wins had come primarily in Ford

Galaxies built by Holman-Moody and the Wood Brothers), there wasn't a ready supply of parts they could bolt on the E-Body cars. Said Tarozzi, "We built everything. I drew it up, and Remington or one of the other guys built it. It was uncanny how everything fit, and mostly on the first try."

The "business office" of the #48 AAR 'Cuda. (Photo Courtesy Barrett-Jackson Auction Company)

Now restored: The Keith Black–developed and All American Racers–built "LA" engine, destroked from 340 ci with a shorter-stroke crankshaft and connecting rods to meet SCCA's 305.5-ci (5-liter) displacement limit. (Photo Courtesy Barrett-Jackson Auction Company)

All-American Racers fabricated what they needed for the race AAR 'Cudas' chassis, plus factory Chrysler parts that they made changes to. "Dan had a certain way he wanted the car to behave, and it required a lot of engineering," said Tarozzi. "To my way of thinking, the rear suspension was pretty straightforward for the time. We used horizontal shock absorbers to control wheel hop. We used a Panhard bar for lateral location. We used double-adjustable Koni shock absorbers mounted in alternate [staggered] locations. The rear axle was a race-proven Chrysler unit, with a multitude of gear set ratios for tuning to the particular track.

"The front suspension went through much iteration, with the intent to provide the individual drivers with what they wanted in feel and drivability. The first car (Plymouth) had the anti-dive suspension, while the next two Plymouths had the more-conventional suspension. They were both okay, but we did not have much time to do all the testing necessary before the first race, so it was all a compromise."

And when Bob Tarozzi said they built everything, that also included the destroked 340 LA small-block engines. "Keith Black was doing all the engine and engine parts development for the Dodge and Plymouth teams, but our engines were built in our shop," he recalled.

"It was getting into late January or early February, and we [AAR] had no engine. What's more, we hadn't even heard one run on the dyno. We needed an engine to put in the chassis, so we could get the car set up for the March test, and I had no engine, not even a dummy. Finally, I told Pete Hutchinson that if he wanted to test in March, I needed an engine. He fired back that Keith Black was doing the Dodge engines, and he had sent us the parts to do ours. I told him again that we didn't have an engine, and since the Plymouth chassis was the only one to be used in testing, he better get me an engine. So he did, but it pissed off a

THE ROAD-RACING AAR 'CUDAS CONTINUED

Back in the day: Dan Gurney at speed at Laguna Seca. (Photo Courtesy Butch Noble/Mazda Raceway at Laguna Seca)

bunch of people, including Dan [Gurney]. The engine we got was a development engine. But it was all we had, and so we used it."

Thanks to the skills of Tarozzi, Phil Remington, and the rest of the All-American Racers team, the #42 and #48 AAR 'Cudas were ready for the 1970 season's first race. "When the season began in April at Laguna Seca, we were ready. Probably more ready than most, except Ford," Tarozzi recalls.

Unfortunately, the AAR 'Cudas trailed the Ford Mustang Boss 302s at Laguna Seca, with Swede Savage bringing the #42 'Cuda home in fourth place, one lap down to winner Parnelli Jones' Mustang, while Gurney's race ended after just 21 laps thanks to a transmission failure.

Problems plagued the AAR 'Cuda team after Laguna Seca, both mechanical and financial. On the track, they failed to finish at Lime Rock (Gurney's clutch let go after 64 laps while Savage's engine gave way after 32 laps), and at Bryar (Loudon), when the #48 car, driven by Savage, lost its engine after 33 laps. That late-May race in New Hampshire also saw the AAR team cut back to one car, due to the stream of sponsor dollars from Chrysler beginning to dry up. "We qualified on the pole a few times in the first half of the season, and ran pretty good," notes Tarozzi. "But then Chrysler pulled the financial plug, we were cut to one car, and any momentum we had was lost."

Savage again DNF'd at Mid-Ohio in the #42 car, thanks to an oil leak, and again at Bridgehampton in the #48 car (differential failure).

The July 5 race on the Donnybrooke track at Brainerd, Minnesota, marked the first finish by an AAR 'Cuda since Laguna Seca, as Savage finished fifth in the #42 car, three laps behind Milt Minter's winning Camaro. Then, two weeks later, Savage had his best run of the season at Road America at Elkhart Lake, Wisconsin, finishing second in the #42 car only .58 second behind Mark Donohue's winning Javelin.

Then the bad luck returned. Savage crashed the #42 car in practice before the August race at St. Jovite, Quebec, forcing the team to scramble to get the #48 ready for the race. Unfortunately, their work did not result in a high finish for Savage; or a finish at all, as he only ran 27 laps before pulling the car off the track for the day.

Fortunately, when the AAR team brought their third car, another #42 'Cuda for Savage to Watkins Glen, he made another strong run, finishing only one lap down, but in sixth place.

By the time the end of the 1970 Trans-Am schedule approached, times were tough not just for the factory-backed teams, but for the series itself. One early-season race, at Lewisville (Dallas), Texas, in late April had been canceled, and the September 20 race at Sears

Point Raceway in Sonoma, California, was also scratched, with the later-in-the-season race at Seattle International Raceway in Kent, Washington, being moved up to the Sears Point race's former date, with the season finale set for Riverside in early October.

By then, the sponsor money from Chrysler was gone, with no more coming for 1970. "That Riverside race was to be Dan Gurney's last race ever [as a driver]," says Bob Tarozzi. "He had personally funded the last two races with our second car, because he wanted to run at Kent and Riverside. Our whole team rallied around him. We all held out some hope that Chrysler would fund at least one team in 1971, so the competition between the Dodge camp and us was as fierce [as it was] with the Fords and Javelins.

"The two-car Dodge team was better at Kent, but we finished fourth and fifth at Riverside. It didn't matter. Chrysler walked away, as did all the other factory teams except Javelin. I walked, or was nudged away, too."

As was mentioned in this book's 1970 Challenger chapter, Chrysler (at first) told its Trans-Am teams that it was going to sponsor just one team for the 1971 season, that being the team that finished the highest in the final manufacturer's points standings. However, that ray of hope disappeared when Chrysler ended all factory Trans-Am support, and cut its NASCAR sponsorship back to just one Plymouth and one Dodge, both to be built by Richard Petty's shop, and to be raced by Petty and Buddy Baker. Adds Tarozzi, "It had been a great year, and we were proud of our accomplishments, but we didn't win, and the series that was born for the manufacturers was dying without them."

Without the factory support, or any commercial-product sponsorship like Petty received from STP in 1972, the All-American Racers' AAR 'Cudas never again raced in the SCCA Trans Am Series. But their racing history didn't end there.

The cars were shipped back to Chrysler, with one of them becoming a publicity and test vehicle for Goodyear, while the other was shipped to Europe, where it raced in production-based road races for a number of years with a 426 Hemi instead of the destroked 340.

From Goodyear's hands, that AAR 'Cuda was eventually restored by Ed Skanes, who also restored the ex-Sam Posey #77 Challenger T/A seen in Chapter 2.

Ed's son, Bryan, recounted to David Tom how his membership in the Special Interest Auto Club (devoted to the history, restoration, and enjoyment of E-Body Mopars), and an ad that ran in that club's publication in 1982, led him to two rare E-Body race cars. "One day in 1982, I received my issue, and to my surprise there was an article about a surviving AAR 'Cuda race car still being raced in the SCCA GT-1 class out of Indianapolis, as well as a surviving Dodge Challenger Trans-Am race car sitting near Houston, Texas. I read the entire article again and again.

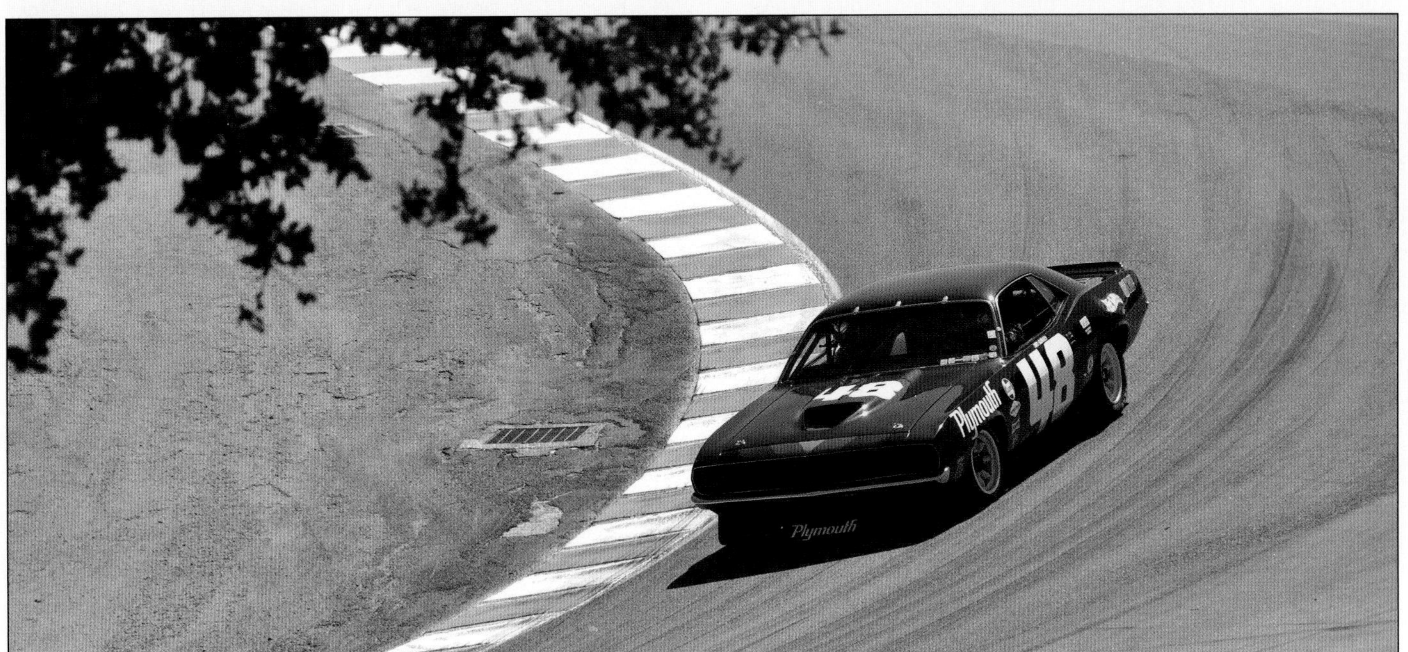

In action in a Historic Trans-Am race at Mazda Raceway Laguna Seca: The restored #48 AAR 'Cuda, at speed on the Corkscrew. (Photo Courtesy Barrett-Jackson Auction Company)

THE ROAD-RACING AAR 'CUDAS CONTINUED

"I wondered how much of their originality still remained. I was aware that it was common for these cars to have modifications performed or updated parts put on them as needed. But two small words kept catching my eye each time I read the article: 'For Sale.' I could not believe this. Here were two historical Mopar race cars that I thought I would never see, and they were both for sale. My dream was just to see one, but now the thought of owning one or both crept into my mind. What a dream that would be."

When father and son Skanes went to see the AAR 'Cuda, it was all they imagined it was, and more. "The AAR 'Cuda looked so cool and was so low to the ground," recalls Bryan Skanes. "As I was looking it over, I noticed an AAR manufacturer tag on the firewall. Wow! Gurney had numbered them.

"The roll cage looked so intricately installed. Plus, the smell was unique. Suddenly, the owner asked if we would like to hear it run. I responded, 'Yes, please.' The owner slid into the driver's seat and fired the 'Cuda up. Oh my Lord. What a beautiful sound. My heart just about skipped a beat when the raw horsepower came to life. My life changed forever upon hearing that sound. As the AAR 'Cuda slowly moved outside into the sunlight, I walked over to my dad and stated, 'I don't care what it takes, we must buy this car. We can sell [our] Superbird, the Daytona, and Hemi 'Cuda, whatever it takes. We must buy this car.'"

The deal was made, and the Skanes towed the AAR 'Cuda home, where they planned, then started, its meticulous, five-year-long restoration. Once finished, they would take it to Mopar-related events around the country as a static show car whose engine would be fired up while at the show.

But in 1985, the project took a dramatic turn, not unlike the "Corkscrew" at Laguna Seca. "We got a phone call from David Tom, who lived in Cincinnati, Ohio. He informed us that he owned the 1970 Chaparral Camaro driven by Jim Hall and Vic Elford. He asked about our plans for the AAR 'Cuda race car. We informed him that we were going to restore it and show it at Mopar shows around the country.

"He thought there was another option to consider: Why not enjoy the car for what it was meant to do? That was to restore it back to 1970 'as-raced' condition, and put it on a racetrack. Vintage racing, as it was called, allows an old race car to still get out and have fun at speed. Fans would get to watch and relive what Trans-Am racing was like back in the late 1960s and early 1970s. They would see the Camaros, Mustangs, Javelins, Cougars, Barracudas, Challengers, and Pontiac Trans Ams at war again.

Plus, it allowed the owners or drivers to experience what it was like to drive these great cars. This was such an interesting idea."

A later trip to the vintage races at Mid-Ohio cinched it, and they were immersed in the vintage Trans-Am community. Bryan says, "As the years passed, we visited more racetracks, met more owners of the other Trans-Am race cars, found new friends, and enjoyed life as we would have never thought possible before. We soon realized that we had become the keepers of the flame of racing history, preservationists you could say, of a racing era. We were the source that people relied on, and they expected us to know the complete history of the car. We had the responsibility to always do our best in presenting these beautiful works of rolling art on the track."

Instead of a show car that was only under power when driven on or off a trailer, this AAR 'Cuda ran again in the manner it was built for: at speed, on the nation's best road courses. As of the publication of this book, it wears Swede Savage's #42 and color scheme and is owned and vintage-raced by Bill Ockerland. "This particular car was not very highly modified, or destroyed, or anything, after the 1970 season," he says, which made its later restoration a straightforward matter.

What's it like to drive the restored #42 car? "It's good," says Ockerland. "It's different than the Chevys and Fords in the way it works. The Mopar engine has a lot more torque, so it definitely pulls stronger down low. We've had to rebuild the shocks; that's one thing we figured out at the test day that they needed to be rebuilt. We'll have a little bit more to work on handling-wise, but it looks [like] it will handle quite well, and it has very good brakes."

Ockerland has plenty of good things to say about the #42 car's restored race engine. "The torque of this engine is far greater than that of the Ford [302 Boss]. The Chevy [Z28] has good torque, but this is stronger than the Chevy, in that regard." He adds, "The engine issues [that All-American Racers had in 1970] are now solved these days. It would be like if they'd continued on in 1971, how they would have ended up getting it to run."

As for the 'Cuda that raced with a 426 Hemi after its Trans-Am days, it's also been restored, to how it was when Dan Gurney finished fifth at Riverside in it in the last race of the 1970 SCCA Trans-Am season, Dan Gurney's last-ever race in competition as a driver. It is also the last of the E-Body Plymouths that All-American Racers built and raced. "There were three cars built. Swede rolled one of the cars, and [at that time] they hadn't put the third car into commission, which is the car I have," says its current owner, Craig Jackson, in an interview with this author. "Toward the end of the season they did, and that's this car."

Raced only at Seattle (Kent) and Riverside by Gurney in 1970, its days as a competition car were far from over. "The car was sold

The ex-Dan Gurney #48 AAR 'Cuda graces Mazda Raceway at Laguna Seca during the Rolex Monterey Reunion. (Photo Courtesy Barrett-Jackson Auction Company)

to Chrysler of France, and it raced [in the 24 Hours of] LeMans as a Hemi 'Cuda," notes Jackson. "They took out the destroked 340. It was competitive, but it didn't finish.

"Then, it raced in B/Salon in the Shell Series for many years. And then, it was found in a winery garage and brought back to the United States."

Fortunately, those who raced it after Dan Gurney didn't crash it, or otherwise tear it up. "It was pretty much all original, but some changes had been made to it to make it FIA-legal to race in Europe, like changes to the roll bar, and lights for the numbers [in order to] race at LeMans," says Jackson. "But all of the [AAR-made] components were still on the car.

"When the car came back to the States, it came back with the original race engine back in the car, because it had been put on an engine stand the entire time that it raced with a Hemi. So, I have the original race engine."

With all the original parts on hand, the ex-Gurney AAR 'Cuda was restored by the owner who subsequently sold it to Jackson. "He got all the original blueprints from one of the guys at Gurney's," says Jackson, who notes that it also had its original blue paint on it as well. "When he started to go through the car, he discovered the original paint and livery was underneath [the paint that was on it]."

Even though it wears its 1970-season-finale colors, is it in the condition that it would have raced in 1971, had Gurney and AAR found sponsorship to race in Trans-Am that year? "Yes," says Jackson enthusiastically. "The car is a very competitive car. He only had one year to sort them out, and they suffered from reliability issues more than anything."

Issues that you can see have been resolved, once you see and hear it run in Historic Trans-Am events on the nation's leading racetracks.

CHAPTER 4

1971 DODGE CHALLENGER

Massive Muscle and New Updates

Change was in the air all across the U.S. auto industry for 1971, and it did not favor muscle cars. Several factors were bringing the muscle car era to a close, and 1971 proved to be the last year of the genuine high-performance Mopars, thanks to factors like high insurance premiums and surcharges, as well as the need to devote company resources to complying with emission standards set by the Clean Air Act of 1966.

Back then, insurance surcharges were added not only for cars with high-performance powertrains (often described as those with any engine that produced more than 300 hp) but also for cars equipped with manual transmissions and/or console-mounted automatics, and even to cars equipped with a factory tachometer.

A Slightly Revised Challenger Returns in 1971

To many observers, the 1971 Challenger lineup looked little changed from its debut year of 1970. One new model appeared for 1971, a base-series coupe, notable for its fixed rear quarter windows, standard 198-ci Slant Six, and options like a day/night inside mirror and cigarette lighter (both standard on all other Challengers). It would be the most-affordable Challenger, a price leader aimed at the low-line Firebird and Javelin coupes.

In keeping with auto-industry common wisdom of the time, visible changes were limited to a new grille and taillights, Instead of the simple, concave grille of 1970, the 1971 Challenger was "faced" by a grille that the *1971 Dodge Dealer Data* book described as having "a one-piece plastic frame, dual headlight frame of stamped aluminum, and a two-piece plastic grille with stamped aluminum bezel."

In back, the taillights were slightly restyled, and the backup lights were centered in the taillights instead of centered between them. Challenger R/T models received a new set of simulated fiberglass louvers just forward of the rear wheelwells, that looked like ones to be used for rear-brake cooling but having no mechanical function at all. Those simulated louvers only appeared on the 1971 Challenger R/T coupe, as the convertible version of the performance Challenger was discontinued after 1970.

For 1971, few visible changes were made to the Dodge Challenger. This 1971 Challenger R/T shows off its new grille, the R/T's simulated scoops just forward of the rear wheels, and the painted-steel-wheel-with-hub-cap wheel treatment, which was the standard wheel choice with the 426 Hemi in 1971 with the W21 Rallye wheels as the only option. (Photo Courtesy Mecum Auctions)

Also disappearing from the Challenger model lineup: the Special Edition. However, the SE's "formal" roof treatment, including a functional center headliner-mounted consolette, would be available on base-series and R/T hardtops as an option group.

As Chrysler had curtailed (and eventually ended) sponsorship of the Autodynamics Challenger T/A racing team in SCCA's Trans-Am series during the 1970 season, so was the production Challenger T/A dropped from the 1971 Challenger lineup. That move was made after preliminary 1971 product information had been prepared, including a photograph and related information about the 1971 Challenger T/A that appeared in early versions of that year's Challenger, full-line Dodge, and Dodge Scat Pack sales brochures, which went to press in August 1970.

With the Challenger T/A's discontinuation, its fiberglass hood and rear spoiler, special TA cylinder

Inside, the Challenger was unchanged from 1971, with its front high-back bucket seats carrying over from 1970. The Pistol-Grip Hurst shifter for the 4-speed manual transmission was repositioned a little closer to the driver for 1971, while the amber reverse-indicator light returned for 1971 in the center of the dash. (Courtesy Mecum Auctions)

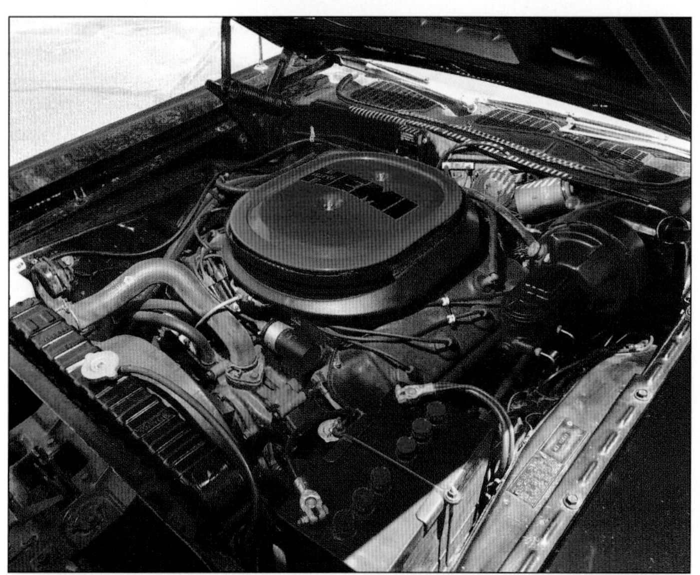

Once again, the 426 was the top engine choice for the Challenger R/T for 1971, for $789.95 over the standard 383. The fender tag on the inside of the left front fender (lower right of photo) identifies this car as an original TX9 Black exterior/H6X9 Black all-vinyl interior E74 426 Hemi car built at Hamtramck on December 11, 1970. It also indicates that this car was built with the D21 4-speed manual transmission, A34 Super Track Pack (which also included a 4.10-geared Dana 60 rear end), B51 Power brakes (drum), C55 Bucket seats, G11 Tinted glass, G31 Right-hand manual chrome sport mirror, G33 Left-hand remote-control chrome sport mirror, J25 3-speed windshield wipers, J45 Hood tie-down pins, J46 Locking gas cap, J54 Sport hood, M21 Roof drip moldings, M25 Wide sill moldings, N41 Dual exhaust, N42 Chrome exhaust tips, N85 Tachometer, R11 AM Radio, R31 Rear seat speaker, V68 longitudinal stripe delete, and a heavy-duty 26-inch radiator. (Photo Courtesy Mecum Auctions)

What graced a 1971 Challenger's engine bay if the base-series coupe, hardtop, or convertible were chosen: the "flat" hood, which so many modern-day builders and "resto-modders" replaced with either the factory Shaker or twin-scooped R/T hoods, or the 1970 fiberglass T/A hood.

The Challenger's taillights and backup lights were redesigned for 1971, with the backup lights now centered in each of the taillights, instead of centered between them. Black-painted taillight panel was a 1971 Challenger R/T design cue, and the chrome exhaust tips with special rear valance carried over from 1970.

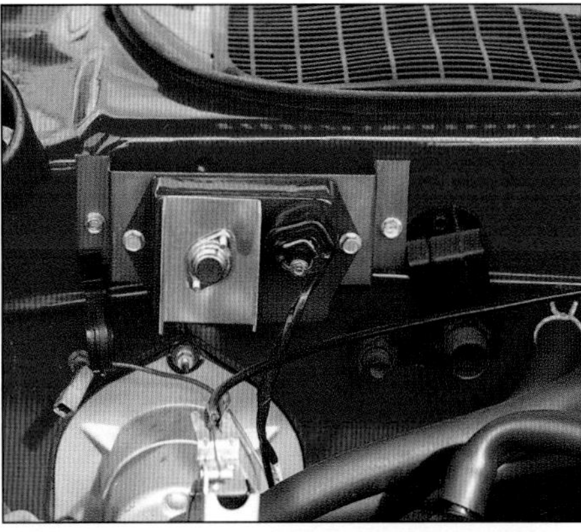

Before the spring of 1971, 340 Challengers received a control module like this one for their engine's non-electronic ignition systems. A running change did away with this module, as well as the ignition's breaker points and condenser.

On another 340 'Cuda is seen an Electronic Ignition System's control box and related wiring. From about May 1971 onward, all 340 Challengers had this installed on the line at Hamtramck Assembly.

block and heads and side-exit exhaust were also dropped as regular-production items, though they continued to be available through Dodge's Hustle Stuff parts program. However, the T/A's special fast-ratio power steering assembly survived and was added to 340 Challengers as a running change on February 1, 1971.

The 340 Challengers were also the recipients of other changes before the end of the 1971 model year. One was the replacement of their Carter AVS 4-barrel carburetor with Carter's new ThermoQuad 4-barrel at the start of 1971 production. Designed around a lightweight plastic body, it would eventually become the 4-barrel used on all regular-production Chrysler V-8 engine platforms within the next year.

Two other carburetor changes took place during 1971 for base-series Challengers. The 318's standard fuel/air mixer

Wearing the orange paint characteristic of a Chrysler high-performance engine is the 1971 340. The year 1971 was the last time it was available with high (10:1) compression, large-port heads with 2.02-inch intake valves, and "performance-style" exhaust manifolds. Note power brake booster on the firewall's right side, power steering pump at lower-right, and the lack of a factory-installed Airtemp air-conditioning system, whose compressor would have been located at the front-center of the engine.

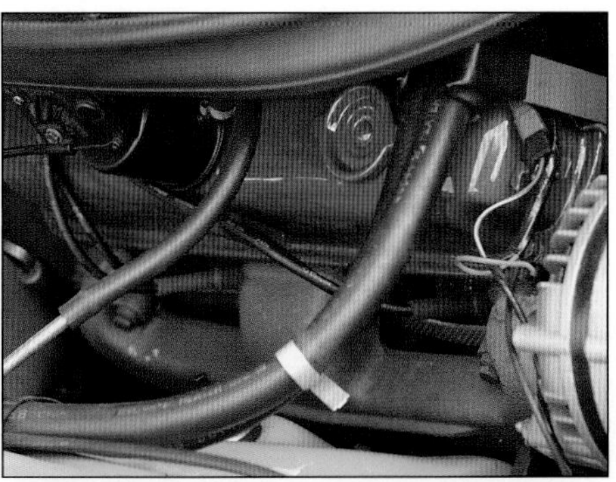

A look at the 340's factory right-side exhaust manifold. Changes to the 340 for 1972 deleted these in favor of the more-restrictive manifolds used on the "station wagon" 360 engines.

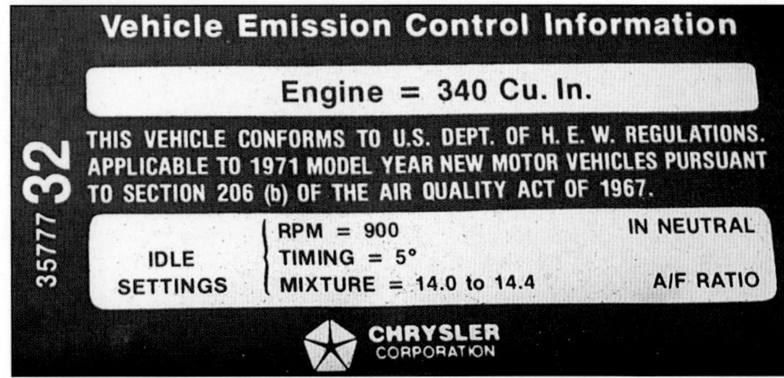

Vehicle Emission Control Information
Engine = 340 Cu. In.
THIS VEHICLE CONFORMS TO U.S. DEPT. OF H. E. W. REGULATIONS. APPLICABLE TO 1971 MODEL YEAR NEW MOTOR VEHICLES PURSUANT TO SECTION 206 (b) OF THE AIR QUALITY ACT OF 1967.
IDLE SETTINGS
RPM = 900
TIMING = 5°
MIXTURE = 14.0 to 14.4
IN NEUTRAL
A/F RATIO
35777 32
CHRYSLER CORPORATION

How to keep a 340 in tune, per Chrysler: This sticker, with idle specifications for mechanics to refer to, also stated that the car it was affixed to met federal emission-control standards as of the date of its manufacture.

The Challenger R/T was only available as a hardtop for 1971, with simulated rear-quarter-panel air scoops and new side stripes standard on Dodge's performance E-Body. Returning for 1971 were the optional "High Impact" colors (this one is painted (the lightest of the two greens), along with 14-inch five-spoke wheels, the Shaker hood, and the J81 rear spoiler. (Photo Courtesy David Newhardt)

From the side, only the side stripes and simulated rear quarter panel scoops indicate this Challenger R/T is a 1971 model. The Code J81 rear spoiler was also available as a factory-installed option, or a do-it-yourself item at a Dodge dealer's parts counter. The Code A44 rear window louvers were also available as dealer-installed items or as accessories at a Dodge dealer's parts department to be owner-installed, but they were not legal for use on cars registered in Pennsylvania in 1971. (Photo Courtesy David Newhardt)

Rear styling updates for 1971 included revised taillights with backup lights centered inside them for all Challengers while the Challenger R/T's taillight panel was now painted flat black. A special rear valance panel under the bumper was also standard on non-California-sold R/Ts equipped with the chrome exhaust tips that graced the dual-exhaust systems of the 383s, 340s, 440 Six Packs, and 426 Hemis. (Photo Courtesy David Newhardt)

The factory-installed 440 Six Pack rests beneath the massive Shaker hood scoop's air cleaner, which protrudes through a factory-stamped hole in the hood. The forward edge of the Shaker scoop sits where an air conditioning compressor would otherwise reside, so the H51 Airtemp Air Conditioning option was not available on Challengers equipped with the Shaker hood. (Photo Courtesy David Newhardt)

Six color choices (blue, dark green, beige, brown, black, and white) were available for the standard Challenger hardtop, convertible, and R/T's front bucket/rear bench seat interiors. Only two color choices (green and black) were offered for the available split-bench front seats, which were only available with a column-mounted TorqueFlite automatic. (Photo Courtesy David Newhardt)

changed from a Carter unit to one manufactured by GM's Rochester division, similar to the ones that topped base Chevrolet and Pontiac V-8s. And, during the 1971 model year, some Carter carburetors for the Slant Six models were in short supply, so Holley carburetors were substituted on the assembly line and mentioned in Technical Service Bulletins to dealers regarding them and the parts to service them.

High Impact colors may have been rarely seen in 1971 due to their extra ($14.05) cost, but they are valuable features on E-Body Challengers today. This Challenger convertible was painted "Top Banana" at Hamtramck in 1971, and its factory hue shines as it did when new. Note the front bumper is two-toned, the "Elastomeric" (urethane-covered) bumper option had the lower surface of the bumper painted to match the car body, with the grille side of the bumper painted black to match the area surrounding the grille. (Photo Courtesy Barrett-Jackson Auction Company)

In the spring of 1971, two significant performance features were added to the 340. One was a dual-breaker distributor, optional on TorqueFlite 340s only. The other was Chrysler's Electronic Ignition System, which eliminated the ignition system's breaker points and condenser and added an electronic control module under the hood on the firewall. This was aimed at delivering a "hotter" spark to the cylinders and to lengthen spark plug life. By the end of the 1973 model year, every Chrysler Corporation passenger car and light truck's engine would be equipped with this system, part of Chrysler's "Extra Care in Engineering."

The other performance engines in the Challenger lineup were carried over from 1970, but they were fewer in number. Gone was the 4-barrel 440 Magnum, as the triple-carbureted 440 Six Pack was the only available RB-series big-block. And the 426 Hemi was still available, though only in R/T coupes.

Still available were Chrysler's TorqueFlite automatic transmissions and New Process Gear-built A-833 4-speed manual gearboxes, though both received significant mechanical upgrades for 1971. The automatics received a part-throttle kickdown feature that Chrysler said would provide

This close-up of an A62 rallye gauge cluster shows it unchanged for 1971; it has the same 150-mph speedometer and four-function fuel level/oil pressure/ammeter/ coolant temperature gauge cluster flanking the same 8,000-rpm tach that still doesn't show a "redline" (maximum safe operating speed) for the engine. (Photo Courtesy David Newhardt)

Taillight panel detail of the Plum Crazy 1971 Challenger convertible seen earlier in this chapter. Trunk lock cylinder above "Challenger" script accepted only one key: the one with the round head on it. (The ignition key doubled as the front door key.) As with all Chrysler products of the time, the flat side of the key went on the bottom while using it. (Photo Courtesy David Newhardt)

Detail of the leading edge of the right front fender, showing front bumper's location relative to it. Starting in 1973, the Challenger's front bumper was repositioned forward, to make room for a steel reinforcing bar behind it that was necessitated by the federal bumper standard that took effect in 1973. (Photo courtesy David Newhardt)

"more economical acceleration." It also eliminated a "bog" that could happen when accelerating, such as going from 30 to 50 mph or more while passing.

The 4-speeds' updates included a gear set "borrowed" from the 4-speeds used in the 1970 Challenger T/A whose gear ratios were closer together, which helped to limit engine RPM drops during upshifting. The A-833's Hurst-built Pistol Grip shifter was moved closer to the driver, so upshifts and downshifts would require less of a reach than before.

And the standard 3-speed manual gearbox also saw revisions for 1971, with a redesign of its gear teeth for less tooth angle, aimed at improving upshifting and downshifting.

There were other updates inside, under, and on Challenger's Unibody for 1971. Standard front torsion bars were made smaller in diameter, from .88 inch to .86 inch, for a "softer and more comfortable ride," while all power steering-equipped Challengers received a new steering gear that gave "a more positive feel of the road in the straight ahead position."

The option list saw a new front floor-mounted cassette player/recorder join the sound system choices for 1971, available with a detachable microphone that turned it into a mobile dictating machine. An "old" feature became a new option on hardtops: the 1970 Special Edition's "formal" roof treatment with vinyl top, and smaller rear window, which was joined in the A78 "Formal Roof" option group by the consolette mounted on the headliner between the front seats.

One new color was added to Challenger's High Impact color selection for 1971: Citron Yella. Two other hues, however, were no longer regular production options. Panther Pink, a midyear addition in 1970, became a special-order-only color, while SubLime was dropped altogether.

A significant addition to the 1971 Challenger option list repeated and foreshadowed a future Dodge sales and marketing practice: the Challenger Radio Group. It combined the available AM or AM/FM radio options with power steering, variable-speed windshield wipers and a chrome remote-control left-side rearview mirror in a package whose sticker price was lower than if those options were purchased by themselves. This was similar to the "White Hat Special" option packages that Dodge had offered on Darts, Polaras, Coronets, and Chargers during the

Do you like the looks of the interior trim (seen here) that was standard on the 1971 Challenger R/T and on all base-level Challengers except the price-leader coupe that year? The "bean counters" at Highland Park liked it; or, rather its sales performance, as this was the only upholstery pattern and material on Challenger's interior trim selector after 1971. White seats, door panels, and side panels proved very difficult to keep clean in normal vehicle use.

late 1960s, where two-tone or vinyl-roof Dodges with this appearance package were available at a special package price.

In coming years, similar Dodge Basic Group, Easy Order, or Luxury Equipment option packages would combine available features, including TorqueFlite automatic transmissions, whitewall tires, and optional wheel covers, in a package whose sticker-price savings (especially when the TorqueFlite was no extra charge) would be a big selling point.

A well-equipped 1971 Dodge Challenger convertible sports the Shaker hood with hood pins atop its 340, while Goodyear-shod Rallye road wheels fill its fenderwells. Only 2,165 Challenger convertibles in all were built for 1971. How many of them were built with this one's combination of options and colors? (Hint: You may be looking at the only one known to exist with this combination.) (Photo Courtesy Mecum Auctions)

But there was one significant deletion that neither Dodge nor Chrysler mentioned in any factory literature for potential customers. The five-year, 50,000-mile limited powertrain warranty that had been a major Chrysler Corporation selling point since 1963 was now a thing of the past. Not only did Chrysler drop it, but Ford, General Motors, and AMC also scaled back their factory warranty protection, which had reached similar levels of coverage. For 1971, all Chrysler Corporation passenger-car powertrain warranties were for 12 months or 12,000 miles, whichever came first. Except for the 440 Six Pack and 426 Hemi, those engines were offered with six-month, 6,000-mile powertrain warranties that were only available to the original purchaser.

Models, Options and Pricing

When the 1971 models went on sale at Dodge dealers from coast to coast in October 1971, new car buyers saw a slightly smaller selection of Challengers than the year before, with vehicle and option prices close to those of 1970. (Prices quoted here are from the *1971 Dodge Salesman's Pocket Guide*, and do not include federal excise tax, state and local sales taxes, registration, title, inspection, and license plate fees.)

The new Challenger coupe was the line's price leader, whose sticker prices started at $2,727 for the 198 Slant Six one, or $2,853 for one powered by a 318-ci V-8. The Challenger hardtop saw a slight price drop in both 6-cylinder and V-8 models, with base-version sticker prices dropping three dollars from 1970 on both, to $2,848 and 2,950, respectively.

A chrome-bumper 1971 Dodge Challenger R/T crosses the auction block at a Barrett-Jackson collector-car auction in Palm Beach, Florida. Vinyl tops were popular options on R/T and non-R/T Challenger hardtops alike in 1971. This particular R/T is powered by the standard 383-ci "B" series big-block V-8, which was still a potent performer despite a compression ratio drop (and switch to regular gas from premium) for 1971. (Photo Courtesy Barrett-Jackson Auction Company)

With the R/T letters seen here, the body-side performance tape stripe was standard on the Challenger R/T, though the Code V68 Stripe Delete option was available for those who wanted their E-Body Dodge's flanks unadorned. Without the "R/T" letters, those stripes were just $14.25 extra on the Challenger convertible and hardtop, and $28.50 extra on the coupe.

Highly optioned Challengers like this 1971 R/T are stars and bring big money at auction. This one is equipped with the 426 Hemi, factory-installed sunroof, and front and rear spoilers, as well as 60-series raised-white-letter tires on 15-inch Rallye road wheels. (Photo Courtesy David Newhardt)

From this angle, you can see that the 1971 Challenger's Shaker hood was more than just the base-series hood with a hole cut in it, thanks to Dodge's exterior styling team. Note the factory-installed electric sunroof, rarely seen today because of its high sticker price ($461.45). (Photo Courtesy David Newhardt)

Moving up the line, the 1971 Challenger convertible's pricing started at $3,105 for the 225 Slant Six one (a $15 drop), while the base 318 drop-top's sticker started at $3,207, again a $15 drop over 1970 prices. The only Challenger that saw a base-price increase for 1971 was the R/T hardtop, whose sticker now started at $3,273, a $7 increase.

There were no changes under the hood for the 426 Hemi in the second year of the E-Body Dodge Challenger. At $778.75, it was the most expensive item on Challenger's option list, and it came with only a 6-month powertrain warranty, instead of the 12-month/12,000-mile one that covered all other 1971 Challenger engines except the 440 Six Pack. (Photo Courtesy David Newhardt)

1971 Option Packages

Two option packages offered in 1970 were dropped for 1971: the A32 Super Performance Axle Package and the A35 Trailer Towing Package. For the latter, it's likely that buyers

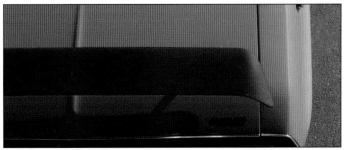

There are no Chrysler Engineering lab reports that show how effective the Code J81 Rear Spoiler is in creating downforce to help high-speed stability and handling yet the flat-black bolt-on item has proven to be a popular addition to Challengers over the years. That's regardless of whether or not the car was built with it and has the J81 code number on its fender tag and broadcast sheets to prove it. (Photo Courtesy David Newhardt)

If you see a side stripe and rear-quarter-panel louvers like these on any other Challenger than a 1971 R/T, chances are that car was "resto modded" to give it a look similar to that of this original one. Some called this car with its Hemi Orange/white color scheme a "Creamsicle," but only the rear tires were likely to melt given the torque that its 426 Hemi puts out. (Photo Courtesy David Newhardt)

Not only did the new-for-1971 longitudinal stripes add style to that year's Challenger R/T, owners of other year E-Body Challengers have added them to their cars to upgrade the appearance. If functional, the rear scoops at the bottom of this picture would direct cold outside air onto the car's rear brakes, keeping them cool and improving their performance. (Photo Courtesy David Newhardt)

Stainless steel hood pins were a must for stock-bodied race cars. In case the hood latch failed at high speeds, the hood would stay off the car's windshield. Option Code J45 added a dual-purpose look to Challenger R/Ts equipped with them, while adding only $19.20 to the car's sticker price. They were also available at Dodge dealer's parts counters, or as dealer-installed accessories. (Photo Courtesy David Newhardt)

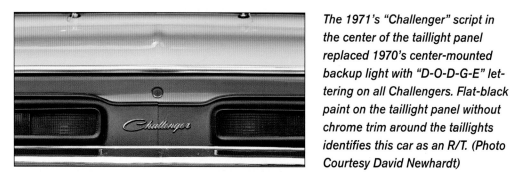

The 1971's "Challenger" script in the center of the taillight panel replaced 1970's center-mounted backup light with "D-O-D-G-E" lettering on all Challengers. Flat-black paint on the taillight panel without chrome trim around the taillights identifies this car as an R/T. (Photo Courtesy David Newhardt)

The final year not only of the Code E87 440 Six Pack engine option, but also for the Code N96 Shaker hood, was 1971. From 1972 onward, if you wanted to put a Shaker hood on a new Challenger, you had to scrounge one off a wreck in a junkyard, or find the New Old Stock or New Original Replacement Stock (NOS/NORS) parts on a Dodge dealer's shelf. (Photo Courtesy David Newhardt)

Dressed up with optional C16 console and Slap Stik shift for the TorqueFlite automatic transmission, this 1971 Challenger R/T's cabin also includes the A62 Rally gauge cluster with tachometer, S83 Rim-blow steering wheel and leather-and-vinyl seats. Radio is the optional R11 push-button Music Master AM receiver. (Photo Courtesy David Newhardt)

A close-up look at the console-mounted Slap Stik that could shift the TorqueFlite automatic transmission manually (once engaged with the button on the end of the shifter) or automatically with it in Drive. The Slap Stik mechanism was intended to give quicker shifts into Second and Drive without missing them and engaging Reverse or Park at speed instead (with expensive consequences for the gearbox)! (Photo Courtesy David Newhardt)

looking for a new Dodge to tow a trailer opted for a bigger Coronet or Polara, or a D-series pickup truck, over the smaller Challenger. For the former, the ultra-strong Dana 60 rear end was still available in the A33 Track Pak, for 4-speed cars and in the A34 Super Track Pak (which also included 4.10 rear gears) for automatics. Sticker prices on those two performance-axle option groups also dropped for 1971, with the A33 package's price dropping from $142.85 to $137.90, while the A34 package's $201.75 price for 1971 was nearly $35 less than in 1970. Also, the A31 Hi Performance Axle package with its 3.91 rear gears for 383 Challengers saw its price drop from $102.15 to $85.15, and the A36 Performance Axle Package for automatic 440s and Hemis (and 4-speed or TorqueFlite 340s and 383s) now cost as little as $41.70 with a Hemi to $75.25 with the 340 or 383.

This 1971 Challenger convertible has a lot going for it: a 426 Hemi under its hood, an attractive and desirable color combination, and plenty of rubber in the rear wheelwells to handle the Hemi. It's an example of a "tribute car" that was originally built with an engine other than a Hemi, but was retro-fitted after Mopar Performance brought out its 426 Hemi crate engines in the early 1990s that could bolt up to the B/RB engine crossmember (K member). The 15-inch chrome five-spoke wheels are reproductions; those wheels were only offered in the 14-inch diameter in 1971. (Photo Courtesy David Newhardt)

The chrome trim around the taillights is a giveaway that this car is not a factory-built 1971 Dodge Challenger R/T, whose taillights resided in an all-flat-black taillight panel. That, and the larger-than-stock-diameter exhaust system visible under the right-side door. On every other appearance cue for 1971, this car's builders got it right. (Photo Courtesy David Newhardt)

Inside, the four-pod A62 Rallye gauge cluster, D21 4-speed manual transmission, R11 AM radio, and C16 Center console are the only visible options. Wood-grained steering wheel was a standard Challenger feature on all but the base coupe. (Photo Courtesy David Newhardt)

White seats and door panels added style but were difficult to keep clean. Regardless of exterior color, all Challengers ordered with white interiors received black dashboards, steering columns, and carpets, and their available C16 Center console was also black, while it was color-keyed to the other interior colors. (Photo Courtesy David Newhardt)

The Challenger script badge adorned the taillight panel, and the taillights received minor changes for 1971. (Photo Courtesy David Newhardt)

The high-performance Challengers featured hood pins to keep the hood firmly secured during extreme or racing use. The deeply inset grille featured chrome accents; a chrome trim piece followed the leading edge of the hood and fenders as well. (Photo Courtesy David Newhardt)

Sunroof-equipped Challengers were also equipped with the Federally mandated shoulder belts. This Challenger also has the optional Code R22 stereo cassette player/recorder located on its center console (at right of photo). When have you seen another Hemi-powered 1971 Challenger R/T with this combination of rare options? (Photo courtesy David Newhardt)

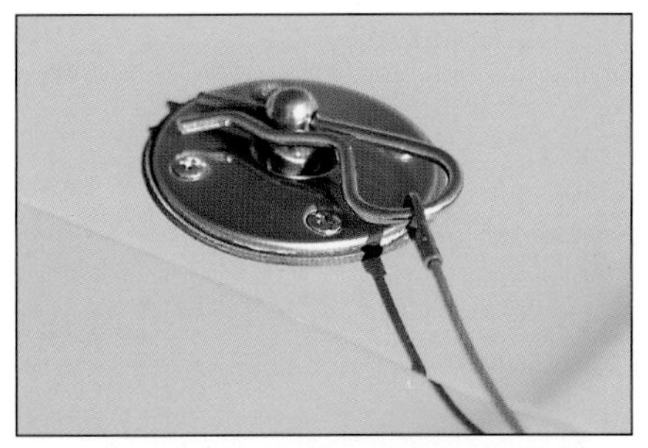

During the late 1960s, hood tie-down pins were either standard items on factory-built muscle cars, or low-priced items that could be added by dealer or owner for their function and race-ready looks. With big-power engines including the 426 Hemi and440 Six Pack still available, these items were still on Challenger R/T's option list for 1971.

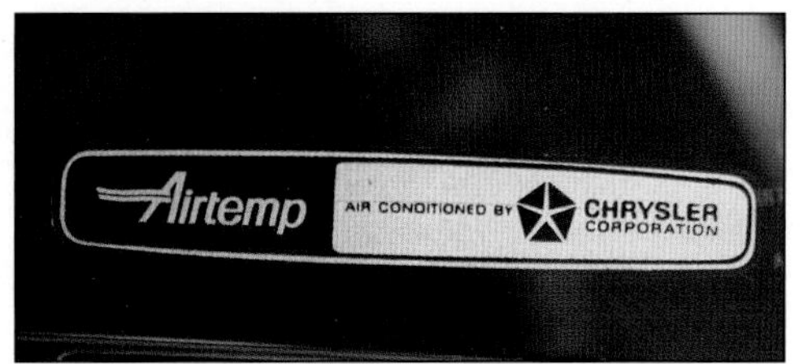

Once again for 1971, Challengers and other Dodges that had Chrysler's Airtemp air conditioning system installed at the factory bore this decal on the inside of the right rear window. Not only was it something that gave that car's owner, driver, and occupants bragging rights on hot and humid days, it also made "factory air" cars that much easier to spot on a dealer's lot.

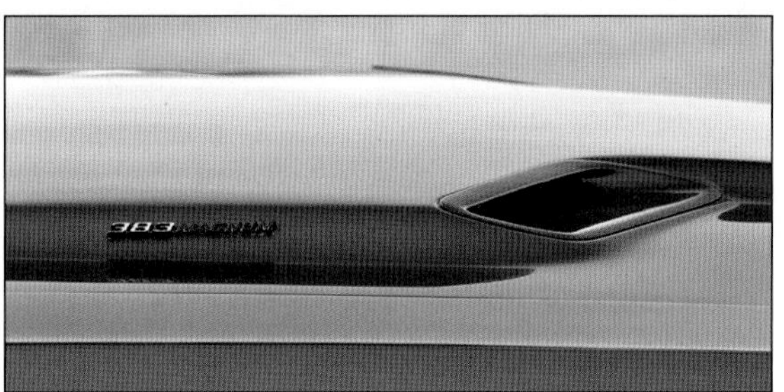

The optional J54 Sport hood sits atop an optional E65 383 Magnum V-8. The venerable 383's final year in the Dodge engine lineup was 1971. It was replaced by a 400-ci version of the Chrysler "B" engine series big-block for 1972. (Photo Courtesy David Newhardt)

Other options that didn't make the cut for 1971 included the A66 340 engine package. Those package contents were included when the E55 340 was ordered on either the R/T hardtop or on base Challenger hardtops and convertibles; N88 Automatic Speed Control; two-tone paint on base hardtops and the R/T's available rear bumblebee stripe; the S83 Rim-Blow Steering Wheel and S79 Partial Horn Ring; and any optional wheel treatment on 426 Hemi-equipped Challengers, other than the W21 Rallye wheels or steel wheels with hub caps, per the *1971 Dodge Salesman's Pocket Guide.*

New option packages for 1971 included the A78 Formal Roof Package (mentioned above), which added $127.50 worth of style to Challenger and Challenger R/T hardtops. Also new were two elastomeric bumper packages available on base Challenger models: Code A21 coated the front bumper in urethane before body-color paint went on it and black paint went on the grille (and $50.05 went on the sticker price), while the A22 option code meant that both bumpers received the urethane-then-paint treatment, the grille and taillight panels each received black paint, while the sticker saw a $94.00 upcharge. Those body-colored bumpers were also optional on R/Ts: Code M71 ($40.70) for the front only, M73 ($81.40), or both.

Although Challenger T/A didn't return for 1971, its fiberglass hood and front spoilers appeared on the 1971 options list. The Code N94 Fiberglass Hood with Fresh-Air Pak was not available on Slant Six Challengers or with the A05 Challenger Protection Group, and it added $173.20 to base Challengers equipped with the 383, or $152.95 when ordered on an R/T or with the 340 on a base Challenger. The T/A's "chin whisker" front spoilers, now wearing Code A45 and combined with the free-standing rear "spoiler" (and not the "ducktail" rear spoiler the T/As had) added $54.65 to the sticker, while the rear J81 spoiler by itself was a $34.35 factory option (and also available as a dealer-installed item, too). Neither spoiler package was available with the A78 Formal Roof Package, by the way.

The Shaker hood (Code N96) was back for 1971, for just $94.00 extra on R/Ts and 340 base Challengers, or $114.20 with a 383 on the base Challenger series. The Shaker was not available on Slant Six or 2-barrel cars, and H51 Airtemp air conditioning wasn't available with it because the Shaker's base took up room at the front of the engine where the AC compressor would otherwise go. (The hood wouldn't shut and latch with both the Shaker and AC.)

Performance-oriented appearance options that were new for 1971 also included the A44 Louver Package, which added a set of rear-window louvers to R.T. and base-series hardtops but was not available in Pennsylvania. The A44 added $73.70 to Challengers equipped with the A04 Radio Group package, $88.65 without it.

Feature-oriented option groups saw a price drop for 1971. The A01 Light group now cost 10 bucks less ($30.20) for its array of convenience lights inside and out, while the A04 Challenger Radio group, which also included power steering and variable-speed wipers, along with the buyer's choice of sound systems, was just under $200 ($193.60) without the A62 Rallye Gauge package, or $183.00 with it, plus upcharges for the available AM/FM stereo radio or cassette tape player/recorder.

Among the 1971 Challenger's selection of à la carte options, some had hefty price increases. That included the H51 Airtemp Air Conditioning, whose $374.40 price was nearly $20 higher than in 1970; S77 Power Steering (at $106.95, a $16 increase); and the D34 TorqueFlite automatic transmission's price with the Slant Six jumped by nearly $20, to $209.00; on V-8s, it went up to $229.35.

The chrome snap-open fuel filler (Code J46) was still available as a factory-installed option for 1971. It could also be dealer-installed or purchased at the parts counter for owner installation. (Photo Courtesy David Newhardt)

Taillight panel detail of the Plum Crazy 1971 Challenger convertible seen earlier in this chapter. Trunk lock cylinder above "Challenger" script accepted only one key: the one with the round head on it. (The ignition key doubled as the front door key.) As with all Chrysler products of the time, the flat side of the key went on the bottom while using it. (Photo Courtesy David Newhardt)

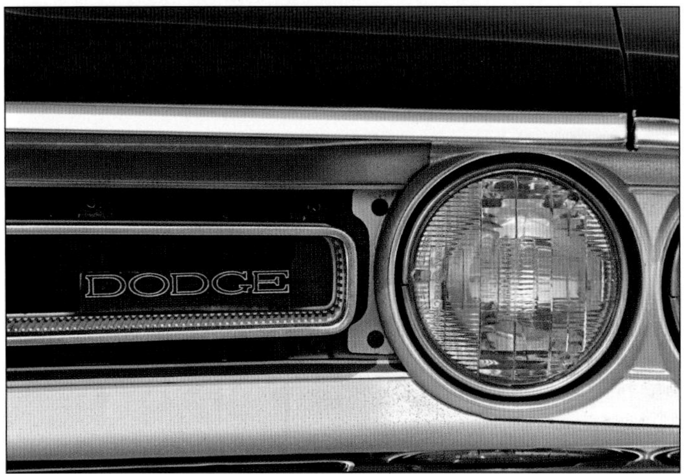

Close-up of the non-R/T Challenger's grille for 1971. A new grille with chrome inserts and "DODGE" letters inside it replaced 1970's concave grille. All Challengers had four headlights, the high beams mounted inboard (at right of photo). (Photo Courtesy David Newhardt)

Detail of the leading edge of the right front fender, showing front bumper's location relative to it. Starting in 1973, the Challenger's front bumper was repositioned forward, to make room for a steel reinforcing bar behind it that was necessitated by the federal bumper standard that took effect in 1973. (Photo Courtesy David Newhardt)

If you wanted a cassette player/recorder in your Challenger's factory sound system instead of the then-industry-standard 8-track tape player, Dodge had you covered for 1971. The newly available tape unit, housed in a pod mounted on the center console or on the floor forward of the shifter, cost $231.60 extra when combined with the AM radio in the Code R26 sound-system option, or $337.05 when combined in Code R36 with the factory AM/FM stereo radio. The R33 detachable microphone was a $10.75 factory option (and was also available as a dealer-installed accessory) while rear speakers were priced at $13.85 for the R31 single speaker or $25.05 for Code R33 dual rear speakers.

If you were to do price comparisons between identically equipped Challengers from 1970 and 1971, you'd likely end up with a worksheet that included these figures:

Base Challenger hardtop with 318, TorqueFlite Automatic, Airtemp air conditioning, and the A04 Radio Group, plus power front disc brakes, power steering, vinyl top, tinted glass whitewall tires and full wheel covers, very likely a combination of options that you'd see on a car in a dealer's inventory. The 1970 price was $3,913.05; the 1971 price was $3,985.45.

Challenger convertible with 340, 4-speed, Sure-Grip rear differential, Rallye gauges and Rallye wheels, and the A04 Radio Group. The 1970 was $4,114.90; the 1971 price was $4,097.85.

"Dandy" Dick Landy was the standard bearer for Dodge in the Pro Stock classes with his 1971 Challenger. He piloted the Hemi-powered Pro Stock/Super Stock cars, but in 1971 Landy faced a weight penalty program that unfairly disadvantaged the Challenger in class racing. He soon returned to match racing. (Photo Courtesy Bob McClurg)

Challenger R/T hardtop with 426 Hemi, 4-speed, Super Track Pak, AM radio, and no other options. The 1970 price was $4,584.75; the 1971 price was $4,523.90.

Drag Racing Domination . . . Again

Although factory support for the SCCA Trans Am program was gone, the factory-backed Hemi Challengers that began racing in NHRA's and AHRA's Pro Stock and Super Stock classes in 1970 kept going for 1971, along with "Performance Clinics" held at, or in conjunction with, local Dodge dealers in cities where they raced.

Foremost among the Challenger racers (and who presented the bulk of the "Performance Clinics" across the country) was "Dandy" Dick Landy, who'd been a fixture on the drag strips of Southern California since the 1950s. Back then, it seemed like there was a drag strip almost anywhere in the Golden State's "Southland": San Fernando, Irwindale, Pomona, Carlsbad, Lions Drag Strip in Long Beach, Orange County International Raceway, San Gabriel, Riverside; the list was long of the tracks that racers could run at, almost any day or night of the week, in some cases.

And run they did, in homebuilt cars in the Fuel, Gas, and Altered classes, and in production-based cars in the "doorslammer" (Stock) classes. The first three of those classes might have the most imaginative and exotic-looking cars (as well as the fastest and quickest), but it was in the Stock classes where novice and experienced racers alike could compete with their street-driver, in classes designed to match them up with racers of similar skill and equipment.

Dick Landy competed at San Fernando and other tracks between the mountains and the sea. He began winning more and more rounds in Stock class competition, which drew the attention of the team based in Highland Park that made Mopars go fast(er) on the strip. But it wasn't just a matter of winning rounds; it was how "Dandy Dick" won. He used his natural mechanical skills to wring more and more power from his engines, along with applying that power to the pavement that pushed his Plymouth to more and more round and race wins. He earned the "Dandy" nickname from *Hot Rod* scribe Eric Dahlquist for his immaculately prepared race cars and crew that went after, and won, Best Appearing Car and Best Appearing Crew prize money the way they went after wins on the track.

When the new E-Body Dodge Challenger appeared for 1970, along with heads-up classes in both NHRA and AHRA, where 426 Hemi Challengers could compete with their engines and wheels in their stock locations, along with a 7-pounds-per-cubic-inch weight rule, it was a natural for the new class, and Landy a natural to build and race one.

Landy's Challenger won only one race in NHRA Pro Stock in 1970, a season dominated by Sox & Martin's Hemi 'Cuda. (See Chapter 5.)

Indianapolis 500 Pace Car

For the 60th running of the Indianapolis 500-Mile Race in 1971, the Dodge Challenger convertible was front and center, serving as not only the Official Pace Car for the race, but also the Official Car of the "500" Festival. Those "festival cars" were given to Indianapolis Motor Speedway directors and other

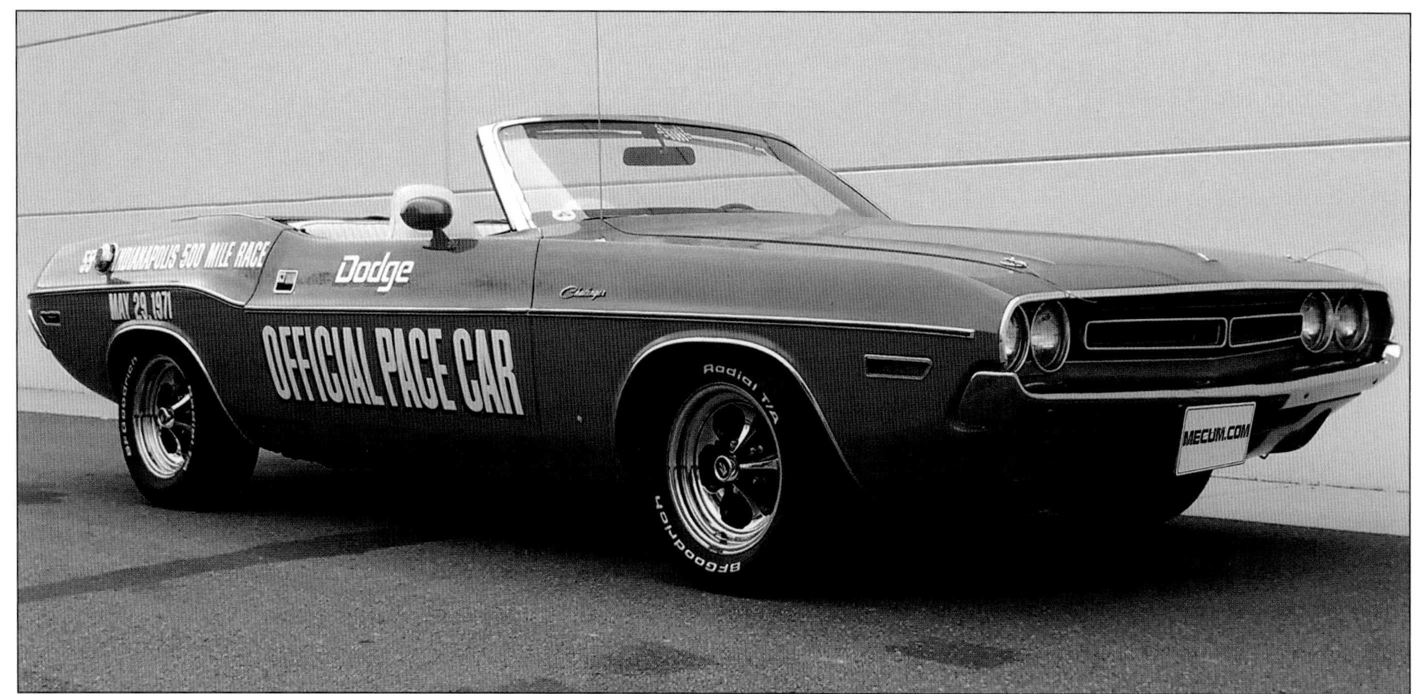

This is one of the "festival cars" that was part of the 1971 Indianapolis 500 Pace Car program put together by four Indianapolis-area Dodge dealers in early 1971. Note the Hemi Orange color with white graphics and white interior trim. Also note the aftermarket Keystone Klassic wheels, which are period-correct for 1971, as were the BFGoodrich Radial T/A tires, which wore different sidewall lettering in 1971. (Photo Courtesy Mecum Auctions)

dignitaries to drive during the month of May 1971 and appeared at race and 500 Festival–related events at that time.

In preceding years, manufacturers had not only supplied the Official Pace Car, its backup, and the "Festival cars," but also backed that program with large advertising budgets, as Chrysler had in 1963 when the Chrysler 300 Sport Series convertible paced the race.

When it came time to plan for the 1971 500, no manufacturer presented an Official Pace Car program to the Speedway, so a group of four Indianapolis-area Dodge dealers (Palmer Dodge, Capitol Dodge, McGinty Dodge, and Shadeland Dodge) picked up the slack and put together their own Official Pace Car/Festival Car program.

Those four dealers ordered 50 Dodge Challengers, all painted High Impact EV2 Hemi Orange with white interiors and tops. Two of them had 4-barrel 383s: the actual and backup Pace Cars; three had the 340, and the remaining festival cars were powered by the base 318. The two designated as the Official Pace Car and the backup were both built with drum brakes.

Eugene Piurowski, who owns one of the festival cars, told allpar.com there's a reason why features such as the Shaker hood scoop, elastomeric bumpers, and engines such as the 440 Six Pack and 426 Hemi, were not specified by the four dealers. "The reason that they were not 'loaded' models was that Chrysler did not supply the cars. None of the manufacturers wanted to supply cars that year as the muscle car market had dried up and publicity was being directed toward Dusters, Vegas, and Pintos. So the four local Indy dealers (led by Eldon Palmer of Palmer Dodge) purchased the fifty cars themselves."

Indianapolis-area collector Steve Cage, who owns the actual pace car, as well as the backup and look-alike 500 Festival Queen's Car, says that availability of Challenger convertibles in early 1971 was a problem. As he related to theindychannel.com, "Chrysler at the time was having trouble producing all of the cars, so the dealers went out and bought cars all over the country."

Given the lack of E-Body convertible sales up until then, it is possible that Highland Park had already decided to wind down drop-top production in anticipation of the Challenger and Barracuda lines becoming hardtop-only for 1972.

As for what happened on the day of the 500, the pace car was involved in an accident. Instead of a past 500 champion such as previous pace-car driver Sam Hanks driving the Challenger pace car, Palmer Dodge's Eldon Palmer was driving it and pacing the Indy 500 starting field in preparation for the start.

As the starting grid rounded Turn Four to take the green flag and start the race, the pace car was supposed to accelerate as it rounded the turn, then make a sharp left turn onto the pit road and then decelerate as the 33-car field roared past. This Palmer did, but he did not see the cone he had placed next to pit road as a reference point telling him where to start braking. Without the cone, Palmer missed the reference point, and the Challenger (with the 500's Chief Steward Harlan Felgler, as well as former astronaut John Glenn and ABC Sports commentator Chris Schenkel aboard) zoomed down the pit road, running out of room to safely stop.

Palmer then had a desperate, split-second decision to make: He could exit the pits and return to the track. Or he could try to make an emergency stop and in a hurry. Palmer locked up the Challenger's brakes and slid into a photographer's stand at the end of the pit lane and the entrance into Turn One on the infield. While no one in the stands or the car was killed, about 20 photographers were injured, and it was an unfortunate incident in the history of the Speedway.

Following the 500 (won for the second year in a row by Al Unser) Palmer kept the Challenger that he had driven, eventually restoring it and later selling it to Steve Cage, who promised the Palmer family that he was not going to sell it. Instead of taking the Official Pace Car, or one of the identical festival cars, as part of the winner's prize package, Al Unser received a yellow 1971 Dodge Charger, which has also been restored, and which Cage also owns.

1971 Challenger R/T, Reviewed

Motoring media attention toward the 1971 Challenger was nowhere near as extensive as it was toward the 1970 version, owing to the E-Body's second-year-in-production status and few major changes made to the 1971 Challengers.

In fact, the major motoring titles paid far more attention to the revised Charger, and new-for-1971 Dodge Demon and Colt, than they did to the second-year Challenger. Of note to the press were the all-new styling the Charger wore over the "pulled-ahead" B-Body platform that was shared with the E-Body; the minimal changes (e.g., front grille, taillights, nameplates) needed to the Plymouth Duster to make a Dodge out of it; and the late-in-the-year-arriving, built-by-Mitsubishi subcompact that gave Dodge a small car to compete against imports like the Volkswagen sedan ("Beetle"), Toyota Corona, and Datsun 510, and domestic-branded rivals such as the Chevrolet Vega, Ford Pinto, AMC Gremlin, and Plymouth Cricket.

One significant test of the 1971 Challenger did not appear in print; rather, it appeared on television, in a segment on the syndicated *Car & Track* program that veteran Michigan broadcaster and racetrack announcer Gordon "Bud" Lindemann hosted each week in many TV markets around the country.

In scenes that were filmed during late 1970 or very early 1971 (judging by the mustard-and-white 1970 Michigan license plates that were on the test car), the red Challenger R/T hardtop was put through its paces in one episode's 5-minute road-test segment.

Here's Bud's narration of that road-test film, which was loaded with run-by shots of the Challenger during acceleration, braking, and cornering tests, accompanied by the natural

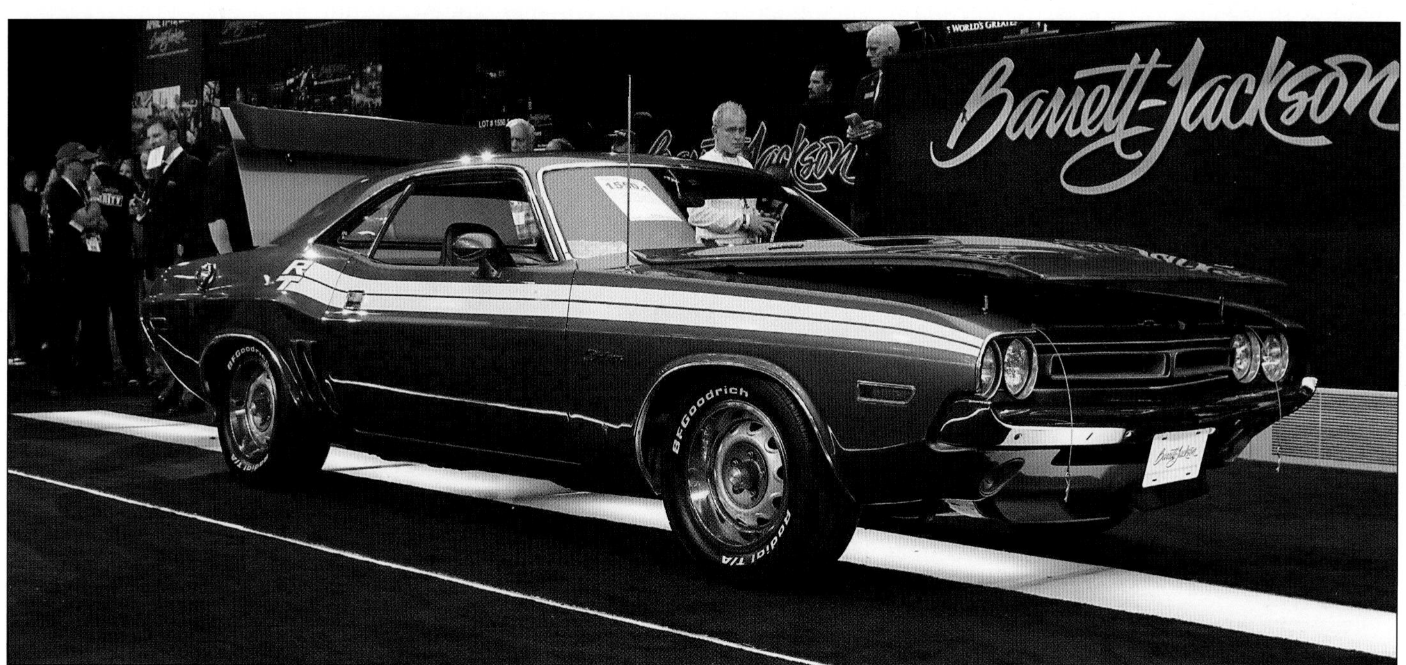

The 383 not only powers the 1971 R/T seen here crossing the block at a Barrett-Jackson Collector Car Auction, but it was the engine that powered the Challenger R/T that Bud Lindemann and his* Car & Track *crew road-tested during the 1971 TV season for their syndicated half-hour motoring and motorsports show, which was a staple of weekend television viewing in many of the nation's largest TV markets. A video of that test would make a great addition to the literature accompanying any 1971 Challenger R/T. (Photo Courtesy Barrett-Jackson Auction Company)

Thought this was a 1971 Challenger R/T convertible? Optional body-side stripes copied those of the R/T without those two letters at the aft end. The year 1971 marked not only the last one that the Challenger was available as a convertible, it was also the last year for the optional Plum Crazy color in the High Impact paint selection. High warranty costs from repainting cars whose Plum Crazy paint had either "chalked," faded, or peeled off led Chrysler to drop the color after 1971. (Photo Courtesy David Newhardt)

sound of that 383, as well as by production music similar to that used by NFL films:

"If you think this 1971 Dodge Challenger is hot, you're right. But it offers more than just a pile of muscle. The Dodge Boys put a lot of engineering know-how into this one, and it paid off in just about every department. Our driver twisted this Challenger every way but loose, and it looks like this:

"With tight money, and insurance premiums that are out of sight, the curtain could be falling on the 'supercar' era. But, nonetheless, they're still pure fun. And this Dodge Challenger has to be a contender for 'Pony Car of the Year.' It looks an awfully lot like last year's model. But then, what's wrong with that?

"In most pony cars, this 383 engine would cause heavy characteristics in the nose. But the Challenger is built to match the output of its bigger engines. In fact, with the 340 engine up front, the handling difference is hardly noticeable. When we brought our pony up to the line, it was happy time, and our speedometer found 30 mph in 2.8 seconds.

"That Hurst shifter was so smooth, we thought it was mounted in butter.

"On our second run, we nailed 45 in 4.7 [seconds].

"When we popped the clutch on our third time out of the hole, those big rubber doughnuts [Tires on the test car were bias-ply 70-series whitewalls, not the wider and lower-profile 60-series raised-white-letter tires that were the top choice on the Challenger option list.] bit hard into the asphalt, and that eight-fisted screamer had us to 70 in eight seconds flat. Our best shift point was at about 5,600 rpm.

"The car not only came out of the hole like its tail was on fire, but it negotiated the pylon course with comparative ease. After the first run, we shortened the distance between the cones by 10 feet, and the Challenger pushed through at 50 mph. Rebound, as well as recovery, was excellent.

"Braking in our test car left quite a bit to be desired. From 30 mph, it took 49 feet to stop. We had power-assisted discs up front, with 10-inch drums in the rear. From 50 mph, it took 86 feet to grind to a halt. The brakes pulled to the right, and noticeably so on high-speed stops. After five consecutive 70-mph panic stops, heat build-up was intense, [and] the pedal faded. This stop [where the test car slewed to the left, then did a 180-degree spin before stopping] took 211 feet!

"What it lacked in the braking department, it made up in cornering. This little pony was beautiful in the turns. Our driver ran it deep and hard into the pockets, and with that 383 cubic incher up front, he brought it through in a four-wheel drift with power on. This pony twisted through the corners on unequal-length A-arms, longitudinal torsion bars [and rear leaf springs], tubular shocks and an anti-sway bar [front and rear]. In high-speed corners, and with the slack out of the suspension, body lean was excessive, but it didn't affect roadability.

"The 1971 Challenger is one of the best pony cars we've tackled yet . . . "

A Hemi Challenger Company Car

As the other U.S. automakers offered to qualified employees, Chrysler had a "company car" plan where they could lease any new company-built vehicle, typically for a period of one year.

One of those employees was transmission and powertrain engineer Bob Cox, whose first choice for his first-ever company car in 1971 would be built with a 426 Hemi, backed by an A-833 4-speed manual transmission that he'd helped refine over the years. However, an E-Body car wasn't his first choice. "When I first became eligible for it, I ordered a Road Runner," he recalled in an interview with this author. "I was anticipating it, waiting for it. The guy over in company cars called up and said, 'We have a problem. St. Louis Assembly [where Bob's Road Runner was scheduled to be built] doesn't have any more Hemi engines. Do you want a 440?' I said, 'Not really.' He said, 'Think it over and call me back tomorrow, and let me know what you want to do.'

"I got to thinking. They use the Hemi in the E-Bodies, and they build those at Hamtramck. I had a friend there who I'd gone to the [Chrysler] Institute with, and I called him up and asked, 'Do you have any Hemi engines there?' He called back a few hours later and said, 'We have five engines, three automatics and two manuals.' So, I went back to the company-car guy and I said, 'Let's put it into an E-Body, and let's switch it over.' They did, and I got the car.

"It was TorRed, the orange-ish red, with a black interior. It had the Track Pak, no air conditioning, and it ran 13.70s/108 mph down at Milan [Dragway] through the exhausts on street tires. A friend of mine in the lab had a set of slicks that we put on it, and it ran 13.20s with the slicks.

"It was right at the top end of third gear, it really wanted to be shifted. I wasn't in the lights when it needed to be shifted; it was a toss-up whether you went through the lights in third gear, or in fourth. In third gear, you just had to level it out, and in fourth gear it was still pulling, but you lost a little bit of time shifting it.

"I got the car in the first week of June 1971. If it wasn't the last Hemi car built, it may have been the next-to-the-last one built."

He considered buying and keeping it once the lease was up. Unfortunately, he experienced something that many would-be retail Hemi buyers experienced. "It only had about 4,000 miles on it when I turned it in, and it would have been around $4,000. I could have afforded it," he adds.

Argent-silver paint around the headlights and grille indicates a non-R/T 1971 Challenger. This one wears the available J54 two-scoop Sport hood, body-side stripes, and W21 Rallye road wheels shod with raised-white-letter tires. Only 2,165 Challenger convertibles were built for 1971, a total too low for Chrysler to keep it in production beyond the end of the E-Body's second year. (Photo Courtesy David Newhardt)

Rear styling for non-R/T 1971 Challengers was highlighted by new taillights integrating the backup lights, residing in a chrome-trimmed flat-black taillight panel that was also new for 1971. Chrome exhaust tips with special cut-out rear valance panel was included with the convertible's optional 340 and 383 V-8s (Photo Courtesy David Newhardt)

"I called my insurance guys up, and they asked what engine it had in it, and I said a V-8. They asked what size, and I said 426 [ci]. They said, 'The Hemi?' They then said that they wanted $1,500 a year for insurance for it. So I told them, don't bother.

"It would have been nice if I could have just put it in my garage, but I had to have a driver. Plus, I had a race car (a stock car) on the other side of the garage."

As it turned out, that Challenger R/T instead went to the company-car marshaling yard located near the Lynch Road Assembly Plant. There, it was either sold to another Chrysler employee, or shipped to a Dodge dealer as a low-mileage "brass hat" used car.

Challenger Sales by the Numbers

If Challenger's sales, and those of its competitors, were disappointing in 1970, they were flat out disheartening for 1971. Per *The Standard Catalogue of American Cars 1946–1975,* a total of 29,883 1971 Challengers were built and sold, with 2,165 of them convertibles and 4,630 R/T hardtops, nearly a 66-percent drop from 1970's total.

Specific numbers regarding how many performance-engined 1971 Challengers were built (as cited in Paul Zazarine's *Musclecar History: Barracuda and Challenger*) detailed how bad the sales slump was. The base 1971 Challenger series saw 547 built with the 4-barrel 383 and a TorqueFlite automatic (9 coupes, 412 hardtops, and 126 convertibles), while just 156 base Challengers received the E65 383 and the D21 4-speed (8 coupes, 107 hardtops, and 41 convertibles.)

As for the Challenger R/T hardtop for 1971, its totals were 2,450 with the 383 (1,985 TorqueFlites, 465 4-speeds), 250 with the 440 Six Pack (129 4-speeds, 12 TorqueFlites), and 71 with the 426 Hemi (59 4-speeds, 12 TorqueFlites).

Although General Motors and its Fisher Body Division had solved the problem of wrinkled rear quarter-panel stampings that kept the second-generation Pontiac Firebird out of the showrooms for the first five months of the 1970 model year, a strike by the United Auto Workers against General Motors that started in September 1970 curtailed the supply of new 1971 Firebirds at a critical time early in that model year.

There were 53,135 Firebirds of all kinds built and sold for 1971. Although that was an increase over the number of second-generation Firebirds produced the year before, remember that the all-new Firebirds did not go on sale until late February 1970. Pontiac and General Motors management, likely hoping that the 1970 sales figure would increase to near 100,000 for a full year in 1971, were no doubt disappointed. This in a year that saw Pontiac drop to fourth place in the U.S. new-car sales race, behind Chevrolet, Ford, and a resurgent Plymouth.

It wasn't a strike that hurt sales of the all-new Mercury Cougar for 1971, but likely the "Cat's" larger size as mentioned above, as well as the overall slowdown in sporty-car sales. The 1971 Cougar sales tallied 34,008 base-series hardtops, 1,723 base convertibles, plus 25,416 XR-7 hardtops and 1,717 XR7 convertibles, for a total of 62,874. That was down nearly 10,000 cars (almost 14 percent) from the 1970 Cougar total of 72,365, per the *Standard Catalog of American Cars 1946–1975*.

The bloom was clearly off the rose when it came to sales of the Big Three's upscale pony cars.

In production for more than a decade before the first Challenger was built, the 383 was only available for one more year not only in the Challenger, but in all of the other Dodge and Plymouth E-, B-, and C-Body lines. This 383 Magnum delivers plenty of rear-wheel power but on regular gas. Only the 340, 440 Six Pack, and 426 Hemi required premium fuel in 1971. (Photo Courtesy David Newhardt)

The standard interior on Challenger hardtops and convertibles was this all-vinyl front bucket/rear bench seat combination, with the wood-grain three-spoke seeing wheel also standard. Compare location of the 4-speed's Pistol Grip shifter with the locations of those in the 4-speed 1970 Challengers and Barracudas previously seen in this book. An update for 1971 moved the shifter closer to the driver. (Photo Courtesy David Newhardt)

CHAPTER 5

1971 BARRACUDA
Small-Block, Big-Block and Hemi Glory

Like its Dodge sibling, the Barracuda retained the equipment that made it one of most revered muscle cars of the era. In fact, it had nearly all the same engine, transmission, trim, and color options of the previous year. However, for the Barracuda lineup, there was no more AAR 'Cuda, even though initial product plans called for a 1971 version and many of its special parts like the TA cylinder block, 3x2-barrel carburetor intake system, and side-exit exhaust system were still available through the "Hustle Stuff" parts program. The LA (Lightweight A) small-block lineup included the 318 and 340. It also meant no more 440 Magnum engine option, reducing 'Cuda's engine choices to three, which still included the 440 6-barrel and 426 Hemi.

Also gone was the Gran Coupe's convertible model, and the remaining Gran Coupe hardtop's standard engine was now the 318, instead of the 225 Slant Six. Speaking of the Slant Six, the 198-ci version finally appeared in the Barracuda lineup, as the standard engine in a new-for-1971 base-series coupe model. Intended as a sales-spurring price leader, the Barracuda coupe was notable for what it didn't have,namely, roll-down rear quarter windows (they were fixed in place), and a large selection of optional equipment.

Barracuda found itself shunted to the back of Plymouth's promotional efforts for 1971, with advertising and sales brochure copy for it focusing on its updated styling that featured four headlights and a "gill-like" grille in front and mildly updated taillights in back.

New for the 1971 'Cuda was the four-headlight front styling (shared with the rest of the Barracuda line), front-fender "gills," and the available "billboard" rear-quarter graphics that replaced the 1970s "hockey stick." (Photo Courtesy David Newhard)

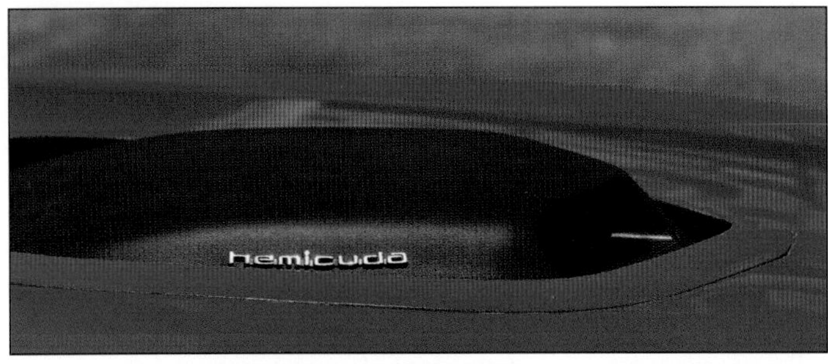

How rare is the 1971 Hemi 'Cuda? Only 114 were built with the Hemi. (Photo Courtesy David Newhardt)

Close-up view of the 1971-only four-headlight and six-"gill" grille that graced all Barracudas that year. Black item at outer edge of front valance is one of the "chin whisker" front spoilers that were part of the 1970 AAR 'Cuda package and were available as dealer-installed options in 1971.

'Cuda-exclusive auxiliary driving lights for 1970 were separate options, either dealer-installed or factory-installed, for all Barracudas for 1971. Light mounting location is approximately where the large rubber bumper guards were located on 1973–1974 Barracudas.

In back, Barracuda's taillights and backup lights received this redesign for 1971, which turned out to be a one-year-only feature. Black-painted taillight panel was standard on 'Cuda models.

This 1971 Hemi 'Cuda shows off the optional rear quarter graphics. They are as attention grabbing to the eye as the 426 Hemi's exhaust note is to the ear! (Photo Courtesy David Newhardt)

For 1971, updates to the Plymouth Barracuda were mainly visual. Seen here is the Hemi 'Cuda convertible that wears the new four-headlight front end styling that flanks a "gilled" grille, and non-functional front fender "gills" that were unique to the 'Cuda. Rear quarter-panel "billboard" graphics were a 'Cuda option that announced the choice of engine under the hood (383, 340, 440, or Hemi). (Photo Courtesy Mecum Auctions)

The available Rallye Instrument Cluster isn't on this Hemi 'Cuda. Was the car's original owner trying to avoid an insurance surcharge for having a tachometer? (He would have received a surcharge for the Hemi and the 4-speed.) The wood-grain steering wheel made its last original-equipment appearance in 1971. (Photo Courtesy David Newhardt)

Underhood plumbing was increasing for all American-built cars every year, not just under "Cuda hoods. The emission-control systems were required to meet increasingly tougher federal standards. The 426 Hemi had a Cleaner Air System just like the other engines in the 'Cuda and Barracuda lineup. (Photo Courtesy David Newhardt)

A close-up of the standard Barracuda and 'Cuda dash shows the stock 120-mph speedometer, as well as the fuel, temperature, and alternator gauges. Indicator lights (or "idiot lights") in the fourth round pod monitor other engine functions. The Music Master (Code R11) AM radio's left-offset knobs were a Chrysler exclusive. The anti-theft ignition key release lever could be operated by two fingers while switching the ignition off. (Photo Courtesy David Newhardt)

The Hurst-built Pistol Grip four-speed shifter was back again for 1971. (Photo Courtesy David Newhardt)

Getting the biggest promotional push were Plymouth's all-new B-Body Satellites, on a longer version of the same platform the Barracuda used. They had arrived for 1971 along with the subcompact Cricket, built by Chrysler's Rootes Group in Britain. The Cricket was a replacement for Chrysler's canceled "25 Car" small-car project, which was intended to compete against the all-new Ford Pinto and Chevrolet Vega, as well as imports from Volkswagen, Datsun, and Toyota.

One big change for Barracuda and all 1971 Plymouths that wasn't trumpeted was the demise of the five-year/50,000-mile limited powertrain warranty. A Plymouth mainstay and selling point since 1963, rising costs had caused the bean counters in Highland Park to cut factory warranty coverage for the 1971s down to 12 months/12,000 miles, whichever came first, on all regular-production cars, and far less coverage (6 months/6,000 miles for the original owner only) for the 440 6-barrel and 426 Hemi.

Power for 1971: Still Nine Engines

While the 440 Magnum was dropped from the 'Cuda's engine options, another engine debuted in the Barracuda for 1971. The 198-ci Slant Six was the standard engine in the new 125 gross horsepower (105 net) was bound to make performance-minded buyers ignore it altogether, unless they were planning to remove it and swap in a Hemi.

What else did the 198-inch Slant Six offer? "Regular gas operation, for cleaner exhaust vapors, more economy," said the *1971 Plymouth Dealer Data Book*. Other than the same features that the longer-stroke (by nearly 1/2 inch) 225 Slant Six had, including a forged-steel crankshaft, a "rugged, deep-skirt engine block," a long-branch intake manifold "for better fuel distribution and operating efficiency," as well as solid lifters and a full-flow oil filter, there was nothing else in the 198's standard features that differed from those of the 225. That engine, by the way, soldiered on unchanged for 1971, except for the change in horsepower figures, which dropped from 145 (gross) to 110 hp (net).

Also returning for 1971: the standard V-8, once again the LA-series 318-ci small-block, whose power numbers took a big

Factory 1971 Hemi 'Cuda wheel choices were simple: anything as long as they're 15 x 7 inches. Shown here isthe optional Code W21 Rallye Road wheel, a $54.25 option over the stock painted steel wheel with hub cap, that also required the available W34 space-saver spare tire (which was $12.55 extra). (Photo Courtesy David Newhardt)

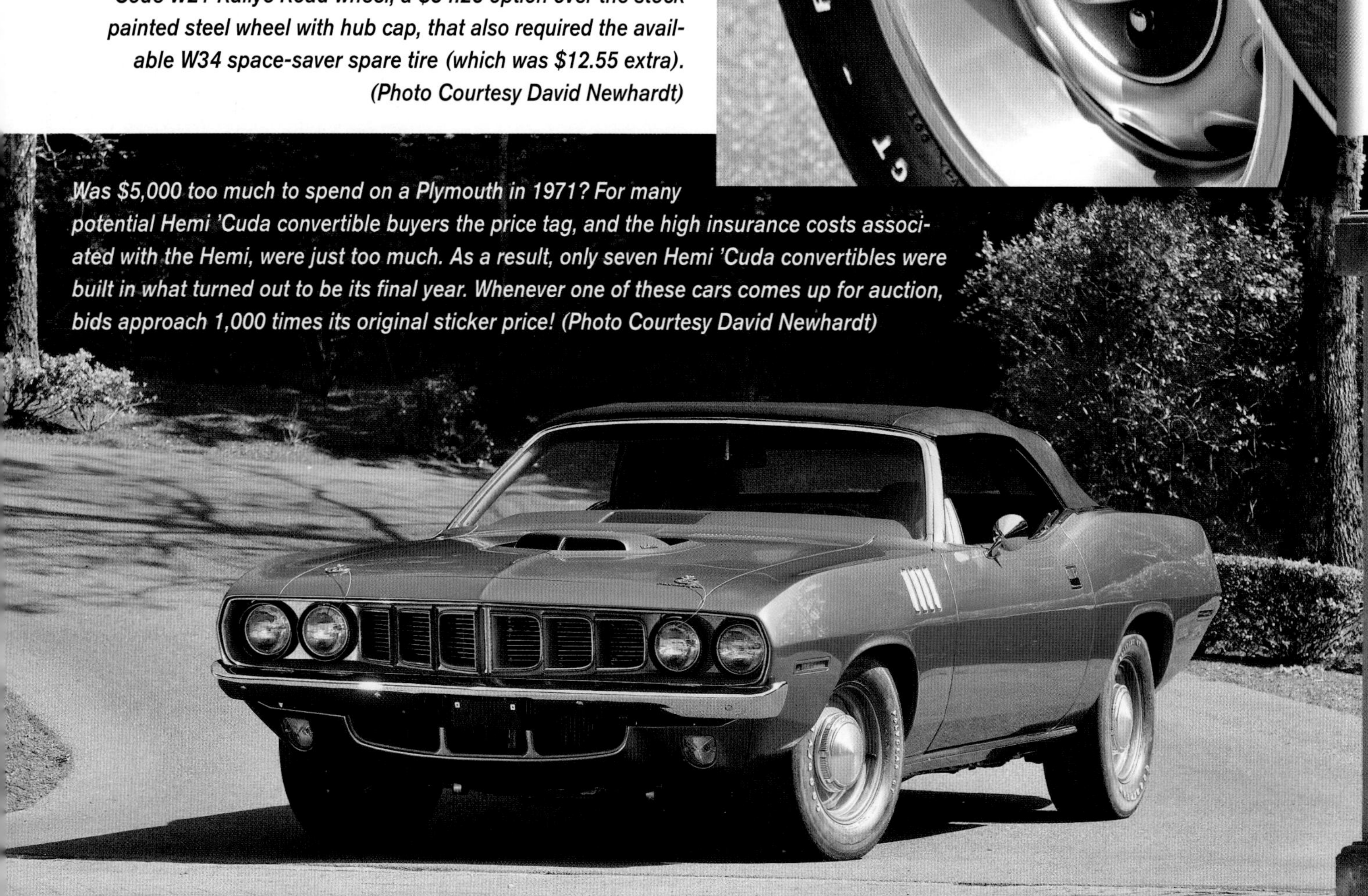

Was $5,000 too much to spend on a Plymouth in 1971? For many potential Hemi 'Cuda convertible buyers the price tag, and the high insurance costs associated with the Hemi, were just too much. As a result, only seven Hemi 'Cuda convertibles were built in what turned out to be its final year. Whenever one of these cars comes up for auction, bids approach 1,000 times its original sticker price! (Photo Courtesy David Newhardt)

No "billboards," and no Rallye wheels. This Hemi 'Cuda convertible is almost invisible, until you turn the key and the Hemi comes to life. B5 Blue exterior color was a popular Plymouth color choice through the 1960s and 1970s. (Photo Courtesy David Newhardt)

With the "Shaker" hood scoop/air cleaner removed, the 426 Hemi looks downright hungry! Note the two huge Holley four-barrels on an inline intake manifold. Also note that there's still room in the engine bay for a power brake booster (top right, just behind the master cylinder). (Photo Courtesy David Newhardt)

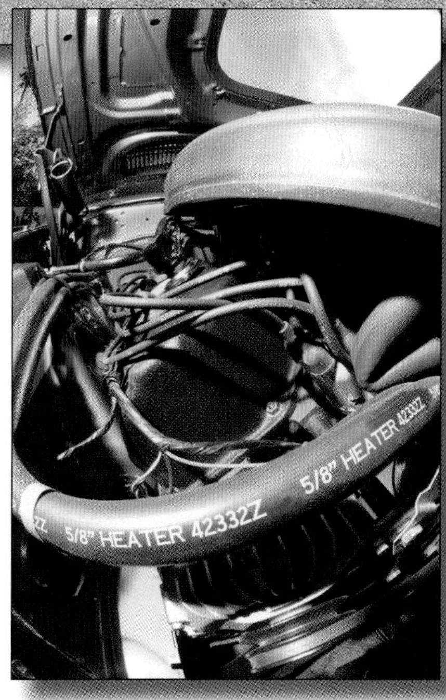

This is the inside of the Hemi 'Cuda's engine bay with the fight-side valve cover at center. Heater tubing at foreground routed coolant from the engine to the heater core under the dash. 426 Hemis were not ideal cold-weather engines and, they were a bear to try and start on chilly mornings. (Photo Courtesy David Newhardt)

Fender tag data indicates that this is a true, factory-built 1971 Hemi 'Cuda convertible, one of seven ever built, and one of just two with a 4-speed gearbox. Other items on this March 4, 1971–built 'Cuda include the Super Track Pack with a 4.10-geared Dana 60 rear end, Rallye Instrument Cluster, power brakes, tachometer, fresh-air ("Shaker") hood, and a power top. "Hemi Fender" on second tag means this car also received special front fenders with inner lips that were rolled inward for tire clearance. (Photo Courtesy David Newhardt)

drop from 230 (gross horsepower) to 155 (net) and whose standard carburetor changed from a 2-barrel Carter to a 2-barrel made by GM's Rochester Division).

Meanwhile, the available 383s saw their number decrease from three to two. The premium-fuel "Magnum" version standard in the 'Cuda gave way to a 8.5:1-compression, regular-gas-fueled engine that, while it did have a "high-lift, high-performance" camshaft in it, its factory horsepower output dropped from 330 gross to 250 net. The 2-barrel 383 carried over from 1970, with its horsepower ratings dropping from 275 (gross) to 190 (net), and had its crankshaft changed from a forged steel item to a cheaper-to-make cast-iron one during the 1971 model run. The milder-performance 4-barrel 383 that was optional on Gran Coupes and base-level Barracudas was discontinued, while the E61 2-barrel 383 saw its crankshaft changed from forged steel to cast iron, just as the E61 option in the Challenger was changed for 1971.

Fortunately for performance buyers, the three premium-fuel engines that were available on the 'Cuda (the 340, 440 6-barrel, and 426 Hemi) saw little in the way of changes for 1971. The 340 gained a new carburetor, the Carter Thermo-Quad, which replaced 1970's Carter AVS 4-barrel, to start the 1971 model year, while the 440 6-barrel's and 426 Hemi's induction systems carried over from 1970.

The most significant of the engine changes for 1971 came very late in the model year, when Chrysler made its new Electronic Ignition System (which delivered a "hotter" spark to the cylinders and did away with a conventional ignition's breaker points and condenser) standard on all 340s, as evidenced by a Plymouth Technical Service Bulletin (TSB 71-19-4, dated June 23, 1971), which told service managers and mechanics what was included in the new system and how to service it. Within three years, the Electronic Ignition System was standard equipment in every Plymouth. Another late-year addition to the 340 was the dual-breaker distributor, which was also standard on the 440 6-barrel and 426 Hemi.

[Author note: Starting in 1971, American automakers began reporting their advertised horsepower and torque figures in "gross" and "net" form per a Society of Automotive Engineers (SAE) standards change. "Gross" was determined with a test engine on a dynamometer without a factory-installed exhaust system, or items such as a factory fan, alternator, or other items that use engine power. "Net" figures reflected a test engine, still by itself on an engine dynamometer, but with those items installed.]

Transmissions: The Same, Yet Different

The transmission lineup that backed the Barracuda's engines (standard 3-speed manual, optional 4-speed manual, and TorqueFlite automatic) appeared unchanged on the outside, but there was plenty new inside them. TorqueFlites for 1971 gained a part-throttle-kickdown feature, which the *1971 Plymouth Dealer Data Book* said provided "quick pickup in traffic without fully accelerating the engine [and] provides instant response to the throttle after a slowdown." In practical terms, all you had to do to induce a downshift and resulting rise in engine RPM (and increase in sound) was to press down on the accelerator only until the kickdown feature dropped the TorqueFlite into second gear, thereby enabling quick and easy two-lane-road passing while letting the driver keep their hands on the steering wheel.

The A-833 4-speed received two significant upgrades from those that went in the 1970 Barracudas. One involved a new gear set developed for the AAR 'Cuda and was a midyear running change in 1970, whose gear ratios were closer together (2.44 First, 1.77 Second, 1.34 Third, and 1.00 [Direct] Fourth), which meant that engine speed wouldn't drop as much while upshifting as it did with the pre-1971 A-833. For the start of 1971 production, its shifter was moved closer to the driver, cutting down the reach needed to shift from second to third gears, or downshift to second from third.

Chrysler's powertrain engineers even paid attention to the standard 3-speed manual gearbox for 1971, redesigning its gear set for less tooth angle on the gear teeth, for easier and smoother upshifting and downshifting.

Color-keyed "racing mirrors," flush door handles, and 33-inch-radius ventless side glass were the features that many people who took a look at this 1971 'Cuda hardtop tended to look at, after one major feature of this car caught their attention: the 426 Hemi under the hood, denoted by "Hemi 'Cuda" badges on the Shaker hood scoop, and the rear-quarter "billboard" graphics, which announced that the Hemi powered this car. (Photo Courtesy Russo & Steele)

Body and Chassis: Changes and Carryovers

Once again, Barracuda was built using Chrysler's Unibody unit-body system and seven-step, dip-and-spray corrosion protection, and with the front torsion bar/rear leaf suspension that every Plymouth had been built with since 1957. Only, for 1971, the standard torsion bars were slightly smaller in diameter, like on its Challenger siblings, for a smoother ride.

'Cuda models once again featured a heavy-duty suspension system that contained front and rear sway bars on 340 and 383 'Cudas. The so-called "Hemi" suspension, comprised of extra-heavy-duty front torsion bars, rear leaf springs (with six leaves on the left and seven on the right), extra-heavy-duty shocks and a front sway bar, was still on the option list, as were the performance axle packages.

As in 1970, the A36 Performance Axle Package included a Sure-Grip and 3.55-geared 8¾-inch rear end (so named from the diameter of its ring gear), Hemi suspension, and a high-performance radiator with a seven-blade fan and fan shroud for 340 and 383 'Cudas with 4-speeds or TorqueFlite automatics, and was not available with air conditioning, while the A31 High-Performance Axle Package substituted 3.91 rear gears for the 3.55s and was also available on 440+6 and Hemi 'Cudas with the TorqueFlite automatic.

For the serious acceleration enthusiast, the A33 Track Pak and A34 Super Track Pak option groups were available once again for the 440 6-barrel or Hemi 'Cudas. Built around the legendary Dana 60 rear end, both Track Paks included a high-performance radiator/fan/shroud and Hemi suspension, along with a dual breaker distributor. The big difference between the two Track Paks was the rear gear ratio: The A33 Track Pak's Dana 60 had 3.54 gears in it, while the Super Track Pak's Dana 60 had a 4.10 gear set inside when code A34 was selected.

A significant chassis change was made to 340 Barracudas during the model year. From February 1, 1971, onward, 340 E-Body cars with power steering now received the quicker power-steering box from the now-discontinued AAR 'Cuda. It provided better road feel over the previous E-Body power-steering hardware, while cutting down the number of steering wheel turns lock-to-lock from 3⅓ to 3.

For years, Plymouth's thinking regarding second-year models after a major styling change was to carry over the colors and trims that had sold well the year before. Thus, the array of interior-trim choices available for 1970 largely carried over to the 1971 Barracudas.

The new base-level coupe models were only available with the standard-level all-vinyl front bucket/rear bench seats, with no cloth, leather, or split-front-bench seating option available in that price-leading model.

The new front grille is the only visible change to 'Cuda's front end from this vantage point. Hood tie-down pins weren't just for looks; they kept the hood from flying backward into the windshield if the hood latch ever failed while the car was moving. Note the fit of the bumper to the front fenders and compare it with the front bumper fit of the 1973–1974 'Cudas seen later in this book. (Photo Courtesy David Newhardt)

Non-functional front fender "gills" were a 1971-only styling cue for 'Cuda. The 60-series tires on 15 x 7 inch painted steel wheels were available on 'Cuda for the last time in 1971. (Photo Courtesy David Newhardt)

Vinyl side "Billboards" on 'Cuda models advertised either the engine's piston displacement for 340, 383, or 440 engines (or "Hemi" with the 426 Hemi). Popular among restorers and resto-modders alike, these vivid side graphics have been reproduced in recent years, with the exact colors and look of the originals.

While the Gran Coupe continued on as a separate model for 1971, its standard interior trim set (leather-and-vinyl front bucket and rear bench seats) were now optional on 'Cuda and base Barracuda hardtops as well.

"Elastomeric" bumpers were optional again in 1971, and not just on the 'Cuda. Like on the Challenger, they were available as either a urethane-covered-and-body-colored front bumper alone, or front-and-rear bumpers that wore a urethane coating between their foundation steel and acrylic enamel color coat. Meanwhile, the through-the-hood Shaker hood scoop was now available on all 'Cudas, not just the Hemi ones (where it was standard).

Unfortunately, the AAR 'Cuda's fiberglass hood, and its "ducktail" rear spoiler and side-exit exhaust system, were not available as regular production options in 1971, though savvy shoppers could get the hood through their Chrysler-Plymouth Dealer's parts department. The twin-scooped steel hood that was standard on 'Cuda for 1970 was now available on base and Gran Coupe models.

Exterior features that were new for 1971 included new deluxe 14-inch wheel covers that looked like a UFO's exhaust port and were shared with the Valiant and Satellite lines. The AAR 'Cuda's standard painted steel wheel/chrome trim ring/standard hub cap wheel treatment was now an option, with either 14- or 15-inch wheels, though the AAR 'Cuda's "staggered" tire sizes (E60x14 front, G60x15 rear) were not available as a factory option in 1971.

The biggest news inside the Barracuda for 1971 was the newly available cassette player/recorder. As with the Challenger, it was available with either an AM or AM/FM stereo radio, was fitted in a pod that sat just forward of the floor shifter location, and had a detachable microphone available as an additional option.

Aside from that, interior changes for 1971 were limited to the formerly optional wood-grain steering wheel now standard on the 'Cuda and the base Barracuda hardtop and convertible, while the rim-blow steering wheel became standard on the Gran Coupe.

Shaking things up atop this 'Cuda's 340-ci V-8 is the Code N96 Shaker hood scoop, seen here with the hood up. Note the Electronic Ignition System's orange control box on the firewall (at left). This car is a late-production 1971 car that had running changes, as well as the fast-ratio power-steering gear, which all 340 E-Body cars received in February of that year.

When it came to exterior colors, one new High Impact color joined the selection (Citron Yella), while Moulin Rouge, a midyear-1970 addition, was now special-order-only and not a regular-production item, while SubLime was no longer available.

Also no longer available: the "Mod Top" floral-pattern vinyl roof option. Available on Barracuda since 1968, it failed to attract enough buyers to keep that vivid floral-pattern trim available as a factory option. The matching floral-pattern vinyl seat trim option that Plymouth offered in 1968 and 1969 never made it into E-Body production.

Models, Options and Pricing

As with the 1971 Challenger, Barracuda's manufacturer's suggested list (sticker) prices for 1971 held the line, compared with those of 1970. In fact, while the price of a number of mechanical options like air conditioning, the optional 4-speed manual or TorqueFlite automatics, and available rear-axle ratios went up slightly, prices on the base Barracuda hardtop and convertible, the Gran Coupe hardtop, and the 'Cuda hardtop and convertible were actually lower in 1971 than in 1970.

One can chalk that up to a desire to make up for what turned out to be overly optimistic 1970 sales volume with a higher volume in 1971, where buyers would (hopefully) be more willing to buy a new Barracuda, thanks to the new lower starting prices. (See this chapter's last section to see how well that worked.)

A price leader among the 1971 Barracudas was the base-level coupe, whose sticker price started at $2,633 for the 198 Slant Six version, or $2,759 with a 318 V-8. For the $112 you didn't pay for the base hardtop, the coupe left off the rear quarter-window cranks (those windows were fixed in place), the cigar lighter, dual horns, and day/night inside rearview mirror that were all standard on the hardtop, and substituted an engine that produced some 40 hp less than 1970's standard Slant Six (which was a $39 option for the 1971 coupe).

Starting prices for the other 1971 Barracudas were lower than the 1970 base prices: the base-level hardtop's sticker now

Ground-level view of a 1971 'Cuda shows the revised taillight and backup-light design that was only used for this year. Also seen are the chrome exhaust tips that were routed through rear valance panel, which had holes for them stamped into it. In later years, owners of base-level Barracudas and Barracuda Gran Coupes that were factory-equipped with single exhausts wished that they had this valance on their cars, as many aftermarket dual exhaust set-ups installed on these cars did not look as "clean" as this factory installation. (Photo Courtesy Russo & Steele)

started at $2,745 for the Slant Six one, or $2,846 with a V-8, both nearly $20 less than in 1970. Similar price cuts were seen on the sticker prices for the Gran Coupe hardtop (which started at $3,008 for 1971, a $27 cut) and on both 'Cudas (the hardtop was now priced at $3,134 while the drop-top's MSRP started at $3,391), both some $30 to $40 less than in 1970.

If you wanted big power in your 'Cuda, your choices were the standard E65 383 4-barrel, the E55 340 ($44.35 extra and available only on 'Cuda); the E87 440 6-barrel V-8 ($253.20 extra, a slight increase over 1970's $249.55 tariff); and the E74 426 Hemi, the priciest of all the 1971 Barracuda options at $883.90. Neither the Hemi nor the 440 6-barrel was available with the standard 3-speed manual transmission; your choice was either the available D21 4-speed manual gearbox for $198.10 more, or the D34 TorqueFlite automatic, which was $229.35 extra with either the 440+6 or the Hemi.

'Cuda's optional axle and suspension packages were back for 1971, mostly. The S15 Extra-Heavy-Duty Suspension option for 340 and 383 'Cudas was no longer available, but the S13 Rallye Suspension option for 1971 included the Hemi's heavy-duty torsion bars, rear leaf springs, and shock absorbers. Pricing on the axle-packages ranged from $75.25 extra for the A36 Performance Axle Package on 340, 383, and 440 6-barrel cars ($41.70 with the Hemi), to $75.25 for the A31 High Performance Axle Package for 340s or 383s only; to $137.80 for the A33 Track Pak and its 3.54-geared Dana 60 for big-engined 'Cudas, to $201.75 for the A34 Super Track Pak and its 4.10-geared Dana 60.

The A32 Super Performance Axle Package did not return for 1971, and neither did the A35 Trailer Towing Package. Other options that did not reappear for 1971 included N89 Automatic Speed Control, M46 'Cuda Air Scoop, Quarter Panel and Black Lower Paint, C15 Deluxe Seat Belts, S79 Partial Horn Ring, and the A05 Barracuda Protection Group and A46 Exterior Trim Group options.

Magazine Road Tests

As the motoring press chose to focus on what was new for 1971, such as the aforementioned "subcompact" cars from Chevrolet, Ford, and AMC, their coverage of carried-over cars like the 1971 Barracuda concentrated on what was new and what changes emission-control rules and rising insurance costs were doing to performance, as a result.

When it came to the Barracuda, 1971-era road tests concentrated on the "hidden" performance engine in the line-up: the 340-ci V-8. *Hot Rod*'s Steve Kelly said in the January 1971 issue, "What this car does is deliver a no-compromise performance exhibition at all stages, be it handling, drag racing, street riding, or cross-country junketing." He added, "The 'Cuda 340 is a far better-driving machine than either the 440 or 426 'Cudas, and at least equals the performance you might expect from an assembly-line-stock Hemi 'Cuda."

Kelly's test noted the new-for-1971 Carter ThermoQuad 4-barrel carburetor, which had replaced the Carter AVS 4-barrel that had been standard on the 340 in 1970, had smaller primary jets than the AVS (1.38 inches versus 1.44 inches), but much larger secondaries (2.25 inches versus 1.69 inches). "It sure helps. It helps lower emission readings, especially at low engine speed, and keeps the top end running better when the demand is high. It is also a good icebreaker for Carter, and

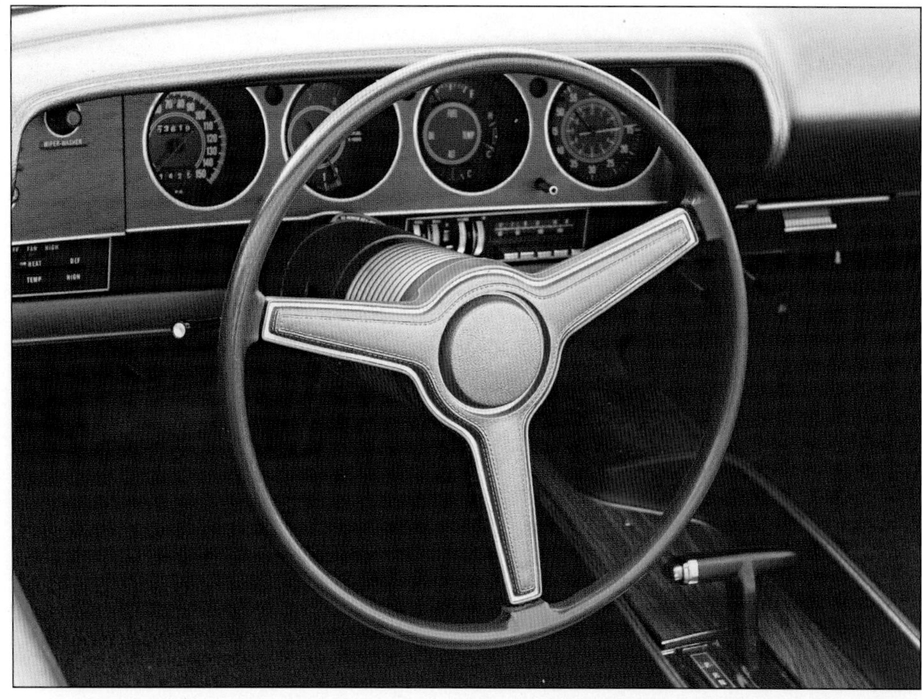

The 'Cuda's front cabin for 1971 included the available Rallye instrument cluster and center console, the latter containing the Slap Stik shifter for the heavy-duty TorqueFlite automatic the car was built with. Wood-grained three-spoke steering wheel was standard, as it was in 1970, but it was discontinued after the 1971 model run.

PRICING THE 1971 BARRACUDAS

If you want an example of how 1971 Barracuda sticker prices would look, here are some examples, as selected by the author, and by *Motor Trend* in its "How to Buy Your New Barracuda" buyer's guide, which was published in the December 1970 issue.

Back then, the 340 'Cuda was praised for its balanced handling and quick acceleration. These days, 'Cuda 340s bring top dollar from knowledgeable collectors when they come up for auction, like this 340 'Cuda convertible did when it crossed Barrett-Jackson's auction block. By the way, this isn't the same Sassy Grass Green 1971 'Cuda convertible seen earlier in this chapter. That one had a 383 under its hood and an accompanying 383 "billboard" on its right rear quarter. (Photo Courtesy Barrett-Jackson Auction Company)

Motor Trend Choice: Street Performance

"If you want a package that can corner as well as go straight, we'd recommend the 275-hp 340-ci V-8 with the Shaker scoop, again with the slap-shifter. Back this up with the A31 Performance Axle Package, and add the spoiler, cast aluminum wheels, and E60s. Secure it all with the hood pins, buying your own tiny locks. Don't forget the Rallye Instrument Cluster. For more go-straight action, we would put the 385-hp 440-ci V-8 with the 990 CFM "Six Pack" in place of the 340. With the 440, you order a different axle package, code named A36."

The prices for base vehicles and optional features are per the *1971 Plymouth Salesman's Pocket Guide*, which include 7-percent federal excise tax (which was repealed on August 15, 1971), but do not include state and local sales taxes or registration, title, license plate and state-inspection fees, or transportation charges.

Author notes: All 1971 Barracuda optional wheels were steel, not cast aluminum, which the 1969 "Recall" wheels were made of.

If you were ordering a Dodge Challenger, you would order the 440 Six Pack. Plymouth called the E87 engine option the "440 6-barrel." Plymouth *never* used the name "Six Pack" to describe that engine, or the 340 6-barrel that was in 1970's AAR 'Cuda. Ever.

Base Vehicle ('Cuda)	$3,134.00 hardtop, 3,391.00 convertible
E55 340 4-barrel V-8	44.35
E87 440 6-barrel V-8	253.20
D34 TorqueFlite Automatic Transmission	229.35
A31Performance Axle Package (with 340)	75.25
A36 Performance Axle Package (with 440)	75.25
A62 Gauges, Rallye Cluster with tach	76.75 with 440; 87.30 with 340
B51 Brakes, Power	41.55
B41 Brakes, Front Disc	22.50
S77 Power Steering	96.55
P37 Top-Power, convertible only	48.70
W21 Wheels, Rallye Road	54.25
T87 E60x15 RWL Bias-Belted tires	139.65
Total	$3,971.10 (340 hardtop) $4,228.10 (340 convertible) $4,436.95 (440 hardtop) $4,485.64 (440 convertible)

Author's Choice: Big-Block Performance

'Cuda hardtop, very well equipped with the 440 6-barrel:

Base Vehicle	$3,134.00
E87 440 6-barrel V-8	253.12
D21 Transmission, 4-speed manual	198.10
A33 Track Pak	137.80
C16 Center Console	53.05
B41 Front Disc Brakes	22.50
B51 Power Brakes	41.55
S77 Power Steering	96.55
G11 Tinted Glass (all windows)	36.85
C62 Seat, 6-Way Adjustable Driver's	32.20
J45 Pins, Hood Tie-Down	15.20
Paint, High Impact	13.85
Stripes, Quarter Panel Sport	37.55

PRICING THE 1971 BARRACUDAS CONTINUED

This 1971 Hemi 'Cuda convertible is painted in a factory High Impact color. This InViolet example was one of just 374 'Cuda convertibles built in 1971, and one of only 11 of those that rolled out of Hamtramck Assembly that were Hemi 'Cuda convertibles. The 15-inch wheels were the only size available with the Hemi, either with Code W21 Rallye road wheels or the stock steel wheel-with-hubcap seen here. (Photo Courtesy Barrett-Jackson Auction Company)

G36 Mirrors, Painted Sport, LH Remote	25.75
N96 Hood, Shaker	96.00
R26 Radio-AM w/Stereo Cassette	140.60
W21 Road Wheels, Rallye	54.25
U82 E60x15 RWL Bias-Belted Tires	51.65
W34 Spare Tire, Collapsible	12.25
Total	$4,452.82

Motor Trend Choice: Track Performance

"You were wondering perhaps when we would get to the 425-hp 426 Hemi? For drag strip work, we would mate it with the A34 Super Track Pack, the 4-speed and spec F60 treads. We would also insist on the Rallye Instruments and power front disc brakes. Racing mirrors could cut that extra .001 of a second?"

Author note: F60x14 tires were not available on 'Cuda, with any engine, E60x14 was largest OEM tire size available in 1971.

Base Vehicle	$3,134.00
E74 Engine, 426 Hemi V-8	883.90
D21 Transmission, 4-speed manual	198.10
A34 Super Track Pak	201.75
B41 Front Disc Brakes	22.50
B51 Power Brakes	41.55
S77 Power Steering	96.55
J45 Pins, Hood Tie-Down	15.20
G36 Mirrors, Sport, LH Remote	25.75
N96 Hood, Shaker	Standard with Hemi
U82 E60x15 RWL Bias-Belted Tires	51.65
W34 Spare Tire, Collapsible (required w/U82)	12.25
Total	$4,683.20

Author's Choice: Dream Come True

'Cuda convertible, extremely well-equipped with a 426 Hemi and 4-speed.

Base Vehicle	$3,391.00
E74 Engine, 426 Hemi V-8	883.90
D21 Transmission, 4-speed Manual	198.10
A34 Super Track Pak	201.75
C16 Center Console	53.05
B41 Front Disc Brakes	22.50
B51 Power Brakes	41.55
S77 Power Steering	96.55
J45 Pins, Hood Tie-Down	15.20
A22 Bumper Group, Elastomeric, Front & Rear	81.40
Paint, High Impact	13.85
Stripes, Quarter Panel Sport	37.55
G36 Mirrors, Outside Painted Sport, LH Remote	25.75
N96 Hood, Shaker	Standard with Hemi
R26 Radio-AM w/Stereo Cassette	140.60
U82 E60x15 RWL Bias-Belted Tires	51.65
W34 Spare Tire, Collapsible	12.25
Total	$5,266.55

The 1971 'Cuda was highlighted by the available "billboard" rear quarter graphics. In this case, they indicate a 383 under the hood. While 1971 marked the first year for four-headlight styling, it also marked a number of Barracuda lasts, namely, the convertible body style, engines larger than 340 ci, and many of the High Impact colors like the Sassy Grass Green seen here. Those items make cars built with them, such as this 'Cuda 383 convertible, quite valuable in the eyes of collectors. (Photo Courtesy Barrett-Jackson Auction Company)

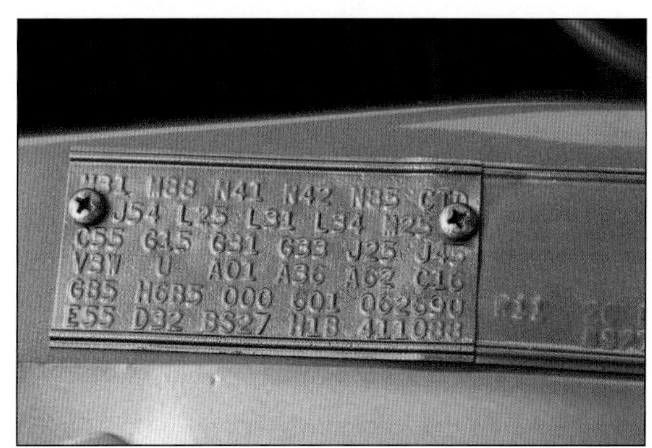

A 1971 'Cuda was well-equipped when it rolled down the line at Hamtramck Assembly on June 1, 1971, per the car's fender tag (which is affixed to the left front fenderwell under the hood). Options seen on it are the E55 340, heavy-duty TorqueFlite (Code D32), A01 Light Package, A36 Performance Axle Package with 3.55 rear gears, A62 Rallye instrument cluster, C16 center console, G15 tinted windshield, G31/G33 dual chrome sport mirrors, C55 bucket seats (in H6B5 bright blue vinyl), J54 sport hood (replaced by owner with Shaker), N85 tachometer, N41/N42 dual exhausts with chrome tips, M31 belt moldings, M88 decklid moldings, L34 road lights, M25 wide sill moldings, R11 AM radio, and painted Bright Blue Poly (GB5) with a white convertible top (V3W). The "601" code on the second line is the car's build date: June 1, 1971.

because it is now an original-equipment item, the price of the ThermoQuad may go down. Other than carburetion, the 1971 340 engine is like it was in 1968."

On the quarter-mile, the 340 shone, when entrusted to a driver like *Hot Rod's* John Dianna. Following a removal of the test car's spare tire, jack, and everything else in the trunk, Dianna ran the 'Cuda (which had 1,500 miles on it by that time) hard. Kelly continued, "Johnny then banged out a 14.53-second elapsed time, with a speed of 98.57 mph. The next trip was worth 14.41 seconds and 99.44 mph." Subsequent runs, after allowing time for the car to cool off and removing the stock air cleaner, dropped the ET down to 14.41 seconds and upped the trap speed at the end of the 1/4-mile to 99.44 mph.

"The Pure Stock record for the 'Cuda 340 class at Lions Drag Strip [a legendary track that was located near sea level in Long Beach, California, where the car was tested] is 14.09 [seconds] and a speed of 99 mph. At least we beat one end of the record. Had we gone deeper, say to the point of [ignition]

Only 114 Hemi 'Cudas were built in 1971 and only 59 of those pared the Hemi with an A-833 four-speed manual gearbox, as represented by this very special car. (Photo Courtesy David Newhardt)

timing or tire pressure experimentation, we would have bettered both marks."

Kelly also gave a tip to prospective Ronnie Sox wannabes regarding the best way to shift the A-833 4-speed manual transmission while under full power, a skill that Sox used to win round after round, and race after race, with his Pro Stock 'Cuda. "Chrysler Corporation 4-speeds are notoriously evil from gear to gear, because the gears are so large it's hard to get the synchros to line up quickly enough to make consistent power shifts. The higher the engine speed, the more time needed to synchronize (i.e., slow down) the next gear.

"Dianna began short-shifting the car on his third run, which eventually resulted in sub-14.20 second times. Not only did this prove beneficial to quarter-mile times, it put shift points closer to the peak torque curve. . . . Original shift points were [at] 6,000 rpm, and when we lowered them; 5,300 to 5,500 rpm was where the best times were earned. Short-shifting effected a temporary cure, but to further help the matter a Competition shifter might allow more consistent shifts without fear of gearbox damage. Even then, short-shifting will help stock-condition times."

The 'Cuda 340's manners away from the track also earned praise from *Hot Rod's* Steve Kelly. "It is a good road car, yet the rear suspension is stiffer than on the Z-28 [Camaro] and Boss 302 [Mustang], so wide tar strips and quick bumps are felt more in the 'Cuda. After a week's possession of the car, however, we didn't notice this.

"Steering is good, with only a hint of understeer. The rear [sway] bar and fat tires induce some oversteer to the car's angle of twisting around bends, so a driver never feels as if he's sliding his front wheels where they're not expected to go. Successive hard stops don't do a thing to the brakes except warm them up, after which they work better than when they are relatively cool."

Improvement in build quality was also noted in Kelly's test. "Chrysler Corporation has evidently taken steps to improve body quality. They have more to do, but this production-line car didn't leak air or water. Wide doors with large side glass probably aren't the easiest assemblies to install, and the ones on this car were wont to shake when rolled down or when the doors were shut."

Kelly summed up the 1971 'Cuda 340 this way: "Barracudas of all shapes and sizes are now in a declining part of the new-car market. This is too bad, but it is fact. Despite there being fewer people buying this kind of car now than two years ago, there's no apology needed from this car's manufacturer for it being the fault of the product. A 'Cuda 340 is a super super-car."

High-Performance CARS' assessment of the 1971 'Cuda 340 also touched on the car's handling prowess. "The 'Cuda 340 is a handling machine, not a stoplight street racer," it said in its road test in its June 1971 issue. "Handling and suspension are the 340-inch 'Cuda's bag." They added, "It's a far better handling car than the 'big Gun' models stuffed with 383, 440 or 426 Hemi power. . . . It's obviously lighter than the bigger-engine jobs and even 90 pounds lighter than the standard 383 4-barrel ['Cuda] version. Where the 340 excels is in the handling department. It hardly leans, only slightly oversteers, and stops . . . and stops . . . and stops. The power discs do their thing in grand style. In addition to the heavy springs and shocks, Plymouth also throws in .088-inch torsion bars and front and rear stabilizer bars. The bars are not available on the 440 and 426 Hemi models.

"Everything costs, and the suspension is no exception. And we're not talking about money. You pay in other ways. Like reacting to every tar strip, pothole and other normal road disturbance. All this translates into a certain degree of discomfort (if you're over 30) and lots of rattles. Usually, the stiffer the suspension, the more the rattles. This 'Cuda rattles. And the super-size doors with huge glass panels certainly didn't help any. The door/glass situation makes for a serious problem in the way of fit and water and air sealing. The 'Cuda suffers in those areas."

The Carter ThermoQuad 4-barrel came in for scrutiny by *High-Performance CARS*, too. "The only change for 1971 is a carburetion substitution, made mainly for pollution control. Strangely enough, it also seems to help in the performance department. This year, the throne is occupied by a Carter ThermoQuad, with smaller primaries and larger secondaries than the AVS model it replaces. This means increased low-end response and cleaner top-end running, but not any improvement in top end power."

Unfortunately, the *High-Performance Cars* staff who wrote the article without credit weren't impressed by the A-833 4-speed, or having to short-shift it on the drag strip for best results. "Overall, it wasn't fun to drive. The 4-speed shifted better than its predecessors, but still left much to be desired."

Per their test data and commentary in the story, they were never able to get their 340 'Cuda to run quicker than the high-14-second range, unlike *Hot Rod*'s Steve Kelly and John Dianna, who did.

What else was High-Performance Cars not impressed by? How about that new-for-1971 front end styling? "All we want to know is why Plymouth couldn't leave well enough alone. They killed the frontal appeal with four headlights and a goofy grille treatment. Last year's front end was sleek, smooth, and hairy, tying the whole package together." They also didn't like the Shaker hood scoop or 4-speed either. "The shaker scoop does little more than add unnecessary weight, more cables, and extra bucks onto the already impressive sticker. The 4-speed is still one of the bigger wastes on the option list."

It concluded, "The trunk and back seating are almost non-existent, but the wheelwells can handle the biggest possible tires. Racers will appreciate that. But how many 'Cudas can Plymouth sell to racers?"

Sales by the Numbers

There's only one word to describe 1971 Barracuda sales, when comparing them with those of 1970: terrible.

Only 14,808 1971 Barracudas were built, a steep drop over 1970's 55,499 total. Per Paul Zazarine's *Musclecar Color History: Barracuda & Challenger*, that total worked out to 592 Barracuda coupes, 6,508 Barracuda hardtops, 722 Barracuda

From the rear, the 1971 'Cuda still featured dual exhausts through the rear valence panel under the bumper and a matte black-painted taillight panel as standard features. The new vinyl rear-quarter "billboard" stripes were $37.55 extra. (Photo Courtesy David Newhardt)

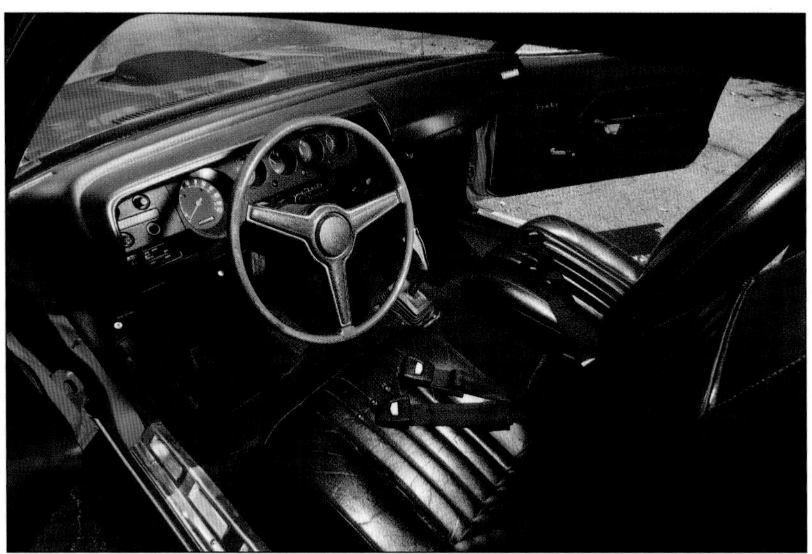

Performance meets style in this Hemi 'Cuda's cabin. Seats are the available leather/vinyl front buckets/rear bench, and simulated woodgrain covers the dash around the Rallye Instrument's cluster and console the same way it covers the steering wheel rim and Hurst "Pistol Grip" shifter. (Photo Courtesy David Newhardt)

convertibles,1,331 Gran Coupes, 5,383 'Cuda hardtops, and 292 'Cuda convertibles.

Only 206 base Barracudas received the A65 383 4-barrel V-8 (among them, 93 had 4-speeds), while only 114 Gran Coupes were powered by that regular-gas 383. 'Cuda engine selections included 3,435 with the 340 (2,005 hardtops and 102 convertibles with the automatic, 1,141/30 with the 4-speed and 154/0 with the 3-speed), 1,422 with the 383 (1,168 hardtops/87 convertibles with 383/TF, 501/33 with 383/4-speed and 67/16 with the 383/3-speed), 254 with the 440 6-barrel (129/12 with TF and 108/5 with 4-speed), and only 114 1971 were built with the 426 Hemi (48/5 with TF, 59/2 with a 4-speed).

A further breakdown of options ordered by Barracuda buyers for 1971 (and listed in the *1972 Plymouth Advance Product Information* flyer that Chrysler-Plymouth Dealers received during the late spring/early summer of 1971) showed that the TorqueFlite automatic transmission was installed in 78.9 percent of 1971 Barracudas, while 78.1 percent of them were built with power steering, 40.2 percent were factory-equipped with the W21 Rallye Road Wheel option, and nearly all 1971 Barracudas (97.2 percent) were equipped with one of the available factory-installed sound systems ranging from the single-speaker R11 pushbutton AM radio to the high-zoot R36 AM/FM stereo radio with stereo cassette tape player and recorder.

Meanwhile, 31.9 percent had an optional V-8 under its hood; 22.4 percent had power front disc/rear drum brakes; 31.4 percent had tinted glass; 29.8 had Airtemp air conditioning; and 49.1 percent had vinyl tops.

Color-wise, again per *1972 Plymouth Advance Product Information*, True Blue Metallic (GB5) was the most popular color, sprayed on to 10.4 percent of the 1971 Barracudas. Following it, in order of popularity, were the High ImpactTorRed (Code EV2), 10.1 percent; Rallye Red (Code FE5), 9.6 percent; Curious Yellow (Code GY3, High Impact), 8.7; In-Violet Metallic (Code FC7, High Impact), 7.2 percent; Sherwood Green Metallic (Code GF7), 6.6 percent; Bahama Yellow (Code EL5, High Impact), 6.4 percent; Autumn Bronze Metallic (Code GK6), 5.9 percent; Amber Sherwood Green Metallic (Code GF3), 5.8 percent; Gold Leaf Metallic (Code GY8), 4.9 percent; Sassy Grass Green (Code FJ6, High Impact), 4.8 percent; Sno White (Code GW3), 4.4 percent; Tawny Gold Metallic (Code GY9), 3.8 percent; Evening Blue Metallic (Code GB7), 2.8 percent; Glacial Blue Metallic (Code GB2), 2.6 percent; Winchester Gray Metallic (Code GA4), 2.2 percent; Formal Black (Code TX9), 2.1 percent; Tunisian Tan Metallic (Code GT2), 1.6 percent; and Lemon Twist (FY1, High Impact), .1 percent

The sales picture wasn't any rosier at General Motors, Ford, or AMC for their 1971 pony cars.

Losing over two months to a strike didn't help Camaro's sales. In a year when Chevrolet sold three million cars and trucks, and in the first full-model-year of second-generation F-Body production, Camaro accounted for only 107,495 of Chevy's total, including 18,404 Rally Sports, 8,377 Super Sports, and 4,862 Z28s. Camaro buyers (per the *Standard Catalog of American Cars 1946–1975*) were particular in the features they wanted: more than 103,000 1971 Camaros had V-8s in them, nearly 91,000 had either Chevy's venerable Powerglide or GM's more-modern TurboHydraMatic automatic transmissions; more than 93,000 were equipped with power steering; 10,614 had 4-speed manual gearboxes; and 42,537 rolled out of GM's assembly plants with factory air conditioning.

The much-changed Ford Mustang saw another sales drop, to a total of 149,676 1971s, down over 22 percent from 1970's 190,727. The base Mustang coupe was the line's top seller, with 65,696 rolling out of Ford's Metuchen, Dearborn, and San Jose assembly plants. The next biggest seller was the Mach I SportsRoof (36,449), the base-series SportsRoof fastback (23,956), the plushed-up Grande coupe (17,406), the base convertible (6,121), and the Boss 351 SportsRoof (1,806).

Then, in third place, ahead of Barracuda, came the AMC Javelin. Despite AMC's continued support of the Penske Javelin team in SCCA's Trans-Am series, only 28,866 Javelins in all were built in 1971. That included 7,105 base-series Javelins, 17,707 midrange Javelin SSTs, and 2.054 Javelin AMXs.

From top to Bottom: No tach? No problem, as long as an aftermarket rev counter goes in. Underhood plumbing (and lots of it!) was common on 1971-vintage U.S.-made cars. The Hemi 'Cuda medallion has been reproduced in recent years, but only 114 'Cudas received it at Hamtramck in 1971. (Photo Courtesy David Newhardt)

Changes were in the wind for 1972, not just for Barracuda but for Mustang and all of those competing with it. These weren't going to be good changes for any of the Big Three's pony cars, except to the bean counters who were only too happy to cancel models, body styles, and optional features if the preceding year's sales numbers didn't give them a reason to continue them.

"Owning" Pro Stock/Super Stock

If the SCCA's Trans-Am Series seemed like a natural for the 340 E-Body Barracuda (especially with Dan Gurney's All American Racers team building the cars and Dan and Swede Savage driving them) the Hemi 'Cuda was a natural fit for NHRA's Pro Stock class and its counterpart in AHRA and IHRA-sanctioned drag racing.

Because U.S. manufacturers, especially Chrysler, began getting more and more involved with production-based drag racing cars as the 1960s dawned, the Stock classes turned from a division where local hot shoes drove production-based cars into one where local hot-shoes driving production-based Plymouths were consistently beating their Ford and GM competition. In more than a few instances, setting up all-Mopar final rounds where two Plymouths, or a Plymouth and a Dodge, would run for class championships or "Mr. Stock Eliminator" titles.

For 1970, both NHRA and AHRA had classes for factory-based steel bodied Super Stock cars: NHRA's Pro Stock and AHRA's Super Stock Eliminator, and GT-1 class. Running heads-up with no "handicap" starts, these classes were intended to give pro teams, such as Sox & Martin, a class where the quickest of the "doorslammers" would pack the race fans into the grandstands the same way that Top Fuel Dragster did. This was especially so after the NHRA ended its ban on using nitromethane as a fuel after the 1963 season and Funny Car did it after it became an NHRA Eliminator.

Like Ronnie Sox and Buddy Martin themselves, the E-Body Barracuda was a natural for Pro Stock, especially with the 426 Hemi, Dana 60 rear axle assembly, and ultra-heavy-duty, 18-spline A833 4-speed manual transmissions on the list of factory-installed equipment starting in 1970, and a customer could order a Hemi car built on the line at Hamtramck, for no more than $5,000.

By way of comparison, their Blue Oval competition, the Ford Mustang Boss 429, needed to have its Blue Crescent engine installed at a separate facility away from Ford's Dearborn, Michigan, assembly plant. There, the 428 Cobra Jet V-8 the car was built with was removed, the front shock towers cut and moved outboard (as well as other modifications that could not be done on the assembly lines), and the massive engine installed before the car was returned to Ford for shipment to the selling dealer.

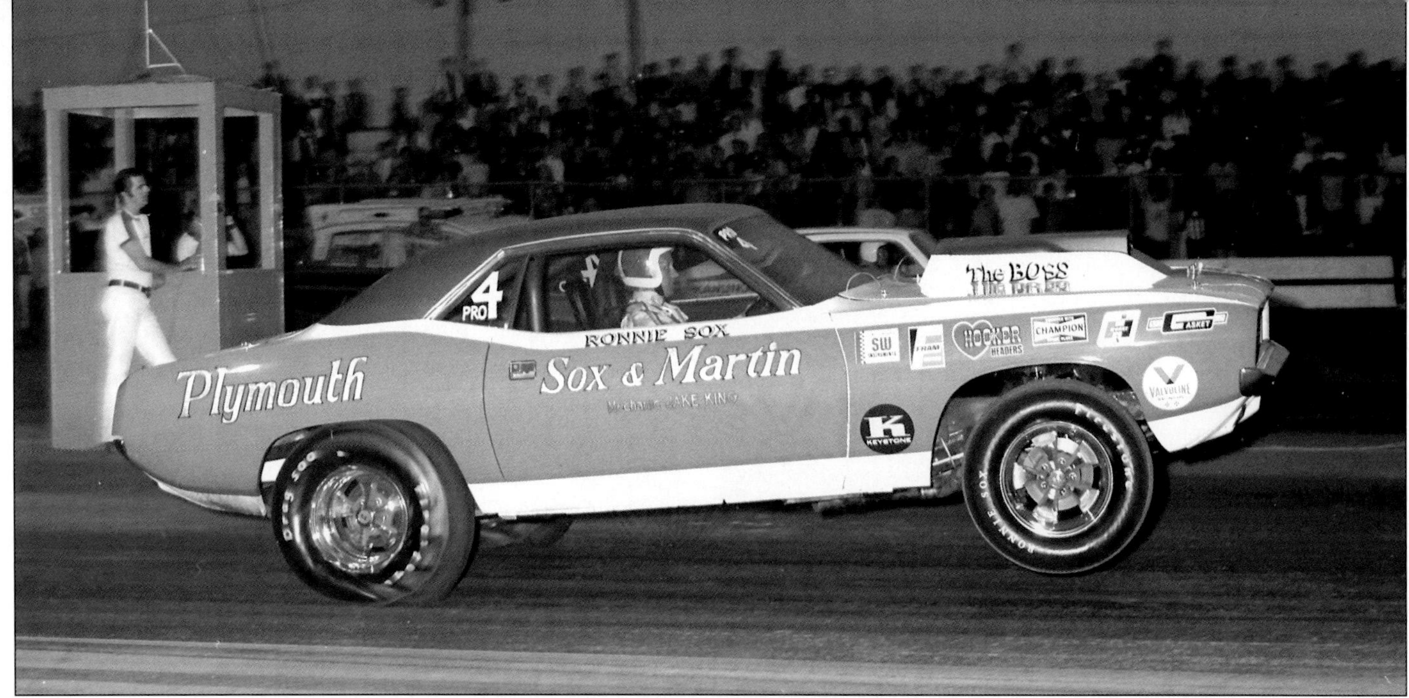

During their heyday, Sox & Martin won at the "big" tracks like Indianapolis Raceway Park, California tracks like Lions Drag Strip in Long Beach, Pomona Raceway, and Famoso Raceway near Bakersfield, as well as tracks in or near small towns from coast-to-coast. (Photo Courtesy Bob McClurg)

As for Chevrolet, the Mark IV big-block V-8s they raced with in the late 1960s were not regular-production Camaro options, but special, limited-run Central Office Production Order (COPO) builds that were an end-run around standard GM ordering and production procedures. In 1969, their COPO for the all-aluminum ZL-1 427-ci engine nearly caused heart attacks among the nation's high-performance Chevrolet dealers, who saw an option they hoped would be priced under $600 cost about 10 times that on a so-equipped base Camaro's invoice and sticker price. For 1970, Chevrolet's highest-output big-block V-8s (the 454-ci LS6 and LS7 versions) weren't even available on the 1970 Camaro as a COPO after the second-generation Camaro entered production in late 1969, but only through Chevrolet's parts operation as a "crate engine."

Armed with a new Hemi 'Cuda for 1970, Sox & Martin took the tracks by storm. In NHRA Pro Stock competition, they won the NHRA's Springnationals and World Finals, and made it to the finals at the Winternationals, and Gatornationals with their Hemi 'Cuda, while adding a U.S. Nationals Pro Stock win at Indianapolis Motorsports Park with a 1970 Plymouth Duster driven by teammate Herb McCandless. They capped 1970 off with a win at NHRA's Supernationals with their updated-to-1971 Hemi 'Cuda.

But it was in AHRA's Super Stock Eliminator division and GT-1 class where Sox & Martin and their Hemi 'Cuda had their biggest success in 1970. Out of ten AHRA national events where they entered, Sox & Martin won Super Stock Eliminator a staggering seven times, with three runner-up finishes (one of those with their Duster), along with four GT-1 class wins.

If that wasn't enough, *Super Stock & Drag Illustrated*'s Nationals was the site of yet another Sox & Martin Pro Stock win in 1970 with their Hemi 'Cuda.

Once again in 1970, Sox & Martin incorporated Performance Clinics into their national-event and match-race schedule. They appeared at dozens of them, at Chrysler-Plymouth dealers and at racetracks hosted by the local dealers, where they passed along their knowledge of engines, transmissions, chassis set-ups, driving techniques, and other information that clinic attendees could use to run better, run quicker, run faster, and win more often.

The 1971 model year saw the return of Sox & Martin to the strip (and to the dealers' Performance Clinics) with their updated-for-1971 Hemi 'Cuda. Racing in NHRA Pro Stock, they scored six wins, and NHRA's World Championship in Pro Stock for the second straight year in national-event competition, plus many more round wins in match races across the country on weekends when NHRA wasn't holding their big events. Same for IHRA events in 1971, seven wins in seven races for the red/white/blue Hemi 'Cuda.

Unfortunately for Sox & Martin, as well as every other drag racer who raced and won with a Hemi E-Body, changes were approaching for 1972 that were intended to "even out" the competition in Pro Stock by making the 426 Hemi cars carry more weight. (Some say that constant whining and complaining by a certain Chevrolet team based in southeastern Pennsylvania had a lot to do with it.)

Also unfortunate: The demise of the Performance Clinics. With the end of the 1971 season, Chrysler chose not to conduct them any longer, and they passed into memory. But not before more than a few die-hard Mopar devotees not only found out what they needed to win on the strip, but what it took to win consistently.

CHAPTER 6

1972 DODGE CHALLENGER

A Different Pony Car for a Different World

By the 1972 model year, the curtain was quickly closing on the muscle era, and consequently the 1972 Challenger lineup was greatly affected and thus curtailed. Engine options and performance greatly diminished in 1972. Engine options dropped from seven to three, and thus only the 225-ci slant-6, 318, and 340 V-8s remained. Compression ratios were softened so these engines could be run on unleaded gas and horsepower was now calculated by SAE net calculations. The Rallye series replaced the R/T trim level, several performance axle packages were dropped, and a convertible was no longer offered.

Styling Update: A Third-Year "Freshening"

Styling updates for the 1972 E-Body cars were well underway when the 1970 Dodge Challengers began rolling off the Hamtramck and Los Angeles assembly lines in August 1969. With the lead time needed to turn Styling concepts into production vehicles (which common auto-industry wisdom put at 24 months, even for minor changes), Dodge's stylists were already hard at work on the 1972 Challenger's looks by then.

Diran Yasajian, who managed E-Body styling in the Dodge Exterior Styling Studio at the time of the third-year upgrade, told this author that the new front end and taillight styling for 1972 resulted from a normal design program. "The designers made sketches and put them on the wall, the big bosses came in and picked them [those they approved of], and they clayed them up. That was the process that we used for all cars."

The new grille extended below the line of the front bumper, giving the 1972 Challenger what some called a "hungrier" look than its 1970–1971 predecessors. In back, the long, rectangular taillights gave way to a pair of oval-shaped light pods, the outboard ones containing the turn signals and brake lights, the inboard ones the back-up lights, on either side of chrome "D-O-D-G-E" lettering that was centered in the taillight panel.

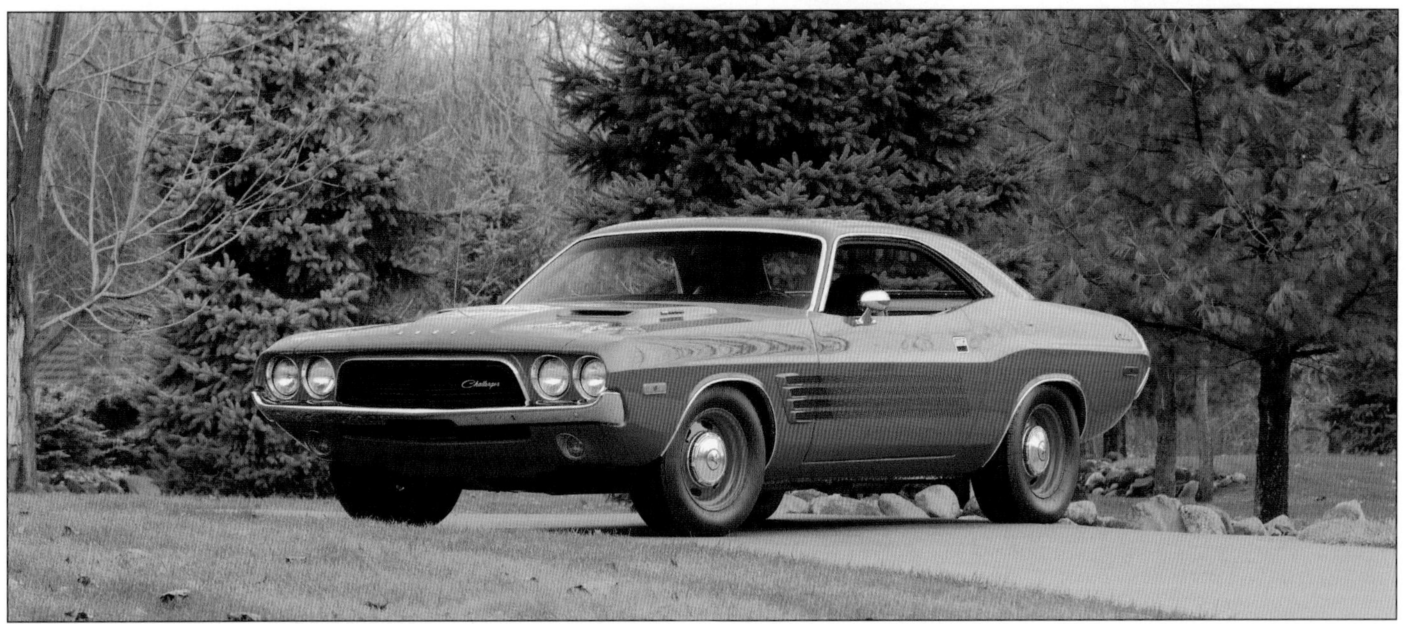

For 1972, the Challenger was pared down to one body style, and two models: base Challenger and Challenger Rallye, which replaced the R/T. This Hemi Orange Rallye wears the slotted 15 x 7–inch Chrysler factory 1978–1989 "Police" wheels. That direct-replacement swap easily replaces the stock 14-inch wheels that were the only size available in 1972. (Photo Courtesy Mecum Auctions)

Before the first Dodge Challengers entered production in the summer of 1969, succeeding-year styling updates were already well underway in the Dodge Exterior Styling studio. Here's one of Bob Ackerman's early renderings for the 1972 update, hinting at the size of the grille that would eventually make it into production, and may have been one of the choices for the standard Challenger and Challenger SE. (Photo Courtesy Bob Ackerman)

Another one of Bob Ackerman's renderings prepared while the 1972 styling update for the Dodge Challenger was underway. This one shows a grille that more closely resembles the black-painted grille that went into production as the standard Challenger Rallye grille. Also note the Shaker hood scoop above the grille. The thought of that scoop, and the big-power engines that went under it, disappearing from the Challenger's option list was not even a remote possibility at that point. (Photo Courtesy Bob Ackerman)

A study in contrasts: the Hemi Orange and matte-black colors on this 1972 Challenger Rallye's body and taillight panel. The dual exhaust system was a carry-over from 1970 and 1971, which made the regular-gas 340 under the hood sound like a performer, even if its output fell short of its 1968–1971 predecessor, (Photo Courtesy David Newhardt)

The large grille was the only front-end styling change for 1972 and would be used on all E-Body Dodges from 1972 onward. Grille and surrounding headlight panel fit within the location where the 1970 and 1971 grilles were once installed. (Photo Courtesy Mecum Auctions)

Still only 8 cubic feet in size was Challenger's trunk for 1972, which could have used the formerly available "space saver" spare tire to maximize the available cargo room. Alas, that option did not return for 1972.

For the third year in a row, the Challenger received a new taillight/backup light design. For 1972, they're each located in their own pods. Black-painted taillight panel was standard with Challenger Rallye; on base models, it was painted argent silver.

Even though the snap-open gas cap disappeared from Challenger's option list after 1971, it's still popular with restorers and resto-modders who want to upgrade the looks of their 1972-later E-Body car.

What would a 1972 Challenger convertible have looked like? Probably a lot like this one, which was a 1971 Challenger convertible that had been furnished to the producers of the TV drama **The Mod Squad**, *along with other Dodges, in exchange for on-screen credit. The producers still wanted a convertible, even though Chrysler no longer made one after 1971, so this car was updated with 1972's front and rear styling and used through that show's end of production in 1973. (Photo Courtesy Barrett-Jackson Auction Company)*

Subtraction

But that new styling would only grace one body style, and two variations of it for 1972. Low sales and high-profit vinyl tops had spelled an end to the convertible body style, while low sales led Dodge to drop the bare-bones Challenger coupe after just one year. So the Challenger would be hardtop-only for 1972.

The R/T hardtop was now called the Challenger Rallye, and it gained a set of simulated front fender louvers as a styling cue while losing the simulated rear-wheel vents of the 1971 R/T.

But the biggest changes, and the ones causing the most disappointment to performance-minded new-car buyers, happened inside the sheet metal.

Simulated scoops moved from the rear quarter panel ahead of the rear wheels on the 1971 Challenger R/T, to just behind the front wheels on the 1972 Challenger Rallye. Note tape stripes trailing out of the scoops. Also note the black-painted Dodge logo and outer perimeter of the "dog dish" hubcap, Plymouth's standard cap used the same stamping minus the logo and paint. Later-vintage slotted 15-inch "Police" wheels are an attractive alternative to the 14-inch wheels that Challengers were built with in 1972. (Photo Courtesy Mecum Auctions)

Powertrain Changes for 1972: Adieu, Big Power

After debuting as a late-year running change, Chrysler's Electronic Ignition System was standard on all 340 Challengers for 1972. The 340 also received a new, synthetic anti-scuff additive in its factory oil fill, which Dodge claimed in its *1972 Dealer Data Book* "provide(s) better protection against piston pin scuffing."

But the other changes to the 340 for 1972 were not for the better, in the eyes of many Mopar enthusiasts. Not only was its compression ratio dropped, from 10:1 to 8.5:1 via a piston change, but the 340 received a different set of cylinder heads for 1972. Developed for the 360-ci LA small-block that was now an option in midsize and full-size sedans and station wagons, their 1.88-inch intake valves were considerably smaller than the 1970–1971 340's 2.02-inch intake valves. Those valves, as

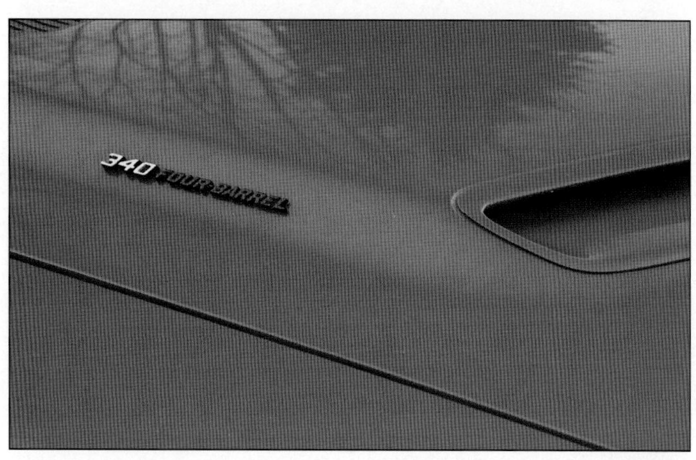

The 340 was still available for 1972. The cylinder heads had smaller valves, more restrictive exhaust manifolds, and a compression ratio drop to 8.5:1. Scoops in the Rallye's hood were non-functional from the factory, but could be opened up to allow cooler outside air into the engine bay. Factory paint charts listing the optional High Impact Hemi Orange color were among the few places the word "Hemi" appeared in 1972. (Photo Courtesy Mecum Auctions)

This 1972 Challenger Rallye has very few options under its hood, including the power brake booster on firewall behind its dual-circuit master cylinder. By 1972, all Chrysler engines were painted blue at the Mound Road Engine Plant in Detroit where they were assembled, instead of the orange color that high-performance engines such as the 340 received in prior years. (Photo Courtesy Mecum Auctions)

a result, allowed less air to flow through the heads, and as a result, power output dropped from 275 (gross) to 245 (net) horsepower. If that wasn't enough, the 360's "log-style" exhaust manifolds, which were also not as free-breathing as the ones used on the 340 since its 1968 introduction, were now on the 340, and a cast-iron crankshaft replaced the 340's forged-steel one in the spring of 1972.

That running change further sealed the fate of the 340 in the eyes of enthusiasts. They bemoaned that it had become a "station wagon" engine worthy of TV's *The Brady Bunch* instead of a performance engine worthy of small-screen-private-eye-show *Mannix*'s title character's dark green convertible.

Yet the 340 was the top "performance" engine in the Challenger lineup for 1972. Gone from the option list were all B/RB big-blocks, both 383s, the 440 Six Pack, and the 426 Hemi. Low production numbers and the approach of stricter emissions standards led the top brass in Highland Park to remove Code E74 Hemi from the E-Body option list for good, as well as the E87 Six Pack. Early 1972 Dodge product literature hinted at the Six Pack's availability in the Charger, but (like the Challenger T/A the year before) it was gone from the lineup when the 1972s went on sale in the fall of 1971. However, two 440 Six Pack 1972 Charger Rallyes are known to exist, per mymopar.com's online listing of V-Code Dodge/Plymouth production.

Also gone for 1972: the 198-ci Slant Six that powered the base-level Challenger coupe.

The small version of Chrysler's Leaning Tower of Power was an A-Body-only engine for 1972. That meant that the 225-ci Slant Six, which had been the standard powerplant in the "most-affordable" Challengers in 1970, was now the base engine once again, though little changed except for Chrysler's ongoing addition of Cleaner Air Package features to meet federal and California emissions limits. The same was true of the base V-8, the venerable LA-series 318-ci small-block.

A 340 Six Pack in a 1972 Challenger? Not as a factory option, but Chrysler's "Hustle Stuff" did offer the Six Pack's carburetors, intake manifold, carburetor linkage, and air cleaner, for those who wanted to bolt on some horsepower that the 1972 changes to the 340 took away. (Also note that this engine has a small aftermarket air conditioning compressor located at the front, one able to fit under the Six Pack's air cleaner (which the factory Airtemp compressor didn't).

From the start of 1972 production onward, all 340s were equipped with Chrysler's Electronic Ignition System at the factory. All North American–built Chrysler Corporation passenger cars and light trucks would get it as standard equipment for 1973.

But those weren't the only mechanical changes in store for Challenger for 1972. Along with the big engines, the Dana 60 rear axle assembly was no longer offered, and the Track Pak and Super Track Pak option packages that included it were gone as well. The 15 x 7–inch wheels, in either W21 Rallye Road Wheel or body-colored-wheel-with-hubcap form, were also no longer available. All 1972 Challengers would ride on 14-inch wheels, regardless of wheel style.

Reduced Interior and Trim Options

Inside, interior trim choices were slashed. The leather-and-vinyl seat trim that had been a hallmark of the 1970 Challenger SE's interior, and were a separate option for 1971, were no longer available. Same with the cloth-and-vinyl seats that were a credit option for SE buyers who did not want leather's added upkeep, as well as R/T and base Challenger buyers looking for

A driver's-eye view through the steering wheel of the four-pod Rallye gauge cluster. The 150-mph speedometer includes a re-settable trip odometer; 7,000-rpm tachometer lacks a factory redline to indicate maximum engine speed; four-gauge pod next to tach includes fuel, oil-pressure, engine temperature, and alternator gauges; and an electric clock occupies the far pod. Over time, factory electric clocks became so "reliable" that they were 100 percent accurate twice a day. (Photo Courtesy Mecum Auctions.com)

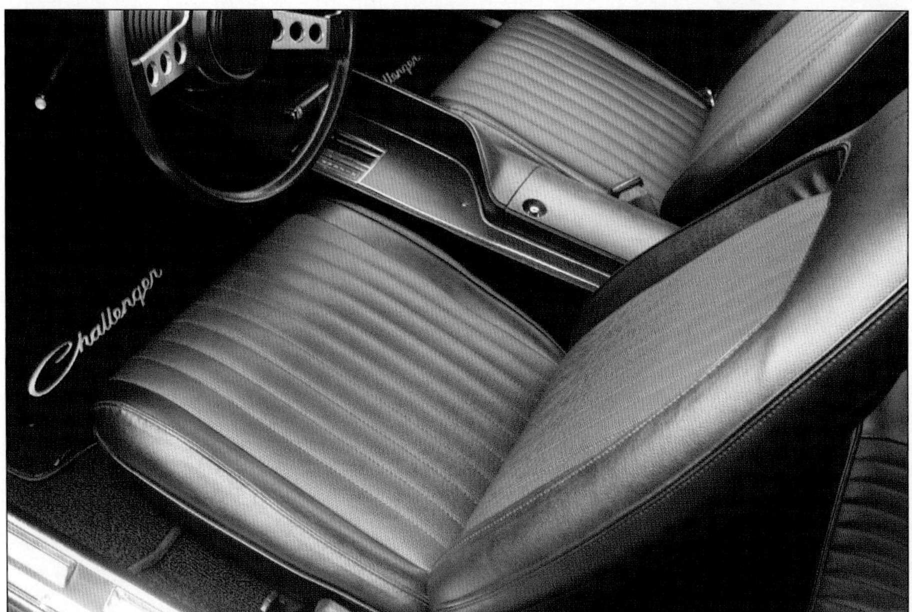

And then there was one . . . one interior trim material (vinyl), and one upholstery pattern (this one). Leather/vinyl and cloth/vinyl seat trims, which had been available in 1971 (and were standard and no-cost options, respectively, on the 1970 Challenger SE) were no longer available, though Challenger's price-class competition (Pontiac Firebird and Mercury Cougar) still offered more than one interior trim, including leather. (Photo Courtesy Mecum Auctions)

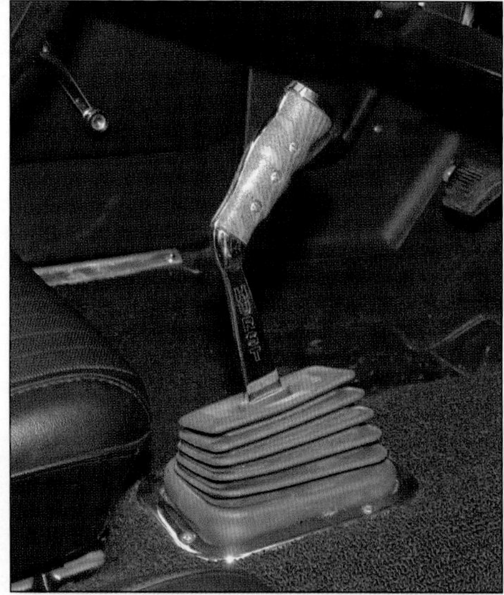

Hurst was still the original-equipment vendor in 1972 for the Pistol Grip shifters installed on the optional A-833 4-speed manual transmission. It's very likely this one stirs a "23-spline" A-833, instead of the heavy-duty "18-spline" version that 440 Six Pack and 426 Hemi cars came with. (Photo Courtesy Mecum Auctions)

The only visible difference between this 1972 Challenger Rallye's interior and those of the 1970 and 1971 Challenger R/Ts and TAs in this book is the two-spoke steering wheel that became standard, and the only steering wheel available that year. All other interior features are the same as before, including the amber reverse-gear-indicator light that's seen on the dash next to the glove box door. (Photo Courtesy Mecum Auctions)

Close-up view of the 1972 Challenger's restyled front end, including the headlight surround and grille. Black-painted grille was standard on Challenger Rallye. Note the radiator bulkhead behind the grille that's painted body color; all Chrysler products back then were painted in their exterior color there, instead of "chassis black" or other dark color. (Photo Courtesy Mecum Auctions)

The optional Rallye road wheel received a new center cap design for 1972, sharing it with not only its E-Body Plymouth sibling but all other Chrysler Corporation A-Body and B-Body cars. The 14-inch diameter was the only size available, as the 15 x 7–inch version was dropped after 1971.

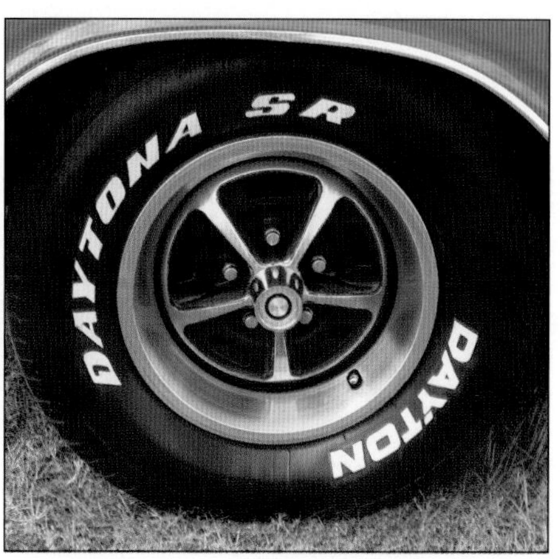

The other optional wheel treatment was the venerable five-spoke "Magnum" design, which had been a Challenger option since 1970. Like the revised Rallye road wheel seen above, it was only available as a 14-inch wheel from 1972 onward.

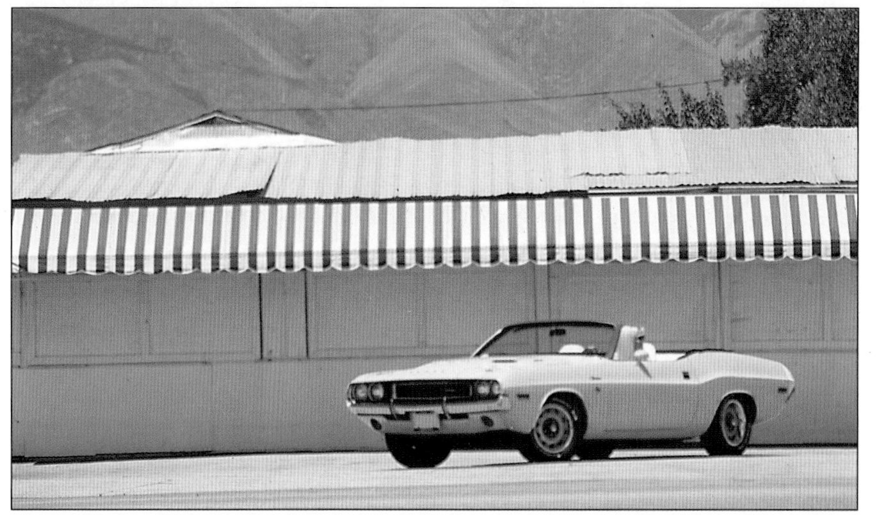

Unlike most used cars of the early 1970s, the 1970 Challenger R/Ts found new life from 1972 onward as collector/"special interest" cars worth preserving and restoring, and they stopped depreciating in value, instead appreciating as more and more enthusiasts turned to them. Also, entrepreneurs began buying up dealer stocks of NOS/NORS parts, to supply customers looking to restore their cars to the condition this 1970 Challenger R/T was when David Newhardt photographed it. (Photo Courtesy David Newhardt)

After 1971, the only places you could find a Dodge Challenger R/T convertible like this one were on used car lots or in private-party car-for-sale ads, as both the convertible body style and the Challenger R/T series left the Challenger lineup when the 1971 model year ended. (Photo Courtesy David Newhardt)

One-year-only items such as this rear taillight assembly (seen here on a 1970 'Cuda) became more valuable as owners and restorers sought new parts to replace missing or crash-damaged items on their car. (Photo Courtesy David Newhardt)

Could you use this photo to imagine what a 1972 Challenger convertible would look like from the right rear? Yes. Imagine the 1972-later rear lamp pods above the bumper. Downward-trending convertible sales and upward-trending factory installations of Airtemp air conditioning made Highland Park's decision to drop the convertible body style an inevitable one. (Photo Courtesy David Newhardt)

Nameplates, series badges, and engine-identification badges like the ones seen here on this 1970 Challenger R/T convertible were among the first items to be reproduced for owners and restorers. (Photo Courtesy David Newhardt)

Compare the grille assembly seen here on a 1970 Challenger R/T with the new-for-1972 grille seen earlier in this chapter. Front bumper, front valence, and headlights were the same for both years. (Photo Courtesy David Newhardt)

a dressed-up cabin. They were gone, along with the split-bench front seat option. That left only the standard all-vinyl front bucket and rear bench seats as the only interior trim choice, though they were available in five colors for 1972: blue, black, white, green, and gold.

Other items deleted from Challenger's features and options for 1972 lists were some items that were still available via Dodge dealers' parts departments. They included front and rear spoilers, the N94 fiberglass hood that first appeared in the Challenger T/A, hood pins, rear-window louvers, and trim rings to surround the factory "dog dish" hubcaps.

These items were also no longer available on Challenger after 1971: the Shaker hood scoop, heavy-duty shock absorbers, Elastomeric (color-keyed) bumpers, six-way adjustable driver's seat, wire wheel covers, power windows, Airtemp air conditioning combined with a Slant Six (or 318), and a manual transmission.

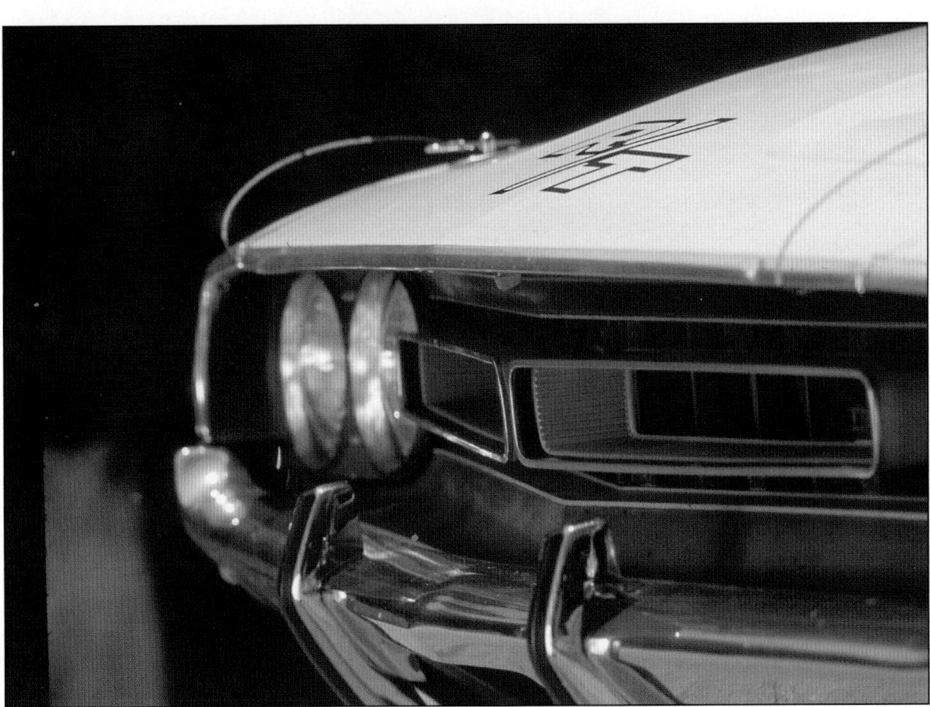

Compare this 1971 Challenger R/T grille with the 1972 Challenger Rallye grille seen earlier in this chapter. Like the 1971 styling update, it was accomplished at minimal cost. (Photo Courtesy David Newhardt)

Models, Options and Pricing

Rising new-car prices had been something that new-car buyers had complained about for years, especially when they saw how much more a mildly facelifted new car's sticker price was over its previous-year predecessor. Many times, that annual new-car price increase, and related rise in the price of optional equipment, was caused by the increasing cost of materials and labor. The new contract that the United Auto Workers reached with General Motors in late 1971, serving as a pattern for new labor deals with Ford, Chrysler, and AMC, called not only for sizable wage increases, but also tied them to the rate of inflation.

Price inflation, not just of new cars and trucks but all consumer goods, was a major concern during 1971. That led to a major action by President Richard Nixon in the summer of 1971. On August 15, he announced that, by executive order, all wages and prices in the United States were frozen for 90 days. So 1972 prices at the start of the model year were little different than those that had been in effect when the last of the 1971 models rolled off the assembly lines.

One item that went away early in 1972: the federal excise tax on new-vehicle purchases. Included in new-car prices for years, it had risen to 7 percent by the time the 1972 model year started, and its abolition served as a price cut. That meant more money in the pockets of potential buyers, but it also meant that

1972 DODGE CHALLENGER WINDOW STICKER

Typical of cars that a Dodge dealer ordered for his inventory, you might see a base-level hardtop outfitted with a 318, TorqueFlite automatic, plus the A06 Basic Group and A01 Light Group option packages.

Here's how those items would have appeared on a window sticker in the spring of 1972 (Pricing information is from *Edmund's 1972 New Car Prices* [May Edition]):

Here's the 1972 version of the 340 that Dodge's sales literature spoke about in such glowing terms. A change to cylinder heads with 1.88-inch intake valves (smaller than the 2.02-inch intake valves used on the 340 since its 1968 introduction) cut power, as did the drop in compression and the "log-style" exhausts manifolds seen here. On the firewall, just behind the right-side valve cover, is the Electronic Ignition System's control module. (Photo Courtesy Mecum Auctions)

Top performer in the Challenger line for 1972 was the Challenger Rallye, seen here in High Impact Hemi Orange with the later-vintage 15 x 7-inch steel Chrysler "Police wheels" wearing year-correct Dodge hubcaps. The "Snap-open" fuel filler on the right quarter panel was discontinued after 1971. The taillight panel was painted black on Rallye models, as was the grille in front. (Photo Courtesy Mecum Auctions)

Base Challenger (V-8)	$2,790
Options	
Vinyl top	80
D34 TorqueFlite Automatic	203
B41 Power Brakes, Front Disc	62
T34 F78x14 WSW Tires	41
A06 Basic Group*	294**
H51 Airtemp A/C	365
G11 Tinted Glass	36
C16 Console	52
Total:	$3,923

** Includes A01 Light Group; G35 chrome LH remote mirror; R11 Music Master AM radio; S77 Power Steering; J55 Undercoating and Hood Silencer Pad; W11 Deluxe Wheel Covers; J25 Variable-Speed Wipers*

*** A06 was no bargain; per* Edmunds, *those options alone were $268.*

Here's what a performance-minded buyer might have ordered with his 1972 Challenger Rallye, including a 340, 4-speed gearbox and the A36 Performance Axle Package. On the sticker, it would have looked something like this:

Base Challenger Rallye	$3,068
Options	
High Impact Paint	3
E55 340 V-8 Package*	210
D21 4-Speed Manual	193
T87 F70x14 RWL Tires	11
H51 Airtemp AC	365
A36 Performance Axle Package**	60
C16 Console	52
G11 Tinted Glass	36
J97 Rallye Gauges w/Clock	95
G35 Dual Painted Sport Mirrors, LH remote	25
S77 Power Steering	104
R35 AM/FM Stereo Radio	191
R32 Dual Rear Speakers	32
W21 Rallye Road Wheels	53
Total	$4,498

** Includes T86 F70x14 WW tires, S13 Rallye Suspension, N23 Electronic Ignition System*

*** Includes D91 Sure-Grip*

A look inside a 1972 Challenger Rallye through the driver's door. This car was not equipped with the center console, but the same Pistol Grip shifter handle was used as with the console. (This was different than the B-Body/bench seat 4-speeds of that era, which used a much longer Pistol Grip handle. Note manual window crank on right-side door: power windows were no longer an option on Challenger after 1971. (Photo Courtesy Mecum Auctions)

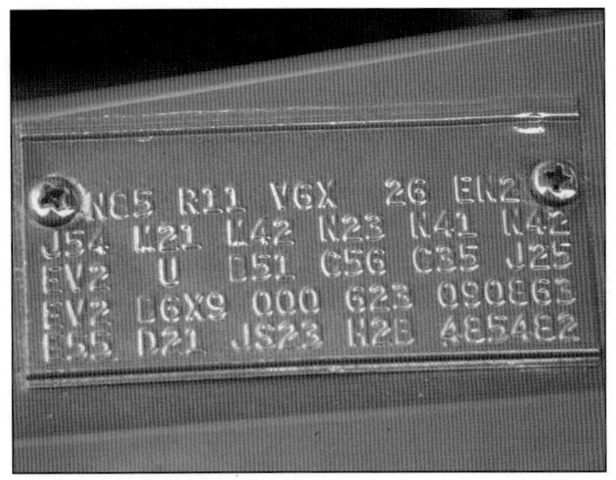

Decoding this Challenger's fender tag shows that it's a Rallye hardtop (JS27) built with a 340 (Code E55) 4-speed manual transmission (Code D21), painted Hemi Orange (Code EV2) with a black interior (Code B6X9), which was ordered and built with power brakes (Code B52), bucket seats (Code C56), three-speed windshield wipers (J25), roof drip rail moldings (Code M21), front stone shield moldings (Code N23), Electronic Ignition System (Code N23), dual exhausts with chrome tips (Codes N41 and N42), tachometer (Code N85), AM radio (Code R11), longitudinal black stripes (Code V6X), and a 26-inch high-performance radiator ("26" in top line of codes). Build date was June 23, 1972 ("623" on second line), at Hamtramck Assembly ("B" code in fourth block of digits on the row from the bottom).

Chrysler and other manufacturers had to update and revise their prices to take that tax's demise into account.

So how could a buyer option a new Challenger to their liking in 1972? It came down to two choices: the base-level hardtop and the Rallye hardtop.

Sales by the Numbers

With a pared-down model and options line-up, Dodge built and sold 26,658 Challengers in 1972, per the *Standard Catalog of American Cars 1946–1975:* 18,535 base hardtops and 8,123 Rallyes, down about 12 percent from 1971's sales total. It wasn't as big a percentage drop as Firebird and Cougar suffered that year (see below), but it still wasn't anything for Dodge dealers and devotees to write home about.

The strike at GM's Norwood, Ohio, assembly plant, plus the downturn in the pony car market segment, resulted in Pontiac building and selling 29,951 1972 Firebirds: 12,000 base models, 11,415 Esprits, 5,250 Formula Firebirds, and 1,286 Trans Ams (per the *Standard Catalog of American Cars 1946–1975*). That was a reduction of 44 percent from 1971's total of 53,135.

Meanwhile, Cougar's 1972 totals (again, per the *Standard Catalog of American Cars 1946–1975*) added up to 53,702, down 13 percent from 1971's 62,874, with 23,731 base hardtops and 1,240 base convertibles, and 26,802 XR-7 hardtops and 1,929 XR-7 convertibles sold by the nation's Lincoln-Mercury dealers.

Would there be a Dodge Challenger for 1973? And, would there still be competitors from Pontiac and Mercury? The 1972 sales figures didn't look good enough for more than a less-than-enthusiastic "yes," thanks to trends in the new-car business that were barely on the horizon when the E-Body cars were in the planning stage in 1967 and Chrysler's response to them.

High insurance premiums and surcharges kept potential buyers away from the high-performance versions, and a recession that some observers linked to the late-1970 United Auto Workers strike against General Motors (which had a ripple effect beyond GM's network of divisions and outside suppliers) kept buyers away, too.

Instead of emphasizing performance, Chrysler instead began touting its longtime engineering expertise in the print and broadcast ads of its car and truck models with the catch phrase "Extra Care In Engineering."

That slogan appeared in Dodge showrooms not only along with the facelift Challengers for 1972, but also a Dodge line-up which included a totally redesigned line of D-Series (two-wheel-drive) and W-Series (four-wheel drive) pickups, whose styling bore a "family resemblance" to the Dodge passenger-car line-up, and whose available features (and standard ride) made it more car-like than any Dodge light truck before it. Same for the B-Series Sportsman and Tradesman vans, which had been introduced during 1971 and carried over virtually unchanged. And, at the opposite end of the size spectrum, was the Dodge Colt. The Mitsubishi-built subcompact, only available on the West Coast at first in 1971, was now available in all 50 states for 1972.

As for the rest of the Dodge lineup, the full-size C-Body Polara and Monaco received a sheet metal freshening, with the top-line Monacos now equipped with hideaway headlights, a styling feature that Ford and General Motors had moved away from on their big cars. The midsize B-Body Coronet and Charger received new grilles and other minor trim changes, with the biggest visual change reserved for the new "formal roof" on the Charger SE. In reality, it was a resculpting and enlarging of the Charger's rear roof pillar that included smaller rear quarter windows and less rearward visibility. A-Body Dodge Darts, Swingers, and Demons received a new grille and not much else.

For the first time since Horace and John Dodge began building automobiles that wore their name in 1914, there was not an open-body car available in the Dodge lineup for 1972. Some industry observers at that time blamed it on customers choosing air-conditioned hardtops and sedans over drop-top body styles, many of them wearing vinyl roof coverings that gave them a convertible-like appearance without the cold-weather and wet-weather problems that convertible body styles had become notorious for. Others pointed to Federal Motor Vehicle Safety Standards that had yet to be adopted, much less proposed, which would have required roll-over protection for all occupants, and likely done away with open-body cars with folding fabric roofs from rolling down Hamtramck's (or any other) assembly line.

Speaking of Hamtramck Assembly, it became the sole plant making Dodge Challengers in 1972, as Chrysler's Los Angeles Assembly Plant in California closed for good before the end of calendar year 1971. A magnitude-6.5 earthquake centered under Sylmar, California, in the early morning hours of February 9, 1971, damaged the plant, and senior management in Highland Park decided against spending what was needed to repair the earthquake damage. From 1972 onward, other Chrysler plants picked up Los Angeles Assembly's slack.

From Front-Runner to Also-Ran

The drag racing classes that were created around factory-Hemi cars began to see non-factory powertrains and chassis under their OEM sheet metal, beginning in 1972.

Foremost among them was the *Grumpy's Toy* Chevrolet, campaigned by Bill "Grumpy" Jenkins. He was a staunch proponent of the Chevy small-block V-8, which he'd built into a giant killer in the mid-1960s, and surprised many a Hemi or big-block Ford opponent on the strips. But when Pro Stock classes were created by NHRA, IHRA, and AHRA, "Da Grump" was there with a big-block Camaro.

But it was his Chevrolet Vega Pro Stock race car, which debuted in 1972, that helped lead to the Hemi's demise as a competitive engine in those classes. Instead of merely swapping in a small-block Chevy V-8 into the Vega's unit body (which was not a factory option then, nor ever was, in the Vega), Jenkins fabricated a full-tube chassis and roll cage to go under the stock Vega sheet metal, a chassis that combined strength and light weight. That car's success, combined with the sanctioning bodies increasing the weight that Hemi cars had to carry from 1970's 7 pounds per cubic inch of engine displacement, led to Hemis like Dick Landy's Challenger seeing fewer and fewer final rounds as the year wore on.

This year, 1971, was the last year that Dick Landy campaigned a Challenger in NHRA Pro Stock.

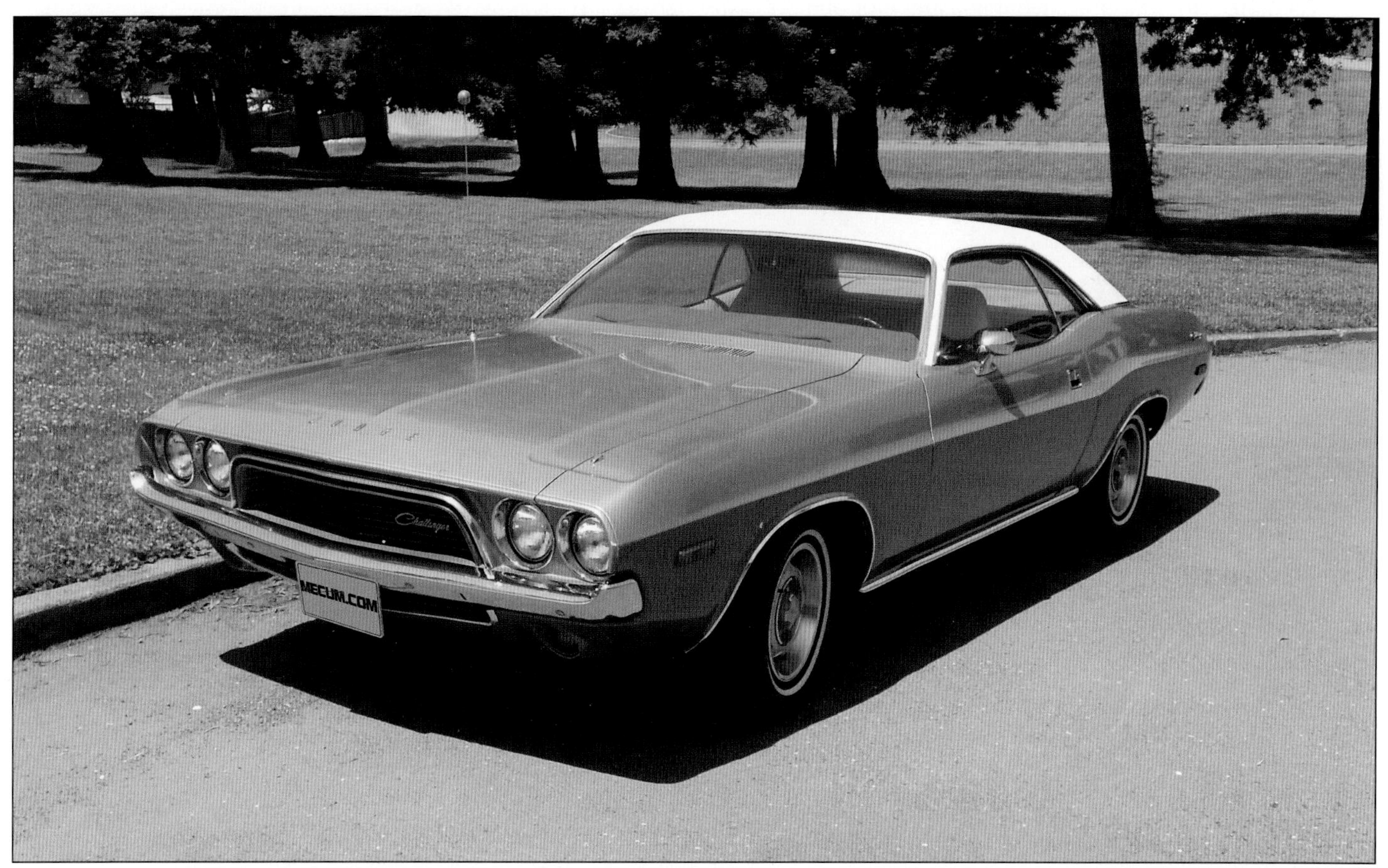

What are the rarest Challengers these days? Along with the Hemi and Six Pack 1970 and 1971 R/Ts, and the 1970 TA, how about a base 1972 Challenger hardtop with its original factory equipment? This one is typical of one that a Dodge dealer would order for their inventory, dressed up with a vinyl top, whitewalls, and Rallye road wheels, but with a 318 under the hood and, very likely, factory-installed Airtemp air conditioning. These days, many 1972–later Challenger owners are "resto-modding" them to look like 1971–earlier R/Ts and TAs, or adding their own 21st Century customizing touches like large-diameter billet aluminum wheels. (Photo Courtesy Mecum Auctions)

CHAPTER 7

1972 PLYMOUTH BARRACUDA

A Changed and Revised Fish

For the 1972 model year, the Plymouth Barracuda experienced a seismic change: The model lineup and selection dramatically shrank. As a result, the Barracuda endured the many changes that its corporate sibling the Challenger had to endure. The big-block engines were discontinued, so the biggest available V-8 for 1972 was a detuned 340. No 383 or 440 was offered and certainly not a 426 Hemi. Beyond the 340, the Barracuda had only two other engines: the 225 six and 318. All engines were calibrated to run unleaded fuel, and horsepower and torque figures were measured according to SAE net method, and therefore the output was paltry. The Barracuda also went through many styling and option changes as well.

The Barracuda and Challenger were both overshadowed by the A-Body cars that had found a strong audience because those were more affordable and economical. The A-Body Plymouth Duster had replaced the "boxtop" Valiant two-door sedan for 1970. A product of Plymouth's styling studios that was created on a shoestring budget, it found a place with small-car and budget-minded buyers with more than 217,000 sold in 1970 and another 196,000 in 1971. It was straight Valiant from the dashboard forward, but from there on back it was a surprisingly roomy five-passenger semi-fastback coupe, which also boasted a huge trunk and a rear tread narrower than the front. That would make it easy for a pair of extra-wide rear tires to be mounted on

Does this look familiar? Many people thought the 1972 Barracuda's front styling was a reversion back to that of 1970. Twin headlamps replaced the 1971-only four-lamp design, while the grille added a set of "gills" in the middle. This would be the front-end styling that all Barracudas would wear for the duration of the E-Body's production lifetime.

Visible changes to the 1972 Plymouth Barracuda included new stripe and wheel center designs, but the big changes had to do with what was dropped after 1971, namely the convertible body style, all engines bigger than the 340, the Dana 60 rear axle assembly, the Gran Coupe and base fixed-window coupe models, as well as options like power windows, cloth/vinyl and leather/vinyl seats, and 15-inch wheels.

wide but standard-offset wheels, to take best advantage of the engine's power and prevent a tendency to want to swap ends while cornering at speeds above 40 mph.

Performance-wise, Duster was a sleeper; a car that didn't look like it could out-accelerate existing muscle cars, but it did. With the 340 under its hood, and a heavy-duty suspension comparable to what was under the 1969 'Cuda 383, the Duster 340 only took about 7 seconds to go 0–60, turned quarter-mile times in the high-14/low-15-second range, and carried a sticker price well below Barracuda's.

Duster's sales performance, as well as that of its A-Body siblings Valiant and Scamp (the latter Plymouth's version of the Dodge Dart Swinger two-door hardtop, introduced in 1971), impressed dealers and executives in Highland Park alike. Their numbers were aided by option packages like the A04 Easy Order Package, which for 1971 included a TorqueFlite automatic for no extra charge. That point was emphasized in television ads by an empty TorqueFlite case flying on camera and landing with a cast-aluminum *clunk* next to the announcer making the televised sales pitch when he mentioned they would "throw in" the automatic gearbox at no extra charge.

Packaging popular options would prove to be a strategy that kept Plymouth's sales up during the coming year, and would reinforce its role as Chrysler's low-price value brand, even if the sticker prices on the most heavily optioned Plymouths were now creeping over the $5,000 mark, as were those on comparable Chevrolets and Fords.

So it was during the spring of 1971, when the advance information for 1972 was mailed out from Highland Park to the Chrysler-Plymouth dealer body. Along with information on the upcoming 1972 models, which would begin shipping to them after model changeover that summer, it contained information regarding the numbers of each car line that was equipped with the available factory options. (It also included information on how many cars were painted in what colors, which was cited in the preceding 1971 Barracuda chapter.) Using that advance information, dealers would then plan how they would order the first of the next year's new cars for their inventory.

They would also use it to shed a tear over the passing of the factory performance era.

That communication confirmed that the 426 Hemi, 440 6-barrel, and both 383s would not return to the Barracuda lineup for 1972. (The 383, a Plymouth mainstay for more than a decade, was replaced by a 400-ci version of the "B-series" big-block V-8 for 1972.) Neither would many of the performance-related options, such as the Track Pak and Super Track Pak option groups, return for 1972.

Although the 426 Hemi was no longer a regular-production option, it was evident that Chrysler planned to keep production of it going at their Marine and Industrial Engine Plant at Marysville, Michigan, where all 426 Hemi engines were built. The advance information from Chrysler stated, "The Hemi engine will not be available as a production option, but will be available on a special order basis for stock and drag racing."

New Additions (and Subtractions) for 1972

Just as with its E-Body sibling, Dodge Challenger, the list of models, features, and options no longer available was a long one. What the *Confidential Plymouth 1972 Advance Information*

As the sun was setting on this photo shoot, so had the sun set on Plymouth's "Mustang fighter" by the time this one was built in 1972. Like the same-year Dodge Challenger, only one interior material was available: all-vinyl, in the same pattern used on the Dodge.

With the reduction in interior trim options came a simplifying of Barracuda's interior door panels. Still molded in polypropylene, they were color-keyed to match the seat trim selected, without any wood-grain trim or other dress-up items. Door and rear quarter windows were crank-up only for 1972, as the power window option was discontinued. Meanwhile, Ford and Chevrolet offered power windows, and upgraded interior trim options, on their Mustang and Camaro.

Bulletin told the dealers was that the convertible body style, base-level Barracuda coupe, and the top-level Gran Coupe hardtop would not return for the E-Body Barracuda's third year.

The options list was pared down, as well, just as Dodge had cut back Challenger's.

Appearance items like front and rear spoilers, two-tone paint, chrome pedal dress-up accents, hood pins, Elastomeric color-keyed bumpers, as well as the available chrome deck-lid luggage rack, rear window louvers, wheel trim rings, and wire wheel covers were dropped.

The list of interior features and options that would not return for 1972 was substantial. No more power windows, 6-way adjusting driver's seat, rim-blow steering wheel, or AM/FM stereo radio with cassette player. The microphone for the remaining cassette player option was now a dealer-installed extra.

But the list of mechanical features and options took the most visible cuts. Along with the 426 Hemi 440 6-barrel and all 383s, the Shaker hood was also discontinued, as were heavy-duty shock absorbers, the Dana 60 rear axle assembly and related axle/performance option groups, the 11-inch drum brakes, all axle ratio options lower (numerically higher) than 3.55:1, the extra-heavy-duty suspension that Hemi and big-block cars received, road lamps, engine block heater, and the collapsible spare tire.

At the other end of the performance spectrum, the 198-ci Slant Six was no longer available in the Challenger lineup, as were power-assisted drum brakes.

Inside, all interior trim choices except all-vinyl front bucket/rear bench seats were no longer available. That meant no more split-bench front seats or seats upholstered in cloth and vinyl or leather and vinyl.

Engine Changes

The 340 for 1972 was no longer the high-output performance engine it had been since its 1968 introduction. Although the advance information bulletin didn't mention it, the 340 was a different engine. That was thanks to the replacement of its cylinder heads with those from the 360-ci LA-series small-block V-8, whose valves were smaller, especially the intake valves, which shrank from 2.02 to 1.88 inches. The 360 heads' passages were not as free flowing as the 340 heads' were, because the 360 had been designed and engineered as a "grocery-getter" instead of a performance engine as the 340 had been.

Also, during the 1972 model year, the 340's crankshaft was changed from a steel forging to a ductile-iron casting as of April 11, 1972. That was just like what happened to the 383 the year before and would eventually happen to the 440 and Slant Six as well. Forged-steel crankshafts had been a Chrysler hallmark for years, and while forging created a strong and durable part (especially at high RPM), the cast-iron cranks cost less to make. This was an example of "bean counter engineering," where a cheaper-to-produce part is substituted for a premium component in the name of saving a few cents here and there and nothing more.

As with the late 1971 340s, Chrysler's Electronic Ignition System was standard on the 1972 340, as well as the 400 4-barrel, 440 4-barrel, and 440 6-barrel engines available in the B-Body and C-Body Plymouths, the latter of which had yet to

Two-spoke variation of the "Tuff" steering wheel used on Plymouth's Duster and Satellite/Road Runner lines became not only the standard steering wheel for 1972, it was the only steering wheel available. No more three-spoke, wood-grain, or "rim blow" versions were on the option list. Behind it is the standard Barracuda gauge cluster, unchanged since 1970.

Still in use was the twin-scooped hood that was introduced with the 1970 'Cuda. It still topped 'Cuda's engine bay, but was also available on the base Barracuda as part of the J51 "Sport Decor Package" (which this car was built with), or included with the optional 340, or as a separate $20 option with the 318. Non-functional scoops could be opened up by removing the metal inserts in the scoops, which would allow cooler outside air into the engine bay while driving. Any type of "forced-air induction" using these scoops was up to the owner's ingenuity and fabricating skills.

be discontinued at the start of 1972 production. The advance information bulletin cites it, in a section titled, "What the Electronic Ignition Does," which dances around any mention of better performance: "The electronic ignition system transmits a uniform and controlled spark impulse to each spark plug, assuring more complete combustion of the fuel. As a result, less contaminants remain in the exhaust gases for emission into the atmosphere, [and] there's less pollution.

"The electronic ignition also eliminates the distributor points and condenser, which are usually the first parts to fail and require replacement. Thus, the need for frequent tune-up is significantly reduced."

So what new features were on the way for 1972? The advance information bulletin pointed them out, few that they were. A new "performance hood treatment" was now an option, as was the scooped 'Cuda hood. An inside hood release was also new for 1972, along with a blue metallic vinyl top material. Standard features now included a single three-point lap-and-shoulder belt for driver and front passenger (instead of the separate lap and shoulder belts of 1970–1971), and a two-spoke version of the "Tuff" steering wheel that was available in the A-Body Duster and B-Body Satellite/Road Runner lines.

Styling Update: Forward, into the Past

For 1972, Barracuda's "new grille treatment" looked like a return to 1970's front-end styling. It featured two headlights flanking a split grille divided by a center piece with six gill-like slots in it. In back, the horizontal taillights and backup lights were replaced by four round lights: one taillight and one backup light per side.

Diran Yasajian, who was the manager of E-Body styling in the Plymouth Exterior Styling Studio back then, told me in a January 2015 interview that the process to revise Barracuda's looks for 1972 was not prompted by negative reaction to the 1971 Barracuda's front-end styling.

Models, Options and Pricing

All prices mentioned here are courtesy of *Edmunds 1972 New Car Prices* (May 1972 edition). They reflect the repeal of the 7-percent federal excise tax just as 1972 production began, and may have been rounded off by Edmunds to the nearest dollar.

A base Barracuda hardtop cost $2,710 with the 225 Slant Six; $2,808 with a 318 V-8. The 'Cuda hardtop (which began the 1972 model run with the 340 standard, but the 318 replaced it as standard early in the 1972 model run, with the 340 now available only in an option package) cost $2,753.

Under the Media Microscope

Compared to the 1970 and 1971 E-Body cars, published road tests by the major car magazines were fewer and further between in 1972. Probably the most significant, and most brutal, was *Car and Driver*'s road test of a 340/4-speed 'Cuda for its

The slit-style rear lamps used in back were also gone for 1972, replaced by a pair of round lamps on each side: the outboard ones containing the stop light and turn signal, and the inboard ones contained the backup lights. Base-level Barracuda's tail lamp panel was painted body color for 1972, while that on the 'Cuda was painted black. As with the new front-end styling, this is what all Barracudas would wear above their rear bumpers until the end of E-Body production in 1974. Also note the lack of cut-outs in the valance panel beneath the bumper, indicative of a car that was not factory-equipped with the 340, and its dual exhaust system with chrome rectangular exhaust tips.

Detail of the "gills" at the center of the 1972 Barracuda grille. As was industry practice back then, front grilles were now made of injection-molded plastic instead of stamped steel, aluminum, or die-cast metal. This may have saved weight and cost at the time, but plastic grilles not only were subject to the ravages of collision damage but also tended to become brittle and crack when subjected to extreme cold weather for long periods of time.

One thing unchanged about 'Cuda for 1972: Its rear taillight panel was still painted black and would stay that way through the end of E-Body production in 1974.

The name was the same for 1972, but the Barracuda was not the muscle car it was before.

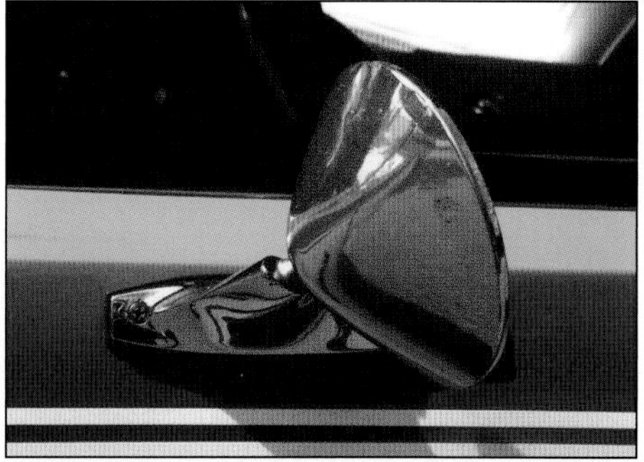

Standard outside rearview mirror was this chrome manually adjustable one, which was also standard on Plymouth's A-Body Valiant/Duster/Scamp compacts and B-Body Satellite/Road Runner. Also used in 1970 and 1971, this would be the standard one until the end of E-Body production.

January 1972 issue. Any hopes of a positive review were dashed by the story's subhead: "The end of the road is in sight and no one, it seems, is looking for the detour."

Instrumented test data showed a somewhat-respectable 0–60 mph time of 6.9 seconds, a quarter-mile time of 15.5 seconds at 91.9 mph, and an 80–0 stopping distance of 279 feet. Observed top speed was 125 mph, and estimated fuel economy was in the 10–15 mpg range.

Detail of the standard 1972 Barracuda tail lamps and the panel that they're mounted in. This was a new stamping, replacing the one used for 1970 and revised for 1971. Also note the location of the rear bumper relative to the body. In coming years, it would be moved outboard, as reinforcements were added behind it to comply with Federal Motor Vehicle Safety Standards (FMVSS) that mandated low-speed impact protection, which became effective in 1973.

But the text, which ran in *C/D* without a byline, was brutal toward the car, and toward Plymouth and Chrysler management. Some of the story's memorable quotes included:

"Even brief exposure behind the wheel will reveal Plymouth's secret: the Barracuda is a sheep in wolf's clothing. It's easy to be fooled at first by the 150-mph speedometer. The trick tachometer with its numbers rotated racer-style to place the 6,500-rpm redline at the 11 o'clock position; and the business-like Hurst shifter standing at attention, its Bowie-knife grip ready for whatever rapid gear changing may be necessary to win.

"The whole package reeks of performance . . . performance that allowed your insurance agent to move into the high-rent subdivision and kept police summons books looking thin. But, with the exception of Ronnie Sox' car, there will be precious little conquering by the emasculated 1972 Barracuda. If outside it looks like the street eliminator, underneath you will find a back-of-the-pack impostor.

"It's apparent that Plymouth is offering only a thin shell of last year's car for the shrinking sporty car market. By substituting parts from other models and simplifying the assembly operations with fewer options, Plymouth plans to make money on the Barracuda, even if sales for the entire sporty car segment plummet.

"The 340 lives, but in name only. Plymouth gave rein to the accounting department, and the bean counters slipped out the good parts before their very eyes.

"As a result, for 1972, Plymouth is selling lackluster 360 components under the 340's nameplate, and whereas the 340 engine was once a highly responsive small V-8, now it can no longer be considered a performance engine."

Car and Driver did find something worth praising, however, the Electronic Ignition System, which it noted was justified by the emission-control benefits from constant dwell angle and less spark scatter.

"Everyone will gain from increased reliability, since breaker points have been ash-canned in favor of a maintenance-free magnetic pulse generator in the distributor," the review said. "This ingenious device supplies a signal at firing intervals which is amplified by a semi-conductor module to control a conventional ignition coil. An RPM limiter is scaled into the

Even before the 1970 Barracudas entered production, Plymouth stylists were already at work on updates for 1971 and later. This styling sketch, dated November 12, 1969, shows a grille-opening shape similar to what eventually appeared on the 1971 Plymouth Satellite and Road Runner hardtops. The asymmetric hood scoop may have directed cold air to a Slant Six engine, as the scoop sits about where that engine's carburetor and intake manifold would be. (Photo Courtesy Brett Snyder)

September 1969 saw this sketch created in Plymouth's Exterior Styling studio, of a possible future version of the Barracuda. With the coming of federal safety standards requiring 5-mph impact protection, this design would have needed to be modified extensively if it had been approved for production before those standards took effect. (Photo Courtesy Brett Snyder)

Could a 1972 or later Barracuda have worn rear styling like this? From August 1969, this Plymouth Exterior Styling sketch does indeed foreshadow a future look, of the mid-size "B-Body" hardtops that appeared for the 1975 model year. Note the location of the backup lights above center of rear bumper. (Photo Courtesy Brett Snyder)

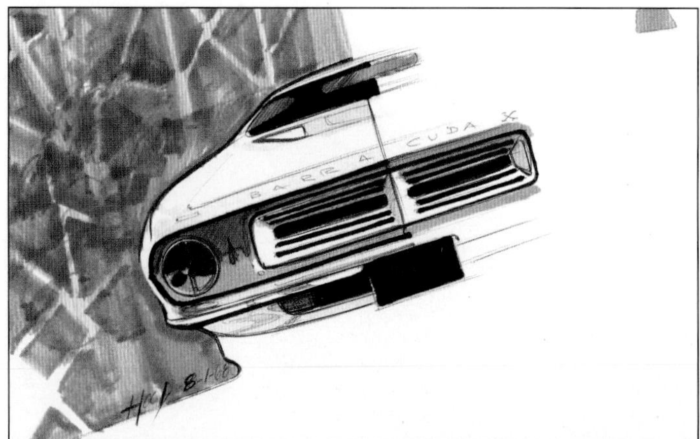

Another single-headlight front styling theme was explored in this Plymouth Exterior Styling sketch from August 1968. Full-width appearance could be simulated by placing a mirror at the sketched car's centerline, a common technique in passenger-car styling studios of the time. Note lack of "gills" anywhere on the grille. (Photo Courtesy Brett Snyder)

Despite the lack of big-power engines that were available in 1970 and 1971, the 1972 Plymouth Barracuda was still a good-looking car. This one was factory-equipped with the "Sport Appearance Package," which added the 'Cuda's scooped hood and new-for-1972 side stripes. Alas, the "hockey stick" and "billboard" side graphics were no more. Rallye wheels' center cap design was also new for 1972.

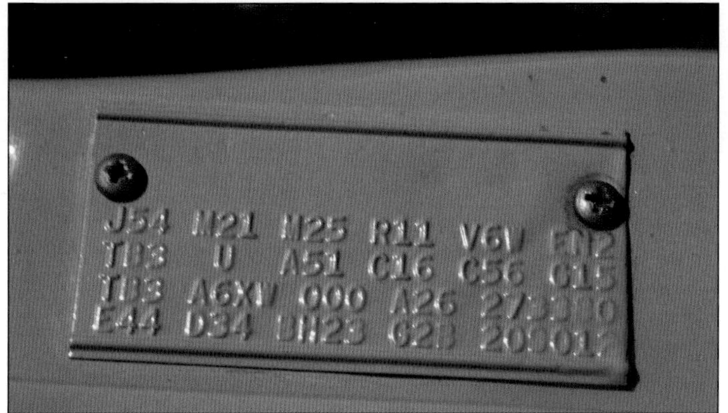

This one was factory-equipped with the Code J51 Sport Appearance Package, which added the 'Cuda's scooped hood and new-for-1972 side stripes.

system, and at a pre-set limit of 6,400 rpm the control module interrupts all messages to the coil, ceasing ignition until the revs drop."

That was about it for praise, as the review heaped scorn on the 'Cuda's chassis, noting the decrease in handling capability with the demise of the extra-heavy-duty suspension, 15-inch wheel, and 60-series tire options. "Suddenly we are back to 1968, and the fast-backed fish. Transition from a desirable handling stance to a tail-out attitude now begins at a lower speed, and any major power applications while cornering must include a corresponding steering correction. A faster steering ratio would ease the driving chores, but a variable-ratio, high-effort power steering gear is a development Chrysler hasn't justified at this point. Catalytic mufflers and air bags come first."

As for its brakes, *Car and Driver* said that was where 'Cuda still provided excitement, not from "eyeball-popping deceleration," but from the rear-wheel lock-up on hard braking that hampered directional stability.

Car and Driver summed up its feelings about the 'Cuda for 1972 with these words, which likely were not received well in Highland Park: "We feel Plymouth's actions are particularly unwise. Their attempts to generate broad appeal for the Barracuda by compromising every aspect has been a stone around the car's neck since its beginning. Early Barracudas shared so many Valiant components that the styling had sufficient sporty appeal only for 80-year-old widows. The new body was handicapped by dated styling concepts and an engine compartment most suitable for the greatest mass of cast iron to leave the foundry.

"If sporty car interest must fade, the obvious response would be a more competitive entry with glowing advantages over the sales leaders. The 340 engine was just such an advantage, and many judged it to be the very best small-block engine one could buy. But Plymouth has allowed the major attraction of the car to wither, with only an accounting department justification."

Sales by the Numbers

Did the paring back of the Barracuda model lineup and options list result in a sales increase?

Believe it or not, almost 4,000 more than the 1971 total of 14,808. That worked out to 10,622 base-series Barracudas and 7,828 'Cudas, 18,450 E-Body Plymouths in all, a nearly 20 percent gain. That uptick in sales was likely enough to convince

1972 PLYMOUTH BARRACUDA WINDOW STICKER

Base Hardtop with 318 V-8	$2,808
D34 TorqueFlite automatic	203
A04 Basic Group*	188
A51 Sport Decor Package**	67
H51 Airtemp Air Conditioning	365
G11 Tinted Glass	[AU: cost?]
T34 F78x14 WSW Bias-Belted Tires	No charge
B41 Power Brakes, Front Disc	62
C16 Console	52
W23 Chrome-Style Road Wheels	91
Vinyl Top	80
High Impact Paint Color	13
Total	$3,929

** Includes LH remote mirror, variable-speed windshield, wipers, AM radio,and power steering*

*** Includes scooped 'Cuda hood and 'Cuda's body-side stripes*

Base 'Cuda Hardtop	$2,753
E55 340 Engine Package*	210
D21 4-Spd. Manual Transmission	193
T87 F70x14 Rwl Bias-Ply Tires	97
A36 Performance Axle Package**	60
B41 Power Brakes, Disc Front	62
C16 Console	52
F25 70 Amp Battery	13
G36 Mirrors, Dual Racing Style, Body Color, LH Remote	25
H51 Airtemp Air Conditioning	365
G11 Tinted Glass	36
J52 Inside Hood Release	10
J97 Rallye Instrument Panel	85
M51 Power Sunroof W/Vinyl Top	434
R36 Radio-AM/FM Stereo	191
R32 Dual Rear-Seat Speakers	24
S77 Power Steering	104
W21 Rallye Road Wheels	53
Total	$3,929

** Includes S13 heavy-duty suspension*

*** Includes D91sure-Grip Differential*

upper management in Highland Park that the E-Body (or, at least Plymouth's version of it) was worth bringing back for 1973.

Regarding what percentage of Barracudas had what features, a *1973 Plymouth Advance Information* publication from Chrysler, sent to the dealers late in the 1972 model run, showed 80.2 percent of Barracudas were built with the TorqueFlite automatic transmission: 34.0 percent with Airtemp air conditioning; 55.6 percent with the standard 318 V-8, and 39.1 percent with the optional 340; 82.6 percent were equipped with power steering; 97.2 percent with a factory-installed radio; 85.9 percent had either full wheel covers or optional road wheels; 53.7 percent had a vinyl top; and 67.8 percent had a center console.

As for the percentages of what color Barracudas were built at Hamtramck Assembly for 1972, that advance-information publication listed two available shades of blue: Basin Street Blue (Code TB3) and True Blue Metallic (Code GB5) as the top two color choices, with 12.1 percent and 11.9 percent, respectively, of the 1972 production total. Rallye Red (Code FE5) was next with 11.5 percent, the only other color that was sprayed on to more than 10 percent of the 1972 Barracudas.

The High Impact TorRed (Code EV2) and Lemon Twist (Code FY1) colors were next, with 9.1 percent and 8.2 percent, respectively, then came Sherwood Green Metallic (Code GF7), 6.3 percent; Tawny Gold Metallic (Code GY9) and Blue Sky (Code HB1), 5.6 percent each; Gold Leaf Metallic (Code GY8), 5.1 percent; Chestnut Metallic (Code HT8), 4.9 percent; Honeydew (Code GY4), 4.8 percent; Formal Black (Code TX9), 4.2 percent; Amber Sherwood Metallic (Code GF3), 3.9 percent; Winchester Gray Metallic (Code GA4), 3.2 percent; Spinnaker White (Code EW1), 2.4 percent; and Mojave Tan Metallic (Code HT6), .9 percent.

Barracuda's other price-class competitors did not see such rosy sales-percentage gains as their E-Body competitor. In fact, 1972 turned out to be the worst year ever for one of them, Camaro.

General Motors started Camaro production on time for 1972, but a strike at the Norwood, Ohio, assembly plant that also built the Pontiac Firebird and Chevy Nova, which began on April 8 of that year (over increased assembly-line speed, lay-offs, and weld-shop automation) was not settled until well after 1973 model-year production began at other GM plants. When Norwood Assembly reopened, some 1,100 unfinished cars that were in various stages of assembly were scrapped instead of completed, as General Motors determined that they could not be retrofitted to comply with the federal 5-mph bumper standards, or other new or updated federal safety and emission-control standards, that were effective for 1973.

That, and the softening market for pony cars, led to only 68,651 1972 Camaros being built (per the *Standard Catalog of American Cars 1946–1975*), a 63-percent drop from 1971's total of more than 107,000, and a far cry from the more than 200,000 Camaros built and sold for 1967–1969. The 1972 total included 11,364 Rally Sports, 6,562 Super Sports, and 2,575 Z-28s. Further breakdown of that strike-shortened year showed 63,882 Camaros were built with V-8s, 11,388 with 4-speed manual transmissions, 59,857 with an automatic transmission, and 31,737 with factory-installed air conditioning.

The 1972 sales totals for the Ford Mustang weren't much better. The final Mustang tally for that year was 125,405 per the *Standard Guide*. That worked out to a base-series total of 57,350 coupes, 15,622 SportsRoof fastbacks, and 6,401 convertibles, plus 18,045 Grande coupes and 27,675 Mach I's. It also added up to nearly a 16-percent drop over 1971's 149,678, and a far cry from the more than 417,000 built in Mustang's first year.

And the AMC Javelin? During 1972, 22,964 Javelin SSTs and 3,220 Javelin AMXs, for a total of 26,184 (per the *Standard Guide*), rolled out of AMC's Kenosha, Wisconsin, assembly plant, including 4,152 built with the Pierre Cardin–designed interior trim option and 100 SSTs built as police interceptors for the Alabama State Police. Javelin's 1972 numbers were a slight drop from the 1971 total of 26,867, but enough to keep Barracuda in fourth place in this four-car market sub-segment.

Demise of the 'Cuda in NHRA Pro Stock

While 1970 and 1971 had been memorable years for all Plymouth and Dodge drag racers who competed in NHRA's Pro Stock class with 426 Hemi E-Body cars, especially Sox & Martin, 1972 turned into a disaster, thanks in large part to rule changes effective with the season-opening Winternationals.

As NHRA's *National Dragster* explained, "After the first two seasons of Pro Stock competition in 1970 and 1971, there was no doubt that the factory hot rod category was a big hit with the fans. But NHRA officials were concerned that the overwhelming success of the Dodge and Plymouth entries, which had won 12 of the 15 races held during those two years, could hurt the class.

"Said then-NHRA Competition Director Steve Gibbs, 'At the end of 1971, there was no doubt that Chrysler had achieved total domination of Pro Stock, and the class was bound to suffer. We decided to implement weight breaks to encourage some other makes to get back into the program.'

"NHRA accordingly switched from the original 7.0 [pounds of car weight per cubic inch of engine displacement] factor for all types of cars, to 6.75 for small-block entries and 7.25 for cars with big-blocks.

"Only one small-block entry showed up at the 1972 season opener in Pomona: Jenkins' 331-cid Chevrolet Vega. Said Jenkins, 'I was going to build the Vega whether NHRA went with a weight-break format or not. I could've used it for match races.'

"Tuning problems held Jenkins to a qualifying best of 9.90, which put him in the 17th position of the 32-car field and forced him to race Stu McDade, driver of Billy Stepp's Dodge Challenger that had qualified No. 1 with a 9.59. But Jenkins made some pivotal suspension changes prior to the first round and managed to quicken his pace to a 9.63 to defeat McDade's 9.75. Jenkins went on to defeat four more Hemis to score a crowd-pleasing victory, the first of six wins in eight races that earned him the 1972 NHRA Pro Stock championship.

"Ford later got into the act with small-block Pintos campaigned by the likes of Bob Glidden, Gapp & Roush, and ['Dyno Don'] Nicholson, who won the NHRA Pro Stock title in 1973."

Sox & Martin only won one race during the 1972 season, IHRA's U.S. Open at Rockingham, North Carolina. During the season, they switched to an LA-small-block Duster, as well as a Hemi Dodge Colt, but Jenkins' Vega (using an engine that was never offered by Chevrolet as a factory option in it) was too dominant that season.

Another big change happened in Pro Stock the following season, with the arrival of the Lenco manual transmission, whose planetary gears and individual shifters for each gear enabled any competitor to shift as fast as Ronnie Sox, but without the risk of parts damage and transmission failure that a missed shift could bring. Sox & Martin installed a Lenco in their Duster that year, but did not experience much of an increase in performance.

Ronnie Sox and Buddy Martin, the dominant team in the first two seasons of NHRA's Pro Stock class, never saw the winner's circle again after 1972, and they closed down their race team in 1975.

Even with the available vinyl side striping, base-level Barracuda's nameplate shone on, moved to the door's upper-front area for 1972.

CHAPTER 8

1973 DODGE CHALLENGER
Performance Under Pressure

Whether the Challenger would return for another year was in doubt. But it did return, albeit as a shadow of its former self from two years earlier. For 1973, the Slant Six was dropped, the 318 became the base engine, and the 340 was the optional V-8. The 340 could be optioned with a 4-speed transmission or a TorqueFlite automatic transmission. Grille, bumper, and taillights remained largely the same, but the Challenger Rallye was now offered as an option package.

To put the situation into perspective, the E-Body sales were poor from the previous year, so more than a few Dodge dealers were wondering whether there would be a Challenger for 1973. Its lackluster sales performance since its introduction, as compared to initial sales projections that saw it and its E-Body sibling, Barracuda, selling 200,000 or more cars a year between them, gave them reason for concern.

The American automotive industry was going through an upheaval and ever-changing market conditions. However, Chrysler was determined to keep pace. For 1973, Chrysler's corporate "Extra Care In Engineering" phrase was more than just a tagline to Dodge's ads, along with their slogan "Dodge. Depend On It." The Electronic Ignition System, introduced on the 340 late in 1971, was now standard equipment on all models of all car lines, a selling point for salesmen, and a reason for dealers' parts departments to start cutting back on their inventories of replacement ignition points and condensers, which the Electronic Ignition System had eliminated.

Engineers in Highland Park had been busy on the big C-Body and B-Body Dodge lines, adding extra rubber insulators throughout the chassis to create the "Torsion Quiet Ride," which C-Body Chryslers and Y-Body Imperials had featured since 1970. Those additional rubber pieces, designed and engineered into the existing midsize and full-size platforms, resulted in those cars riding smoother and at a cost of increased isolation from the road.

The Challenger was still an attractive car for 1973, which wore its impact-absorbing bumpers well. This Challenger Rally hardtop wears a set of 15-inch Rallye wheels, as well as the 1970-1971 "snap open" fuel filler, neither of which were on the factory options list for 1973, but could easily be found at Dodge dealers' parts departments. (Photo Courtesy David Newhardt)

The FMVSS 215-compliant front bumper for 1973 is hardly distinguishable from its 1972 predecessor, save for the large rubber blocks on the bumper and the bumper's mounting farther forward of the front fenders. (Photo Courtesy David Newhardt)

"Dull gray" is not a name that applies to this Challenger. Silver Metallic paint adorns this Challenger Rallye. Goodyear Eagle tires are later additions; Goodyear didn't introduce its high-performance Eagle tires until several years after the end of E-Body production. (Photo Courtesy David Newhardt)

The year 1973 was the final one for the 340 in not only the Challenger, but in the entire Dodge and Plymouth lineup as an upgraded higher-output 360 was set to replace it for 1974. A factory-installed Airtemp air-conditioning compressor sits between the engine and radiator. (Photo Courtesy David Newhardt)

Although some later Challenger owners added the chrome snap-open fuel filler to their cars, they were looking for locking gas caps to go under them once the oil shock of October 1973 hit and gasoline thefts became a problem. (Photo Courtesy David Newhardt)

A closer look at the front end of this 1973 Challenger shows how the FMVSS 215 reinforcements moved the front bumper outward, and the huge rubber bumper guards/blocks flanking the front license plate location, which enabled it to pass the 5-mph-impact compliance tests without adding a front bumper like the one added to the Mercury Cougar to meet the new bumper regulations. Seeing a 1973 or 1974 Challenger with those bumper blocks still installed is rare, as owners have removed them for appearance's sake. (Photo Courtesy Mecum Auctions)

Was this a possible 1973–later Dodge Challenger design concept? This styling sketch by Chet Limbaugh shows a taillight/back-up light/bumper design that could have been considered for 1973, given the May 1970 date of the sketch and the typical American auto industry 24-month lead time to turn such a styling concept into production parts. Bumper appears to be possibly reinforced to meet the FMVSS 215 bumper standards that went into effect for 1973, without spoiling the Challenger's overall looks the way competitors' "park bench" bumpers did. (Photo Courtesy Chet Limbaugh)

They also had to make all of Dodge's existing car lines comply with yet another new Federal Motor Vehicle Safety Standard. FMVSS 215 required front-and-rear low-speed collision protection on all 1973-model passenger cars built after January 1, 1973.

Nonetheless, the Challenger would appear for 1973, alongside a Dodge lineup whose revisions ranged from new grilles and taillights to Torsion Quiet chassis rubberization.

Additions and Deletions

At first look, the 1973 Dodge Challenger did not appear very different from its 1972 predecessor. Visible changes were few. The front bucket seats were now constructed with a molded-in-place, full-volume urethane foam front and back, replacing the hard plastic back panel used since 1970. Also, fire-retardant chemicals were applied to all of the interior's soft trim pieces such as the seats, cushions, seat backs, floor coverings, and trim panels. Instead of being a separate model, the Challenger Rallye was demoted to option-package status for 1973 and given code A57.

But underneath the sheet metal, there were plenty of changes. Not only was the Electronic Ignition System standard on all engines, so were induction-hardened valveseats. These provided a greater resistance to wear and better compatibility with low-lead and unleaded gasolines. That wear resistance was needed as tetraethyl lead had previously served as an insulator from wear. With that chemical being phased out of the nation's gasoline supply, those valveseats were now passed through a large electromagnet after they were formed, and then rapidly quenched. That created a hardened layer at and just below the surface, giving those parts the wear resistance needed for use with gasolines that had less and less amounts of tetraethyl lead in them as time went on.

The Challenger's standard and optional engines had electric-assist chokes on their carburetors for 1973, added in the name of hydrocarbon and carbon monoxide emissions reductions during starting and warm-up. As the *1973 Dodge Dealer Data Book & Car Selector* explained to would-be Challenger buyers, "The electric assist choke shortens the period of choke operation when the outside temperatures are above 63 degrees Fahrenheit."

Speaking of Challenger's engines, they were now down to two, with the 225 Slant Six no longer available. Base engine was now the 318 V-8, and the 340 was optional with or without the A57 Rallye Package.

Front disc brakes were now standard on all Challengers, with rear brakes continuing to be the old style drum-and-shoe type. As front brakes contributed much more to a car's stopping power than rear brakes, the bean counters in Highland Park determined that the extra expense of disc brakes on the rear wheels was not worth the investment, not at that time.

The tried-and-true TorqueFlite automatic transmission received a number of upgrades and updates for 1973. Among them: a new fluid filter with 50 percent more filtering area for improved fluid (and transmission) life; its internal vent was redesigned to prevent fluid loss during hard braking from fast vehicle speeds; and the A-904 version used behind the 318 received a new internal seal which had a longer life at low ambient temperatures.

But the most visible change to Challenger for 1973 were a pair of large rubber blocks on both the front and rear bumpers, added to comply with the new federal bumper standard.

Dawn of the Big Bumper Era

During the 1950s, and before the National Traffic and Highway Safety Act was passed by Congress and signed into law by President Lyndon B. Johnson in 1966, passenger-car bumpers had been integrated more and more into a car's overall styling, their role as frame-mounted, low-speed protectors of a car's radiator and fuel tank diminishing. They became, in many instances, another exterior body panel, and little more than a chrome-plated place to hang license plates and bumper stickers from.

Unfortunately, those stylishly integrated bumpers provided little, if any, protection at collision speeds as low as 5 mph. Rather, they would transmit the force of impact through their attaching brackets, to the front fenders, grille, and radiator, as well as to the rear quarter panels, trunk lid, taillight panel, and, in some instances, the fuel filler. That led to repair bills in the hundreds, and even thousands, of dollars to replace crash-damaged parts.

The nation's automobile insurance companies were as enthusiastic to pay out claims for those low-speed crashes as they were to pay out claims arising from muscle car crashes, and they began raising rates and adding surcharges to policies of cars that were the most expensive to repair after a low-speed crash. They also pressured Washington, especially the National Highway Traffic Safety Administration (NHTSA), to do something about it.

The result was the Federal Motor Vehicle Safety Standard (FMVSS) 215, issued on April 9, 1971, effective with the new passenger cars produced on or after January 1, 1973, and designated 1973 or later models. It required dynamic protection for safety-related parts (i.e., lamps and reflectors; fuel, cooling and exhaust systems; plus the vehicle's hood, trunk, and doors) against 5-mph front impacts, and 2½-mph rear impacts, with the passage of compliance testing mandatory before production was to begin.

As it was built with Chrysler's Unibody construction, there was no separate frame on Challenger to attach any hydraulic impact-absorbers, such as the ones General Motors and Ford used on their full-framed passenger cars. What Chrysler's engineers did to make Challenger, and its E-Body sibling Barracuda, FMVSS 215 compliant was to make the bumper thicker, adding a reinforcing bar behind it, moving them outward slightly, and attaching two large, solid-rubber bumper guards.

Thanks to those four large rubber blocks, the Challenger's overall length increased from 191.3 to 198.2 inches, per the *1972* and *1973 Dodge Dealer Data Book & Car Selector*, but curb weight did not increase over 1972. Both of those publications listed the 318 Challenger's curb weight at 3,220 pounds.

The Challenger and its "rubber baby buggy bumpers" passed their FMVSS 215 compliance tests, and Challenger went on sale for 1973 in September 1972.

In the following years, many 1973 Challenger owners would remove the rubber bumper guards, to improve the appearance of their cars.

Models, Options and Pricing

Just like Challenger's styling was little changed for 1973, its available features and colors were much the same as they were for 1972.

A 1973 Challenger T/A? If Dodge had kept it in the Challenger lineup, here's how one may have looked for Challenger's fourth year in production. Similar "resto-modding" had given owners cars that look like "muscle era" ones.

Optional "accessory groups" became more prominent, with the A57 Rallye Package joining the A01 Light Package and A04 Basic Group "package deals" on Challenger's option list.

The A57 Rallye Package consisted of the twin-scoop hood that had originally been standard on the 1970 Challenger R/T; a black-painted front grille; simulated front fender scoops; a body-side strobe stripe; the Rallye Instrument Cluster with tachometer; heavy-duty suspension that included larger front torsion bars, heavy-duty rear leaf springs, tubular shock absorbers, front and rear sway bars; and F70x14 whitewall tires, with F70x14 raised-white-letter tires available for an extra charge. Wheels were still 14 x 5½ inches, and anyone who wanted a wheel and tire combination similar to the E60x15 tires on 15 x 7-inch rims that were available on the 1970–71 Challenger R/T would have to get them from the aftermarket.

Not included in the A57 Rallye package was the 340, which was available as a separate option. However, the A36 Performance Axle package was still available on 340 Challengers, Rallye package or not. It included 3.55:1 rear gears inside the 8¾-inch rear axle assembly's Sure-Grip limited-slip differential; a 26-inch-wide high-performance radiator with fan shroud; and if power steering was ordered, an air-to-fluid power steering fluid cooler.

The two other accessory groups for 1973 were the A01 Light Package, and the A04 Basic Group. Included in the Light Package were ashtray, glove box, trunk, and ignition lights (the latter with a time delay); instrument panel floodlight with time delay; a trunk light; and fender-mounted turn signals. None of these courtesy lights were available separately, if you wanted one, you had to get them all.

The A04 Basic Group combined options and features that were available separately, but not with the 340. The 318 Challengers ordered with it received a Music Master AM radio; power steering; 3-speed windshield wipers and electric washers; whitesidewall tires; undercoating and an under-hood insulating pad; a left-side chrome remote-control rearview mirror; plus the A01 Light Package.

Along with the accessory groups and the 340, the Challenger's option list still contained Airtemp air conditioning; power steering; power brakes; 4-speed manual transmission with Hurst Pistol Grip shifter; TorqueFlite automatic transmission, column or console-shifted; tinted glass; dual outside rearview mirrors (chrome or painted body color); a choice of Music Master AM, AM with stereo cassette player, or AM/FM stereo radios and a choice of single or dual rear speakers; heavy-duty-suspension; the Rallye gauge cluster (available separate from the A57 Rallye package); vinyl top; and wheel treatments ranging from body-colored steel wheels with "dog dish" caps to deluxe wheel covers, five-spoke, or Rallye road wheels, all available with either blackwall, whitewall, or raised-white-letter bias-belted tires.

Color-wise, the Challenger for 1973 was available in a choice of 15 colors: Light Blue (Code B1); Super Blue (Code B3); Bright Blue Metallic (Code B5); Bright Red (Code E5); Pale Green (Code F1); Light Green Metallic (Code F3); Dark Green Metallic (Code F8); Bronze Metallic (Code K6); Parchment (Code L4); Eggshell White (Code W1); Top Banana, the only remaining High Impact color (Code Y1); Light Gold (Code Y3); Gold Metallic (Code Y6), and Dark Gold Metallic (Code Y9).

Vinyl tops were available in either black, white, dark green, or gold. A vinyl-body side molding was available in black only; available paint stripes came in either blue, green, gold, black, or white; and a "performance" body-side tape stripe was only offered in black.

1973 DODGE CHALLENGER WINDOW STICKER

The following Manufacturer's Suggested Retail Prices (MSRP), or "sticker" prices for the base 1973 Dodge Challenger, and all available options, are estimates. Estimates were made using the prices given in the *Standard Catalogue of American Cars 1946–1975*, as well as the data in *Edmunds 1972 New Car Prices (May Edition)*.

Base Challenger (V-8)	$3,011
Options	
Vinyl top	81
D34 TorqueFlite Automatic	203
B41 Power Brakes, Front Disc	62
T34 F78x14 WSR Tires	41
A06 Basic Group*	197
H51 Airtemp A/C	369
G11 Tinted Glass	38
C16 Console	59
Total (Estimate)	$4,061

** Includes A01 Light Group, G35 Chrome LH Remote Mirror, R11 Music Master Am Radio, S77 Power Steering, J55 Undercoating and Hood Silencer Pad, W11 Deluxe Wheel Covers, J25 Variable-Speed Wipers*

Base Challenger	$3,011
Options	
A57 Rallye Package	182
High Impact Paint	13
E55 340 V-8 Package*	181
D21 4-Speed Manual	203
T87 F70x14 RWL Tires	No Charge with A57
H51 Airtemp AC	369
A36 Performance Axle Package**	63
C16 Console	59
G11 Tinted Glass	38
J97 Rallye Gauges w/Clock	Included with A57
G35 Dual Painted Sport Mirrors, LH Remote	28
S77 Power Steering	109
R35 AM/FM Stereo Radio	194
R32 Dual Rear Speakers	32
W21 Rallye Road Wheels	53
Total (Estimate)	$4,535

** Includes T86 F70x14 Tires and S13 Rallye Suspension*
*** Includes D91 Sure-Grip*

As mentioned above, many owners took the bumper blocks off the front and rear of their 1973 Challengers to improve their looks. Here's one whose bumpers have been treated to such an "addition-by-subtraction" process. This Challenger also received a number of pre-1973 items such as the 15-inch Rallye road wheels with 1970–1971 center caps, snap-open gas cap, 1970 R/T-style side and hood striping, and rear deck-lid spoiler, which give it a factory-appearing "resto-mod" look. (Photo Courtesy Barrett-Jackson Auction Company)

1973 Challenger Rallye in Review

The lack of new features led more than a few automotive-enthusiast publications to only test one E-Body car or another for 1973, if they even tested them at all, so published road tests of that year's Challenger are few. However, that lack of newness didn't stop Bud Lindemann and his *Car & Track* television crew from testing a 340/TorqueFlite Challenger Rallye from the Dodge press fleet on the 1.5-mile Waterford Hills Road Race Course near Clarkston, Michigan, for *Car & Track's* 1972–1973 season.

Here's what Bud had to say about their test of that metallic gray with black vinyl top 1973 Challenger Rallye:

"This body style was the result of last year's wind-tunnel testing. It's aerodynamically clean, good looking, and they repeated it for this year's offering. [Author note: It is unclear if Chrysler did any wind-tunnel testing on E-Body cars, as research to prepare this book did not turn up any evidence of such testing.]

"This Mopar pony is available in two forms: the Challenger and the Rallye Challenger. The latter, we feel, will command most of the sales attention.

"Ours was equipped with the snappy 340-ci V-8, with 4-barrel carburetion, coupled to a TorqueFlite transmission and a 3.23 axle ratio. This eight-banger came out of the hole well. Throttle response was good, 0 to 30 mph took 4.5 seconds. The console-mounted Slap Stik shifter was a delight. We hit 50 mph in 7.2 [seconds].

"Winding up through the gears produces excessive engine noise, with some vibration through the steering wheel. The 70 mph came in 13.4 seconds. [That "excessive engine noise" would likely be a pleasant sound to an E-Body enthusiast, as it was produced by the dual exhaust system used with all 340 Challengers since 1970. One shudders to think what a 426 Hemi 1973 Challenger Rallye would have sounded like!]

"Our car had power front discs [brakes], and they do make a difference. It dumped the heat rapidly. [Stopping from] 30 mph ate up 47 feet. Nose dive did not seem as pronounced from the inside as it did on film, which seemed a little odd for a car with strong suspension like this. From 50, [it stopped in] 102 feet.

"The brakes were cold on this 70-mph stop, and our driver brought the Challenger to a stop in 211 feet, with the usual Chrysler rear axle hop. Pedal fade was hardly noticeable.

"Through the pylon course, we found the steering response to be excellent. However, the power assist left little or no road feel. Returnability was slow. Body lean with this heavy-duty suspension system was slight. Even when we pushed the speedometer up 10 mph faster, stability remained good, as you can tell by this action freeze.

"Handling is far better in the Rallye model. The strong suspension on the Rallye includes heavy-duty shock absorbers, as well as a front sway bar, and a rear sway bar comes with the 340-inch engine. We also had the F70x14 bias-belted tires, remote-control racing mirrors, along with rally wheels. [Wheels on the test car were the W23 5-spoke type, not the W21 Rallye Road Wheel.]

"We felt that the clean styling of the Challenger was cluttered by some of the exterior cosmetics like side scoops and the power bulge hood.

"Beefier leg muscles made for good handling during high-speed cornering. However, the ride was rough, and could be considered by some passengers to be objectionable. Especially in the rear, but then, anybody in the rear [seat] would be so busy looking for a place to put their legs that they might not notice the ride. Front seats, on the other hand, were very comfortable. Chrysler has a new, full-foam, computer-designed front seat that really fits, offering good back, as well as lateral, support.

"To sum it up: If you're looking for a smooth, quiet ride with a spacious interior, this Challenger will not be your next car. However, if pony cars turn you on, and you like the spirited performers, this Rallye might just punch your buttons!"

Sales Results by the Numbers

Rumors of the demise of the upscale end of the pony car market segment were, in the words of Mark Twain, greatly exaggerated for 1973. Not only did Challenger show a sales increase, so did the Pontiac Firebird and Mercury Cougar.

The Challenger's 1973 total was 32,596, per the *Standard Catalogue of American Cars 1946–1975*, an 18-percent gain over 1972. As the Challenger Rallye was an option package instead of a separate model, no breakout was given for its exact production total.

However, that total was only good enough for third in that three-car market segment. Firebird sales rebounded in 1973 to 46,313 for the entire Firebird line, again per the *Standard Catalogue*. For the first time since 1968, Firebird had been produced over a "normal-length" model year, one not shortened by strikes or preproduction foul-ups, or extended to keep new product rolling into the showrooms as a result of a preproduction foul-up. That 1973 total included 14,096 base Firebird coupes, 17,249 Firebird Esprits, 10,166 Firebird Formulas, and 4,802 Trans Ams. In all, 1973 Firebird sales were up 35 percent from 1972.

Leading that upscale pony car trio was the Mercury Cougar, whose 60,628 total (again, according to the *Standard Catalog*) included 21,069 base-series Cougar coupes and 1,284 base Cougar convertibles, and 35,110 XR-7 coupes and 3,165 XR-7 convertibles. In all, Cougar sales rose 11.4 percent in 1973, a move that some might attribute to that year being the final year that Cougar and Mustang would share the same platform.

However, events before the end of calendar 1973 would prove those increased sales figures for model year 1973 to be a period of calm before a massive storm hit the U.S. auto industry.

CHAPTER 9

1973 BARRACUDA

A Coda for the 'Cuda

For 1973, the Barracuda continued to evolve. With more Barracuda buyers opting for either of the two LA-series small-block V-8s, Chrysler management dropped the Slant Six as the Barracuda's standard engine after the 1972 model run, replacing it with the 318. The model year also brought new features: the FMVSS 215-compliant bumpers, front and rear; a new, optional body-side tape stripe that was available (in either black or white) as a separate option on Barracuda and 'Cuda, as well as included in the A51 Sport Equipment Package that included the scooped hood that was standard on 'Cuda; full-foam front bucket seats, as on the Challenger and front and rear bumper blocks.

A change on all 1973 Chrysler-built cars and trucks that new-car buyers likely did not notice, but collectors and restorers in years to come would, was an expanded "door tag," which stated that the car was in compliance with that year's applicable federal safety and emission-control standards as of the day it was built. From 1968 to 1972, this tag included the car's Vehicle Identification Number (VIN), as well as a numerical code relating to what month and year the car was built. For 1973, the larger door tag included a numeric "MDH" code line at the bottom, which signified the month, day, and hour (in 24-hour time) of final assembly. Thus, a "021211" code on that line meant that car was assembled on February 12 between 1100 and 1200 hours local time. That information could be used by Chrysler and its dealers to pinpoint cars that would need repairs covered under a Technical Service Bulletin, or worse, subject to a recall.

Features, Colors and Options

If you liked the available options and features on the 1972 Barracuda, you were certain to like them for 1973. No major changes were made in the available accessory groups and option packages: the A01 Light Package, A04 Basic Group, A36 Performance Axle Package for the 340 cars, and the A51 Sport Decor Package, were all unchanged.

The 340 was now available on the base Barracuda series, as well as on the 'Cuda. The only item of standard equipment that was different on the two E-Body Plymouth lines for 1973 was

Nowadays, seeing a base-level 1973 Barracuda with all its Sport Decor Group trim intact is rare, as more than a few surviving examples have been customized or "resto-modded" by their owners. This 318 example graced Barrett-Jackson's collector-car auction in Las Vegas in 2010 in top condition and is an outstanding example of a late-production non-'Cuda E-Body. (Photo Courtesy Barrett-Jackson Auction Company)

For 1973, the 'Cuda appeared little changed, but the new FMVSS 215-compliant bumpers added more than 8 inches to the E-Body's overall length. Vinyl body-side stripe and vinyl top choices were carried over from 1972, as were the W21 Rallye road wheels and raised-white-letter F70-14 tire options. (Photo by Mack Poholko)

the scooped "Performance-styled" hood that was standard on the 'Cuda. All other sound system, wheel and tire, and comfort and convenience options carried over from 1972 unchanged. As for the array of colors for the Barracuda and 'Cuda for 1973, the all-vinyl front bucket/rear bench seats were available in your choice of blue, dark green, black, and white (gold was no longer available).

Outside, 17 colors of acrylic enamel paint were on the 1973 Barracuda paint selection: Silver Frost Metallic (Code A5); Blue Sky (Code B1); Basin Street Blue (Code B3); True Blue Metallic (Code B5); Rallye Red (Code B9); Mist Green (Code F1); Amber Sherwood Metallic (Code F3); Forest Green Metallic (Code F8); Autumn Bronze Metallic (Code K6); Sahara Beige (Code L4); Spinnaker White (Code W1); and the extra-cost High Impact Lemon Twist (Code Y1), Honey Gold (Code Y3), and Golden Haze Metallic (Code Y6). Leaving the color selection for 1973 were Winchester Gray Metallic, Mojave Tan, and the High Impact TorRed.

Vinyl tops were offered in black, white, dark green, and gold, with blue not returning for 1973.

Such was the "new" Barracuda and 'Cuda for 1973. Much like the rest of the Plymouth lineup, very few visible changes had been made for 1973. So, where was the time, money, and effort going at Chrysler that formerly resulted in distinctive-appearing new cars every year? Likely to the same place where GM's, Ford's, and AMC's similar resources went.

Keeping Uncle Sam Happy

Overall, there was a decided lack of newness in all U.S. automakers' offerings for 1973. Money that might have gone into fresh styling was diverted to federal safety and emissions standards compliance. The only all-new cars available that year were General Motors' midsized A-Body cars, which included "personal luxury" coupes for Buick and Oldsmobile comparable to the Chevrolet Monte Carlo and Pontiac Grand Prix. Their debut had been pushed back a year by the 1970 UAW strike, which delayed the engineering-and-tooling phase of that new platform's development.

Bedazzling with Brilliance

Even more than before, emphasis on Chrysler's long-time reputation for outstanding engineering appeared in all phases of Plymouth advertising and promotion in 1973. One was hard-pressed to find any mention of vehicle performance, as had been common through the late 1960s into 1970.

The slogan "Extra Care In Engineering . . . It Makes A Difference," was also splashed across every Chrysler Corporation car and light truck line, and television commercials touting it were added to the rotation of product-centered spots that aired on local and network television.

At the dealers, "Extra Care In Engineering . . . It Makes A Difference" was on banners hung from showroom walls, and included in product information such as the *Dealer Data Book,* whose engineering-advances section ran some 35 pages, much longer than the Barracuda's 12-page product-information section.

The 1973 *Plymouth Dealer Data Book* detailed such Barracuda-related advances as the Electronic Ignition System, which was now standard on all North American–built Chrysler Corporation passenger cars and light trucks; "Unibody" unit-body construction and the multi-stage anti-corrosion process production bodies received; plus torsion bar front/elliptical rear leaf spring suspensions.

Where you did find mention of vehicle performance was in the *Dealer Data Book* section about the 340-ci V-8, which was still shared with the Road Runner and Duster 340.

The 1973 front red-accented grille was another carryover from 1972, as was the twin-scooped sport hood, which was included with the 'Cuda or optional on the base Barracuda series. Underbumper fog lights were an aftermarket addition, and aided the sealed-beam headlights while driving in less-than-ideal weather. (Photo by Mack Poholko)

From this angle, the 1973 Barracuda's and 'Cuda's FMVSS 215-compliant bumper and the plastic filler panels between it and the rear quarter panels are the most noticeable. The outward relocation of the bumper was necessary because of the addition of a steel reinforcing bar to help the rear end of the car sustain a 2½-mph impact with no damage to the car. These tires are F70-14s. Blackwall versions in this size were not available as factory options; only whitewall or raised-white-letter versions came from the factory. (Photo by Mack Poholko)

"Here, for the performance enthusiast, is a compact-block engine with very large 4.04-inch cylinder bores. The large bores are teamed with large intake manifold passages, large intake and exhaust valve ports, and low-restriction dual exhausts to breathe freely right up through the 340's high-speed power ranges. 'Breathing' is a term that describes how an engine takes in fuel and air and exhausts burned gases . . . and the Plymouth 340 breathes very efficiently."

That passage about "large intake and exhaust valve ports" must have been written by someone who either did not know about the larger ones on the 1968–1971 340s, or who chose to (or was ordered to) ignore the 2.02-inch intake valves used in the earlier 340, one source of that engine's tremendous power.

That section about the 340 also described its aluminum-on-steel bearing material as "the type used on the Plymouth high-performance cars raced by Richard Petty." However, Richard Petty did not race a Plymouth after the next-to-last 1972 NASCAR Winston Cup Series race at Rockingham, North Carolina, on October 22, 1972. From then until his team switched to Chevrolet engines under Chevrolet or Oldsmobile sheet metal in 1978, the #43 STP car that they raced, and won two NASCAR Winston Cup Championships with, was a Dodge.

In the Press

Compared with the motoring-press coverage of 1970 and 1971, coverage of the Barracuda was scant to nonexistent during the 1973 model year. Why, writers and editors likely said, should we bother with a car that is barely changed from 1972 and has a far-shorter list of available powertrains and other options from its 1970 introduction?

If they did, their coverage might have read like Bud Lindemann's narration for *Car & Track*'s filmed road test of the 1973 Dodge Challenger Rallye, which was cited in the previous chapter.

Or, it might have been as harsh as *Car and Driver*'s criticism of the 1972 'Cuda was.

One publication that did write about Barracuda for 1973 was *Motor Trend,* which covered it (briefly) in its Buyers Guide for 1973. It emphasized Chrysler's engineering advances, much like the factory literature did. "As in other Chrysler Corp. lines, all engines will get the new electronic ignition system which only requires a drop of oil for the distributor bearings every 24,000 miles. V-8 engines will have the induction-hardened valveseats, which came only with [Slant Six] last year. This usage will permit lifting the requirement that leaded gasoline be used for every fourth fill of the tank. A new electric choke assist cuts down on emissions during starting and warm-up, and a heater element shortens the period of choke operation when the outside temperature is above 68 [degrees Fahrenheit].

"You have a choice between a floor-shifted 3-speed manual transmission and the 3-speed TorqueFlite [automatic] with both engines, and a 4-speed manual is available with the 340. The latter, incidentally, puts out 240 hp compared to 150 hp for the 318, and it does this with surprising economy. About 15 mpg can be expected at steady cruising speeds because you're only operating on two of the [carburetor's] four barrels in that range. To compare this output in terms of today's still unfamiliar SAE [Society of Automotive Engineers] net rating system, the 500-ci monster used in the Cadillac Eldorado claims only 235 hp.

"Disc brakes are standard on the Barracuda, and they're power-assisted on the 'Cuda. Also with the 'Cuda, you get the otherwise optional handling package, which consists of heavy-duty torsion bars and leaf rear springs, and a front and rear sway bar. Additional 'Cuda options include a special locked 3.51 differential (*Motor Trend*'s term for the 3.55:1-geared,

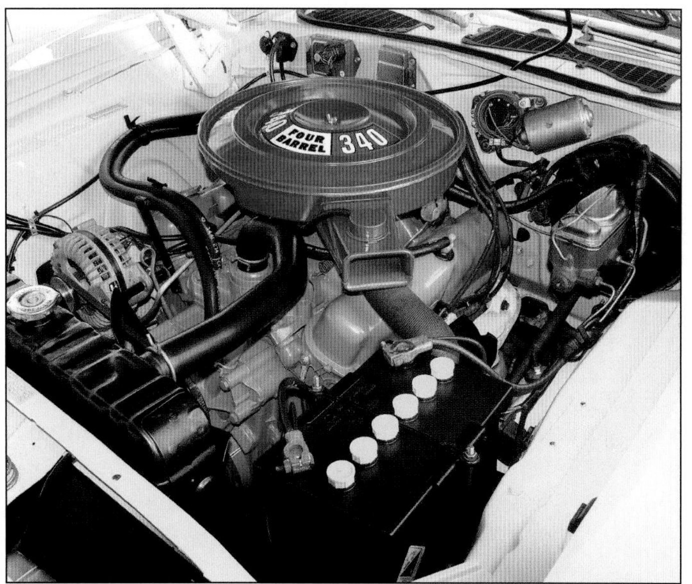

Back for one last year, in 1973, was the regular-gas 340, which first appeared for 1972. All 1973 Chrysler engines were painted blue; no more orange-painted high-performance engines. In fact, the standard 318 appears similar, except for its smaller, black-painted air cleaner. The battery is a reproduction of the original Mopar battery installed at Hamtramck. (Photo by Mack Poholko)

Exhaust manifolds were the same ones used beginning in 1972, and more than a few 'Cuda owners replaced them with either aftermarket steel-tube headers or 1968–1971 factory manifolds. The green-and-white decal on the passenger-side front fender well contains the emissions-control compliance statement, as well as tune-up settings for the 340 that (per Chrysler) ensured compliance with that standard while giving good-for-1973 performance. (Photo by Mack Poholko)

Sure-Grip differential 8¾-inch rear end), 26-inch-high performance radiator with fan shroud, and a cooler for the power steering pump, if that accessory is so ordered.

"Impact bumpers for both models rely entirely on bracket reinforcement plus large solid rubber guards to give the required protection. The rubber pieces, while not particularly attractive, can be compressed up to 60 percent without damage, and they also protect the other fellow. Plastic body-colored strips are used to fill the additional space between the bumper and the body. These bumpers are the only styling change on the 1973 Barracuda, but they make the new model instantly recognizable. Other exterior improvements include newly designed wiper blades, developed to minimize smear and streaking while improving wind lift characteristics. Also, a new thermo-setting acrylic dispersion enamel is used for the color [paint] coats. This is claimed to be more resistant to parking lot dings.

"A new standard [front] seat for the Barracuda has a molded-in-place front and back, instead of those knee-knocking hard backs used in the past. The car doesn't have much rear-seat legroom (only 28.9 inches), so the softer the inevitable contact, the better. A lever-type seatback release replaces the pushbutton system previously used with bucket seats. For added theft protection, a stronger deck-lid lock is enclosed in a steel housing.

"'Cudas have full engine instrumentation plus a tach in an attractive layout that's optional on the base model with either engine. A tilt steering wheel, rare in this type of car, is also optional, but you can't get power windows or door locks. [Author note: A tilt steering wheel option was never offered on the E-Body Barracudas and Challengers, or on the A-Body Barracudas either. They were options on the Chevrolet Camaro and Ford Mustang.] A fairly wide assortment of styled wheels, a so-called cosmetic package with stripes and a special hood, and the usual assortment of radios and tape players complete the option list."

That was it. No mention of acceleration or quarter-mile times, handling prowess, fuel economy, or overall roadability.

Models, Options and Pricing

Retail price information for the 1973 Barracudas is limited. At the time of this writing, the only information of this kind that was available was in the *Standard Catalogue of American Cars 1946–1975* and was limited to base sticker price plus very few options. For this section, the 1973 percentage increase on mechanical, electronic, and appearance options was calculated using the *Standard Catalogue* data, as well as that from *Edmunds 1972 Car Prices* (May Edition), and that percentage was added to the 1972 sticker prices (per *Edmunds*).

Given that demand for Barracudas, and its pony car competition was not as high as it was just three years earlier, it is very likely that Chrysler-Plymouth dealers were encouraged to make generous deals below sticker price, but above invoice price, to keep this relatively slow-selling line of Plymouths from clogging dealers' inventory lots month after month.

This dash with a Rallye gauge cluster, console, and Hurst Pistol Grip shifter carried over not only from 1972, but from all the way back in 1970. (E-Body enthusiasts insist this is because Chrysler got them right the first time.) The accordian-shaped section of the steering column was for impact-energy absorption, just as it was with every E-Body car built before and after. Note the non-AC/heater/defroster controls at passenger-side of the dash. The condition of the pedals and the mat underneath it indicate that this car is not a "trailer queen." (Photo by Mack Poholko)

Still no redline on the 7,000-rpm tach, though the markings are a different color above 5,500 rpm. The radio is the optional R11 Music Master pushbutton AM, whose left-offset knobs were a Chrysler exclusive. The lever at the top of the steering column is part of the built-in anti-theft protection and could be engaged to remove the key with just two fingers. (Photo by Mack Poholko)

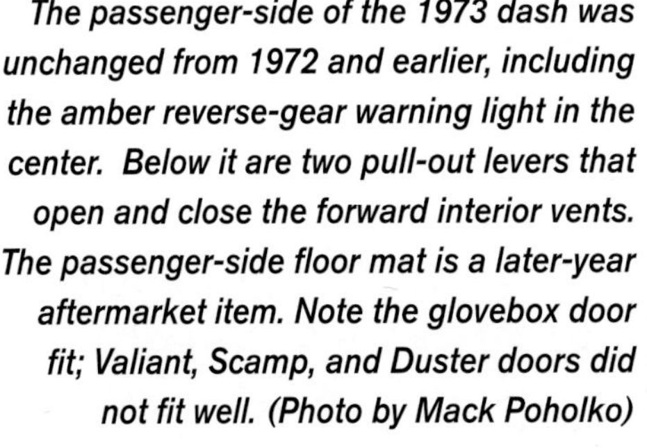

The passenger-side of the 1973 dash was unchanged from 1972 and earlier, including the amber reverse-gear warning light in the center. Below it are two pull-out levers that open and close the forward interior vents. The passenger-side floor mat is a later-year aftermarket item. Note the glovebox door fit; Valiant, Scamp, and Duster doors did not fit well. (Photo by Mack Poholko)

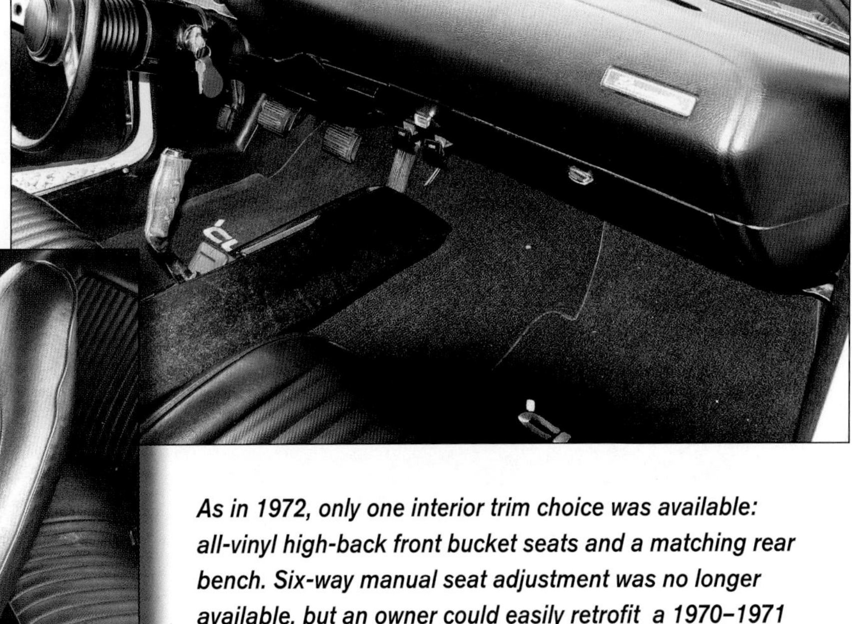

As in 1972, only one interior trim choice was available: all-vinyl high-back front bucket seats and a matching rear bench. Six-way manual seat adjustment was no longer available, but an owner could easily retrofit a 1970–1971 adjuster if one could be found. The steering wheel is the same E-Body version of the Tuff wheel used beginning in 1972 and was still the only one offered. The space between the shifter and the console door is the closest thing to a cup holder in the cabin. (Photo by Mack Poholko)

Sales Results

Along with their roundup of the 1973 Barracuda's features and options in their Buyers Guide, *Motor Trend* had this information about the pony car market as a whole at the start of the 1973 model year.

The same rear window glass was used in 1973 as had been used since 1970. The rear shelf holds openings for optional rear-seat speakers and were typically cut out if an owner added aftermarket speakers behind the back seat. (Photo by Mack Poholko)

"Plymouth has released some interesting statistics on the 'pony,' or specialty-compact market which explain why Barracuda was continued for 1973, and also why certain models and options have been discontinued. Specialty compact sales for the entire industry peaked at 10.5 percent in 1967 and then, more or less simultaneously with insurance companies all but refusing to cover that type of car at any price, sales plummeted to 4.2 percent [of the new-car market], a point reached early in 1972. They have now turned around at 4.3 percent. Barracuda, coincidentally, claims 4.3 percent of the segment.

"In 1972, buyers chose about evenly between the [base series] Barracuda and the more-expensive 'Cuda model. Counting [the base] Barracuda alone, 85 chose the 318-ci V-8, 8.9-percent 6-cylinder power, and 6.1 percent the optional 340 4-barrel. This last [engine], of course, was and is standard on the 'Cuda, so its popularity is much greater than the above figure would indicate. As might be expected, 6-cylinder power will no longer be offered in the single hardtop coupe body style. The choice by Plymouth's admission is small, but it claimed to be right on target for the men and women in their mid-twenties who statistics show buy this car.

"Chrysler Corp. is keeping its collective fingers crossed on the Barracuda for the coming model year. If sales drop further, it's sure to go because a decision must be made soon whether tooling for future models is warranted or not."

For 1973, Barracuda sales did increase, up to 21,713 per the *Standard Catalog of American Cars 1946–1975*, of which 11,587

If you wanted a Plymouth that could comfortably seat three across, you typically didn't buy a Barracuda; a Satellite or Fury sedan was a roomier choice. The center of the rear seat bottom sits directly over the rear floorpan's driveshaft tunnel and did not have as much "give" as the outboard seating locations did. Interior side panels were still one-piece molded plastic pieces. (Photo by Mack Poholko)

No change in trunk size for 1973. It was still around 8 cubic feet of room for luggage. The Space-saver tire was no longer a factory option, but could be obtained from Chrysler-Plymouth dealer parts departments or from aftermarket tire stores. The round plastic plugs cover the holes used to drain primer after the body was dunked in electrostatic-primer tanks during assembly as part of its anti-corrosion process. The trunk mat was a simple vinyl item, not a piece of carpet to match the cabin. (Photo by Mack Poholko)

were base Barracudas and 10,626 were 'Cudas. That was a nearly 15-percent increase of 1972's 18,450 final Barracuda sales tally.

Mustang also saw a sales boost in 1973, up around 7 percent to 134,867 total (51,430 base coupes, 10,820 base SportsRoof fastbacks, 11,853 convertibles, 25,274 Grande coupes, and 35,440 Mach I fastbacks, per the *Standard Catalogue).*

With Camaro in full model-year production for only the third time in its history, General Motors built and Chevrolet sold 96,751 1973 Camaros per *TheCamaro.com.* That was nearly 30 percent more than the strike-shortened 1972 figure of 68,656 listed in the *Standard Catalogue.* The website *The-Camaro.com's* 1973 production figures for Camaro include

The vinyl "rub rail" molding that was a factory option for 1973 served to protect the car's fenders, doors, and quarter panels from parking-lot dings. A splash shield located just aft of the front wheelwell is an aftermarket item. Post-1971 Barracudas and 'Cudas are good candidates for owner-inspired "restomodding," so E-Body cars in this configuration, resembling ones commonly seen during the 1970s, are almost as rare as surviving original 440 Six Barrel and 426 Hemi cars. (Photo by Michael Thomas)

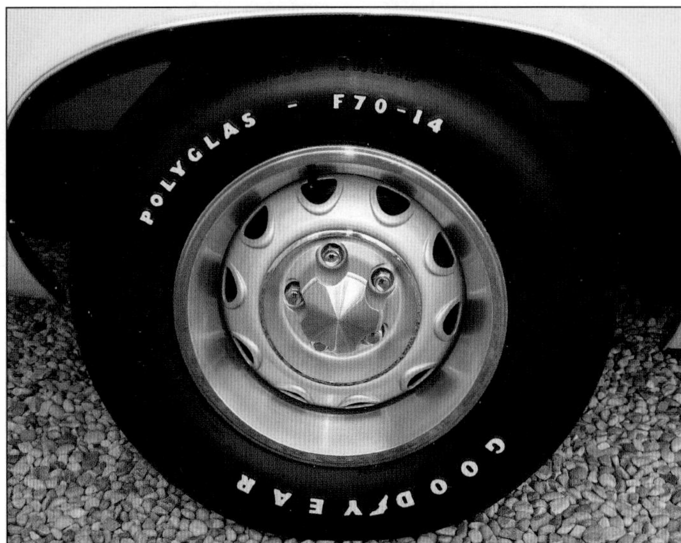

The optional W21 Rallye road wheel returned for 1973 in 14-inch form, with the same center cap that debuted in 1972, and the chrome lug nuts, argent silver finish, and outer trim ring that had been included with it since 1970. Goodyear Polyglas (polyester-cord body with fiberglass belts under the tread) was also a factory option on Duster 340s and Road Runners in 1973. This tire is likely an aftermarket reproduction; Goodyear discontinued this style before the end of the 1970s. (Photo by Mack Poholko)

When Carlisle Events put together a special 50 Years of Barracuda display for its Chrysler Nationals in 2014, this was the 1973 representative in that special collection. Note the W23 five-spoke road wheels, which were a popular option then and are popular in reproduction form today. (Photo by Ed Buczeske/Courtesy Carlisle Events)

Not all 1973 'Cudas wore the body-side tape stripes; they could be optioned-off at the time the car was ordered. This one has had its front bumper blocks removed, a common practice by owners to improve appearance. Whitewall tires and 14-inch deluxe wheel covers are the same as were used on B-Body Plymouth Satellites that year and were also available again for 1974. (Photo by Michael Thomas)

For 1973, the Code A51 Sport Appearance Package returned for the base Barracuda series, complete with twin-scooped hood atop its standard 318 V-8 and side stripes "borrowed" from the 'Cuda. (Photo Courtesy Jeanne and Dana Breska)

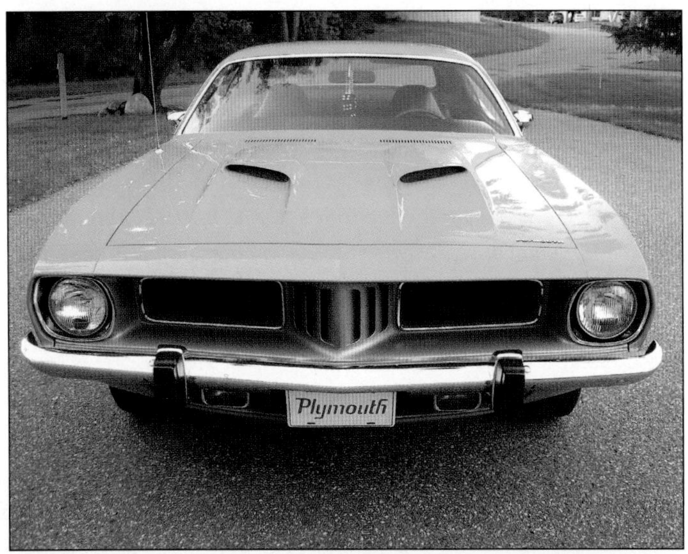

From the front, the original front bumper with its massive rubber blocks is still on this 1973 Barracuda, it and the rear bumper add about 9 inches to the E-Body Plymouth's overall length. The scooped hood is identical in styling and function to the one shown on the A51-equipped 1972 Plymouth Barracuda earlier in this book. (Photo Courtesy Jeanne and Dana Breska)

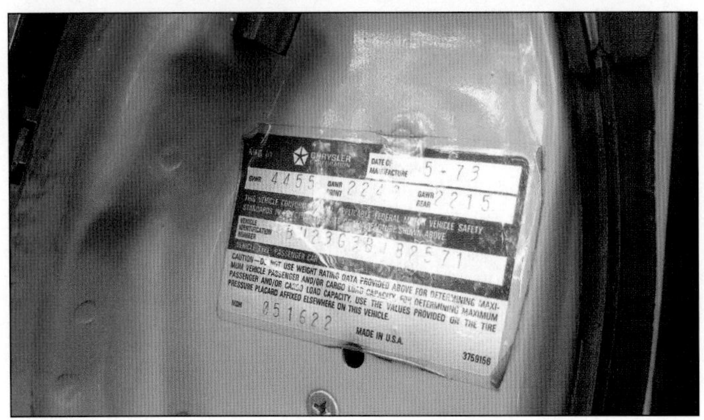

The standard 318 (such as this 40,000-mile original seen in Dana and Jeanne's 1973 Barracuda) is increasingly rare in its original, unmodified condition. Many owners remove theirs for a rebuild, then add chrome valvecovers and other accessory brightwork. This is an unadorned original. (Photo Courtesy Jeanne and Dana Breska)

The view from the rear is almost the same as that of the 1972 Barracuda seen previously. The chrome-tipped dual exhaust system was a later upgrade, as 318s were factory equipped with a single exhaust system and a rear valance under the bumper with no cutouts for dual exhausts. The original rear bumper guards are still in their factory location, and the plastic filler between the bumper and the rear body is still in its original (gray) color. (Photo Courtesy Jeanne and Dana Breska)

Among the firsts for Barracuda for 1973 were standard front disc brakes, standard Electronic Ignition System, and this new factory tag on the left front doorjamb. Along with the car's VIN, gross weight ratings, and a statement about the car's Federal Safety and Emissions standards compliance was the door tag. Per this tag, this car rolled off the line at Hamtramck on May 16, 1973, between the hours of 2200-2300 (10-11 p.m. Eastern Daylight Time). (Photo Courtesy Jeanne and Dana Breska)

64,424 base Sport Coupes (3,614 with a 6-cylinder engine and 60,810 V-8s), 32,327 Camaro Type LTs, 11,364 Rally Sports, and 11,574 Z-28s. (No breakdown on how many Z-28/Rally Sports were built.)

Meanwhile in Kenosha, AMC built 30,902 Javelins for 1973, of which 25,195 were base Javelins and 5,707 were AMXs. That also was a significant boost over 1972, just over 15 percent more than the 26,084 built in 1972.

Small-blocks seemed to be one key to this end of the pony car market's success in 1973. Would that success continue into 1974?

What happens when an owner "resto-mods" his 1973 Barracuda? In this case, he added 17-inch American Racing Wheel "Torq-Thrust" wheels (which, combined with the ultra-low-profile tires, fit the E-Body fender wells very well), 1971-style rear-quarter "billboard" graphics, and a Cal-Tracs rear suspension system. That's along with a very potent powertrain under that vivid red sheet metal. (Photo Courtesy Barrett-Jackson Auction Company)

1973 BARRACUDA AND 'CUDA WINDOW STICKER

Base Barracuda Hardtop with 318 V-8	$2,935
D34 TorqueFlite Automatic	215
A04 Basic Group*	197
A51 Sport Decor Package**	70
H51 Airtemp Air Conditioning	369
G11 Tinted Glass	38
T34 F78x14 WSW Bias-Belted Tires	No charge with A01
B41 Power Brakes, Front Disc	65
C16 Console	59
W23 Chrome-Style Road Wheels	91
Vinyl Top	81
High Impact Paint Color	14
Total (Estimate)	$4,134

** Includes LH remote mirror, variable-speed windshield, wipers, AM radio, and power steering*

*** (Includes scooped 'Cuda hood and 'Cuda's body-side stripes*

Barrett-Jackson's annual Scottsdale, Arizona, collector-car auction brings out the finest in restored, preserved-original, and specially constructed collector cars, drawing interest, and bidders, from around the world. This 1973 'Cuda is seen here in its moment in the spotlight while up for bids. Note the red-painted grille accents, another 'Cuda standard feature. (Photo Courtesy Barrett-Jackson Auction Company)

Base 'Cuda Hardtop	$3,120
E55 340 Engine Package*	85
D21 4-Spd. Manual Transmission	203
T87 F70x14 RWL Bias-Ply Tires	102
A36 Performance Axle Package**	63
B41 Power Brakes, Disc Front	65
C16 Console	59
F25 70-Amp Battery	15
G36 Mirrors-Dual Racing-Style, Body Color, LH Remote	27
H51 Airtemp Air Conditioning	369
G11 Tinted Glass	38
J52 Inside Hood Release	11
J97 Rallye Instrument Panel	89
M51 Power Sun Roof w/Vinyl Top	434
R36 Radio-AM/FM Stereo	194
R32 Dual Rear-Seat Speakers	28
S77 Power Steering	109
W21 Rallye Road Wheels	53
Total (Estimate)	$5,064

** Includes S13 HD Suspension*

*** Includes D91Sure-Grip Differential*

CHAPTER 10

1974 DODGE CHALLENGER

Still Running Against the Wind

The Challenger returned for its final year largely unchanged with similar trim and options. The 4-barrel 360 replaced the 340, and it delivered more torque that was ideally suited for street driving. And the 318-ci was retained as the base engine. While the Challenger's 1973 sales increase brought a sliver of optimism, the fate of Dodge's pony car had been sealed when the 1974 version began rolling out of Hamtramck Assembly in the late summer of 1973. A total of 11,354 Challengers were produced for 1974.

Other changes were few. An updated federal bumper standard now called for 5-mph impact protection front and rear, so Challenger's rear bumper was revised to comply with it. Also, corporate cost cutting meant only two sizes of V-8 engines for the LA and B/RB engine series.

For 1974: What's New

That meant that the 340 was no more, replaced by an all-new Code E58 360 4-barrel High Performance V-8. According to Dodge's 1974 *Dealer Data Book,* it was "a larger-displacement version of Dodge's famous 340 V-8. The extra piston displacement gives the 360 more break-away power than its predecessor, the 340." It added the 1972-later 340's cylinder heads, Carter ThermoQuad 4-barrel carburetor, long-duration camshaft, shot-peened crankshaft, windage tray, and dual exhausts to what had been regarded since its 1971 introduction as a "Brady Bunch station wagon engine."

What else was new with Challenger for 1974? Carburetors on both the 360 and 318 were new "solid fuel" versions of the Carter 2-barrel and ThermoQuad 4-barrel, which the *1974 Dodge Dealer Data Book* said provided "improved fuel metering control and more reliable operation with lean fuel mixtures," which in turn kept harmful emissions low.

Atop both engines were new air cleaners. Their oval-shaped inlet snorkels cut down on intake-air restriction and improved power without increasing engine noise. One other underhood change was two throttle-return springs instead of one, "to provide additional reassurance that the throttle is returned to the closed position when the driver's foot is removed from the accelerator," per the *Dealer Data Book*.

For 1974, Challenger's A57 Rally Package carried over its scooped hood and simulated side scoops from 1973, as that year had done from 1972. This example has been subtlely resto-modded, yet has a period correct look to it. Car courtesy Streetside Classics.

The Challenger also gained a pair of larger rubber blocks on the rear bumper to meet the 1974 5-mph front and rear federal bumper standards.

Then there were the front seat belt/starter interlocks, mandated by FMVSS 208, which prevented the car from starting unless the driver and front-seat passenger were both buckled up. This one item, standard across the entire Chrysler passenger-car line for 1974 (as well as GM's, Ford's, AMC's, and every 1974-dated import's) was likely the single most hated feature ever added to a production car. It caused no small amount of inconvenience to drivers who were used to buckling up after they started the engine and added aggravation if a bag of groceries, or a family pet, was on the passenger seat. Dealer service technicians, and service-station mechanics, were paid cash "under the table" to disarm it by unplugging a connector under the seat and taping up the ends with electrical tape. The

This car was assembled at Hamtramck on January 9, 1974, less than three months before Chrysler's management ended production of the E-Body cars and devoted Hamtramck to A-Body production for the rest of 1974 and for 1975. Spiking gasoline prices from October 8, 1973, onward (the first "oil shock") cut off the Challenger's sales that year, in much the same way that my Police-model 2007 Dodge Charger appears to be intercepting this car. Car courtesy Streetside Classics.

This detail of the rear taillight and backup light was a Challenger styling mainstay since 1972. The slot in the rear bumper under the backup light is the provision for the factory-installed bumper jack to be located when raising the rear of the car to change the left rear tire. Car courtesy Streetside Classics.

The taillight panel was once again painted matte black on A57 Rallye Package Challengers for 1974, and their under-bumper rear valance panel again contained cutouts for a pair of chrome exhaust tips. Those tips are at the end of a 3-inch-diameter stainless steel exhaust system that would have rattled every window in the Hamtramck Assembly complex back in the day! Car courtesy Streetside Classics.

This side view of the right rear corner shows how the rear bumper fits in relation to the rear quarter panel, with a soft-plastic strip covering the gap between them. The 5-mph impact-absorbing bumpers at each end added nearly 9 inches to the Challenger's overall length, compared with the 1972 models built before FMVSS 215 became effective. Car courtesy Streetside Classics.

seat belt/starter interlock provision of FMVSS 208 was repealed by NHTSA before the end of the 1974 model year, after howls of protest from taxpayers and lawmakers alike prompted the bureaucrats to act.

Those, and the change of the VIN's sixth character, denoting model year, from a "3" to a "4," were the extent of the visible changes to Challenger for 1974.

Options, Features and Colors

If you liked Challenger's color selection for 1973, you were bound to like what was offered for 1974. Carrying over were the four all-vinyl interior color choices (black, white, blue, and green), and four vinyl top choices (black, white, gold, and green).

Available acrylic enamel colors on the Challenger were heavy on the "earth tones" that were in fashion in the early and mid-1970s. The 1974 color selection was Gold Metallic (Code YJ6), Dark Gold Metallic (Code JY9), Sienna Metallic (Code KT5), Dark Moonstone Metallic (Code KL8), Burnished Red Metallic (Code GE7), Frosty Green Metallic (Code KG2), Avocado Gold Metallic (Code KJ8), Deep Sherwood (green) Metallic (Code KG8), Lucerne Blue Metallic (Code KB5), Powder Blue (Code KB1), Yellow Blaze (Code KY5), Golden Fawn (Code KY4), Parchment (Code HL4), Bright Red (Code FE5), Eggshell White (Code EW1), and Black (Code TX9). Notable by their absence were the extra-cost High Impact colors. Top Banana Yellow had been the only one available in 1973; now it, too, was gone from the Challenger's color palette.

The options list for the fifth-year Challenger was a familiar, and short, one. The E58 360-ci V-8 was the only engine option, while the 4-speed manual transmission or 3-speed TorqueFlite automatic were the only gearbox options other than the standard 3-speed stick.

Extra-cost options were Airtemp air conditioning; Sure-Grip differential; power steering; power front disc/rear drum brakes; rear window defogger (now required on all cars sold in New York state); tinted glass; undercoating with hood insulator pad; inside hood release; Rallye instrument cluster; "Performance" hood with scoop (the same hood that dated back to the 1970 Challenger R/T); a choice of outside rearview mirrors including dual "racing" mirrors, either chromed or painted body color; body-side moldings; a choice of Music Master AM or AM/FM stereo radios without a tape player; rear seat speakers; body-side

Appearing for one year only: the Code E58 360-ci V-8, which replaced the 340 as Challenger's optional engine and top performance choice. This nameplate was also a one-year-only item; it was not used on any A-or B-Body Dodge or Plymouth that was equipped with that engine. Car courtesy Streetside Classics.

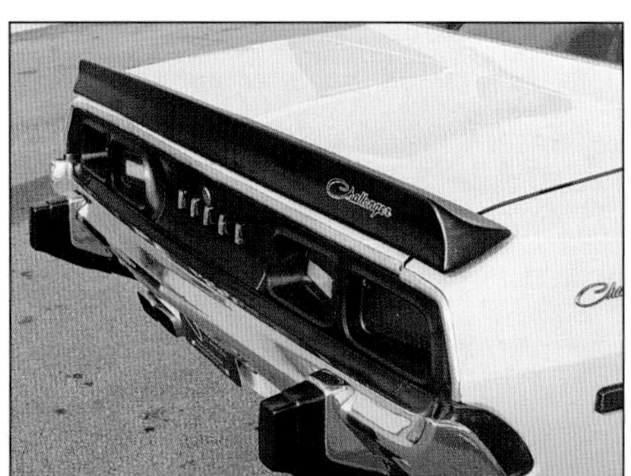

For 1974, the Challenger's rear styling was also a carry-over, but the rear bumper was moved outboard ever so slightly from its 1973 location to allow for a bigger reinforcing bar that was needed to make it comply with the 5-mph rear-impact standard dictated by FMVSS 215 for 1974. The rear spoiler is a reproduction of the one seen on the 1970 Challenger T/A earlier in this book. It is a period-correct addition; they were available from the aftermarket or from Dodge dealers' parts departments. Massive rear bumper guards are among the first items that modern-day builders remove from a 1974 Challenger when "resto-modding" it. Car courtesy Streetside Classics.

On the outside, the stock Yellow Blaze color contrasts with the A57 Rallye Package's black side stripes. Car courtesy Streetside Classics.

Five-spoke road wheels were optional once again on the Challenger in 1974, but this car was not equipped with them at Hamtramck, per its fender tag. These 15-inch aftermarket reproduction wheels were only available in the 14-inch-diameter size in 1974. This front tire, a BFGoodrich Premier Touring high-performance radial, is a P215/70R15 size that fits well within the stock front fenderwell and gives a period-correct look. ThePentastar valve-stem cap is an aftermarket dress-up item. Car courtesy Streetside Classics.

This right rear corner view shows the gap between the rear bumper and the right rear quarter panel, as well as the 1970-style "snap-open" fuel filler and 15-inch-diameter five-spoke wheel, which were added to this car as period-correct upgrades. The rear tire, although a modern 70-series radial, fits well within the stock fenderwell, where fat, low-profile G60-14 tires were once factory-installed. Car courtesy Streetside Classics.

My apologies if this driver-seat view of this 1974 Dodge Challenger Rallye's cabin looks a lot like those of its 1972 and 1973 predecessors. No changes were made by Chrysler to the E-Body's cabin during its 1970–1974 production history, other than the two-spoke Tuff steering wheel. The center console was factory-installed on this car, but the Hurst Pistol Grip shifter and 4-speed manual gearbox attached to it replaced the 3-speed manual transmission and straight-stick/round-knob shifter this car was built with. The item on the steering column is an upshift-indicator light, something that aftermarket companies introduced to help tell drivers when to upshift during hard acceleration, instead of relying on engine sound or looking down at the factory tachometer. Car courtesy Streetside Classics.

tape stripes; 3-speed electric windshield wipers; and a choice of dogdish hubcaps, deluxe wheel covers, five-spoke or Rallye road wheels on either blackwall, whitewall, raised white letter bias-ply tires, or whitewall radials.

Does that list look familiar? Other than the radial-tire option, and the 360 replacing the 340, it's identical to the option list from 1973.

Also identical: the A57 Rallye package, whose "performance" hood, "blackout" painted grille, faux front fender scoops, Rallye gauge cluster, Rallye suspension with heavy-duty shocks, and 70-series tires were an encore of the 1973 A57 package, minus the optional High Impact Top Banana Yellow paint option.

This 1974 Challenger Rallye's dash shows it was equipped with the four-pod gauge cluster with 150-mph speedometer, 7,000-rpm tachometer, combined fuel level, oil pressure, coolant temperature and alternator gauges, and electric clock. You can see the optional R35 AM/FM Stereo radio (and its rear-speaker switch), as well as the controls for the standard heater/defroster. Car courtesy Streetside Classics.

The Calm Before the Storm

As the 1973 model year ended with the close of Chrysler's fiscal year on September 30, Chrysler Corporation and its Dodge Division had reason to be optimistic. The previous year had seen sales increases, led by strong sales of the A-Body Dodge Dart line and the B-Body Dodge Charger, especially the Charger SE with three small "opera windows" in each rear roof pillar. Also, the imported Dodge Colt had proven to be a winner in the subcompact market segment, which had Dodge dealers clamoring for more and more of the feature-laden yet low-priced small cars.

Coming for 1974 was an all-new full-sized line of C-Body Dodge Polaras and Monacos. Like their Plymouth Fury and Chrysler Newport/New Yorker counterparts, they did away with the "fuselage" body styling they'd worn since 1969 and wore slab-sided styling that looked very much like the restyled full-sized cars General Motors had introduced for 1971.

Also on the way for 1974 was an all-new subcompact. Colt was totally redesigned by Mitsubishi and was still a feature-filled small car that made ideal competition for imports like the Datsun 510 and Toyota Corolla, and Volkswagen's ancient Beetle and new Dasher.

Dart's sedan and Swinger hardtop models received new rear styling that better incorporated a 5-mph impact-absorbing bumper system mandated by FMVSS 215 for 1974 than its competition from General Motors and Ford, which looked to many observers like chrome-plated park benches.

The Dart Sport coupes received a similarly strengthened rear bumper, but it was "tacked on" to the coupe body's existing rear styling. It looked marginally better than the front and rear bumpers the B-Body Coronet sedans and wagons were saddled with for 1974, which stuck out like sore thumbs, especially in front. Charger carried over for 1974 largely unchanged, its FMVSS 215-compliant bumpers constructed similarly to those on Challenger.

Speaking of engine changes, even though it was no longer available in the Challenger, the Slant Six was now available only in 225-ci form. The shorter-stroke 198-ci version was discontinued when 1973 model-year production ended.

Looking into the future, a replacement for Chrysler's aging A-Body line was already in the works for 1976. Code-named F-Body, its styling was nearly complete in the fall of 1973, and Chrysler engineers were then translating the latest in engineering advances, such as a transverse-torsion-bar front suspension system and the expanded use of electronics under the hood,

If you liked the all-vinyl bucket seats in 1972 and 1973 Challengers, those in the 1974 version would not disappoint you. Standard carpets were nylon loop-pile, commonly used on American cars of the era, and were "press-molded" during fabrication for drop-in-easy installation on the Hamtramck final assembly line. Floor mats atop the carpets are much-later aftermarket versions. Car courtesy Streetside Classics.

Although this Challenger doesn't have the chrome-and-amber reverse-indicator light seen on earlier-year E-Body cars, it does have a set of aftermarket auxilary gauges located just above the center console. They're located where an aftermarket 8-track or cassette tape player would have been installed in 1974. Car courtesy Streetside Classics.

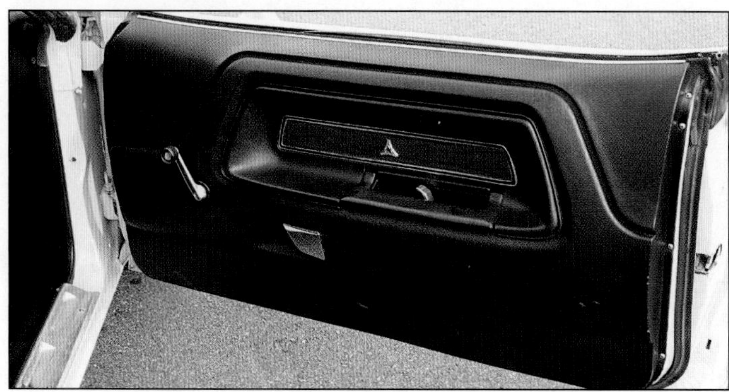

Also unchanged for 1974 were the door panels, which were still a one-piece molded plastic item. Crank-up windows were the only ones available, as power windows were dropped from the Challenger's option list after 1971. The chrome lever next to the armrest is the door lock, which locked the door by pushing down on it, then closing the door. Car courtesy Streetside Classics.

into a line of coupes, sedans, and for the first time since 1966, a small four-door station wagon.

Chrysler also had automotive holdings in Europe, which included the Rootes Group in Great Britain and Simca in France. Plus, their defense, materials, marine, and other non-automotive divisions created the image of a modern, diversified corporation.

The 1974 Dodges went on sale on September 25, 1973. Less than two weeks later, the world changed for good, and not for the good of Chrysler.

Despite styling that had its roots in the 1960s, the 1974 Dodge Challenger Rallye stands out in a crowd of 21st Century cars and trucks. The twin-scoop hood was available on the Challenger in each year of E-Body production. Car courtesy Streetside Classics.

Race Car in a Box

During the 1970s, Chrysler revised its Mopar performance-parts program with the "Direct Connection" program. Under it, aftermarket performance parts makers were able to have their parts included in the Mopar performance-parts catalogue, and not have to ship them to a Mopar/Chrysler parts warehouse. Instead, once a customer ordered one of these parts (denoted by a "P" prefix on the factory part number), the order instead went to the aftermarket parts maker, who then shipped it directly to the dealer. This eliminated the need for Chrysler to stock a large inventory of aftermarket performance parts, which likely would have been slow movers compared to replacement and repair parts sold and distributed through the Mopar parts network. Also, there were a number of Dodge and Chrysler-Plymouth dealers around the country who were also "Direct Connection" parts dealers, who stocked a number of these parts for customers who built and raced Mopars at drag strips and oval tracks around the country.

Back then, racers could also order a "body-in-white" of any current-model-year car in the Dodge or Plymouth line, provided they gave Chrysler about four weeks' notice, so that it could be scheduled for build in one of their assembly plant's body shops. It would then be ready for pickup at the plant,

THE STORM HITS

On October 8, 1973, Israel was attacked by Egypt, Syria, Lebanon, and Jordan on Yom Kippur. The United States, a staunch ally of Israel, pledged its support and supplied needed defense material to Israel, which was fighting the fourth such war against its Arab neighbors since it was established in 1948.

In response, the Organization of Petroleum Exporting Countries (OPEC), whose membership was dominated by nations such as Saudi Arabia and Libya (allies of Egypt, Syria, Lebanon, and Jordan) announced that they were stopping all shipments of oil to the United States, effective immediately.

The result in the United States was the first Oil Shock, where gasoline supplies dwindled and pump prices skyrocketed from the 30- to 35-cents-per-gallon range to 50- to 60-cents per gallon. (That was, if gas stations even had gasoline to sell.) By the end of December 1973, a number of states had instituted odd-even gasoline rationing based on a car's license-plate number, with more to follow; and New York State had lowered the speed limits on all of its roads, highways, and expressways to a mere 50 mph, with other states considering similar moves. That led to the National Maximum Speed Limit (NMSL) of 55 mph in 1974, which Congress coerced the states into adopting by threatening to withhold federal highway funds if they didn't comply.

As a result, new-vehicle sales dropped drastically. Full-sized cars, and anything else in a dealer's inventory with a V-8 under its hood, sat unsold on dealer lots for months while anything with a 4- or 6-cylinder engine moved "across the curb" almost as soon as it rolled onto a dealer's lot.

Thanks to the A-Body Dart and imported Colt lines, Dodge had products that buyers who decided to brave the higher gas prices and buy a new car were interested in. They proved to be exceptional sellers at a time when all three of Dodge's other passenger car lines, as well as their light trucks and vans, sat on dealer lots unsold for month after month after month.

Dodge responded to the change in the market in early calendar 1974 by introducing a "premium" version of the Dart, the Dart Special Edition (SE). What made it special in the eyes of Dodge was its additional sound insulation, velour-and-vinyl split-bench seats, cut-pile carpeting, whitewall radial-ply tires with body-colored wheel covers, standard vinyl roof, and available exterior colors borrowed from the full-size Dodge color selection. What made it special to buyers was the thrifty 225-ci Slant Six that was the SE's standard engine.

including doors, front fenders, hood, and deck lid, but without any paint, primer, body sealer, or undercoating. They could also order individual exterior body components, including rear quarter panels, as needed. For the teams that could afford this, it was a quicker way to build a race car than buying a production car and stripping unneeded parts and weight from it before turning it into a race car.

However, the bulk of short-track oval racers, who raced on weekends at hometown racetracks, such as county fairground ovals and "bull rings" bulldozed out of the soil, were rich in mechanical skill and desire to win, but oftentimes short on funds. Race winnings, sponsorship money, and contingency awards helped. But a simpler and less expensive way for them to get a new race car was elusive.

Early in 1974, the idea of a complete race car that could be sold through the "Direct Connection" parts program was developed. The "Chrysler Kit Car," as it came to be called, would be a complete short track oval-racing stock car, available in various stages of completion ranging from ready-to-weld unassembled, to partially assembled "rolling chassis," to a complete, turn-key, ready-to-race car.

As Denis Hill said in the first paragraph of his cover story on the new late-model stock (LMS) car for *Stock Car Racing* magazine in December 1973, "It's Chrysler's newest gift to the racing enthusiast, a complete late model sportsman [race car] in kit form."

Chrysler engineer Larry Rathgeb came up with the idea for a high-quality, low-cost race car. "Rathgeb is the brains behind the Chrysler racing chassis program, and over the years has developed many of the theories on handling that have helped Richard Petty, Bobby Allison, Buddy Baker, Charlie Glotzbach, and other Mopar racers translate their seat-of-the-pants reactions to race car behavior into a useful system of handling principles and behaviors.

"With short track race car building booming all over the nation, it isn't surprising that Rathgeb became interested in designing an inexpensive short track car that could win. So he sharpened his pencil and began outlining a design and a plan to go with it. His car would be cheap to build. It would be easy to build. And it would be capable of winning."

Rathgeb had not only a wealth of experience to work with (his own, especially) but a treasure trove of solidly engineered OEM (original equipment manufacture) Chrysler parts to

Instead of suffering the fate of so many short track stock cars after their racing days were over, such as relegated to a scrap heap behind a small garage and shop, the prototype Chrysler Kit Car has undergone a total restoration. Using original and period correct parts, it is now in ready-for-its-first-race condition. In the near future, its body color will be changed back to what it wore during its 1973–1974 track test sessions, and it will once again wear number 0. (Photo by Chris Brown)

Under the hood sits a race-built "LA"-series small-block V-8, nestled inside the round tube structure that serves as the front of the car's chassis. Note the cross-bracing in front of the engine, and the extra bracing that surrounds the brake system's master cylinder. Short-track cars not only had to be built to be quick around the track, but also rugged enough to withstand the bumps and bangs of heat races, trophy dashes, and feature races week after week. Also note the left-front shock absorber's attachment to the frame tubing. (Photo by Howard Cohen)

No fancy or expensive mechanical fuel injection system here, just a proven combination of a 4-barrel carburetor atop an aluminum intake manifold, all the better to get the fuel to the cylinders while shaving weight off the front of the car. Prototype Kit Car uses a Holley induction system, including a period-correct "Street Dominator" intake manifold. Also note the valve-cover breathers located in the frame tubing in front of the engine. (Photo by Chris Brown)

Inside the Kit Car prototype, gauge cluster tells the driver what he needs to know: engine speed, oil and coolant temperature, oil and fuel pressure. Note the "Saturday Night Special—By Petty" lettering along the bottom of the gauge panel. Along with the welded-tube frame, the Kit Car uses the "FMVSS 214-beam" side-impact protection built into the Challenger's doors, seen just outboard of the door-opening protection bars. (Photo by Chris Brown)

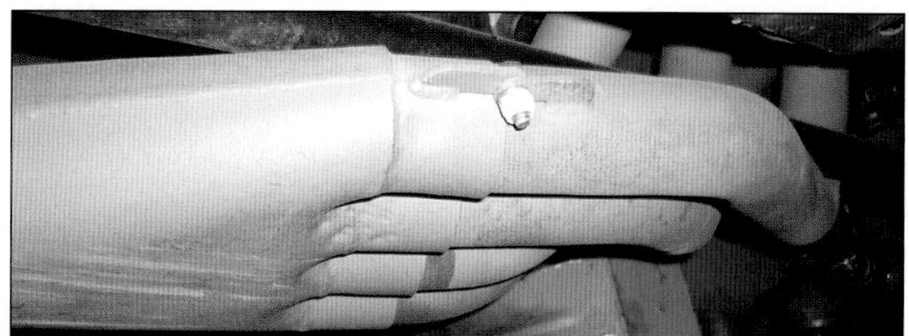

I'm not joking when I say that exhaustive research went into the design of the Kit Car prototype's exhaust system. "Four-into-one" header design was a product of long hours worth of work in Chrysler Engineering's engine labs in Highland Park, whose unmuffled exhaust notes of test engines at high RPM likely spooked animals in the Detroit Zoo, located only a few miles away from Chrysler's engineering shops. (Photo by Chris Brown)

choose from. They included torsion bars, suspension control arms, front spindles, rear leaf springs, front K-frames, as well as the front and rear frame rails that were welded underneath production Unibodies. All were then in production, and not specially fabricated items, which would keep costs down and keep the price racers would pay down, as well.

The first prototype "Kit Car" was assembled in the Petty Engineering shops in Level Cross, North Carolina, in the early months of 1973, and *Stock Car Racing*'s Denis Hill observed an on-track test of it that August. "The car proved capable of beating the track record at both the paved and dirt test tracks used. . . . And we were impressed."

Not where you'd expect to find a Late Model Stock or Sportsman race car. But then, the Petty-built Chrysler Kit Car prototype was no ordinary race car but one worthy of inclusion in this display of Petty-built racing hardware. Extra-long rear leaf springs' rear mounts are located just aft of the rear valance panel under the bumper. Dzus fasteners not only keep the rear deck lid secure on the track, they also save weight by replacing the production hinges. (Photo by Chris Brown)

According to Hill, "What makes all the stock parts work together is Rathgeb's insistence on simplicity and function dictating design. The [steel tube rollover-protection] cage is built to absorb suspension loadings, as well as protect the driver. Many short track racers don't build their roll cages properly, so their suspension can't work. Here, it works."

Hill went on to say that Chrysler had versions of the "Kit Car" in the works for the coming 1974 season that would use production Challenger, Charger, and Dart Sport body components, as well as those of their Plymouth counterparts (Barracuda, Duster, and Satellite), all to be built on chassis with wheelbases ranging from the A-Body's 108-inch to the larger B-Body's 115-inch. Powered by a 340-ci LA-series small-block race engine, it was projected that racers would pay around $5,000 to $7,000 for it, depending on the level of completion they wanted from "rolling chassis" to race-ready. They would be sold through Petty Engineering, who was then the official outlet for Chrysler/Mopar oval-track racing parts.

Lead test driver during the development of the "kit car" was a familiar one to Petty Engineering, Pete Hamilton. He'd raced the #40 Plymouth Superbird that was a team car to Richard Petty's #43, and won the 1970 Daytona 500, as well as both 500-mile races that year at the 2.66-mile, high-banked track known today as the Talladega [Alabama] Superspeedway.

However, for test sessions at Concord Speedway near Charlotte, North Carolina, they needed a driver who had experience running on that dirt track, as well as on other dirt ovals. Rathgeb and Hamilton chose a young driver who, although he hadn't had much success in his racing career to date, showed promise when he ran. The son of a two-time NASCAR Sportsman

Inside the trunk are the fuel cell and electric fuel pump, and the battery (in a protective box). Rear wheelwells are fabricated to give plenty of room for the wide rear tires, while keeping them within the production body profile. Note rear tube members extending through the trunk to the rear bumper. Also note the production weather-stripping around the trunk opening. That had to be weathertight not as much for on-track conditions, but to keep everything dry inside on trips to and from the track while transported on an open trailer or rollback truck on rainy days or nights. (Photo by Howard Cohen)

Getting the prototype "dialed in" between test runs on the dirt track at Concord Speedway, 1974. Chrysler engineer Larry Rathgeb is wearing the tie, and to his left is the Kit Car's lead development driver, and 1970 Daytona 500 winner, Pete Hamilton. Randy Owens (Richard Petty's brother-in-law) is in the foreground working the jack, and fellow Petty crewmember Tex Powell is adjusting the car's front toe-in. (Photo Courtesy Larry Rathgeb/Chris Brown)

Division champion, he was at a point in his life when he had to choose between following his racing dreams, or turning to farming full-time to support his family.

The test sessions went extremely well; the young driver was able to tell the veteran racer and the factory engineer how the Challenger-bodied "mule" handled on the challenging Hickory track surface, information they used in refining the "Kit Car" that eventually went on sale later that year. Plus, the $800 that he was paid for the two test sessions was money he needed, right when he needed it.

That test also opened doors in racing for the young driver, as word got around how well he handled that prototype race car at speed, a car built in the shops of a legend who would win seven NASCAR Grand National and Winston Cup Series Championships during his career.

What would any run on a dirt "bull ring" be without a little metal-to-metal contact? Looks like the #0 car was a little out of shape on one of its test runs and banged the guard rail, but wasn't torn up bad enough to end the test early. Duct tape on the leading edge of the right door was not a Chrysler production item or Mopar performance part, but experienced race mechanics never went to the track without it. (They still don't.) At the right is . . . no, it can't be. He doesn't have his trademark mustache (yet). (Photo by Larry Rathgeb, Courtesy Chris Brown)

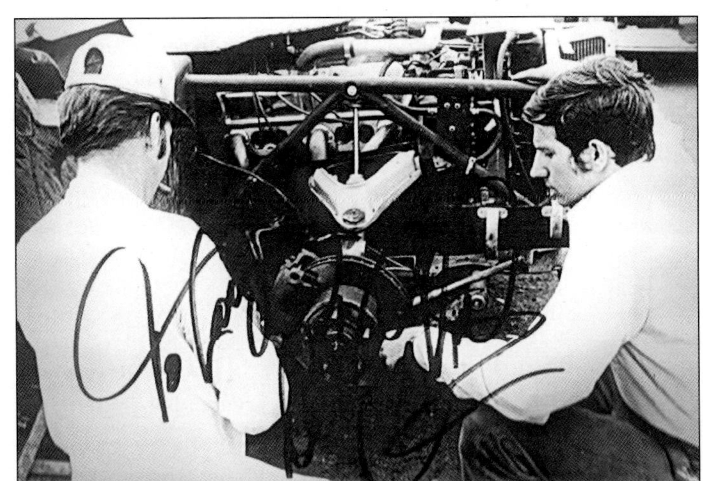

Trackside at Concord Speedway near Charlotte, North Carolina, in 1974 for dirt-track tests of the Kit Car prototype, with a talented local driver at the wheel. That driver, by the way, autographed this picture for Larry Rathgeb during a visit at Talladega in 1994. Note the combination of production parts, including the front upper control arm, used on the prototype's chassis. (Photo by Larry Rathgeb/Courtesy Chris Brown)

Yes, indeed . . . "The Intimidator" drove the Chrysler Kit Car prototype during its 1974 dirt-track tests. Built in the shops that prepared the cars that Richard Petty drove to his seven NASCAR Grand National and Winston Cup Championships, that Challenger-bodied late model Sportsman car bears the signature of the man who would later win the Winston Cup seven times himself. (Photo by Howard Cohen)

The young driver would get offers to drive better equipment, which he began driving to the winner's circle in race after race, eventually leading up to seven of his own championships in NASCAR's top division.

That driver's name? Dale Earnhardt.

As longtime radio newscaster/commentator Paul Harvey would say, "*Now*, you know the rest of the story!"

Sales by the Numbers

The Oil Shock of 1973 hurt all carmakers equally. For a time, no one was buying any new car, large or small, until they could be certain they could get gas for it at their local filling station.

The son of a past two-time NASCAR Sportsman champion, Dale Earnhardt drove the Kit Car on its test laps on the dirt back in 1974, and autographed this picture for Chrysler engineer Larry Rathgeb when he visited "The Intimidator" at Talladega some 20 years later. Those test sessions not only gave Rathgeb plenty of data to take back to Highland Park with him, but also opened doors for the young driver seen here. (Photo by Larry Rathgeb, Courtesy Chris Brown)

After 1973's sales gain, Challenger sales tumbled for 1974. Per the *Standard Catalogue of American Cars 1946–1975*, only 16,437 Challengers were built, a 49.6-percent drop from 1973.

That compared with 26,372 base Firebird Sport Coupes (7,603 of them with 6-cylinder engines), plus 22,583 Firebird Esprit coupes, 14,519 Formula Firebirds, and 10,255 Firebird Trans Ams, 943 of those powered by Pontiac's high-output 455 SD (Super Duty) engine.

1974 DODGE CHALLENGER WINDOW STICKER

Base Challenger (V-8)	$3,143.00
Options	
Vinyl Top	84
D34 TorqueFlite Automatic	215
B41 Pwr Brakes, Front Disc	62
T34 F78x14 WSW Tires	41
A06 Basic Group*	196
H51 Airtemp A/C	384
G11 Tinted Glass	39
C16 Console	59
Total (Estimate):	$4,223

** Includes A01 Light Group, G35 Chrome LH Remote Mirror, R11 Music Master AM Radio, S77 Power Steering, J55 Undercoating and Hood Silencer Pad, W11 Deluxe Wheel Covers, J25 Variable-Speed Wipers*

Base Challenger :	$3,143
Luxury Options	
A57 Rallye Package	190
E58 360 V-8 Package*	259
D21 4-Speed Manual	195
T87 F70x14 RWL Tires	No Charge with A57
H51 Airtemp AC	384
A36 Performance Axle Package**	63
C16 Console	59
G11 Tinted Glass	38
J97 Rallye Gauges w/Clock***	28
S77 Power Steering	109
R35 AM/FM Stereo Radio	202
R32 Dual Rear Speakers	32
W21 Rallye Road Wheels	56
Total (Estimate)	$4,758

** Includes T86 F70x14 WW Tires, S13 Rallye Suspension, N23 Electronic Ignition System*

*** Includes D91 Sure-Grip*

**** Included with A57 G35 Dual Painted Sport Mirrors, LH Remote*

That $4,700+ sticker price is at or near where a very-well-equipped Dodge Charger SE hardtop would have been priced that year, with the top-line B-Body hardtop offering not only available big-block (400 and 440) engines, but also a much larger rear seat and more spacious trunk for the same money.

In all General Motors built and Pontiac sold 73,729 1974 Firebirds, a 37-percent *increase* over 1973. That also meant that Firebird held a nearly 82-percent share of that market segment, to Challenger's nearly 17-percent share.

For what it's worth, the 1974 Mercury Cougar XR-7 sales tally, per the *Standard Catalogue*, was 91,670. That was more than that year's Buick Century Luxus (44,930) and Regal (57,512) two-doors, and almost as many as the Pontiac Grand Prix (99,817), but trailed the Oldsmobile Cutlass Supreme two-door (172,360) and segment-leading Chevrolet Monte Carlo (312,217).

Neither Dodge nor any other Chrysler Corporation brand would be represented in this growing segment of the U.S. new-car market until 1975. As they were with the E-Body to the pony car sales race, Chrysler would be late in entering this competition, as well.

What could have been: A possible second-generation E-Body Dodge? Stylist Bob Ackerman sketched this proposal early in Challenger's history and included hideaway headlights in the front-end design concept. Hideaway headlights had only been used by 1968-later Chargers by then and wouldn't see production again until the 1972–1973 Monacos. (Photo Courtesy Bob Ackerman)

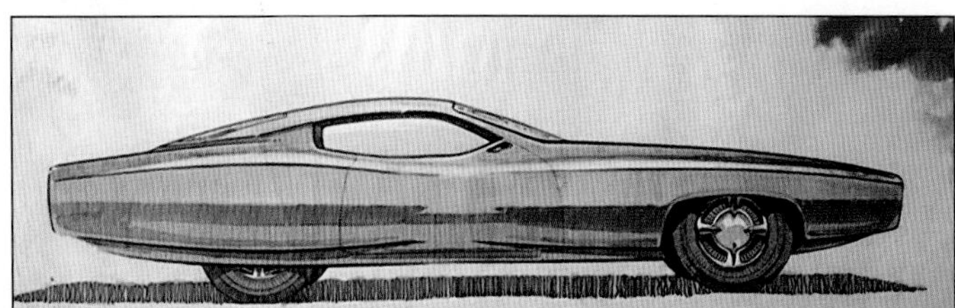

A 1966-dated concept by Chet Limbaugh whose lines may have ended up in the "Cincinnati" styling proposals for a second-generation E-Body that never made production. Named "Cincinnati" for the city where they were shown to a focus group by Chrysler in late 1969, unfavorable reaction to them led to those design concepts never advancing past the full-size clay model (or fiberglass-body prototype made from the full-size clay) stage. (Photo Courtesy Chet Limbaugh)

Challenge Met

A 49-percent sales drop is serious business in any year. But when it came on the heels of the first Oil Shock, and at a time when the E-Body platform as originally designed was at the end of its production life, the bean counters in Highland Park could not sit idly by.

On April 1, 1974, the E-Body Dodge Challenger was no more. The name would be revived before the end of the 1970s, to go on an upscale, two-door sport coupe designed and engineered by Mitsubishi. But to many devoted Dodge lovers, it was not the same.

Not only was the production Challenger discontinued, the "Kit Car" version of it was also canceled. When the "Short Track Stormer that Comes in a box" finally went on sale, it was offered with one wheelbase, 108 inches, with the buyer's choice of Dodge Dart Sport or Plymouth Duster body panels atop it.

Looks sort of like a Barracuda, with the single headlight per side, doesn't it? It's another of Bob Ackerman's Challenger styling proposals that makes one wonder what would have happened if it had reached production. "Split-grille" front styling is Ackerman's take on a look that Pontiac had used as a virtual hallmark in its rise to sales success during the 1960s. Also, this front-end design looks like its cost to manufacture could have made the bean counters on the other side of Chrysler's Highland Park headquarters smile, or at least take notice. (Photo Courtesy Bob Ackerman)

The roofline of this 1968 Chet Limbaugh styling sketch resembles one used on the "Cincinnati" styling prototypes one year later. From the overall look of this concept, this looks like it would have made a formidable challenger to Pontiac's Grand Prix, and, in a shorter-wheelbase version, to the Pontiac Firebird. (Photo Courtesy Chet Limbaugh)

CHAPTER 11

1974 PLYMOUTH BARRACUDA
The Final Fish

As with its Dodge Challenger sibling, Barracuda was largely unchanged for 1974, outside of the absence of High Impact paint colors on its exterior-paint color choices and the E58 360 V-8 replacing the E55 340. The 360 produced 245 SAE net horsepower and the base 318 a measly 150 hp net. For 1974, a mere 11,734 Barracudas rolled off the production line. The energy crisis, rising insurance costs, emissions standards, and a negative public image against muscle cars all culminated in the demise of the E-Body cars and most muscle cars in general.

In times past, when a successful car, or car line, reached a significant anniversary in terms of years in production or numbers of them built and sold, its maker would commemorate it. In the case of a "__ Millionth" car, it might be with a ceremony at the assembly plant when the specially marked milestone car rolled off the final assembly line. Or it could be with a special anniversary model, with a package of features, options, and colors to attract shoppers into a showroom, whether they were interested in that anniversary-edition car or not. (For example, the Anniversary Edition Corvettes produced periodically since 1978.)

Chrysler did none of that when the Plymouth Barracuda turned ten. In fact, there was barely any mention of its existence, again, in company sales literature. And there were few changes again, as well.

A Familiar Look for 1974

Once again, Barracuda was pushed to the back of Plymouth's sales literature, sharing a sales brochure with the Valiant and Duster line for another year. The first of only two pages in it that were dedicated to the E-Body Plymouths proclaimed "A full measure of sport is available in either the 1974 'Cuda or Barracuda."

It then listed the common standard features of both lines, such as front disc brakes, Unibody construction, and the Electronic Ignition System ("for up to 35-percent higher starting voltage than conventional systems"). The 'Cuda's standard

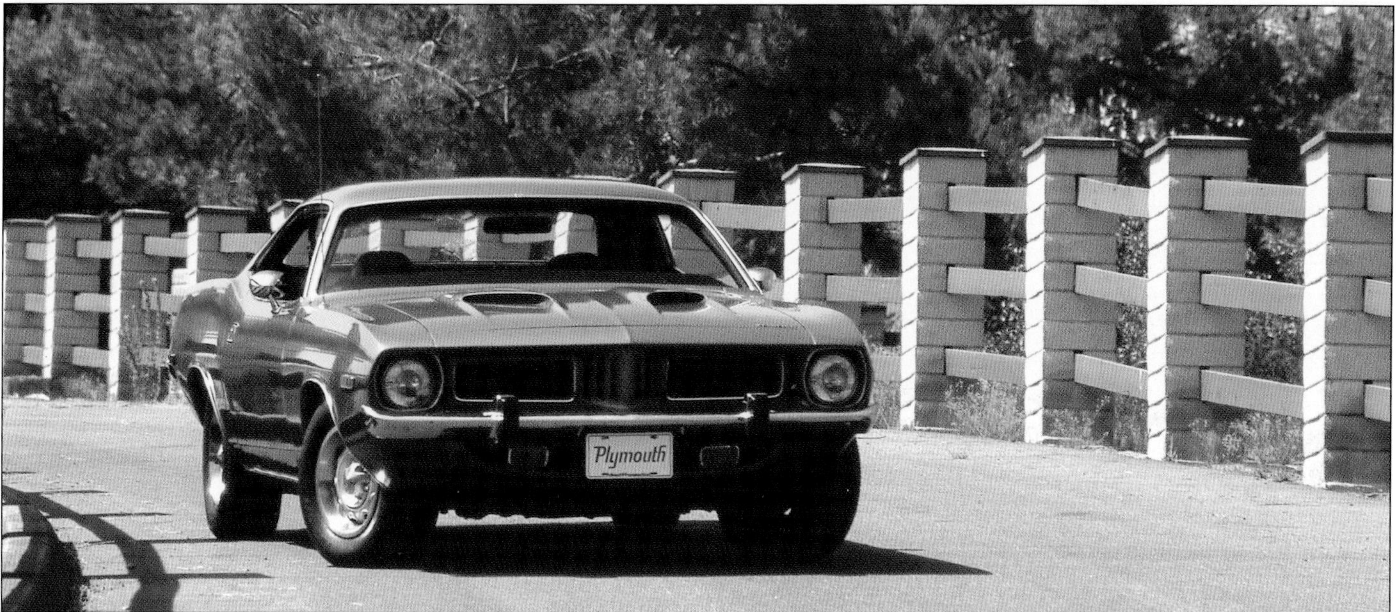

Keeping with the "earth tones" theme of mid-1970s fashions, this 1974 Plymouth 'Cuda is resplendent in Deep Sherwood Green Metallic. Low sales, a $14 extra cost, and peeling problems for some High Impact colors led to their withdrawal from the Barracuda color selection after 1973. (Photo Courtesy David Newhardt)

If Chrysler ever offered a "Tenth Anniversary Edition" of the Plymouth Barracuda for 1974, they would have been wise to start with a well-equipped one like this 1974 'Cuda. Maybe revive some of the High Impact colors (which had been dropped for 1974), along with the cloth-and-vinyl Gran Coupe seat trim from years gone by? Instead, Plymouth's E-Body hardtop was almost a total carryover from 1974, except for the 360-inch V-8 this one has, and the seat belt/ starter interlock system. (Photo Courtesy Mecum Auctions)

On April 1, 1974, Chrysler discontinued the Barracuda, and the E-Body line had shown its rear bumper to the exit door at Hamtramck Assembly for the last time. One wonders if that last Barracuda was a 360 'Cuda like this one, which would have rattled the windows of the former "Dodge Main" plant on its way to the transporter that would take it to the dealer who ordered it. (Photo Courtesy Mecum Auctions)

Just like in 1974: Get in, sit down, shut the door, push in the clutch, turn the key, and . . . a loud buzzer and red "idiot light" on the dash loudly remind you to buckle your seatbelt before the car can start. Once that's done, try again, and the high-pitched "Highland Park Hummingbird" starter motor spins the E58 360 to life as the Rallye gauge cluster's tach and oil pressure gauges show you. Note the horizontal parking-brake release and vertical hood release. Shaping those controls that way permitted drivers to reach down and operate one without (hopefully) pulling the other. (Photo Courtesy Mecum Auctions)

As with the 'Cudas that preceded it, the 1974 version sported a black-painted taillight panel atop its bumper, and the same rectangular chrome exhaust tips and the cut-out rear valance panel that were 'Cuda standard features since 1970. Non-flush door fit onto the body was likely how the car was assembled at Hamtramck; by 1974, build quality there had improved somewhat, but not to the standard that current-generation Chrysler products are built to. (Photo Courtesy Mecum Auctions)

features, along with the scooped hood and heavy-duty suspension system also included "special ornamentation that lets everyone know you're driving a 'Cuda."

That "special ornamentation" must have been in lieu of an exhaust note generated by engines such as the 426 Hemi, the 440 and 383-ci B/RB big-blocks, the 1968–1971 340s, and the 273 "Hi-Po" engine of 1965–1967, which let everyone then know you were driving what some hardcore Mopar devotees believe was a *real* 'Cuda.

Inside, other than a "new vinyl grain" on the front bucket/rear bench seats, the cabin looked the same as 1973. Available once again in a choice of white, black, blue, and green, they featured front bucket seats that the sales literature said "are not only good looking . . . but they are also designed to reduce fatigue and stress as they provide support and comfort."

The factory literature described the available Rallye road wheels and Hurst shifter as "options sure to be appreciated by those who want more sport." Unfortunately, while referring to the Pistol Grip shifter that stirred the optional 4-speed manual transmission, the interior picture below the text showed a cabin with a column-shifted TorqueFlite automatic transmission.

It concluded: "For an illustration of what a 'Cuda or Barracuda can do for your life, ask your dealer for a test drive."

The table in the rear of the sales brochure listed the available options for Barracuda and 'Cuda, which were the same parts sourced from the same suppliers and installed on the same assembly line at Hamtramck as the Challenger, which were listed in the Chapter 10.

If you didn't notice the front bumper (which stuck out even farther than in 1973) and the 1972 and later wheel center caps, you would think that this 'Cuda was a 1970 model. The twin-scooped Sport hood was available on Plymouth's performance E-Body throughout its entire production run. (Photo Courtesy David Newhardt)

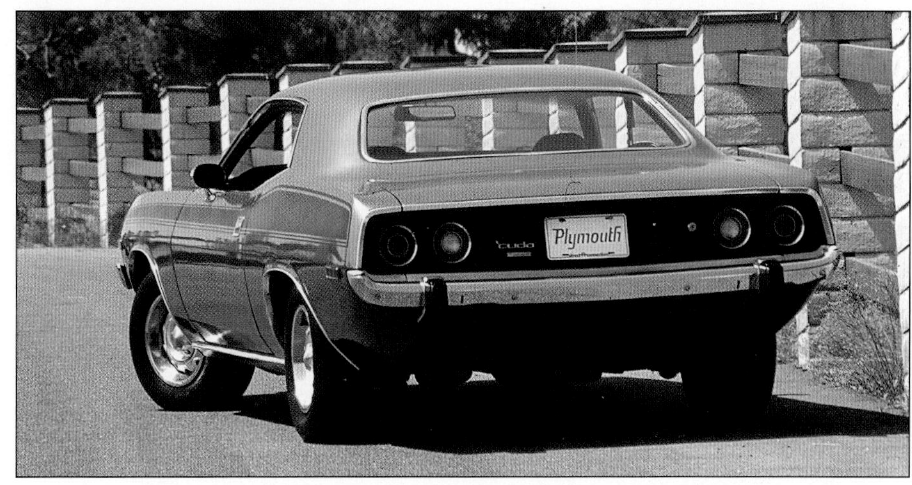

Another subtle upgrade was the rear bumper for 1974, set out a little farther from the body than it did in 1973. That was to permit a bigger reinforcing bar behind the bumper, needed to meet the new 5-mph rear impact-absorption requirement for 1974. (Photo Courtesy David Newhardt)

The color selection for 1974 totaled 16 available solid and metallic acrylic enamel colors, many with the same names Dodge used but no more optional High Impact colors: Powder Blue (Code KB1), Lucerne Blue Metallic (Code KB5), Rallye Red (Code FE5), Burnished Red Metallic (Code GE7), Frosty Green Metallic (Code KG2), Deep Sherwood Metallic (Code KG8), Avocado Gold Metallic (Code KJ8), Sahara Beige (Code HL4), Dark Moonstone Metallic (Code KL8), Sienna Metallic (Code KT5), Spinnaker White (Code EW1), Formal Black (Code TX9), Golden Fawn (Code KY4), Yellow Blaze (Code KY5), Golden Haze Metallic (Code YJ6), and Tahitian Gold Metallic (Code YJ9).

One would have to compare the information in the 1974 Barracuda factory literature, and its presentation, to that which Chrysler released for its De Soto brand for 1961, after Chrysler severely cut back De Soto's model lineup and its divisional operations after sales collapsed in 1958, before Highland Park killed off that longtime medium-price nameplate six weeks after the 1961s arrived in dealerships and didn't sell at all.

In the Press

Of the few feature articles and road tests that car magazines published about the Barracuda after 1972, *Road Test*'s December 1973 story about the 1974 Barracuda line showed some optimism for the E-Body Plymouth, and the market segment it competed in, while running down the changes and updates for 1974 under the heading "'Cudas Don't Grow Old."

"Plymouth's business charts reflect a stirring in the 'sporty car' field. According to them, many young persons still want a car that provides sound transportation, good handling and quick response while looking sharp and individualistic. Their answer is the Barracuda.

"While remaining unchanged in appearance, there are engineering, safety and emission control improvements.

"The [wheelbase is 108 inches, while overall] length has increased to 195.6 inches with the bumper change. There are only two models, the Barracuda and the 'Cuda. The engine in both is the 318 as standard, with the 360 CID 4-barrel the only optional powerplant, replacing the discontinued 340.

"The 360 engine includes a windage tray, shot-peened crankshaft with heavy-duty bearings, dual exhaust and chrome-plated exhaust valvestems.

You've seen it in blue, you've seen it in white, and now here's the Barracuda cabin in black. The amber-and-chrome item near the center of the photo is the reverse-indicator light, a common feature on floor-shift-manual-transmission Plymouths and Dodges for many years. The front bucket seats were only fore-and-aft adjustable from 1972 onward, and the seatbacks did not recline. (Not if the standard seatback latch was working properly.) (Photo Courtesy Mecum Auctions)

In many ways, the 1974 'Cuda looked just like its 1972–1973 predecessors: black-painted taillight panel, chrome exhaust tips, Rallye road wheels, and vinyl side striping. The way you can tell them apart is to look at how far the back bumper sticks out from the body. That, plus the larger rear bumper blocks then used on the 1973 model, denote this one as a 1974. (Photo Courtesy Mecum Auctions)

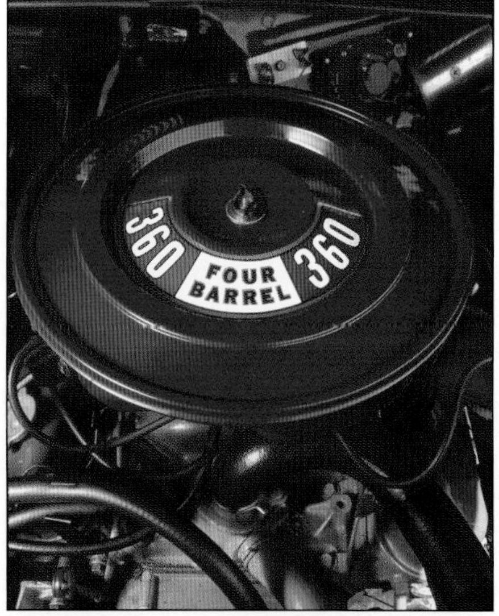

Introduced in 2-barrel form a few years earlier, the 360 took its place as a Plymouth performance powerplant for 1974, with the Code E58 4-barrel version. Under the air cleaner resides the plastic-bodied Carter ThermoQuad 4-barrel carburetor introduced earlier in the decade. (Photo Courtesy David Newhardt)

"Other 360 items include dual valvesprings with surge dampers, high-performance camshaft, special valve keepers, rocker arms, bearing clearances and slip-drive fan.

"Polyester-cord steel-belted radial ply FR78x14 tires, warranted for 40,000 miles by the [tire] manufacturer, are an option.

"A fan shroud which prevents air circulation around the radiator core, and provides cooler underhood temperatures is standard.

"A new brake lining material for disc brakes provides improved friction stability.

"Air cleaner snorkels are redesigned to decrease engine intake noise and resulting in greater engine output. Improved cold weather starting is provided by eliminating the [carburetor's] external bowl vents. 'Solid fuel'-type carburetors provide [a leaner fuel-air] mixture and improve drivability.

"The Barracuda and 'Cuda are planned around the demographics presented by a youthful buying public. They, and anyone else desiring a true high-performance car, should not be disappointed with the offering for 1974."

It must be noted that this item appeared in the *Road Test* dated December 1973. Back then, magazine-industry practices dictated at least a four-to-five month lag between when a story was written and when it appeared in print, with the magazine's cover date at least one month ahead of the month that it appeared. (For example, a December 1973 issue would have hit the newsstands sometime in October or November 1973, the advanced cover date giving that issue a longer "shelf life.") It is very likely, then, that item in *Road Test* was written during the preceding summer, before the 1974 Plymouths went on sale on September 26, 1973, and before the Oil Shock that began two weeks later.

Prices: How Much for That Fish?

As with 1973 retail price information, 1974 retail price information for the Barracuda and 'Cuda is limited. And, for

The engine bay would look like this with the optional E58 4-barrel carbureted 360-ci LA-series small-block V-8 inside it. The single-snorkel air cleaner was new that year, and was used on the E58 360 through 1976 in Dart Sport 360s and Duster 360s. Note the fender tags to the right of the battery. This car is well-optioned, even without factory air. (Photo Courtesy Mecum Auctions)

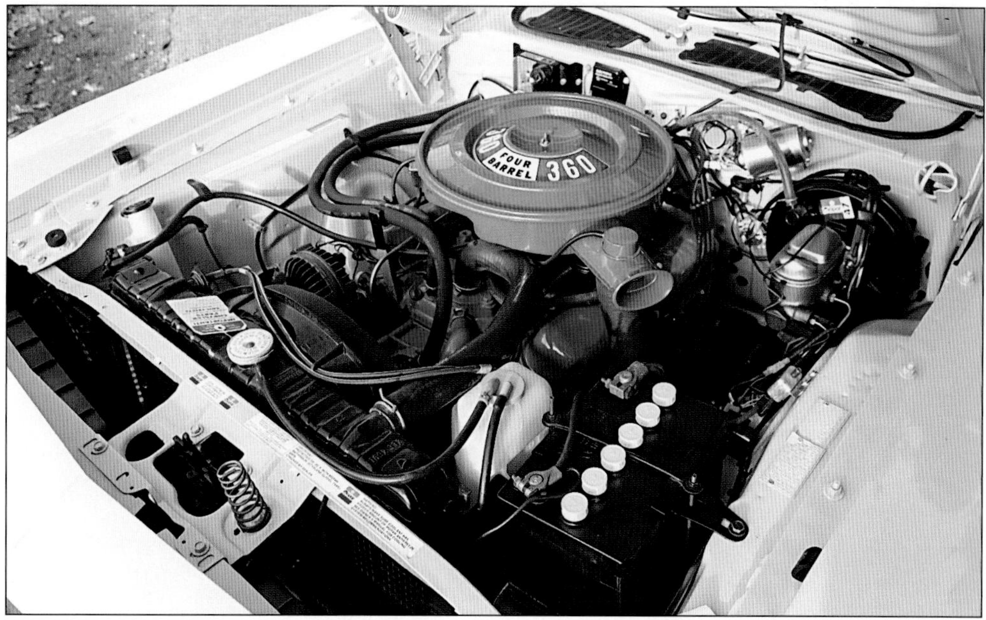

The 4-barrel E58 360 was a potent performer for its time, but performance was not comparable to the 1970–1971 engines. The power steering pump is blocked from view by the coolant-recovery bottle and battery. Two fender tags on the left front wheelwell indicate a well-optioned car. The green-and-white decal on the right front fender well contains the idle specifications and other information relating to the car's Cleaner Air System and its compliance with federal and California emissions standards. (Photo Courtesy Mecum Auctions)

1974 BARRACUDA AND 'CUDA WINDOW STICKER

Base Barracuda Hardtop with 318 V-8	$3,067
D34 torqueflite Automatic	215
A04 Basic Group*	196
A51 Sport Decor Package**	71
H51 Airtemp Air Conditioning	384
G11 Tinted Glass	37
T34 F78x14 WSW Bias-Belted Tires	No Charge with A01
B41 Power Brakes, Front Disc	65
C16 Console	59
W23 Chrome-Style Road Wheels	80
Vinyl Top	84
Total (Estimate)	$4,258

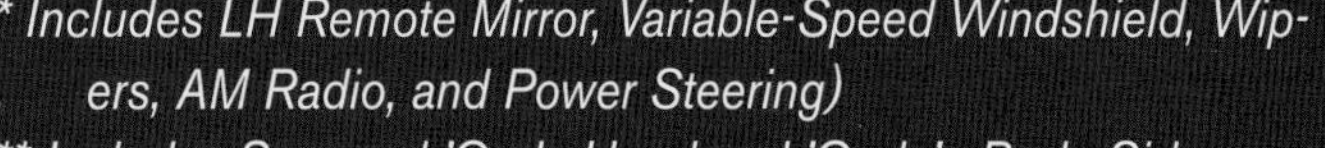

** Includes LH Remote Mirror, Variable-Speed Windshield, Wipers, AM Radio, and Power Steering)*

*** Includes Scooped 'Cuda Hood and 'Cuda's Body-Side Stripes*

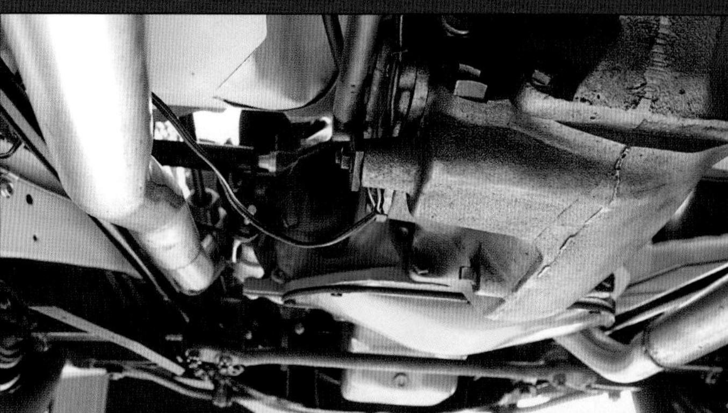

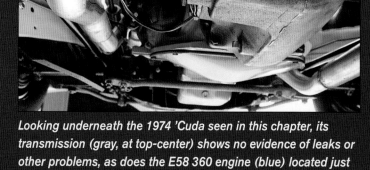

Looking underneath the 1974 'Cuda seen in this chapter, its transmission (gray, at top-center) shows no evidence of leaks or other problems, as does the E58 360 engine (blue) located just ahead of it. Stainless-steel exhaust pipes that flank the engine were likely installed when this car was restored. (Photo Courtesy Mecum Auctions)

Base 'Cuda Hardtop	$3,120
E58 360 Engine Package*	259
D21 4-Spd. Manual Transmission	195
T87 F70x14 RWL Bias-Ply Tires	102
A36 Performance Axle Package**	63
B41 Power Brakes, Disc Front	65
C16 Console	59
F25 70-Amp Battery	15
G36 Mirrors-Dual Racing-Style, Body Color, LH Remote	27
H51 Airtemp Air Conditioning	384
G11 Tinted Glass	37
J52 Inside Hood Release	11
J97 Rallye Instrument Panel	89
M51 Power Sun Roof w/Vinyl Top	434
R36 Radio-AM/FM Stereo	202
R32 Dual Rear-Seat Speakers	28
S77 Power Steering	107
W21 Rallye Road Wheels	56
Total (Estimate)	$5,253

** Includes S13 HD Suspension*

*** Includes D91 Sure-Grip Differential*

Nowadays, many people who discover the 1972–1974 E-Body Mopars like this 1974 Barracuda find them to be stylish, responsive-handling, joy-to-drive cruisers. This one, which crossed the block at Barrett-Jackson's Palm Beach (Florida) Auction, was brought up to "showroom new" appearance before it went up for bid. Finding a low-mileage original in this condition is a major discovery for a Mopar lover, even if it doesn't have a high-performance powertrain in it. (Photo Courtesy Barrett-Jackson Auction Company)

this section, data from the *Standard Catalogue of American Cars 1946–1975* is used again, with percentage-increases for 1974 calculated by using the data in the *Standard Catalogue,* limited though it might be, along with the estimates calculated in the 1973 Barracuda chapter.

Regarding the estimated sticker price above $5,000: It's likely that more than a few Chrysler-Plymouth dealers were shocked by sticker prices above $5,000 on any Plymouth back then, as that dollar figure was where Chrysler-brand sticker prices had reached for a number of years.

This author remembers that back in the spring of 1974, a salesman at Fayetteville (New York) Chrysler-Plymouth shook his head and complained out loud about the $5,200+ sticker price on a loaded, top-of-the-line Fury III that had just been shipped to that dealer. If Chrysler had shipped a 'Cuda with a sticker price in the range estimated above that had not been special-ordered for a customer who wanted such a car, it's likely that dealer would have refused it and sent it back, claiming that, at that price and in the market at that time, such a car was unsalable.

The 1974 Model Year

The big draw into Chrysler-Plymouth dealerships for 1974 was not the Barracuda. Instead, the all-new full-sized Plymouths, Chryslers, and Imperials got the space in front of the showroom windows and in company ads.

As mentioned in the previous chapter, all that changed after October 1973 and the Oil Shock that cut the nation's gasoline supplied, and all but killed any new-vehicle sales except for fuel-efficient small cars.

The only glimmer of optimism for Plymouth as the calendar changed from 1973 to 1974 was strong, for the time, sales of Slant Six A-Body Valiant sedans, Duster coupes, and Scamp hardtops. The imported Cricket was gone from Plymouth's lineup by the end of the 1973 model year, never having caught on in the States. One can thank the devaluation of the British pound, which caused the smaller Cricket's sticker prices to rise into Valiant territory, along with the costs of making it compliant with U.S. emissions and safety standards, for Chrysler's call to stop importing it. Spotty-at-best build quality, common to mass-produced-in-Britain cars of that time, didn't help Cricket's U.S. sales, either.

Sales by the Numbers

The Oil Shock of 1973 had a devastating impact on new-car sales at the time it hit in early October of that year, barely anything was moving off a dealer's lot, regardless of how good its gas mileage was. As it did to Dodge's 1974 sales, the Oil Shock of October 1973 severely impacted Plymouth's sales. Valiants, Dusters, and Scamps with a 225 Slant Six under the hood sold the best, while the larger V-8 powered Satellites, Furys, and Barracudas languished on dealers' lots for months at a time. Voyager and Trail Duster went on sale as scheduled in late 1973, with disappointing results. They would stay in the Plymouth line for several more years to come, however.

Barracuda's sales tally for 1974, per the *Standard Catalogue of American Cars 1946–1975*, was 11,734, of which 6,745 were base-series Barracuda hardtops and 4,989 were 'Cudas. That was the lowest number ever for Barracuda, just over half of 1973's total and less than half of the 23,443 total for 1974's three-month production run. That low number received the attention of the bean counters in Highland Park, and not in a good way.

Javelin's sales were down, too, but not by the percentage Barracuda's were. For 1974, AMC built 27,536 Javelins, 22,566 base-series models, and 4,989 AMXs, off about 11 percent from 1973.

Chevrolet's 1974 Camaro total was 146,598, a nearly 39-percent *increase* over 1973. Per the *Standard Catalogue,* that total included 13,801 Z-28s, as well as 128,810 Camaros of all series with V-8 engines; 11,175 with 4-speed manual transmissions; 11,174 with 3-speed manual gearboxes; 128,659 with GM's Turbo-Hydramatic automatic transmission (Powerglide had been discontinued after 1973); 79,279 with factory-installed Harrison air conditioning, and 151,008 with power steering.

And Mustang II? According to the *Standard Catalogue,* 385,993 of them galloped out of Ford dealers' lots for 1974: 171,671 base-level coupes, 74,799 base three-door hatchbacks, 89,477 luxury-oriented Ghia coupes, and 44,046 Mach I hatchbacks. That total far exceeded 1973 Mustang sales of 134,867 and would be the "high-water" mark of the Mustang II's history.

Barracuda's Final Swim Upstream

Once gasoline supplies became available again in quantity in early 1974, new-car sales recovered somewhat.

But that uptick in sales at Chrysler benefited the A-Body Valiant and Dodge Dart lines, which were bolstered by plushed-up versions (Valiant Brougham and Dart Special Edition) that went on sale in the spring of 1974.

By that time, Chrysler was bleeding cash and could not afford to keep a low-volume car like Barracuda in production. Also, the cost of upgrading existing car lines to meet the tougher 1975 emissions standards, and the increased demand for the A-Body cars, meant that the handwriting was on the wall for the E-Body.

On April 1, 1974 (10 years to the day after the first Plymouth Valiant Barracuda went on sale), Chrysler announced the end of E-Body production. There was no special "Final Edition" model, nor was there any commemoration of the last one to roll off the line at Hamtramck Assembly.

That venerable plant (60 years old in 1974) would now produce only A-Body compacts for the rest of 1974, as well as all of 1975. An all-new product did arrive at Hamtramck for 1976, the F-Body Plymouth Volare and Dodge Aspen.

The "Fish" had swum inland and upstream from the sea that was the new-car market, and died without spawning a successor in the pony car market. Ford itself had abandoned it when they dropped the "big" Mustang in favor of the smaller, Pinto-derived Mustang II, which did not offer a V-8 in U.S.-built and sold Mustang IIs in 1974, while offering a 120-hp 302-ci V-8 in Mustang IIs sold in Mexico that year.

Also at the end of the 1974 model run, AMC discontinued the Javelin, for many of the same reasons (starting with sluggish sales) that Chrysler did away with the E-Body cars. And, like

A "what-if" design concept by Bob Ackerman that hinted at a possible second-generation Barracuda. The shape of the roof line ended up on the ill-fated "Cincinnati" focus-group styling prototypes, while the shape of the headlight area and grille are quite like those of the 1970–1972 Satellite, Belvedere, Road Runner, and GTX two-doors. (Photo Courtesy Bob Ackerman)

This 1971 vintage Bob Ackerman sketch shows a front bumper much like the production 1971–74 Dodge charger had, combined with grille inserts that almost look like the 1971 Barracuda grille's "gills." If this design concept had actually been approved for production, the soonest it would have appeared in production form would have been the 1974 model year, given the common industry practice of taking a minimum of 24 months for a styling makeover to go from sketch to clay, to body engineering, to tool-and-die making, to production. (Photo Courtesy Bob Ackerman)

Would this have been a front end treatment on a second-generation Barracuda Gran Coupe? That will never be known, but this Bob Hubbach sketch incorporates a bumper and grille design that would have had a hard time passing muster with the 1973-and-later Federal 5-mph crash-protection standards. Also, would it have even graced a Barracuda, or a future Plymouth aimed at the Chevrolet Monte Carlo's spot in the new-car market? (Photo Courtesy Bob Hubbach)

The general profile of this Bob Hubbach sketch says "Barracuda," but the shape of the grille, bumper, and quad headlights closely resemble the front-end styling of the production 1973 Plymouth Fury line, minus its own set of rubber bumper blocks, which helped make them FMVSS 215-compliant. "Family resemblance" styling was still a common occurrence in the U.S. auto industries in the 1970s, even if those identical-looking cars didn't share bumpers, grilles, or sheet metal. (Photo Courtesy Bob Hubbach)

Chrysler, production capacity for Javelin at American Motors' Kenosha, Wisconsin, assembly plant was dedicated for a new "wide small car" set to go on sale in the spring of 1975, the Pacer.

But the pony car market segment was far from dead. General Motors had it all to itself until 1979, when Ford introduced its Fox-bodied Mustang and Mercury Capri, car lines that were competitive with Camaro and Firebird in terms of size, features, powertrains, and price. That generation of small, sporty Fords lasted until 1994 (though the Capri was dropped after 1986), when the SN95s succeeded them, which in turn were succeeded by the fifth-generation Mustang in 2005, and an all-new sixth-generation Mustang that was introduced as this book was being written in 2015.

Where did the bumper blocks go? In this case, off the bumpers and far away from this "resto-modded" 1974 Barracuda. Combining the best of the styling cues and performance hardware with modern-day paints and items such as billet aluminum wheels wrapped in high-tech tires, sound systems that bathe you in your favorite tunes, and engines like the modern electronically fuel injected Hemi, or a "stroker" version of Chrysler's legendary V-8s, modern day customizers have plenty to work with if they choose an E-Body Barracuda for their next project. (Photo Courtesy Russo & Steele)

The bumpers say "1974," even without the rubber blocks on them, but the reproduction "hockey stick" rear stripes say "suddenly it's 1970!" as loud as a 500-ci "stroker" version of Chrysler's B/RB big-block V-8 can. Modern-tech wheels and tires offer traction and cornering ability that the 60-series "Wide Ovals" of the E-Body's early years can't match. Note the body's panel fit and gaps between the door, front fender, and rear quarter panel. Someone put some time and effort into making it all fit, much more time than the line workers in Hamtramck Assembly's body shop had. (Photo Courtesy Russo & Steele)

General Motors redesigned the F-Body Camaro and Firebird for 1982, then again in 1993. However, slowing sales led to General Motors dropping the F-Body after the 2001 model year. Camaro was revived for Chevrolet for 2006, and an all-new generation of Camaros also entered production in 2015.

And Chrysler? The company that needed a federally guaranteed loan "bailout" in 1979, which saw the demise of the ancient Hamtramck Assembly Plant under its terms in 1980, seemed to have forgotten its rear-drive high-performance heritage as the 1980s moved into the 1990s, a time that brought the Daimler-Benz "merger of equals" in 1998 that was anything but, the discontinuation of the Plymouth brand in 2001, the Cerberus takeover in 2007, and the FIAT "bailout/takeover" of Chrysler in 2008.

But a number of things happened beginning in the 1990s that gave the Mopar-faithful hope. That started with the V-10 powered Dodge Viper prototype, whose 1992 appearance created such a sensation that it entered production just under two years later, and survived the DaimlerChrysler and Cerberus years as a brutally unrefined two-seat sports car that served as the vanguard of a new era of rear-drive Chrysler performance cars.

In 2003, an all-new V-8 debuted under the hood of Dodge's Ram pickup trucks. Displacing 5.7 liters (345 ci), it was smaller and lighter than the LA small-block V-8s, but its output rivaled that of any of Chrysler's big V-8s. And, because its combustion-chamber design was hemispherical in nature, it received an honored name from Chrysler's past: Hemi.

In 2006 came the rear-wheel-drive LX platform, with many of its chassis components "borrowed" from then-corporate-overlord Mercedes-Benz. The Chrysler version received the legendary "300" moniker, while "Magnum" was the name of the four-door Dodge wagon variant, and "Charger" was the name selected for the Dodge sedan. Purists scoffed at the idea of a four-door Charger until they drove a Hemi one, or tried to outrun a Hemi Dodge Charger police sedan. (They couldn't.)

Then, in 2007, the unthinkable happened. Dodge introduced a two-door version of the LX platform, the LC, whose styling looked remarkably familiar to a legendary Dodge of nearly four decades before, and whose engine selection included that new-generation, two-spark-plugs-per-cylinder Hemi V-8.

It's name? Challenger.

As of this writing, the Challenger is still in the Dodge lineup, with R/T and other variants appearing over the years, and with the 707-hp supercharged "Hellcat" version of the Hemi available.

Chrysler may have been late to the pony car party in the late 1960s and early 1970s, but it is the life of that party now!

APPENDIX A

1970 HIGH PERFORMANCE 'CUDA, CHALLENGER R/T, AND CODE A66 (340) ENGINES

Engine	***340***	***383***	***440***	***440 6-Barrel***	***426 Hemi***
Displacement (ci)	340	383	440	440	426
Horsepower@RPM	275@5000	335@5200	375@4600	390@4700	425@5000
Torque, ft-lbs@RPM	340@3200	425@3400	480@3200	490@3200	490@4000
Compression ratio	10.5:1	9.5:1	9.7:1	10.5:1	10.25:1
Camshaft	High lift, long duration, high overlap (same for all engines)				
Cam duration (degrees; intake/exhaust/overlap)	276/284/52	276/292/54	276/292/54	276/292/54	292/292/68
Lifter type	Hydraulic (Same for all engines; new this year for the 426 Hemi)				
Valve diameter, intake (inches)	2.02	2.08	2.08	2.08	2.25
Valve diameter, exhaust (inches)	1.60	1.74	1.74	1.74	1.94
Carburetion	Single Carter AVS 4-bbl.	Single Holley AVS 4-bbl.	Single Carter AVS 4-bbl.	Triple Holley 2-bbl.	Dual Carter AFB 4-bbl.

Components	***340, 383***	***440, 440 6-Barrel, 426 Hemi***
Distributor	Dual-Breaker/Single-Breaker	Dual Breaker
Air induction (standard)	Underhood	Air Grabber
(optional)	N/A	Air Grabber (none)
Exhaust system	Dual, low restriction, with cast-iron headers and high-flow mufflers	
Transmission (standard)	Heavy-duty 3-speed	High-upshift TorqueFlite automatic
Transmission (optional)	Heavy-duty 4-speed	High-upshift TorqueFlite

APPENDIX B

1970 DODGE CHALLENGER (Base Series, Barracuda Gran Coupe, and Challenger SE) AND PLYMOUTH BARRACUDA STANDARD AND OPTIONAL ENGINES

Engine	***225 Slant Six***	***318 V-8***	***383 2-Barrel V-8***	***383 4-Barrel V-8***
Displacement (ci)	225	318	383	383
Bore x stroke (inches)	3.40 x 4.12	3.91 x 3.31	4.25 x 3.38	4.25 x 3.38
Horsepower@RPM	145@4,000	230@4,400	290@4,400	330@5,000
Torque ft-lbs@RPM	215@2,400	320@2,000	390@2,800	425@3,200
Carburetor	1-barrel	2-barrel	2-barrel	4-barrel
Air cleaner	Silenced	Silenced	Silenced	Dual Snorkel
Camshaft	Standard	Standard	Special	Special
Exhaust system	Single	Single	Single, low-restriction	Dual, low-restriction
Fuel recommended	Regular	Regular	Regular	Premium

APPENDIX C

1970 DODGE CHALLENGER/PLYMOUTH BARRACUDA TRANSMISSIONS

		Basic	*Gran Coupe/SE*	*'Cuda/Challenger R/T*
3-speed manual	Floor mounted	Standard	Standard	Standard
	Console mounted	Optional	Optional	Optional
4-speed manual	Floor mounted	Optional	Optional	Optional
	Console mounted	Optional	Optional	Optional
TorqueFlite automatic	Column mounted	Optional	Optional	Optional
	Console mounted	Optional	Optional	Optional

APPENDIX D

1970-1971 CHALLENGER AND BARRACUDA ACCESSORY GROUPS AND PACKAGES

Basic Group (Code A04)

- Solid-state AM radio*
- Power steering
- Remote-control left outside racing mirror, chrome
- Variable-speed windshield wipers

* *Any available radio may be ordered for an additional charge over the AM radio*

*Light Package (Code A04)**

- Fender-mounted turn-signal indicators
- Trunk compartment light
- Glove box light
- Ashtray light
- Ignition switch light with time delay
- Time-delay instrument panel floodlight
- Map/courtesy light

* *Available in group only; not available as separate options*

Challenger Molding Group "A" (Code A63—Standard on SE)

- Belt molding
- Front splash-pan scoop molding
- Cowl molding
- Rear Astrotone-painted appliqué

Barracuda Exterior Trim Package (Code A46)

- Grille surround molding*
- Rear surround molding*
- Wheel lip moldings
- Deluxe wheel covers

* *Available in group only; not available as separate options; not available on 'Cuda or Gran Coupe*

*Elastomeric Front Bumper Package (Code A21)**

- Elastomeric front bumper, color-keyed to exterior color*
- Remote-control left outside racing mirror, chrome
- Manually adjustable right outside racing mirror, chrome
- Belt molding
- Body-colored mirrors may be ordered with this package for an additional charge

* *Available on Barracuda and 'Cuda in 1970–1971; available on the base Challenger in 1971 only*

*Elastomeric Front and Rear Bumper Package (Code A22)**

- Elastomeric front and rear bumpers**
- Remote-control left outside racing mirror,
- Manually adjustable right outside racing mirror
- Belt molding

* *Not available with rear quarter-panel air scoop*

** *Available in group only; not available as a separate option; this option was only available in red for 1970 Barracudas*

*Rallye Instrument Cluster Package (Code A62)**

- Variable-speed windshield wipers with electric washers
- Tachometer
- Electric clock
- Heater-control floodlight
- 150-mph speedometer
- Trip odometer with push-button reset
- Wood-grain instrument cluster appliqué
- Oil pressure gauge added for full instrumentation

* *Available in V-8 models only*

APPENDIX D CONTINUED

Trailer Towing Package (Code A35)

Maximum gross trailer weight: 2,000 pounds.
TorqueFlite required (n/a with manual transmissions).
Not available with 225 6-cylinder, 440 6-barrel or Hemi.

- Maximum-capacity cooling system: 26-inch heavy-duty radiator, 7-blade torque-drive fan with shroud and hood seal
- Heavy-duty suspension: Heavy-duty rear springs/front torsion bars and anti-sway bar (Standard 340)
- Heavy-duty (drum) brakes: 11 x 3–inch front, 11 x 2–inch rear
- Wide-rim heavy-duty wheels: 14 x 5-1/2 JJ
- Heavy-duty stop-lamp switch
- Heavy-duty turn-signal flasher
- Auxiliary transmission oil cooler
- 3.23 rear axle ratio

Recommended Options

- Engine: 340, 383 (2- or 4-barrel), or 440 4-barrel V-8
- Power steering
- Power brakes
- Front disc brakes
- 50-amp heavy-duty alternator (standard with air conditioning)
- 70-amp/hour battery with rubber separators
- Air conditioning

APPENDIX E

1970–1971 BARRACUDA STANDARD GRAN COUPE FEATURES

- Overhead consolette for the hardtop version, with warning lights for Door Ajar, Seat Belts, and Low Fuel
- Molded hardtop headlining, knit jersey
- Leather bucket seats in black, white, or tan
- Sill molding and wheel opening molding
- Distinctive taillight trim
- Gran Coupe crest on side
- Gran Coupe crest on rear
- Black-textured hardtop rear window molding with optional black vinyl roof.
- Cloth and vinyl bucket seats with a houndstooth pattern on the seating surfaces, as a credit option instead of the standard leather-and-vinyl buckets
- Deluxe all-vinyl bucket seats in a choice of six colors; another credit option instead of the standard leather-and-vinyl trim

APPENDIX F

1970–1971 DODGE CHALLENGER SE

According to the *1970 Dodge Dealer Data Book*, the Challenger Special Edition (SE) was a variant of both the base Challenger hardtop and Challenger R/T hardtop.

The SE was priced $232 higher than the base 6-cylinder and base 8-cylinder Challenger hardtops, and $232 over the base Challenger R/T hardtop. For that extra $232, buyers received a standard vinyl roof with a "formal" (smaller) rear window.

They also received an upgraded interior trim, including:

- Standard leather-and-vinyl front bucket/rear bench seats; cloth and vinyl or all-vinyl seat trims were available as credit options that knocked $48.25 off the sticker price.
- Carpeted lower door inner panel with reflectors.
- Formed headliner with three-lamp (Low Fuel, Door Ajar, Fasten Belts) consolette.

Additional exterior bright trim included:

- Code A63 Molding Group "A" (belt molding, front splash pan scoop molding, cowl molding, and rear "astrotone"-painted molding on taillight panel center)
- SE nameplates on the rear roof panel

Exclusions and differences with the SE were:

- Two-tone paint was not available with SE.
- Code A66 340 engine package was not available with the SE.
- Code M51 Electric Sunroof was not available with the SE.
- Standard wheels with the SE were the same as for the Challenger and Challenger R/T (e.g., painted steel wheel with hub cap); wheel covers and road wheels were optional, at the same prices, as on the base Challenger/Challenger R/T.

Also according to the *1970 Dodge Salesman's Pocket Guide*, sticker prices and availability of other options and option packages on the Challenger SE and SE R/T were the same as for the base Challenger and Challenger R/T hardtops.

1970-1971 DODGE CHALLENGER AND PLYMOUTH BARRACUDA AXLE PACKAGES

Performance Axle Package (Code A31)

Available on all Barracudas and Challengers.

Available with 340, 383 4-barrel with 4-speed manual transmission or TorqueFlite; 440 4-barrel, 440 6-barrel, or Hemi with TorqueFlite. Not available with Trailer Towing Package.

- 3.91 ratio, heavy-duty Sure-Grip rear axle, 8-3/4-inch ring gear
- 7-blade torque-drive fan (standard with Hemi)
- 26-inch high-performance radiator with fan shroud (standard with Hemi)
- Hemi suspension (standard with 440 and Hemi)
- Heavy-duty torsion bar front springs
- Heavy-duty rear springs
- Heavy-duty shock absorbers
- Front anti-sway bar

High-Performance Axle Package (Code A36)

Available with 340 or 383 4-barrel with 4-speed manual transmission or TorqueFlite. Not available with air conditioning* or trailer-towing package.

- 3.55 ratio, heavy-duty Sure-Grip rear axle, 8-3/4-inch ring gear
- 7-blade torque-drive fan
- 26-inch high-performance radiator with fan shroud
- Hemi suspension

Super-Performance Axle Package (Code A32)

Available on with 440 4-bb. or 440 6-bbl or Hemi with TorqueFlite transmission. Not available with air conditioning or trailer-towing package.

- 4.10 ratio, heavy duty Sure-Grip rear axle, 9-3/4-inch ring gear (Dana axle)
- 7-blade torque-drive fan (standard with Hemi)
- 26-inch high-performance radiator with fan shroud (standard with Hemi)
- Power disc brakes
- Hemi suspension (standard with 440 and Hemi)

Track Pak (Code A33)

A performance package designed expressly for those interested in sanctioned drag racing.

Available on 'Cuda and Challenger R/T only.

Available with 440 4-barrel, 440 6-barrel, and Hemi. Not available with air conditioning.

- Heavy-duty, 4-speed manual transmission with Hurst shifter, Wood-grained pistol-grip shift knob and reverse warning light (available in package only with 440 or Hemi engines)
- 3.54 ratio, heavy duty Sure-Grip rear axle, 9 3/4" ring gear (Dana axle)
- 7-blade torque-drive fan (standard with Hemi)
- 26" high-performance radiator with fan shroud (standard with Hemi)
- Dual breaker distributor (standard with 440 6-bbl. and Hemi)
- Hemi suspension (standard with 440 and Hemi)

Super Track Pak (Code A34)

A performance package designed expressly for those interested in sanctioned drag racing.

Available on 'Cuda and Challenger R/T only.

Available with 440 4-barrel, 440 6-barrel, and Hemi. Not available with air conditioning.

- Heavy-duty, 4-speed manual transmission with hurst shifter, wood-grained pistol-grip shift knob, and reverse warning light (available in package only with 440 or Hemi engines)
- 4.10 ratio, heavy-duty Sure-Grip rear axle, 9-3/4-inch ring gear (Dana axle)
- 7-blade torque-drive fan (standard with Hemi)
- 26-inch high-performance radiator with fan shroud (standard with Hemi)
- Dual-breaker distributor (standard with 440 6-barrel and Hemi)
- Hemi suspension (standard with 440 and Hemi)

As for why air conditioning was not available with the Super Track Pak, Track Pak, Super Performance, and High Performance Axle Packages, it's likely that the factory-installed Airtemp air-conditioning compressor's drive belt might come off at high speeds, and the compressor itself may not have been able to sustain continued ultra-high-speed operation. So, not wanting any of the related warranty problems that would result, Chrysler chose to make these option groups not available with air conditioning. Plus, racing-minded 'Cuda and Challenger R/T buyers didn't want the Airtemp system's extra weight under the hood.

APPENDIX H

1971 HIGH-PERFORMANCE 'CUDA, CHALLENGER R/T AND 340 ENGINES

Engine	***340***	***383***	***440 Six Pack/Six Barrel***	***426 Hemi***
Displacement (ci)	340	383	440	426
Horsepower@RPM	275@5,000	300@5,200	390@4,700	425@5,000
Torque, ft/lbs@RPM	340@3,200	410@3,400	490@3,200	490@4,000
Compression ratio	10.3:1	8.5:1	10.3:1	10.25:1
Camshaft	High lift, long duration, high overlap (for all engines)			
Cam duration, intake/exhaust/overlap (degrees)	276/284/52	276/292/54	276/292/54	292/292/68
Lifter type	Hydraulic *(for all engines; new in 1970 for the 426 Hemi)*			
Valve diameter, intake (inches)	2.02	2.08	2.08	2.25
Valve diameter, exhaust (inches)	1.60	1.74	1.74	1.94
Carburetion	Single Carter AVS 4-barrel*	Single Carter AVS 4-barrel*	Triple Holley 2-barrel	Dual Carter AFB 4-barrel

** Replaced by Carter ThermoQuad for 1971*

Components	***340, 343***	***440, 426***
Distributor	Dual-Breaker/Single-Breaker	Dual Breaker
Air induction (std.)	Air Grabber, Underhood	Air Grabber, Air Grabber
Exhaust system	Dual, low restriction, with cast-iron manifolds and high-flow mufflers	
Transmission (std.)	Heavy-duty 3-speed	High-upshift TorqueFlite
Transmission (opt.)	Heavy-duty 4-speed	High-upshift TorqueFlite

APPENDIX I

1971 DODGE CHALLENGER (Base Series, Barracuda Gran Coupe, and Challenger SE) AND PLYMOUTH BARRACUDA STANDARD AND OPTIONAL ENGINES

Engine	***198***	***225 Slant Six***	***318 V-8***	***383 2-bbl. V-8***
Displacement (ci)	198	225	318	383
Bore x stroke (inches)	3.40 x 3.64	3.40 x 4.12	3.91 x 3.31	4.25 x 3.38
Horsepower@RPM	125@4,400	145@4,000	230@4,400	290@4,400
Torque ft-lbs@RPM	180@2,000	215@2,400	320@2,000	390@2,800
Carburetor	1-barrel	1-barrel	2-barrel	2-barrel
Air cleaner	Silenced	Silenced	Silenced	Silenced
Camshaft	Standard	Standard	Special	Special
Exhaust system	Single	Single	Single, low-restriction	Single, low-restriction
Fuel recommended	Regular	Regular	Regular	Regular

APPENDIX J

1972 DODGE CHALLENGER AND PLYMOUTH BARRACUDA ENGINES

Engine	*225 Slant Six*	*318 V-8*	*340 V-8*
Displacement (ci)	225	318	340
Bore x stroke (inches)	3.40 x 4.12	3.91 x 3.31	4.25 x 3.38
Horsepower@RPM	110@4,000	150@4,000	245@4,400
Torque ft-lbs@RPM	185@2,000	260@1,600	290@3,600
Carburetor	1-barrel	2-barrel	4-barrel
Air cleaner	Silenced	Silenced	Silenced
Camshaft	Standard	Standard	Special
Exhaust system	Single	Single, low-restriction	Dual, low-restriction
Fuel recommended	Regular	Regular	Regular

APPENDIX K

1973 DODGE CHALLENGER AND PLYMOUTH BARRACUDA ENGINES

Engine	*318 V-8*	*340 4-Barrel V-8*
Displacement (ci)	318 cubic inches	340
Bore x stroke (inches)	3.91 x 3.31	4.25 x 3.38
Horsepower@RPM	150@4,400	240@4,800
Torque ft-lbs@RPM	265@2,000	295@3,600
Carburetor	2-barrel	4-barrel
Air cleaner	Silenced	Silenced
Camshaft	Standard	Special
Exhaust system	Single, low-restriction	Dual, low-restriction
Fuel recommended	Regular	Regular

APPENDIX L

1973 DODGE CHALLENGER AND PLYMOUTH BARRACUDA TRANSMISSIONS

- 3-speed manual (standard)
- 4-speed manual
- TorqueFlite automatic

APPENDIX M

1970-1974 DODGE CHALLENGER AND PLYMOUTH BARRACUDA REAR DIFFERENTIALS

Standard: Open (non limited-slip)
Optional*: SureGrip (limited-slip)

*Included with trailer towing and performance axle packages; optional rear-axle ratios were no extra charge with SureGrip.

APPENDIX N

1974 DODGE CHALLENGER AND PLYMOUTH BARRACUDA ENGINES

Engine	*318 V-8*	*360 4-Barrel V-8*
Displacement (ci)	318	360
Bore x stroke (inches)	3.91 x 3.31	4.25 x 3.58
Horsepower@RPM	150@3,600	245@4,800
Torque ft-lbs@RPM	265@2,000	320@3,600
Carburetor	2-barrel	4-barrel
Air cleaner	Silenced	Silenced
Camshaft	Standard	Special
Exhaust system	Single, low-restriction	Dual, low-restriction
Fuel recommended	Regular	Regular

APPENDIX O

1974 DODGE CHALLENGER AND PLYMOUTH BARRACUDA TRANSMISSIONS

- 3-speed manual (standard)
- 4-speed manual
- automatic

APPENDIX P

1970–1974 PAINT AND EQUIPMENT OPTIONS

1970 DODGE CHALLENGER AND PLYMOUTH BARRACUDA PAINT CODES

A4 1970 Plymouth: *Platinum Poly*
A4 1970 Dodge: *Silver Poly*

A9 1970 Dodge: *Dark Gray Poly*

B3 1970 Dodge: *Light Blue Poly*
B3 1970 Plymouth: *Jubilee Blue Poly*

B5 1970 Dodge: *Bright Blue Poly*
B5 1970 Plymouth: *Blue Fire Poly*

B7 1970 Dodge: *Dark Blue Poly*
B7 1970 Plymouth: *Jamaica Blue Poly*

C7 1970 Dodge: *Plum Crazy Poly*
C7 1970 Plymouth: *In Violet Poly*

E5 1970 Dodge: *Bright Red*
E5 1970 Plymouth: *Rally Red*

F4 1970 Dodge: *Lime Green Poly*
F4 1970 Plymouth: *Lime Green Poly*

F8 1970 Dodge: *Dark Green Poly*
F8 1970 Plymouth: *Ivy Green Poly*

J5 1970 Dodge: *Lime Green Poly*
J5 1970 Plymouth: *Lime Light Poly*

K2 1970 Dodge: *Go Mango Poly*
K2 1970 Plymouth: *Vitamin "C" Poly*

K3 1970 Plymouth: *Burnt Orange Poly*

K5 1970 Dodge: *Dark Burnt Orange Poly*
K5 1970 Plymouth: *Deep Burnt Orange Poly*

L1 1970 Dodge: *Beige*
L1 1970 Plymouth: *Sandpebble Beige*

1970 DODGE CHALLENGER AND PLYMOUTH BARRACUDA PAINT CODES

P6 1970 Plymouth:
Frosted Teal Poly

Q3 1970 Dodge:
Light Turquoise Poly

R6 1970 Dodge:
Red
R6 1970 Plymouth:
Scorch Red

R8 1970 Dodge:
Burgundy Poly

T3 1970 Dodge:
Tan Poly
T3 1970 Plymouth:
Sahara Tan Poly

T6 1970 Dodge:
Dark Tan Poly
T6 1970 Plymouth:
Burnt Tan Poly

V2 1970 Dodge:
Hemi Orange Poly
V2 1970 Plymouth:
Tor-Red Poly

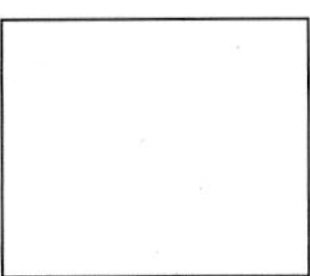

W1 1970 Dodge:
White
W1 1970 Plymouth:
Alpine White

Y1 1970 Dodge:
Bright Yellow
Y1 1970 Plymouth:
Lemon Twist

1970 DODGE CHALLENGER UPHOLSTERY

H6E4
Exteriors: FE5, BL1, EW1, TX9, DT3

H6B5
Exteriors: EB3, EB5, EB7, BL1, EW1, TX9

H6F8
Exteriors: FF4, EF8, BL1, EW1, TX9, DY3, FY4

H6T5
Exteriors: FE5, FF4, EF8, EK2, BL1, FT6, EV2, EW1, TX9, FY1, DY3

H6K4
Exteriors: EK2, FK5, BL1, EW1, TX9

H6X9
Exteriors: All Challenger Colors

H6XW White/ Black*
Exteriors: All Challenger Colors

* *Black Carpet, Instrument Panel, and Steering Wheel.*

1970 DODGE CHALLENGER VINYL ROOF

VIY Gold
Exteriors: *GY4, GY8, with All Interiors*

V1X Black
Exteriors: *Available with All Colors*

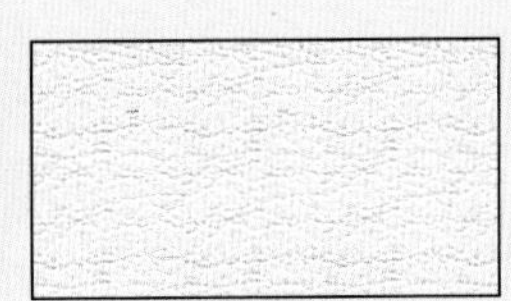

V1W White
Exteriors: *Available with All Colors*

V1F Green
Exteriors: *FF4, EF8 with All Interiors*
Exteriors: *EA4, BL1, EW1, TX9, FY1, DY3, FY4 with Green Interiors*
Exteriors: *EA4, BL1, EW1, TX9 with Black, White & Black Interiors*

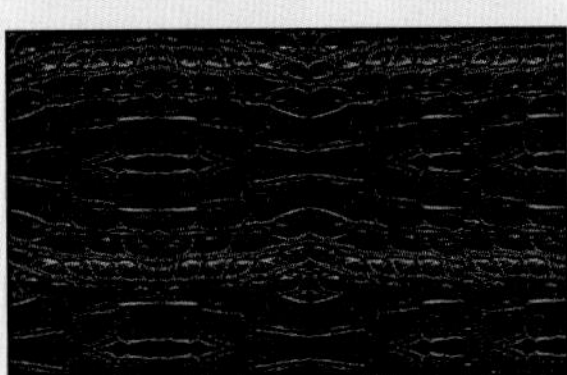

V1G Gator Grain
Exteriors: *FF4, EF8, FT3, FT6, FY4, FY6 with All Interiors*
Exteriors: *BL1, EW1, TX9 with Green, Tan, White & Black Interiors*
Exteriors: *EA4, FQ3, ER6, FY1 with Black, White & Black Interiors*
Exteriors: *EB3, EB5, EB7 with Blue, Black, White & Black Interiors*

1970 PLYMOUTH BARRACUDA UPHOLSTERY

H6B5, H4B5 Blue
Exteriors: *EB3, EB5, EB7, EW1, TX9*

H6E4 Red
Exteriors: *FE5, BL1, EW1, TX9*

H6F8, H4F8 Green
Exteriors: *FF5, EF8, BL1, EW1, TX9*

H6T5 Tan
Exteriors: *BL1, FT6, EW1, TX9*

H6X9, H4X9 Black
Exteriors:
All Barracuda Colors

H6XW White & Black*, H4XW White
Exteriors:
All Barracuda Colors

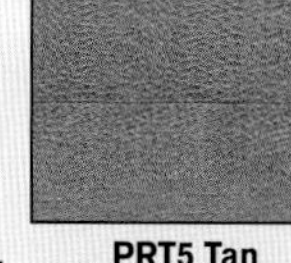
PRT5 Tan
Exteriors: *BL1, FT6, EW1, TX9*

PRX9 Black†
Exteriors:
All Barracuda Colors

PRXW White & Black*†
Exteriors:
All Barracuda Colors

P8A8 Black Frost
Exteriors:
All Barracuda Colors

P6B5 Blue
Exteriors: *EB3, EB5, EB7, EW1, TX9*

P6E4 Red
Exteriors: *FE5, BL1, EW1, TX9*

P6F8 Green
Exteriors: *FF4, EF4, BL1, EW1, TX9*

P6K4 Burnt Orange
Exteriors: *FK3, FK5, BL1, EW1, TX9*

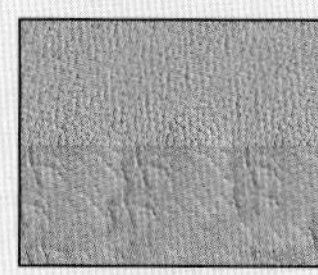
P6T5 Tan
Exteriors: *BL1, FT6, EW1, TX9*

P6XW White & Black*
Exteriors:
All Barracuda Colors

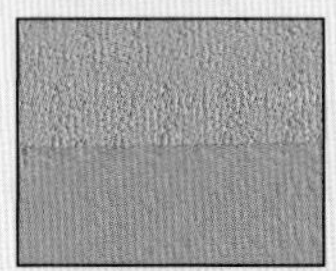
P6YX Gold & Black*
Exteriors:
All Barracuda Colors

P5K4 Burnt Orange
Exteriors: *FK3, FK5, BL1, EW1, TX9*

P5X9 Black
Exteriors:
All Barracuda Colors

** Black on Carpet, Instrument Panel, Steering Wheel*
† Not Available on Barracuda and 'Cuda

1970 PLYMOUTH BARRACUDA VINYL ROOF

V1G Gator Grain
Exteriors: *FF8, FF4, DY3, FY4, FY8, FT3, FT6 with All Interiors*
Exteriors: *BL1, EW1, TX9 with Green, Tan, White & Black, or Green & White Interiors*
Exteriors: *FK3, FK5 with Black, White & Black, or Burnt Orange & White Interiors*
Exteriors: *EV2, EA4, ER5, DY2** with Black, White & Black Interiors*
Exteriors: *EB3**, EB5**, EB7** with Blue, Black, White & Black, or White & Blue Interiors*
Exteriors: *FF6**, with Black, Teal & Black, or White & Black Interiors*

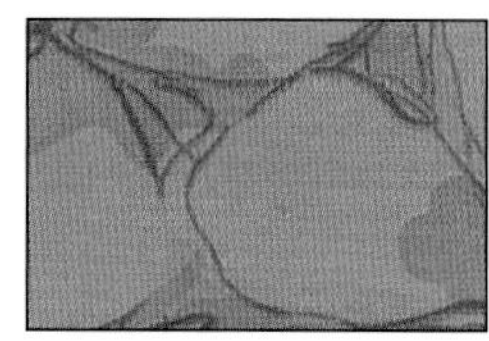
V1Q Mod Blue
Exteriors: *EB3, EB5, EB7, EW1, TX9 with All Interiors*

V1W White
Exteriors:
All Plymouth Colors

V1X Black
Exteriors:
All Plymouth Colors

V1P Mod Yellow
Exteriors: *EF8, FY4, DY3, EW1, TX9, with All Interiors*

*** Available but Not Recommended*

1971 DODGE CHALLENGER AND PLYMOUTH BARRACUDA PAINT CODES

A4 1971 Dodge: *Light Gunmetal Met.*
A4 1971 Plymouth: *Winchester Gray Metallic*

B2 1971 Dodge: *Light Blue Metallic*
B2 1971 Plymouth: *Glacial Blue Metallic*

B5 1971 Dodge: *Bright Blue Metallic*
B5 1971 Plymouth: *True Blue Metallic*

B7 1971 Dodge: *Dark Blue Metallic*
B7 1971 Plymouth: *Evening Blue Metallic*

C7 1971 Dodge: *Plum Crazy**
C7 1971 Plymouth: *In-Violet**

E5 1971 Dodge: *Bright Red*
E5 1971 Plymouth: *Rallye Red*

F3 1971 Dodge: *Medium Green Met.*
F3 1971 Plymouth: *Amber Sherwood Metallic*

F8 1971 Dodge: *Dark Green Metallic*
F8 1971 Plymouth: *Sherwood Green Metallic*

1971 DODGE CHALLENGER AND PLYMOUTH BARRACUDA PAINT CODES CONTINUED

J6 1971 Dodge: *GreenGo**
J6 1971 Plymouth: *Sassy Grass Green**

K6 1971 Dodge: *Dark Bronze*
K6 1971 Plymouth: *Autumn Bronze Metallic*

K5 1971 Dodge: *Dark Burnt Orange Metallic*
K5 1971 Plymouth: *Deep Burnt Orange Metallic*

L5 1971 Dodge: *Butterscotch*
L5 1971 Plymouth: *Bahama Yellow*

V2 1971 Dodge: *Ceramic Red**
V2 1971 Plymouth: *Tor Red**

M3 1971 Dodge: *Panther Pink***
M3 1971 Plymouth: *Moulin Rouge***

T6 1971 Dodge: *Dark Tan Metallic*
T6 1971 Plymouth: *Tunisian Tan Metallic*

W3 1971 Dodge: *White*
W3 1971 Plymouth: *Spinnaker White*

X9 1971 Dodge: *Black*
X9 1971 Plymouth: *Formal Black*

FY1 1971 Dodge: *Top Banana**
FY1 1971 Plymouth: *Lemon Twist**

Y3 1971 Dodge: *Citron Yella**
Y3 1971 Plymouth: *Curious Yellow**

Y4 1971 Dodge: *Gold Metallic*
Y4 1971 Plymouth: *Gold Leaf Metallic*

Y9 1971 Dodge: *Dark Gold Metallic*
Y9 1971 Plymouth: *Tawny Gold Metallic*

999 Special Order (Other Plymouth, Dodge, Chrysler & Imperial paint colors)
* *Extra-cost optional High Impact colors available all year*
** *Extra-cost optional High Impact color only available on special order*

1971 DODGE CHALLENGER COUPE SEAT COLOR CODES

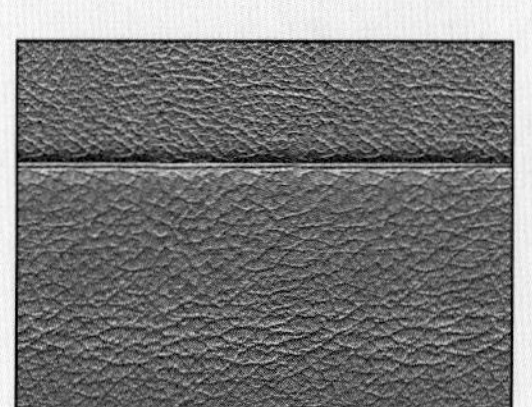

L6B5
Exteriors: *GB2, GB5, GB7, GW3, TX9*

L6F7
Exteriors: *GF3, GF7, GT2, GW3, TX9, GY8*

L6T7
Exteriors: *FE5, GF3, GF7, GK6, EL5, GT2, EV2, GW3, TX9, GY8*

L6X9
Exteriors: *All Challenger Colors*

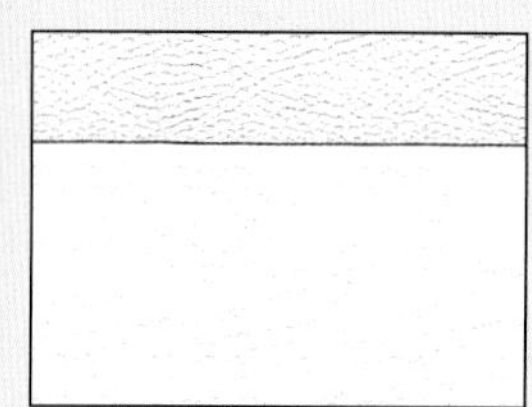

L6XW
Exteriors: *All Challenger Colors*

1971 DODGE CHALLENGER SEAT OPTIONS AND CODES (HARDTOP, CONVERTIBLE, R/T)

H6B5 Bucket
Exteriors: *GB2, GB5, GB7, GW3, TX9*

H6F7 Bucket
Exteriors: *GF3, GF7, GT2, GW3, TX9, GY8*

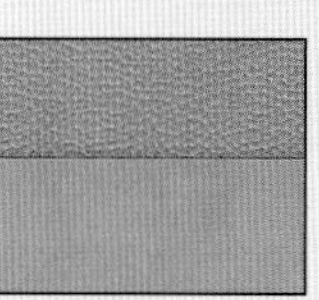

H6Y3 Bucket
Exteriors: *GB7, GW3, TX9, GY8, GY9*

H6T7 Bucket
Exteriors: *FE5, GF3, GF7, GK6, EL5, GT2, EV2, GW3, TX9, GY8*

H6X9 Bucket
Exteriors: *All Challenger Colors*

H6XW Bucket
Exteriors: *All Challenger Colors*

H4F7 Bench
Exteriors: *GF3, GF7, GT2, GW3, TX9, GY8*

H4X9 Bench
Exteriors: *All Challenger Colors*

1971 DODGE CHALLENGER SEAT OPTIONS AND CODES (HARDTOP, CONVERTIBLE, R/T CLOTH/VINYL)

HRX9
Exteriors:
All Challenger Colors

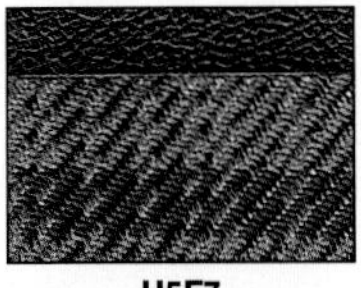

H5F7
Exteriors: *GF3, GF7, GT2, GW3, TX9, GY8*

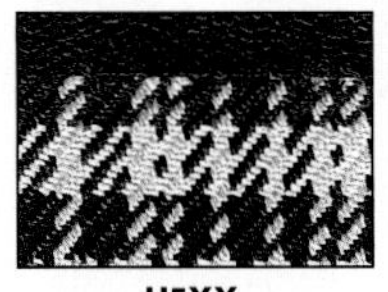

H5XX
Exteriors:
All Challenger Colors

H5X9
Exteriors: *FE5, EV2, GW3, TX9*

1971 PLYMOUTH BARRACUDA AND 'CUDA INTERIOR CODES

H6XV Orange & Black
Exteriors: *EV2*, GW3*, TX9*, GA4***

H6B5-H4B5 Blue
Exteriors: *GB2*, GB5*, GW3*, TX9*, GA4***

H6F7-H4F7 Green
Exteriors: *GF3*, GF7*, GW3*, TX9*, GY8**, GT2***

H6XW-H4XW White & Black
Exteriors: *All Barracuda Colors, except GW3***

H6T7-H4T7 Tan
Exteriors: *EL5*, GT2*, GW3*, TX9*, GF7**, GF3**, GY8**, GK6**, EV2**, FE5**, FY1***

H6X9-H4X9 Black
Exteriors:
All Barracuda Colors

** Recommended for Color Coordination ** Available*

1971 PLYMOUTH BARRACUDA GRAN COUPE SEAT OPTIONS AND CODES

PRX9-SRX9 Black (Leather)
Exteriors:
All Barracuda Colors

PRT7-SRT7 Tan (Leather)
Exteriors: *EL5*, GT2*, GW3*, TX9*, GF7**, GF3**, GY8**, GK6**, EV2**, FE5**, FY1***

PRY3 Gold (Leather)
Exteriors: *GW3*, TX9*, GY8*, GY9*, GF7***

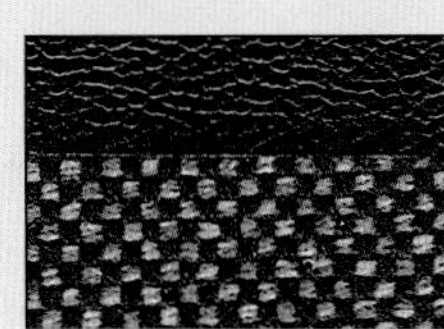

P5X9-H5X9 Black
Exteriors:
All Barracuda Colors

H5XV Orange & Black
Exteriors: *EV2*, GW3*, TX9*, GA4**, GK6**, GT2***

** Recommended for Color Coordination*

*** Available*

1971 PLYMOUTH BARRACUDA GRAN COUPE STANDARD INTERIOR COLOR CODES

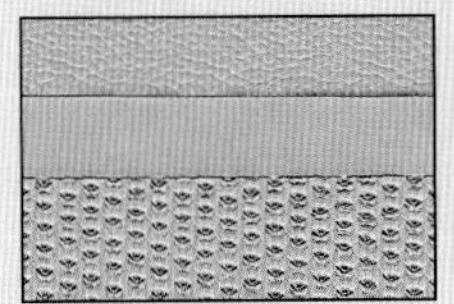

P6Y3 Gold
Exteriors: *GW3*, TX9*, GY8*, GY9*, GF7***

P6B5 Blue
Exteriors: *GB2*, GB5*, GW3*, TX9*, GA4***

P6F7 Green
Exteriors: *GF3*, GF7*, GW3*, TX9*, GY8**, GT2***

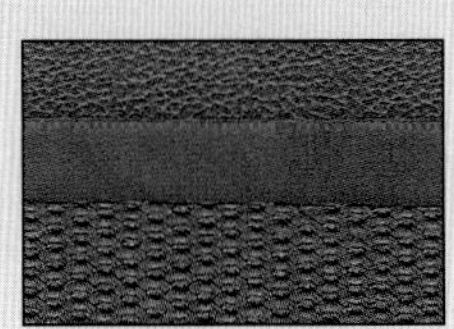

P6T7 Tan
Exteriors: *EL5*, GT2*, GW3*, TX9*, GF7**, GF3**, GY8**, GK6**, EV2**, FE5**, FY1***

P6X9 Black
Exteriors: *All Barracuda Colors*

** Recommended for Color Coordination*

*** Available*

1972 DODGE CHALLENGER AND PLYMOUTH BARRACUDA PAINT CODES

A4 1972 Dodge: *Light Gunmetal Metallic*
A4 1972 Plymouth: *Winchester Gray Metallic*

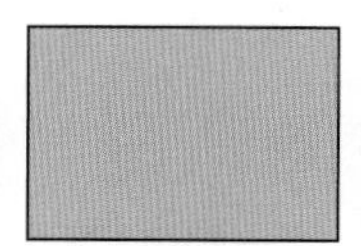

B1 1972 Dodge: *Light Blue*
B1 1972 Plymouth: *Blue Sky*

B3 1972 Dodge: *Super Blue*
B3 1972 Plymouth: *Basin Street Blue*

B5 1972 Dodge: *Bright Blue Metallic*
B5 1972 Plymouth: *True Blue Metallic*

E5 1972 Dodge: *Bright Red*
E5 1972 Plymouth: *Rallye Red*

F3 1972 Dodge: *Light Green Metallic*
F3 1972 Plymouth: *Amber Sherwood Metallic*

F7 1972 Dodge: *Dark Green Metallic*
F7 1972 Plymouth: *Sherwood Metallic*

T6 1972 Dodge: *Medium Tan Metallic*
T6 1972 Plymouth: *Mojave Tan Metallic*

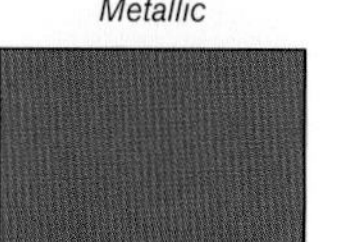

T8 1972 Dodge: *Dark Tan Metallic*
T8 1972 Plymouth: *Chestnut Metallic*

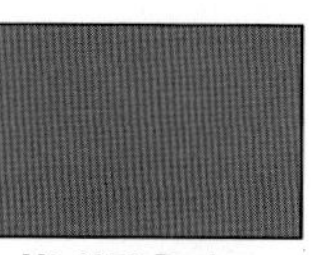

V2 1972 Dodge: *Hemi-Orange**
V2 1972 Plymouth: *Tor-Red**

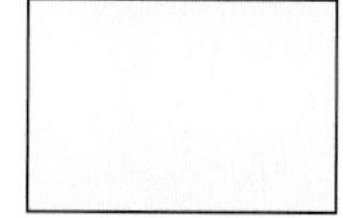

W1 1972 Dodge: *Eggshell White*
W1 1972 Plymouth: *Spinnaker White*

X9 1972 Dodge: *Black*
X9 1972 Plymouth: *Formal Black*

Y1 1972 Dodge: *Top Banana**
Y1 1972 Plymouth: *Lemon Twist**

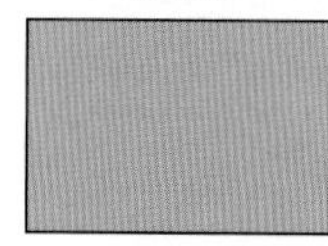

Y4 1972 Dodge: *Light Gold*
Y4 1972 Plymouth: *Honeydew*

Y8 1972 Dodge: *Gold Metallic*
Y8 1972 Plymouth: *Gold Leaf Metallic*

Y9 1972 Dodge: *Dark Gold Metallic*
Y9 1972 Plymouth: *Tawny Gold Metallic*

** High Impact Color; Optional at Extra Cost*

1972 DODGE CHALLENGER INTERIOR CODES

B6B5
Exteriors: *GA4, HB1, TB3, GB5, EW1, TX9*

B6F6
Exteriors: *GF3, GF7, HT6, EW1, TX9, GY4, GY8*

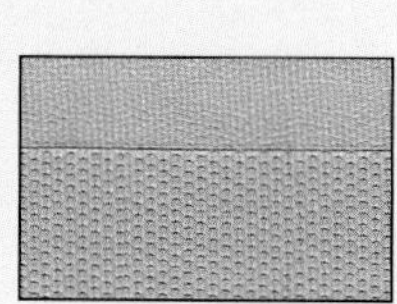

B6Y3
Exteriors: *GF7, EW1, TX9, GY4, GY8, GY9*

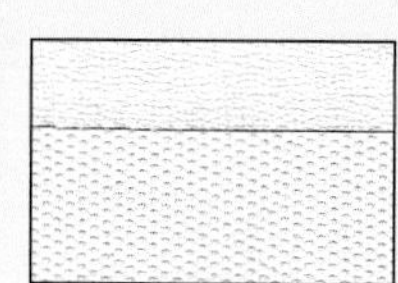

B6XW
Exteriors:
All Challenger Colors

B6X9
Exteriors:
All Challenger Colors

1972 PLYMOUTH BARRACUDA INTERIOR CODES

A6B5 Blue
Exteriors: *GA4, HB1, TB3, GB5, EW1, TX9*

A6F6 Green
Exteriors: *GF3, GF7, HT6, EW1, TX9, GY4, GY8*

A6X9 Black
Exteriors:
All Barracuda Colors

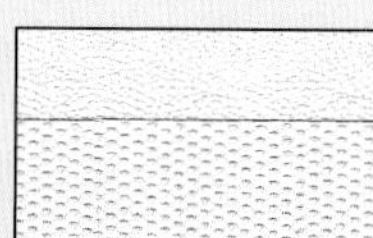

A6XW White
Exteriors:
All Barracuda Colors

1972 PLYMOUTH BARRACUDA VINYL TOP CODES

V1X, V4X Black
Exteriors: *All Plymouth Colors with All Interiors*

V1W, V4W White
Exteriors: *All Plymouth Colors with All Interiors*

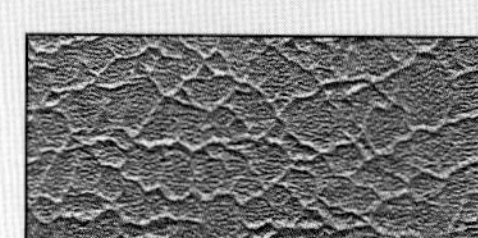

V1B Blue
Exteriors: *GA4, HB1, TB3, GB5, EW1, TX9 with Blue Interiors; TB3, GB5, EW1, TX9 with Black and Black & White Interiors*

1972 PLYMOUTH BARRACUDA VINYL TOP COLOR CODE

V1F Green*
Exteriors: *GF3, GF7, HL4, EW1, TX9, DY2, GY4 with Green Interiors; GF3, GF7, HL4, EW1, TX9 with Black, Black & White, and Parchment Interiors*

** Not Available on Wagons*

1973 DODGE CHALLENGER AND PLYMOUTH BARRACUDA PAINT CODES

A5 1973 Dodge:
Dark Silver Metallic
A5 1973 Plymouth:
Silver Frost Metallic

B1 1973 Dodge:
Light Blue
B1 1973 Plymouth:
Blue Sky

B3 1973 Dodge:
Super Blue
B3 1973 Plymouth:
Basin Street Blue

B5 1973 Dodge:
Bright Blue Metallic
B5 1973 Plymouth:
True Blue Metallic

E5 1973 Dodge:
Bright Red
E5 1973 Plymouth:
Rallye Red

F1 1973 Dodge:
Pale Green
F1 1973 Plymouth:
Mist Green

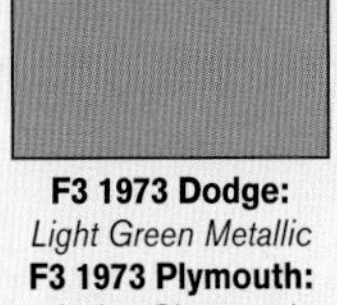

F3 1973 Dodge:
Light Green Metallic
F3 1973 Plymouth:
Amber Sherwood Metallic

F8 1973 Dodge:
Dark Green Metallic
F8 1973 Plymouth:
Forest Green Metallic

K6 1973 Dodge:
Bronze Metallic
K6 1973 Plymouth:
Autumn Bronze Metallic

L4 1973 Dodge:
Parchment
L4 1973 Plymouth:
Sahara Beige

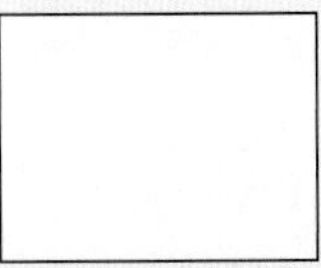

W1 1973 Dodge:
Eggshell White
W1 1973 Plymouth:
Spinnaker White

X9 1973 Dodge:
Black
X9 1973 Plymouth:
Formal Black

Y1 1973 Dodge:
*Top Banana**
Y1 1973 Plymouth:
*Lemon Twist**

Y3 1973 Dodge:
Light Gold
Y3 1973 Plymouth:
Honey Gold

Y6 1973 Dodge:
Gold Metallic
Y6 1973 Plymouth:
Gold Haze Metallic

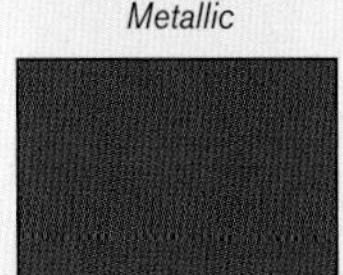

Y9 1973 Dodge:
Dark Gold Metallic
Y9 1973 Plymouth:
Tahitian Gold Metallic

** High Impact Color; Optional at Extra Cost*

1973 DODGE CHALLENGER VINYL TOP COLOR CODES

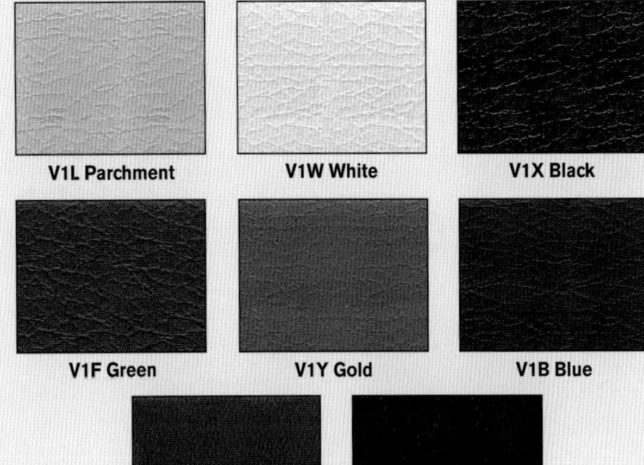

V1L Parchment
V1W White
V1X Black
V1F Green
V1Y Gold
V1B Blue
V1F Green
V1X Black

1973 DODGE CHALLENGER INTERIOR OPTIONS AND CODES

A6B5 Blue
Exteriors: *JA5*, HB1*, GB5*, EW1*, TX9*, TB3**, HL4***

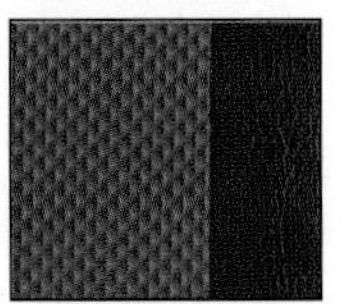

A6F6 Green
Exteriors: *JF1*, GF3*, JF8*, HL4*, EW1*, TX9**

A6X9 Black
Exteriors: *All Challenger Colors*

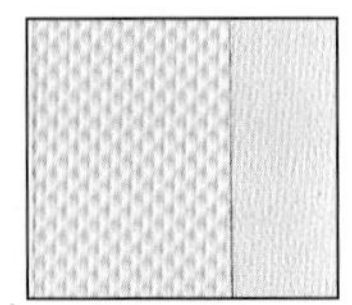

A6XW White
Exteriors: *All Challenger Colors*

** Recommended for Color Coordination*
*** Available*

1973 PLYMOUTH BARRACUDA ALL-VINYL INTERIOR COLOR CODES

A6B5 Blue
Exteriors: JA5, HB1*, GB5*, EW1*, TX9*, TB3**, HL4***

A6F6 Green
Exteriors: JF1, GF3, JF8, HL4, EW1, TX9

A6X9 Black
Exteriors: All Barracuda Colors

A6XW White
Exteriors: All Barracuda Colors

** Recommended for Color Coordination*

*** Available*

1973 PLYMOUTH BARRACUDA VINYL ROOF CODES

V1X Black

V1F Green

V1Y Gold

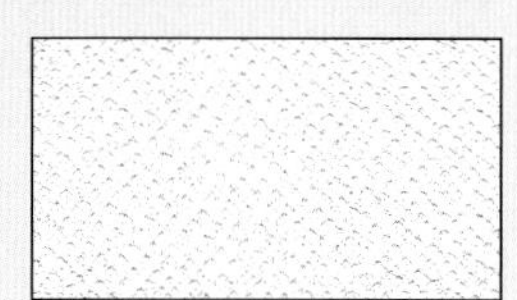
V1W White
Exteriors: All Cricket Colors with Available Interiors

V1X Black
Exteriors: All Cricket Colors with Available Interiors

1973 PLYMOUTH BARRACUDA INTERIOR OPTIONS AND CODES

A6B5 Blue
Exteriors: JA5, HB1*, GB5*, EW1*, TX9*, TB3**, HL4***

A6F6 Green
Exteriors: JF1, GF3*, JF8*, HL4*, EW1*, TX9**

A6X9 Black
Exteriors: All Barrcuda Colors

A6XW White
Exteriors: All Barrcuda Colors

** Recommended for Color Coordination*
*** Available*

1974 DODGE CHALLENGER INTERIOR COLOR CODES

A6B6 Blue
Exteriors: KB1, KB5*, EW1*, TX9*, HL4***

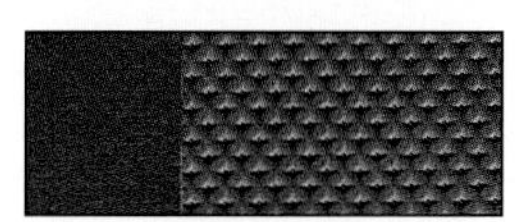
A6G6 Green
KG2, KG8*, HL4*, EW1*, TX9**

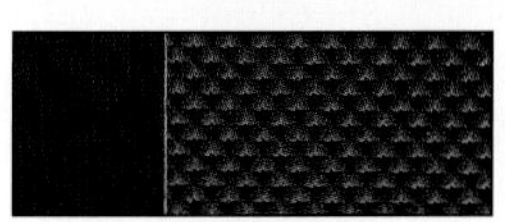
A6X9 Black
Exteriors: All Challenger Colors

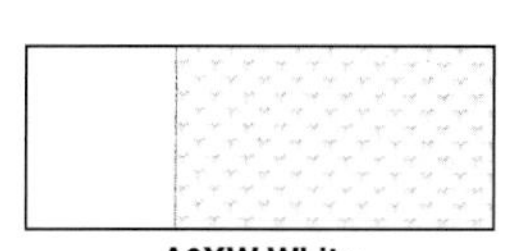
A6XW White
Exteriors: All, HL4***

** Recommended for Color Coordination*

*** Available*

1974 DODGE CHALLENGER AND PLYMOUTH BARRACUDA PAINT CODES

Earth tones yes, High Impact colors no. Dodge's palette of acrylic enamel paints for 1974 excluded those vivid, extra cost colors for the first time since the spring of 1969. Still, there were some bright colors available for Challenger, including Bright Red and Gold Metallic. Each exterior hue was color-keyed to the available interior trims and optional vinyl tops and side striping.

B1 1974 Dodge: *Powder Blue*
B1 1974 Plymouth: *Powder Blue*

B5 1974 Dodge: *Lucerne Blue Iridescent*
B5 1974 Plymouth: *Lucerne Blue Poly*

E5 1974 Dodge: *Bright Red*
E5 1974 Plymouth: *Rallye Red*

E7 1974 Dodge: *Burnished Red Iridescent*
E7 1974 Plymouth: *Burnished Red Poly*

G2 1974 Dodge: *Frosty Green Iridescent*
G2 1974 Plymouth: *Frosty Green Poly*

G8 1974 Dodge: *Deep Sherwood Iridescent*
G8 1974 Plymouth: *Deep Sherwood Poly*

1974 DODGE CHALLENGER AND PLYMOUTH BARRACUDA PAINT CODES

* Also 1973 Spring Color

CONTINUED

J6 1974 Dodge: *Avocado Gold Iridescent*
J6 1974 Plymouth: *Avocado Gold Poly*

L4 1974 Dodge: *Parchment*
L4 1974 Plymouth: *Sahara Beige*

L8 1974 Dodge: *Dark Moonstone Iridescent*
L8 1974 Plymouth: *Dark Moonstone Poly*

T5 1974 Dodge: *Sienna Iridescent*
T5 1974 Plymouth: *Sienna Poly*

W1 1974 Dodge: *Eggshell White*
W1 1974 Plymouth: *Spinnaker White*

X9 1974 Dodge: *Black*
X9 1974 Plymouth: *Formal Black*

Y4 1974 Dodge: *Golden Fawn*
Y4 1974 Plymouth: *Golden Fawn*

Y5 1974 Dodge: *Yellow Blaze*
Y5 1974 Plymouth: *Yellow Blaze*

Y6 1974 Dodge: *Gold Iridescent*
Y6 1974 Plymouth: *Golden Haze Poly*

Y9 1974 Dodge: *Dark Gold Iridescent*
Y9 1974 Plymouth: *Tahitian Gold Poly*

1974 DODGE CHALLENGER VINYL TOP COLOR CODES

V1B Blue

V1G Green

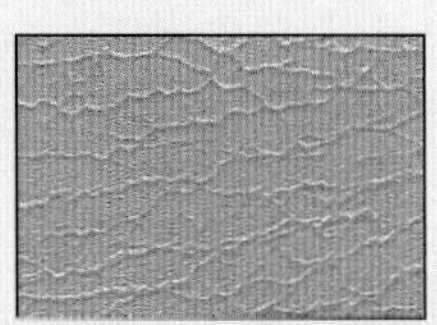

V1Y Gold

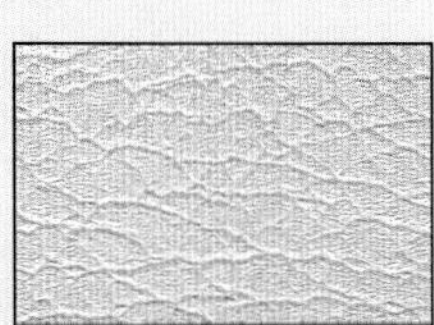

V1L Parchment

V1X Black

V1W White

1974 PLYMOUTH BARRACUDA INTERIOR COLOR CODES

A6B6 Blue
Exteriors: *KB1*, KB5*, EW1*, TX9*, HL1***

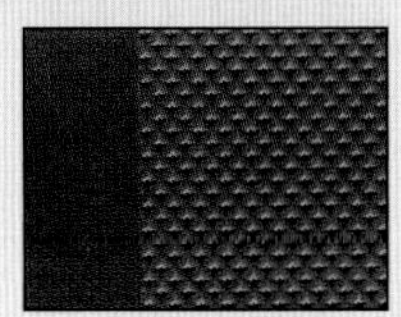

A6G6 Green
Exteriors: *KG2, KG8, HL4, EW1, TX9*

A6X9 Black
Exteriors: *All Barracuda Colors*

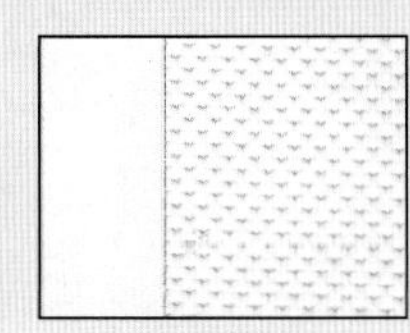

A6XW White
Exteriors: *All*, HL4***

* *Recommended for Color Coordination*

** *Available*

1974 PLYMOUTH BARRACUDA VINYL ROOF CODES

Available vinyl tops for Barracuda's last year were available in these colors. If someone wanted theirs in another color, they would have to settle for one of these, plus enough vinyl dye from their local auto-parts store to do the job.

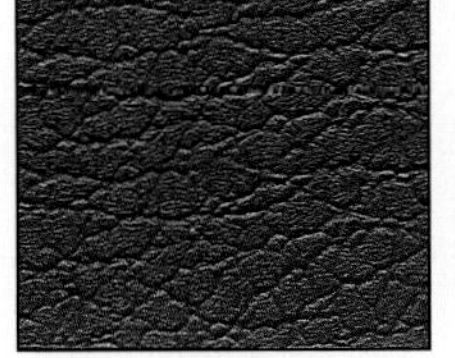

V1B Blue

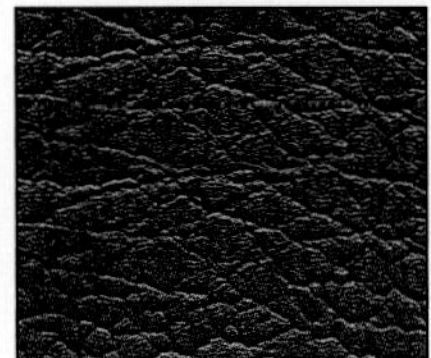

V1G Green

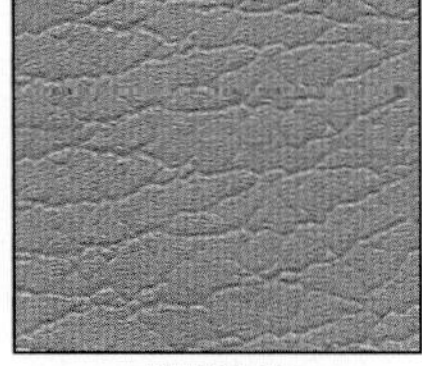

V1Y Gold

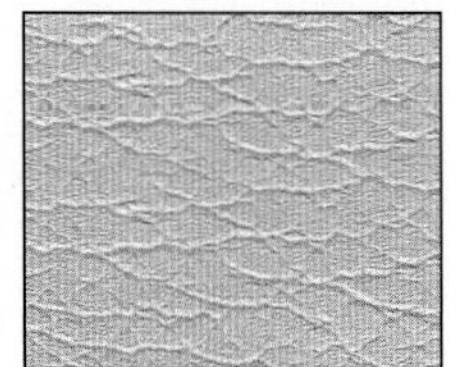

V1L Parchment

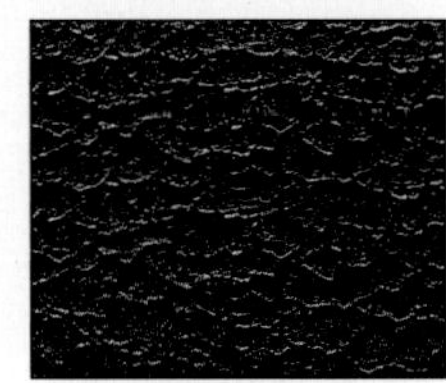

V1X Black

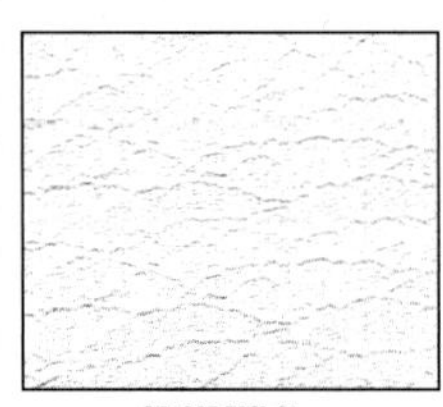

V1W White

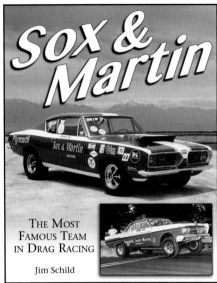

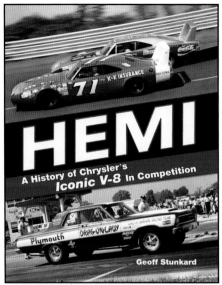

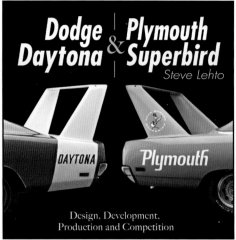

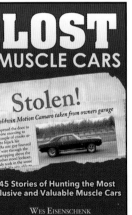